The 2015

First

Bus Handbo

British Bus Publishing

Body codes used in the Bus Handbook series:

Type:

A	Articulated vehicle
B	Bus, either single-deck or double-deck
BC	Interurban - high-back seated bus
C	Coach
M	Minibus with design capacity of 16 seats or less
N	Low-floor bus (Niederflur), either single-deck or double-deck
O	Open-top bus (CO = convertible - PO = partial open-top)

Seating capacity is then shown. For double-decks the upper deck quantity is followed by the lower deck.

Please note that seating capacities shown are generally those provided by the operator. It is common practice, however, for some vehicles to operate at different capacities when on certain duties.

Door position:-

C	Centre entrance/exit
D	Dual doorway.
F	Front entrance/exit
R	Rear entrance/exit (no distinction between doored and open)
T	Three or more access points

Equipment:-

T	Toilet	TV	Training vehicle where seats are removed.
M	Mail compartment	RV	Used as tow bus or engineers' vehicle.

Allocation:-

s	Ancillary vehicle
t	Training bus
u	out of service or strategic reserve; refurbishment or seasonal requirement
w	Vehicle is withdrawn and awaiting disposal.

e.g. - B32/28F is a double-deck bus with thirty-two seats upstairs, twenty-eight down and a front entrance/exit., N43D is a low-floor bus with two or more doorways.

Re-registrations:-

Where a vehicle has gained new index marks the details are listed at the end of each fleet showing the current mark, followed in sequence by those previously carried starting with the original mark.

Annual books are produced for the major groups:

The Stagecoach Bus Handbook
The First Bus Handbook
The Arriva Bus Handbook
The Go-Ahead Bus Handbook
The National Express Coach Handbook

Regional books in the series:

The Scottish Bus Handbook
The Welsh Bus Handbook
The Ireland & Islands Bus Handbook
English Bus Handbook: Smaller Groups
English Bus Handbook: Notable Independents
English Bus Handbook: Coaches

Associated series:

The Hong Kong Bus Handbook
The Malta Bus Handbook
The Leyland Lynx Handbook
The Postbus Handbook
The Mailvan Handbook
The Toy & Model Bus Handbook - Volume 1 - Early Diecasts
The Fire Brigade Handbook (fleet list of each local authority fire brigade)
The Police Range Rover Handbook

Some earlier editions of these books are still available. Please contact the publisher on 01952 255669.

The 2015 FirstBus Handbook

The 2015 First Bus Handbook is part of the Bus Handbook series that details the fleets of selected bus and coach operators. These Bus Handbooks are published by British Bus Publishing. Although this book has been produced with the encouragement of and in co-operation with Firstgroup, it is not an official publication. The vehicles included are subject to variation, particularly as new vehicle deliveries lead to older vehicles being withdrawn. The contents are correct to late May 2015.

Quality photographs for inclusion in the series are welcome, for which a fee is paid. High-resolution digital images are also welcome on CD or DVD. Unfortunately the publishers cannot accept responsibility for any loss and they require that you show your name on each disc.

To keep the fleet information up to date we recommend the publication, Buses, published monthly by Key Publications, or for more detailed information, the PSV Circle monthly news sheets. The writer and publisher would be glad to hear from readers should any information be available which corrects or enhances that given in this publication.

Editorial team: Stuart Martin and Bill Potter

Acknowledgments:
We are grateful to John Birtwistle, Tom Johnson, Steve Richmond, the PSV Circle and the management and officials of First companies for their kind assistance and co-operation in the compilation of this book. The front cover view is by Alan Blagburn, rear cover pictures by Dave Heath and Steve Rice, while the frontispiece is also by Richard Godfrey.

Earlier editions are available from the orderline, 01952 255669 or our web site.

ISBN 9781904875758

© Published by British Bus Publishing Ltd, June 2015

British Bus Publishing Ltd, 16 St Margaret's Drive, Telford, TF1 3PH

Telephone: 01952 255669

web; www.britishbuspublishing.co.uk
e-mail: sales@britishbuspublishing.co.uk

Contents

Allocated to Dublin's AirCoach operation are thirty-five Volvo coaches. AirCoach was purchased in 2003 and provides staff and car park shuttles at Dublin Airport together with a network of high quality express coach services across Eire along with a Dublin-Belfast express route. The AirCoach brand has since been rolled out to other First airport link services in the UK. *Alan Blagburn*

Introduction

FirstGroup plc is the UK's largest surface transportation company with a turnover of over six billion pounds, employing 117,000 staff in Europe and North America. First runs local bus services throughout the UK outside London, and these currently carry almost sixhundred million passengers each year in more than forty major towns and cities from Aberdeen to Penzance, with express coach services also operated in Ireland. Full details of First's operations can be found at www.firstgroup.com.

First is also a major UK train operator, with three passenger franchises: First Great Western, First TransPennine Express and First ScotRail (until 31st March 2015). First also owns Hull Trains, an "open access" operator. Between them these companies operate a significant proportion of the UK passenger rail network with a balanced portfolio of intercity, commuter and regional services, and carry more than 330 million passengers per year. The Croydon Tramlink operated by First on behalf of Transport for London carries over thirty-one million passengers per year.

First's North American business is split into First Student (yellow school buses), First Transit (local bus service operations and fleet maintenance services) and Greyhound. Besides the iconic Greyhound brand, market segmentation has seen the introduction of Bolt Bus and Yo! Bus for long distance coaching in recent years. All three divisions provide services across Canada and North America. First Student alone carries over four million passengers daily with a fleet of over 60,000 school buses.

First was formed in 1995 from the merger of the Badgerline Group plc based in Weston-Super-Mare, and GRT Bus Group plc based in Aberdeen. Badgerline had its roots in the former National Bus Company subsidiary of the same name which was formed in 1986 from the country operations of Bristol Omnibus. As a result of acquisitions, the Badgerline company grew and at the time of the merger comprised the former National Bus Companies Western National, Midland Red West, Bristol Omnibus, Eastern National/Thamesway, Eastern Counties and South Wales Transport, along with the former West Yorkshire passenger transport executive operation privatised as Yorkshire Rider. GRT was originally Grampian Regional Transport, the municipal operation in Aberdeen privatised under the 1985 Transport Act. GRT had also grown by acquisition and comprised the former Leicester and Northampton municipal operations, together with the Alexander (Midland) and Eastern Scottish former Scottish Bus Group fleets.

The new company was named FirstBus plc, this changing to FirstGroup plc in December 1997 to reflect the diversification of the business into rail and airport management. First soon acquired the former passenger transport executive operations in South Yorkshire (Mainline) and the southern part of Greater Manchester Transport. Other operators acquired comprised the former Strathclyde Passenger Transport Executive operations and adjacent Kelvin Central (formerly part of the Scottish Bus Group), former NBC companies Potteries, North Devon/Southern National (Cawlett Group), BeeLine (previously Alder Valley) and Provincial, and the Southampton municipal operation. A new corporate livery was soon introduced, initially on low floor vehicles. The final components of the original UK Bus operations were the privatised London Buses subsidiary Centrewest and on the opposite side of London the recently established Capital Citybus. Smaller operators subsequently bought included Chester City Transport, Hutchisons of Overtown, Truronian of Truro and the local bus services of Finglands of Rusholme.

Aircoach was purchased in 2003. Aircoach provides staff and car park shuttles at Dublin Airport together with a network of high quality express coach services across Eire and a Dublin-Belfast express. The AirCoach brand has since been rolled out to other First airport link services in the UK.

The Overground concept of simplified networks with clear, colour coded route branding, launched in 1999, was the first such unified marketing application within the bus industry. Overground rapidly spread from its Glasgow origin to cover many of First's urban operations, based on frequent, reliable bus services provided with low-floor vehicles at a time when these were relatively uncommon.

The American style Yellow School Bus concept was introduced by First to the UK in 2002, with the first scheme being in Hebden Bridge in West Yorkshire. First now operates a fleet of over 200 such vehicles in the UK on both its own and local authority supported schools services. These services have the same driver every day, the driver holding a list of passengers who are to use the service. The same safety and security features are employed as in the vast US schoolbus fleet, and some of the drivers have been recruited from the parents of the schoolchildren.

The ftr concept with the Streetcar vehicle, introduced in 2007 to York, Leeds and Swansea, has been refreshed, with many of these high quality articulated buses now operating on the "Hyperlink" branded high frequency shuttle between Leeds and Bradford.

The original Group livery was refined over the years to encompass specific variations for interurban (Excel and AirCoach) services, Park & Ride services and RailLink services. A new livery for the UK bus fleet was unveiled in 2012, based on the strong brand image generated since 1998. This initially received considerable exposure through the deployment of two hundred new vehicles to transport visitors to the Olympic Games in London and subsequently at the Commonwealth Games in Glasgow two years later. Now visible throughout First's operations, the new livery reintroduced local branding, emphasising local accountability for the provision of a high quality local service network. Each bus identifies its operating depot and the area, or group of services, where it operates. Examples can be seen in the following pages. The accelerated repaint programme commenced in 2012 has made the new First livery a common sight across the UK.

Building upon First's early involvement in guided busways, with four of these currently in operation in Leeds, Bradford and Ipswich, a new busway scheme linking Gosport with Fareham in Hampshire opened in April 2012, branded as the Eclipse system and developed in partnership with Hampshire County Council. The first route combines segregated busway, traffic signal priority and bus lanes, together with major improvements to passenger infrastructure to bring passengers to their destination on time every time, using a new fleet of high quality dedicated vehicles. First has recently been announced as the provider of services on the Leigh-Manchester busway which is due to start carrying passengers in early 2016. This concept of Bus Rapid Transit is under consideration for other parts of the UK and is growing in popularity in First's USA operations, including the Austin (Texas) BRT Rapid system which has opened a second line since the last edition of this book was published.

Having established the Sheffield Bus Partnership with South Yorkshire PTE, Sheffield City Council and the other operators in 2012, this concept was extended to Rotherham in 2014 and the partnership has already delivered significant patronage growth in six months. First considers strategic partnerships with local authorities to be the way forward, and this approach is being used to deliver significant improvements to the bus networks in West Yorkshire and Greater Bristol amongst many others. The Glasgow network was re-launched as SimpliCity in 2013 with a rationalised and simplified network offering improved services and frequencies over an easily assimilated system of routes, accompanied by major investment in new vehicles.

Fares were also reviewed in many areas in 2013, with the objective of providing value for money products. Operations in Greater Manchester, West and South Yorkshire all saw significant reductions in the price of period tickets with resultant increases in bus use. A more radical approach was taken in Bristol where an extensive public consultation exercise was undertaken, the results of which were evaluated and resulted in a much simplified fares structure for City services and improved discounts for young people. This was introduced in late 2013 and was followed in 2014 by a similar exercise covering operations elsewhere in the former county of Avon. These initiatives have resulted in an increase of over 20% in bus patronage in the Greater Bristol area. Investment in both vehicles and technology continues. Not only is all First's bus ticketing equipment compatible with ITSO Smartcards, but mobile ticketing has now been rolled out across all UK Bus operations and contactless Smartcard technology is in use across South & West Yorkshire, Greater Bristol and Hampshire and for all concessionary travel in England, Scotland and Wales.

Having previously trialled LPG, CNG, fuel cell and battery electric vehicles, together with experimental hybrids, today all First's diesel buses run on ultra-low sulphur diesel. The use of more fuel efficient and less polluting hybrid vehicles continues to grow, with these vehicles now in service in Leeds, Manchester, Bath, Chelmsford, Heathrow and Glasgow. In partnership with City of York Council, electric vehicles were introduced to the York Park & Ride services in 2014, with hybrid vehicles drafted in to City services. Other electric buses are being used on Manchester's MetroShuttle services. Meanwhile, in Aberdeen a partnership with the City Council introduced the first UK use of hydrogen fuel cell buses outside London in Spring 2015. Biomethane generated from human waste is being used to power an experimental vehicle operating in Bristol as part of that city's European Green Capital 2015 programme and the opportunity to expand the use of such renewable energy is under investigation. First has also worked in partnership with local authorities to retrofit many older vehicles with state of the art emissions treatment systems under several government sponsored initiatives in the last three years.

Successful evaluation of the lightweight fuel efficient Wrightbus StreetLite vehicle led to significant orders for these vehicles beginning in 2013. The original design was developed into a full size single deck vehicle and the latest "micro hybrid" variant, which uses waste energy from braking to power vehicle ancillary systems, has helped to cut fuel use and emissions still further. Many of these "micro hybrid" StreetLites have now entered service across First's operations, and have been followed by the first examples of the StreetDeck double decker designed on the same principles of light weight and fuel efficiency, now in service in South Yorkshire and Greater Manchester. In the latter location a comparison is afforded with the latest lightweight Volvo/Wrightbus double decker, and both types have been ordered for 2015 deliveries.

First remains committed to reducing its fuel use, and significant driver training, education and feedback programmes have been rolled out to assist in achieving this aim. The GreenRoad system monitors each driver's braking, acceleration and cornering forces, and, by highlighting where the normal limits of these are exceeded, is used to provide ongoing education and training of drivers, improving fuel economy, road safety and passenger comfort. This alone has resulted in fuel savings of over 5% across the board.

Following extensive passenger research the standard First internal bus layout was revised in 2012 to provide additional space in the front part of the vehicle for passengers with luggage, pushchairs etc and at the same time the specification was updated to include free passenger wifi, with seats upholstered in environmentally friendly e-leather.

In recent years First's UK Bus operations have gone through a period of consolidation. In 2013 the disposal of the London operations was completed with the sales to Tower Transit and Metroline. The final London operations in Dagenham were taken over by Stagecoach later in the year. First re-focussed its attention and investment on operations outside London and 2014 witnessed the biggest single investment in new vehicles in the deregulated market yet. The successful launch of services on the busy southern Wilmslow Road corridor in Manchester, operating across the city centre to the north in Spring 2014 was soon followed by investment in a fleet of new double-deck vehicles to further develop services in this area.

Tim O'Toole became the Chief Executive of FirstGroup plc in 2010, when the founder of the Group, Moir Lockhead retired. Tim brought a wealth of experience to the Group from both the USA and UK and has brought a new approach to the business. Through its "Better Journeys for Life" programme, the UK Bus Division is at the forefront of developments to create a new vision for bus services across the UK, and has demonstrated sustained passenger satisfaction and volume growth. Essential components of this programme include public consultation, improved staff communication and working closely with Governments, local authorities and other local stakeholders to develop partnerships and sustainable transport policies.

Depots and Codes

Company legal name as holder of O licence	Registered operating centres	Code
Aberdeen		
First Aberdeen Ltd	King Street, Aberdeen, AB24 5RP	AB
Scotland East		
Midland Bluebird Ltd	Dunmore Street, Balfron, G63 0TU	BF
Midland Bluebird Ltd	Cowie Road, Bannockburn, FK7 8AD	BK
Midland Bluebird Ltd	Stirling Street, Galashiels, TD1 1QA	GS
Midland Bluebird Ltd	Stirling Road, Larbert, FK5 3NJ	LT
First Edinburgh Ltd	Mall Avenue, Musselburgh, EH21 7DY	MU
First Edinburgh Ltd	Deans Road, Livingston, EH54, 8JY	LV
First Edinburgh Ltd	Linlithgow,	LW
Glasgow		
First Glasgow (No 1) Ltd	South Street, Scotstoun, Glasgow, G14 0AQ	SN
First Glasgow (No 1) Ltd	Cathcart Road, Glasgow, G42 7BH	CA
First Glasgow (No 1) Ltd	Tollcross Road, Glasgow, G31 4UZ	PH
First Glasgow (No 2) Ltd	Glasgow Road, Blantyre, G72 0LA	B
First Glasgow (No 2) Ltd	Birch Road, Dumbarton, G82 2RE	DU
First Glasgow (No 2) Ltd	Castlehill Rd, Overtown, Wishaw, ML2 0QS	O
West Yorkshire		
First West Yorkshire Ltd	Donisthorpe St, Hunslet, Leeds, LS10 1PL	HP
First West Yorkshire Ltd	Henconner Lane, Bramley, Leeds, LS13 4LD	BM
First West Yorkshire Ltd	Bowling Back Lane, Bradford, BD4 8SP	BD
First West Yorkshire Ltd	Old Fieldhouse Lane, Huddersfield, HD2 1AG	HU
First West Yorkshire Ltd	Skircoat Road, Halifax, HX1 2RF	HX
York		
First York Ltd	James Street, York, YO10 3WW	YK
South Yorkshire		
First South Yorkshire Ltd	Leger Way, Doncaster, DN2 6AZ	DN
First South Yorkshire Ltd	Midland Road, Rotherham, S61 1TF	RO
First South Yorkshire Ltd	Olive Grove Road, Sheffield, S2 3GA	OG
Manchester		
First Manchester Ltd	Weston Street, Bolton, BL3 2AW	BN
First Manchester Ltd	Rochdale Road, Bury, BL9 0GZ	BY
First Manchester Ltd	Queen's Road, Manchester, M8 8UT	QS
First Manchester Ltd	Wallshaw Street, Oldham, OL1 3TR	OM
First Manchester Ltd	Wilmslow Road, Fallowfield, M14 5LJ	OX
First Pioneer Ltd	Broadway, Dukinfield, SK16 4UU	TE
Midlands		
First Potteries Ltd	Dividy Road, Adderley Green, ST3 5YY	AG
First Potteries Ltd	Liverpool Road, Newcastle, ST5 2AF	NE
Leicester CityBus Ltd	Humphreys Way, Leicester, LE4 0BR	LE
First Midland Red Buses Ltd	Friar Street, Hereford, HR4 0AS	HD
First Midland Red Buses Ltd	Padmore Street, Worcester, WR1 2PA	WR
Eastern Counties		
First Eastern Counties Buses Ltd	Star Lane, Ipswich, IP4 1BN	IP
First Eastern Counties Buses Ltd	Vancouver Avenue, King's Lynn, PE30 5RD	KL
First Eastern Counties Buses Ltd	Gas Works Road, Lowestoft, NR32 1UZ	LO
First Eastern Counties Buses Ltd	Vulcan Road South, Norwich, NR6 6AE	VN
First Eastern Counties Buses Ltd	Caister Road, Great Yarmouth, NR30 4DF	YA

Carrying Portsmouth Park & Ride livery is 33897, SN14TRX, one from the 2014 intake of Enviro 400 buses.
Steve Rice

Essex

First Essex Buses Ltd	Springwood Drive, Braintree, CM7 2YN	BR
First Essex Buses Ltd	Cherrydown East, Basildon, SS16 5AG	BS
First Essex Buses Ltd	Westway, Chelmsford, CM1 3AR	CM
First Essex Buses Ltd	Telford Road, Clacton, CO15 4LP	CN
First Essex Buses Ltd	Queen Street, Colchester, CO1 2PQ	CO
First Essex Buses Ltd	London Road, Hadleigh, Benfleet, SS7 2QL	HH

Hampshire and Berkshire

First Beeline Buses Ltd	Market Street, Bracknell, RG12 1JA	BL
First Beeline Buses Ltd	Stoke Road, Slough, SL2 5AQ	SH
First Beeline Buses Ltd	Reading Transport Ltd, RG1 7HH	RG
First Hampshire & Dorset Ltd	London Road, Hilsea, Portsmouth, PO2 9RP	HI
First Hampshire & Dorset Ltd	Gosport Road, Hoeford, Fareham, PO16 0ST	HO
First Hampshire & Dorset Ltd	Empress Road, Southampton, SO14 0JW	SO
First Hampshire & Dorset Ltd	Edward Street, Weymouth, DT4 7DP	WH

West of England

First Bristol Ltd	Roman Farm Rd, Hengrove, Bristol, BS4 1UJ	HG
First Bristol Ltd	Easton Rd, Lawrence Hill, Bristol, BS5 0DZ	LH
First Somerset & Avon Ltd	Lower Bristol Rd, Twerton, Bath, BA2 9ES	BA
First Somerset & Avon Ltd	Easton Rd, Lawrence Hill, Bristol, BS5 0DZ	MS
First Somerset & Avon Ltd	Searle Cres., Weston-super-Mare, BS23 3YX	WS

Devon & Cornwall

First Devon & Cornwall Ltd	Boards Road, Bridgwater, TA6 4BB	BW
First Devon & Cornwall Ltd	Union Street, Camborne, TR14 8HF	CE
First Devon & Cornwall Ltd	The Ride, Plymouth, PL9 7JT	PL
First Devon & Cornwall Ltd	Hamilton Road, Taunton, TA1 2EH	TN

Cymru

First Cymru Buses Ltd	Aneurin Bevan Ave., Bridgend, CF32 9SZ	BG
First Cymru Buses Ltd	Withybush Road, Haverfordwest, SA62 4BN	HV
First Cymru Buses Ltd	Acacia Avenue, Port Talbot, SA12 7DP	PT
First Cymru Buses Ltd	Heol Gwyrosydd, Penlan, Swansea, SA5 7BN	RA

Aircoach

Aircoach Ltd	Glengall Street, Belfast, BT12 5AH	BT
Aircoach Ltd	Airport Business Park, Swords, Co. Dublin	D

Depot Codes

AB	King Street, Aberdeen	HX	Skircoat Lane, Halifax
AG	Dividy Road, Adderley Green	IP	Foundation Street, Ipswich
B	Glasgow Road, Blantyre	KL	Vancouver Avenue, King's Lynn
BA	Weston Island, Bath	LE	Abbey Lane, Leicester
BD	Bowling Back Lane, Bradford	LH	Lawrence Hill, Bristol
BF	Dunmore Street, Balfron	LO	Gas Works Road, Lowestoft
BG	Bridgend	LT	Stirling Road, Larbert
BK	Cowie Road, Bannockburn	LV	Deans Road, Livingston
BL	Market Street, Bracknell	MS	Marlborough Street, Bristol
BM	Headconner Lane, Bramley, Leeds	MU	The Mall, Musselburgh
BN	Weston Street, Bolton	NE	Liverpool Road, Newcastle-under-Lyme
BR	Springfield Industrial Estate, Braintree	O	Castlehill Road, Overtown
BS	Cherrydown East, Basildon	OG	Olive Grove, Sheffield
BT	Great Northern Mall, Belfast	OM	Wallshaw Street, Oldham
BW	East Quay, Bridgwater	OX	Oxford Road, Manchester
BY	Rochdale Road, Bury	PH	Tollcross Road, Parkhead, Glasgow
CA	Caledonia, Cathcart Road, Glasgow	PL	Chelson Meadow, Plymouth
CE	Union Street, Camborne	PT	Acacia Avenue, Sandfields, Port Talbot
CM	Westway, Chelmsford	QS	Queen's Road, Manchester
CN	Telford Road, Clacton	RA	Pentregethin Road, Ravenhill, Swansea
CO	Queen Street, Colchester	RG	Reading Transport Ltd
D	Airport Business Park, Dublin	RO	Midland Road, Rotherham
DN	Duke Street, Doncaster	SH	Stoke Road, Slough
DU	Birch Road, Dumbarton	SN	South Street, Scotstoun
GS	Stirling Street, Galashiels	SO	Portswood Road, Southampton
HD	Friar Street, Hereford	TE	Broadway, Dukinfield, Tameside
HG	Hengrove, Bristol	TN	Hamilton Road, Taunton
HH	London Road, Hadleigh	VN	Vulcan Road, Norwich
HI	London Road, Hilsea, Portsmouth	WH	Edward Street, Weymouth
HO	Gosport Road, Hoeford, Fareham	WR	Padmore Street, Worcester
HP	Hunslet Park, Leeds	WS	Searle Crescent, Weston-super-Mare
HU	Old Fieldhouse Lane, Huddersfield	YA	Caister Road, Great Yarmouth
HV	Withybush Ind Est, Haverfordwest	YK	James Street, York

Twenty-three Enviro 300s were allocated to Aberdeen during 2013. Pictured in the city while heading for Dice. 67794, SN13CNK, carries Northern Lights lettering. *John Birtwistle*

Fleet at May 2015

10017	BY	X401CSG	Scania L94UA			Wrightbus Solar Fusion	AN58D	2001

10035-10043 — Volvo B7LA — Wright Eclipse Fusion — AN56D — 2000

10035	BA	W118CWR	10038	HP	W127DWX	10040	HP	W128DWX	10042	HP	W129DWX
10036	BA	W119CWR	10039	HP	W122DWX	10041	HP	W124DWX	10043	HP	W126DWX
10037	BA	W122CWR									

10044	AB	V601GGB	Volvo B10BLA	Wright Fusion	AN53D	1999
10045	AB	V602GGB	Volvo B10BLA	Wright Fusion	AN53D	1999

10047-10052 — Volvo B7LA — Wright Eclipse Fusion — AN56D — 2000

10047	AB	W2FAL	10049	AB	W4FAL	10051	AB	W6FAL	10052	AB	W7FAL
10048	AB	W3FAL	10050	AB	W5FAL						

10108	AB	V608GGB	Volvo B10BLA	Wright Fusion	AN55D	1999
10110	ABu	V610GGB	Volvo B10BLA	Wright Fusion	AN55D	1999

10136-10148 — Volvo B7LA — Wrightbus Eclipse Fusion — AN56D — 2000-01

10136	AB	X136FPO	10141	AB	X141FPO	10144	AB	X144FPO	10148	AB	Y148ROT
10138	AB	X138FPO									

10154-10173 — Volvo B7LA — Wrightbus Eclipse Fusion — AN56D — 2005

10154	AB	SV05DXA	10159	AB	SV05DXG	10164	AB	SV05DXM	10169	AB	SV05DXT
10155	AB	SV05DXC	10160	AB	SV05DXH	10165	AB	SV05DXO	10170	AB	SV05DXU
10156	AB	SV05DXD	10161	AB	SV05DXJ	10166	AB	SV05DXP	10171	AB	SV05DXW
10157	AB	SV05DXE	10162	AB	SV05DXK	10167	AB	SV05DXR	10172	AB	SV05DXX
10158	AB	SV05DXF	10163	AB	SV05DXL	10168	AB	SV05DXS	10173	AB	SV05DXY

A number of articulated buses operate very effectively in selected parts of Britain, although no further examples have been added since 2009. Aberdeen is the home to thirty-two Wrightbus-bodied Volvo B7TLs. 10108, V608GGB, an earlier Volvo B10BLA model is shown. *Mark Doggett*

Illustrating the Volvo B7LAs with Wrightbus Eclipse Fusion body is 10177, WX55HWC which operates the service between the university and the city of Bath. *Dave Heath*

10174-10183

					Volvo B7LA			Wrightbus Eclipse Fusion	AN56D	2005			
10174	BA	WX55HVZ	10176	BA	WX55HWB	10178	BA	AN02EDN			10183	AB	SF05KUH
10175	BA	WX55HWA	10177	BA	WX55HWC	10179	BA	BN02EDN					

11036	CE	SN04XYA	Mercedes-Benz O530 Citaro G	Mercedes-Benz		AN27T	2004	
11037	CE	SN04XXY	Mercedes-Benz O530 Citaro G	Mercedes-Benz		AN27T	2004	
11038	CE	SN04XXZ	Mercedes-Benz O530 Citaro G	Mercedes-Benz		AN27T	2004	

11073-11083

					Mercedes-Benz O530 Citaro G			Mercedes-Benz	AN29T	2008-09			
11073	D	08D67693	11076	D	08D69040	11079	D	08D69972			11082	D	09D5300
11074	D	08D67694	11077	D	08D69043	11080	D	08D69973			11083	D	09D5303
11075	D	08D67697	11078	D	08D69070	11081	D	08D69974					

11085	CE	BX54UDE	Mercedes-Benz O530 Citaro G	Mercedes-Benz		AN49T	2004	Go South Coast, 2014
11086	CEu	BX54UDL	Mercedes-Benz O530 Citaro G	Mercedes-Benz		AN49T	2004	Go South Coast, 2014
11087	CE	BX54UDU	Mercedes-Benz O530 Citaro G	Mercedes-Benz		AN49T	2004	Go South Coast, 2014

11101-11115

					Mercedes-Benz O530 Citaro G			Mercedes-Benz	AN52D	2009			
11101	YK	BG58OLR	11105	YK	BG58OLX	11109	YK	BG58OMD			11113	YK	BG58OMJ
11102	YK	BG58OLT	11106	YK	BG58OMA	11110	YK	BG58OME			11114	YK	BG58OMK
11103	YK	BG58OLU	11107	YK	BG58OMB	11111	YK	BG58OMF			11115	YK	BG58OML
11104	YK	BG58OLV	11108	YK	BG58OMC	11112	YK	BG58OMH					

12001-12018

					Scania OmniCity CN94UA			Scania	AN58D	2005			
12001	BY	YN05GYA	12006	BY	YN05GYD	12011	BY	YN05GYO			12015	BY	YN05GYR
12002	BY	YN05GYB	12007	BY	YN05GYE	12012	BY	YN05GYV			12016	BY	YN05GYS
12003	BY	YN05GYH	12008	BY	YN05GYF	12013	BY	YN05GYU			12017	BY	YN05GYT
12004	BY	YN05GYJ	12009	BY	YN05GYG	12014	BY	YN05GYP			12018	BY	YN05GYW
12005	BY	YN05GYC	12010	BY	YN05GYK								

19000	RA	S90FTR	Volvo B7LA		Wrightbus StreetCar	AN40D	2005	Wrightbus, 2009

First operates the Rail-Air link between Reading rail station and Heathrow airport, a route instigated during the days of the National Bus Company. Pictured leaving Terminal 5 is 20611, LK07CDE, a Volvo B12B with Plaxton Panther bodywork. *Mark Lyons*

19001-19038

			Volvo B7LA			Wrightbus StreetCar		AN40D	2006-07		
19001	BM	YK06AOU	19011	BM	YK06AUC	19020	BMu	YJ07LVM	19029	RA	S100FTR
19002	BM	YK06ATV	19012	BMu	YJ06XLR	19021	BM	YJ07LVN	19030	RA	S10FTR
19003	BM	YK06ATU	19013	BM	YJ06XLS	19022	BMu	YJ07LVO	19032	RA	S20FTR
19004	BM	MH06ZSW	19014	BMu	YJ56EAA	19023	BM	YJ07LVR	19033	RA	S80FTR
19005	BM	YK06ATX	19015	BM	YJ56EAC	19024	BM	YJ07LVS	19034	RA	S30FTR
19006	BM	MH06ZSP	19016	BM	YJ56EAE	19025	BM	YJ07LVT	19035	RA	S40FTR
19007	BM	YK06ATY	19017	BM	YJ56EAF	19026	BM	YJ07LVU	19036	RA	S50FTR
19008	BM	YK06ATZ	19018	BM	YJ56EAG	19027	BM	YJ07LVV	19037	RA	S60FTR
19009	BM	YK06AUL	19019	BM	YJ07LVL	19028	BM	YJ07LVW	19038	RA	S70FTR
19010	BM	YK06AUA									

20021	AB	WSU489	Volvo B12B			Jonckheere Mistral		C53F	2003
20122	VNt	P732NVG	Volvo B10M-62			Plaxton Première 320		C53F	1996

20201-20207

			Volvo B12T			Plaxton Excalibur		C53F	1999		
20201	WR	T701JLD	20202	WR	T702JLD	20205	AB	T705JLD	20207	AB	T707JLD

20300	GS	WX54ZHM	Volvo B7R		Plaxton Profile		C53F	2005
20301	GS	WX54ZHN	Volvo B7R		Plaxton Profile		C53F	2005
20302	LW	WX54ZHO	Volvo B7R		Plaxton Profile		C53F	2005
20307	LW	WX05OZF	Volvo B7R		Plaxton Profile		C53F	2005

20321-20327

			Volvo B7R			Plaxton Profile		C70F	2007		
20321	BK	YN57BVU	20323	RA	YN57BVW	20325	RA	YN57BVY	20327	GS	YN57BWU
20322	BK	YN57BVV	20324	RA	YN57BVX	20326	GS	YN57BVZ			

20351-20374

			Volvo B7R			Plaxton Profile		C45F	2005		
20351	AB	WA05UNG	20357	MU	CV55ABK	20363	LW	CV55ACZ	20369	LW	CV55AMU
20352	AB	WA05UNE	20358	BK	CV55ACO	20364	LV	CV55AFE	20370	GS	CV55AGY
20353	AB	WA05UNF	20359	LV	CV55ACU	20365	LW	CV55AHA	20371	GS	CV55AMX
20354	LW	CU05LGJ	20360	LT	CV55ACX	20366	LV	CV55AFF	20372	AB	CV55ANF
20355	LT	CU05LGK	20361	LW	CV55ACY	20367	AB	CV55AGX	20373	AB	CV55ANP
20356	LV	CV55ABN	20362	LV	CV55AFA	20368	GS	CV55AGZ	20374	AB	CV55AOO

As mentioned in the introduction and illustrated by 20801, YN08OWO, AirCoach branding is now being applied to links in England as well as Ireland. Five Volvo B9Rs are allocated to Chelmsford for route X30 that connects Southend with Stansted Airport. *Mark Doggett*

20412	CEu	S312SCV	Volvo B10M-62	Plaxton Expressliner 2	C44FT	1998	
20417	HOt	P177NAK	Volvo B10M-62	Plaxton Première 350	C53F	1997	Waugh, Greenhead, 1998
20418	HOt	P176NAK	Volvo B10M-62	Plaxton Première 350	C49FT	1997	Waugh, Greenhead, 1998
20457	HOt	R813HWS	Volvo B10M-62	Plaxton Expressliner 2	C49FT	1997	
20463	CM	X193HFB	Volvo B10M-62	Plaxton Expressliner 2	C49FT	2000	

20500-20509

			Volvo B12M		Plaxton Paragon		C53F	2002	
20500	CM	AO02RBX	20503	DUu	AO02RCF	20506	AB	AO02RCX	20508	DU	AO02RCZ

20500	CM	AO02RBX	20503	DUu	AO02RCF	20506	AB	AO02RCX	20508	DU	AO02RCZ
20501	CM	AO02RBY	20504	CEu	AO02RCU	20507	AB	AO02RCY	20509	DU	AO02RDU
20502	CEu	AO02RBZ	20505	AB	AO02RCV						

20514	IP	WV02EUP	Volvo B12M 12.8m	Plaxton Paragon	C49FT	2002	
20515	IP	WV02EUR	Volvo B12M 12.8m	Plaxton Paragon	C49FT	2002	
20550	RG	CU04AYP	Volvo B12B	TransBus Paragon	C44FT	2004	
20551	SOt	CU04AYS	Volvo B12B	TransBus Paragon	C44FT	2004	
20556	CE	TT04TRU	Volvo B12B	Plaxton Panther	C49FT	2004	Truronian, 2008
20557	CE	TT05TRU	Volvo B12B	Plaxton Panther	C48FT	2005	Truronian, 2008
20558	CE	TT55TRU	Volvo B12B 12.8m	Plaxton Panther	C49FT	2005	Truronian, 2008
20561	CE	TT07TRU	Volvo B12B 12.8m	Plaxton Panther	C49FT	2007	Truronian, 2008
20611	RG	LK07CDE	Volvo B12B 12.8m	Plaxton Panther	C53F	2007	
20612	RG	LK07CDF	Volvo B12B 12.8m	Plaxton Panther	C53F	2007	
20613	RG	LK07CDN	Volvo B12B 12.8m	Plaxton Panther	C53F	2007	

20651-20669

Volvo B12BT — Jonckheere JSV — C51FT — 2008-09

20651	D	08D69442	20656	D	08D70357	20661	D	09D2773	20666	D	09D3708
20652	D	08D70256	20657	D	08D70459	20662	D	09D2774	20667	D	09D4282
20653	D	08D70351	20658	D	08D70460	20663	D	09D2777	20668	D	09D4649
20654	D	08D70352	20659	D	08D70461	20664	D	09D3364	20669	D	09D4276
20655	D	08D70354	20660	D	08D70462	20665	D	09D3365			

20801-20805

Volvo B9R — Plaxton Panther — C43FT — 2008

20801	CM	YN08OWO	20803	CM	YN08OWR	20804	CM	YN08OWU	20805	CM	YN08OWV
20802	CM	YN08OWP								

20806	RG	YX11HPO	Volvo B9R				Plaxton Panther			C45F	2011		
20807	RG	YX11HPP	Volvo B9R				Plaxton Panther			C45F	2011		
20808	RG	YN62GYR	Volvo B9R				Plaxton Panther			C45F	2013		
20809	RG	YN62GXS	Volvo B9R				Plaxton Panther			C45F	2013		
20810	RG	YY63WBT	Volvo B9R				Plaxton Panther			C45F	2014		
20811	RG	YY63WBU	Volvo B9R				Plaxton Panther			C45F	2014		

20901-20910

			Volvo B11R				Plaxton Panther			C45FT	2014		
20901	D	141D24	20904	D	141D27	20907	D	141D30	20909	D	141D32		
20902	D	141D26	20905	D	141D28	20908	D	141D31	20910	D	141D34		
20903	D	141D25	20906	D	141D29								

20911-20916

			Volvo B11R				Plaxton Panther			C53FT	2014		
20911	D	142D15753	20913	D	142D15750	20915	D	142D15748	20916	D	142D15749		
20912	D	142D15752	20914	D	142D15751								

23008-23015

			Scania K114 IB				Irizar Century Capacity 12.35	C53F			2003-04		
23008	CEt	YV03UBA	23010	TN	YV03UBC	23012	TN	YV03UBE	23014	TN	MIG9614		
23009	CE	YV03UBB	23011	TNt	YV03UBD	23013	CEt	YN04AJU	23015	RG	YN04AJV		

23019	CM	YN54APX	Scania K114 IB			Irizar Century Capacity 12.35	C49FT	2004		
23020	CM	YN54APK	Scania K114 IB			Irizar Century Capacity 12.35	C49FT	2004		
23021	AB	YN54APF	Scania K114 IB			Irizar Century Capacity 12.35	C49FT	2004		
23201	PLu	YN04YHY	Scania K114 IB			Irizar Century 12.35	C44FT	2004		
23202	PLu	YN04YHW	Scania K114 IB			Irizar Century 12.35	C44FT	2004		
23204	PLu	YN04YHZ	Scania K114 IB			Irizar Century 12.35	C44FT	2004		
23208	CE	WM04NZU	Volvo B12B			Plaxton Panther	C49FT	2004		

23303-23314

			Scania K114 EB				Irizar PB			C49FT	2004		
23303	PLu	YN54NXV	23306	AB	PSU629	23313	CE	YN54NYU	23314	AB	YN54NYV		
23305	AB	PSU628	23307	AB	YN54NXZ								

23315-23320

			Scania K114 EB				Irizar PB			C49FT	2005		
23315	RAu	YN55PXF	23317	CE	YN55PXH	23319	RAu	YN55PXK	23320	RA	YN55PXL		
23316	CE	YN55PXG	23318	RAu	YN55PXJ								

23321-23325

			Scania K114 EB				Irizar PB			C49FT	2006		
23321	RA	YN06CGU	23323	RA	YN06CGX	23324	RA	YN06CGY	23325	RA	YN06CGZ		
23322	RA	YN06CGV											

23330	AB	PSU627	Scania K340 EB			Irizar PB	C49FT	2008		
23401	AB	LSK570	Scania K114 EB			Irizar Century 12.35	C49FT	2004		
23402	AB	LSK571	Scania K114 EB			Irizar Century 12.35	C49FT	2004		

23501-23504

			Scania K340 EB				Caetano Levanté			C49FT	2006		
23501	D	06D120305	23502	D	06D120303	23503	D	06D120304	23504	D	06D120368		

24000	D	05D62327	Setra S315 GT-HD			Setra			C49FT	2005	Evobus, 2006		

24032-24047

			Setra S415HD				Setra			C44F	2004		
24032	BT	KFZ4653	24035	BT	KFZ4361	24044	D	04D22855	24047	D	04D34313		
24033	BT	KFZ4363	24036	D	04D22822								

29004	AB	YJ61FAF	Temsa Safari HD			Temsa			C49FT	2011		
29006	AB	YJ13GUE	Temsa Safari HD			Temsa			C53F	2013		
29007	AB	YJ13GUF	Temsa Safari HD			Temsa			C53F	2013		

30031	NEu	G755XRE	Leyland Olympian ONCL10/1RZ			Leyland			B47/29F	1989		
30560	BF	P190TGD	Volvo Olympian			Alexander RL			B47/32F	1996		
30561	RO	X856UOK	Volvo B7TL			Alexander ALX400			N47/29F	2001		
30562	RO	X857UOK	Volvo B7TL			Alexander ALX400			N47/29F	2001		
30563	RO	X858UOK	Volvo B7TL			Alexander ALX400			N47/29F	2001		

30564-30578

			Volvo B7TL				Alexander ALX400			N49/27F	2002		
30564	RO	WU02KVE	30569	RO	WU02KVK	30573	OG	WU02KVP	30576	OG	WU02KVT		
30565	RO	WU02KVF	30570	RO	WU02KVL	30574	OG	WU02KVR	30577	RO	WU02KVV		
30567	RO	WU02KVH	30571	OG	WU02KVM	30575	RO	WU02KVS	30578	RO	WU02KVW		
30568	RO	WU02KVJ	30572	OG	WU02KVO								

30722	BMs	B46PJA	Leyland Olympian ONLXB/1R			Northern Counties			B43/30F	1985		

The 2015 First Bus Handbook

Carrying Leeds lettering, 30926, X794NWR, is a Volvo B7TL with Alexander ALX400 bodywork. Joining the Yorkshire Rider operation in 2000 it has continuously served the city since. *Alan Blagburn*

30744-30751

Volvo Olympian — Alexander RL — B47/32F — 1996

30744	GS	P196TGD	30745	BFu	P197TGD	30750	BFu	P203TGD	30751	BFu	P204TGD

30791-30815

Volvo Olympian — Alexander Royale — B43/29F — 1997-98

30791	BD	R611JUB	30805	HX	R625JUB	30809	HX	R629JUB	30813	HX	R633JUB
30796	BD	R616JUB	30806	HX	R626JUB	30811	HX	R631JUB	30814	HUt	R634JUB
30800	HX	R620JUB	30808	HX	R176HUG	30812	HX	R632JUB	30815	HU	R636JUB
30802	HX	R622JUB									

30816-30834

Volvo Olympian — Alexander Royale — B43/29F — 1998-99

30816	HU	R636HYG	30821	HU	R641HYG	30823	HU	R643HYG	30832	LW	R652HYG
30817	BD	R637HYG	30822	HU	R642HYG	30826	LW	R646HYG	30834	BD	S654FWY
30818	HU	R638HYG									

30840-30845

Volvo Olympian — Alexander Royale — B43/29F — 1999

30840	HU	T660VWU	30843	HU	T663VWU	30844	HX	T664VWU	30845	HXu	T665VWU
30841	HU	T661VWU									

30846-30870

Volvo B7TL — Alexander ALX400 — N49/29F — 2000

30846	OG	W701CWR	30853	HU	W708CWR	30859	HX	W714CWR	30865	HU	W668CWT
30847	HU	W702CWR	30854	HU	W709CWR	30860	HX	W715CWR	30866	BD	W721CWR
30848	HU	W703CWR	30855	HX	W667CWT	30861	OGu	W716CWR	30867	BD	W722CWR
30849	HX	W704CWR	30856	HX	W711CWR	30862	OG	W717CWR	30868	BD	W723CWR
30850	HU	W705CWR	30857	BD	W712CWR	30863	HU	W718CWR	30869	BD	W724CWR
30851	HU	W706CWR	30858	HX	W713CWR	30864	HU	W719CWR	30870	BD	W726CWR
30852	HU	W707CWR									

30871-30915   Volvo B7TL   Alexander ALX400   N49/29F   2000

30871	BY	W726DWX	30883	DN	W738DWX	30894	BD	X749VUA	30905	DN	W776DWX
30872	BY	W727DWX	30884	DN	W739DWX	30895	BD	W773DWX	30906	DN	W761DWX
30873	BY	W728DWX	30885	DN	W772DWX	30896	BD	W751DWX	30907	DN	W762DWX
30874	BN	W729DWX	30886	LO	W741DWX	30897	BD	W752DWX	30908	BD	X763VUA
30875	BN	W771DWX	30887	CN	W742DWX	30898	DN	W753DWX	30909	BD	X764VUA
30876	BY	W731DWX	30888	LO	W743DWX	30899	DN	W754DWX	30910	BD	W778DWX
30877	BY	W732DWX	30889	LO	W744DWX	30900	LO	W774DWX	30911	BD	X766VUA
30878	BN	W733DWX	30890	BD	W745DWX	30901	LO	W756DWX	30912	BD	X767VUA
30879	BY	W734DWX	30891	BD	W746DWX	30902	CN	W757DWX	30913	BD	W768DWX
30880	BY	W735DWX	30892	BD	W747DWX	30903	BR	W758DWX	30914	BD	W769DWX
30881	DN	W736DWX	30893	BD	W748DWX	30904	DN	W759DWX	30915	BD	X779VUA
30882	DN	W737DWX									

30916-30938   Volvo B7TL   Alexander ALX400   N49/29F   2000

30916	HU	W771KBT	30922	BD	W788KBT	30928	BM	X796NWR	30934	BM	X354VWT
30917	HU	W772KBT	30923	BM	X791NWR	30929	BM	X797NWR	30935	HU	X356VWT
30918	HU	W773KBT	30924	BM	X792NWR	30930	BM	X798NWR	30936	HU	X357VWT
30919	HU	W774KBT	30925	BM	X793NWR	30931	BM	X351VWT	30937	OG	X358VWT
30920	HU	W787KBT	30926	BM	X794NWR	30932	BM	X352VWT	30938	OG	X359VWT
30921	HU	W776KBT	30927	BM	X795NWR	30933	BM	X353VWT			

30939-30965   Volvo B7TL   Alexander ALX400   N49/27F   2001-02

30939	BD	Y794XNW	30946	HU	YJ51RRO	30953	HU	YJ51RSU	30960	OM	YJ51RDU
30940	BD	Y795XNW	30947	HU	YJ51RRU	30954	OM	YJ51RDO	30961	OM	YJ51RDV
30941	HU	Y796XNW	30948	HU	YJ51RRV	30955	OM	YJ51RCU	30962	OM	YJ51RDX
30942	HU	Y797XNW	30949	HU	YJ51RRX	30956	OM	YJ51RCV	30963	OM	YJ51RDY
30943	HU	Y798XNW	30950	HU	YJ51RRY	30957	OM	YJ51RCX	30964	TE	YJ51RAU
30944	HU	YJ51RPY	30951	HU	YJ51RRZ	30958	OM	YJ51RCZ	30965	TE	YJ51RAX
30945	HU	YJ51RPZ	30952	HU	YJ51RSO	30959	OM	YJ51RCO			

31129-31148   Volvo B7TL   Alexander ALX400   N49/27F   2003

31129	OG	YU52VYE	31134	OG	YU52VYK	31140	OG	YU52VYR	31145	RO	YU52VYX
31130	OG	YU52VYF	31135	OG	YU52VYL	31141	OG	YU52VYS	31146	HU	YU52VYY
31131	OG	YU52VYG	31137	OG	YU52VYN	31142	RO	YU52VYT	31147	HU	YU52VYZ
31132	OG	YU52VYH	31138	OG	YU52VYO	31143	HU	YU52VYV	31148	DN	YU52VZA
31133	OG	YU52VYJ	31139	OG	YU52VYP	31144	RO	YU52VYW			

31497	BK	R655DUS	Volvo Olympian	Northern Counties Palatine II	B43/29F	1997	
31518	CE	M847DUS	Leyland Olympian	Alexander Royale	BC47/28F	1994	
31528	ABs	URS318X	Leyland Atlantean AN68C/1R	Alexander AL	O45/29D	1982	
31529	ABs	CRG325C	Daimler CVG6	Alexander B	B37/29R	1965	

31558-31563   Volvo B7TL   Alexander ALX400   N49/29F   2001

31558	BK	X132NSS	31560	BK	X103NSS	31562	BK	X136NSS	31563	BK	X137NSS
31559	BK	X771NSO	31561	BK	X104NSS						

31577	ABt	XSS344Y	Leyland Atlantean AN68D/1R	Alexander AL	B--/--F	1983	
31656	LW	S925AKS	Volvo Olympian	Alexander Royale	B42/29F	1998	
31677	BD	P613WSU	Volvo Olympian	Alexander Royale	B42/29F	1997	
31684	GS	P588WSU	Volvo Olympian	Alexander Royale	B42/29F	1997	

31760-31775   Volvo Olympian   Alexander RH   B47/29F   1997-98   London United, 2003

31760	BDu	R921WOE	31764	BD	R925WOE	31767	BD	R931WOE	31770	BD	R934YOV
31761	BD	R922WOE	31765	BD	R926WOE	31768	BD	R932YOV	31774	HX	R939YOV
31762	BD	R923WOE	31766	BD	R930WOE	31769	BD	R933YOV	31775	HX	R940YOV
31763	BD	R924WOE									

31776-31786   Volvo B7TL   TransBus ALX400   N49/27F   2003

31776	OG	YN53EOA	31779	OG	YN53EOD	31782	DN	YN53EOG	31785	DN	YN53EOK
31777	OG	YN53EOB	31780	OG	YN53EOE	31783	DN	YN53EOH	31786	DN	YN53EOL
31778	OG	YN53EOC	31781	DN	YN53EOF	31784	DN	YN53EOJ			

One of four Volvo B7TLs with Alexander bodywork currently allocated to Lowestoft, 30900, W774DWX, was initially placed in service in Yorkshire. It is seen operating route 99 that links Normanston College with the town. *Mark Doggett*

31787-31804
Volvo B7TL — Wrightbus Eclipse Gemini — N45/29F — 2003

31787	B	YN53EFE	31792	GS	YN53EFK	31797	B	YN53EFR	31801	B	YN53EFW
31788	B	YN53EFF	31793	B	YN53EFL	31798	B	YN53EFT	31802	B	YN53EFX
31789	B	YN53EFG	31794	B	YN53EFM	31799	B	YN53EFU	31803	B	YN53EFZ
31790	GS	YN53EFH	31795	B	YN53EFO	31800	B	YN53EFV	31804	B	YN53EGC
31791	GS	YN53EFJ	31796	B	YN53EFP					

31807	HX	R929WOE	Volvo Olympian	Alexander RH	B47/29F	1997	London United, 2003
31808	HX	R936YOV	Volvo Olympian	Alexander RH	B47/29F	1998	London United, 2003

31820-31830
Volvo Olympian — Northern Counties Palatine — B47/27D — 1997 — London General, 2005

31820	CE	P920RYO	31826	CE	P926RYO	31828	CE	P908RYO	31830	CE	P930RYO
31821	CE	P921RYO								

31836	CE	R336LGH	Volvo Olympian	Northern Counties Palatine	B47/27D	1998	London General, 2005
31841	CE	R241LGH	Volvo Olympian	Northern Counties Palatine	BC47/31F	1998	Ensign, Purfleet, 2005
31846	CE	R346LGH	Volvo Olympian	Northern Counties Palatine	BC47/31F	1998	London General, 2005
31877	CE	R277LGH	Volvo Olympian	Northern Counties Palatine	B47/27D	1998	London General, 2005
31878	CEu	R278LGH	Volvo Olympian	Northern Counties Palatine	B47/27D	1998	London General, 2005

32001-32024
Volvo B7TL — Alexander ALX400 — N49/29F — 2000

32001	LH	W801PAE	32007	LH	W807PAE	32014	LH	W814PAE	32019	LH	W819PAE
32002	LH	W802PAE	32008	LH	W808PAE	32015	LH	W815PAE	32021	LH	W821PAE
32003	LH	W803PAE	32009	LH	W809PAE	32016	LH	W816PAE	32022	LH	W822PAE
32004	LH	W804PAE	32011	LH	W811PAE	32017	LH	W817PAE	32023	LH	W823PAE
32005	LH	W805PAE	32012	LH	W812PAE	32018	LH	W818PAE	32024	LH	W824PAE
32006	LH	W806PAE	32013	LH	W813PAE					

32027	CEu	V124LGC	Volvo B7TL	Alexander ALX400	O43/29F	2000

32031-32046 — Volvo B7TL — Alexander ALX400 — N49/29F — 2000

32031	SO	W801EOW	32035	HO	W805EOW	32039	WH	W809EOW	32044	PT	W814EOW
32032	HO	W802EOW	32036	WH	W806EOW	32041	PT	W811EOW	32045	WH	W815EOW
32033	HO	W803EOW	32037	PT	W807EOW	32042	PT	W812EOW	32046	WH	W816EOW
32034	SO	W804EOW	32038	SO	W808EOW	32043	WH	W813EOW			

32052	WSs	X578RJW	Volvo B7TL 10.2m	East Lancs Vyking	N--/--D	2000

32053-32065 — Volvo B7TL — Alexander ALX400 — N49/29F — 2000

32053	NE	W213XBD	32056	NE	W216XBD	32059	YA	W219XBD	32063	YA	W223XBD
32054	NE	W214XBD	32057	NE	W217XBD	32061	YA	W221XBD	32064	YA	W224XBD
32055	NE	W215XBD	32058	YA	W218XBD	32062	YA	W422SRP	32065	YA	W425SRP

32066-32099 — Volvo B7TL — Alexander ALX400 — N49/29F — 2002

32066	LE	KP51VZO	32075	LE	KP51WAO	32084	LE	KP51WBU	32092	LE	KP51WCN
32067	LE	KP51VZR	32076	LE	KP51WAU	32085	LE	KP51WBV	32093	LE	KP51WCO
32068	LE	KP51VZS	32077	LE	KP51WBD	32086	LE	KP51WBY	32094	LE	KP51WCR
32069	LE	KP51VZT	32078	LE	KP51WBG	32087	LE	KP51WBZ	32095	LE	KP51WCW
32070	LE	KP51VZW	32079	LE	KP51WBJ	32088	LE	KP51WCA	32096	LE	KP51WCX
32071	LE	KP51VZX	32080	LE	KP51WBK	32089	LE	KP51WCF	32097	CE	KP51WCY
32072	LE	KP51VZY	32081	LE	KP51WBL	32090	LE	KP51WCG	32098	LE	KP51WDD
32073	LE	KP51VZZ	32082	LE	KP51WBO	32091	LE	KP51WCJ	32099	LE	KP51WDE
32074	LE	KP51WAJ	32083	LE	KP51WBT						

32100-32112 — Volvo B7TL 10m — Plaxton President 4.4m — N39/24F — 2002

32100	VN	LT02ZCJ	32104	VN	LT02ZCO	32107	VN	LT02ZCX	32110	OG	LT02ZDJ
32101	VN	LT02ZCK	32105	VN	LT02ZCU	32108	OG	LT02ZCY	32111	OG	LT02ZDK
32102	VN	LT02ZCL	32106	VN	LT02ZCV	32109	OG	LT02ZDH	32112	VN	LT02ZDL
32103	VN	LT02ZCN									

32200-32228 — Volvo B7TL 10.6m — Plaxton President 4.4m — N42/27F — 2002

32200	YA	LT52WTE	32208	YA	LT52WTO	32215	OG	LT52WTY	32222	MU	LT52WUG
32201	VN	LT52WTF	32209	YA	LT52WTP	32216	OG	LT52WTZ	32223	MU	LT52WUH
32202	VN	LT52WTG	32210	YA	LT52WTR	32217	OG	LT52WUA	32224	MU	LT52WUJ
32203	VN	LT52WTJ	32211	VN	LT52WTU	32218	OG	LT52WUB	32225	LV	LT52WUK
32204	YA	LT52WTK	32212	YA	LT52WTV	32219	OG	LT52WUC	32226	LV	LT52WUL
32205	YA	LT52WTL	32213	YA	LT52WTW	32220	OG	LT52WUD	32227	LV	LT52XAL
32206	YA	LT52WTM	32214	YA	LT52WTX	32221	LV	LT52WUE	32228	LV	LT52XAM
32207	YA	LT52WTN									

32249-32276 — Volvo B7TL 10.6m — Alexander ALX400 4.4m — N45/24F — 2003

32249	DN	LT52WVM	32256	LH	LT52WWB	32263	DN	LT52WWJ	32270	DN	LT52WWR
32250	DN	LT52WVN	32257	LH	LT52WWC	32264	DN	LT52WWK	32271	DN	LT52WWS
32251	LH	LT52WVO	32258	LH	LT52WWD	32265	DN	LT52WWL	32272	DN	LT52WWU
32252	LH	LT52WVP	32259	LH	LT52WWE	32266	DN	LT52WWM	32273	DN	LT52WXC
32253	LH	LT52WVY	32260	DN	LT52WWF	32267	DN	LT52WWN	32274	DN	LT52WXD
32254	LH	LT52WVZ	32261	DN	LT52WWG	32268	DN	LT52WWO	32275	DN	KDZ5104
32255	LH	LT52WWA	32262	DN	LT52WWH	32269	DN	LT52WWP	32276	DN	LT52WXF

32277	LE	KP51WDF	Volvo B7TL	Alexander ALX400 4.4m	N49/27F	2002
32278	MS	YU52VYM	Volvo B7TL	Alexander ALX400 4.4m	N49/27F	2003

32279-32292 — Volvo B7TL 11.2m — TransBus ALX400 4.4m — N49/27F — 2003

32279	HG	WR03YZL	32283	BA	WR03YZS	32287	LH	WR03YZW	32290	LH	WX53UKL
32280	LH	WR03YZM	32284	BA	WR03YZT	32288	LH	WR03YZX	32291	LH	WR03ZBC
32281	BA	WR03YZN	32285	BA	WR03YZU	32289	LH	WX53UKK	32292	LH	WR03ZBD
32282	BA	WR03YZP	32286	LH	WR03YZV						

32294-32312 — Volvo B7TL 10.6m — TransBus President 4.4m — N44/23F — 2003

32294	LV	LK03NGJ	32299	LV	LK03NGY	32303	SN	LK03NHC	32309	OG	LK03NHJ
32295	LV	LK03NGN	32300	SN	LK03NGZ	32304	SN	LK03NHD	32310	OG	LK03NHL
32296	LV	LK03NGU	32301	SN	LK03NHA	32305	SN	LK03NHE	32311	OG	LK03NHM
32297	LV	LK03NGV	32302	SN	LK03NHB	32308	OG	LK03NHH	32312	OG	LK03NHN
32298	LV	LK03NGX									

Initially placed in service with Centrewest in 2004, most of this batch of Wrightbus-bodied Volvo B7TLs have now been converted to single door and allocated to the Bristol area. Carrying West of England names is 23256, LK53LZV. *Dave Heath*

32328-32348 — Volvo B7TL 10.6m — Wrightbus Eclipse Gemini — N41/28F* — 2003-04 — *32348 is N41/25F

32328	LH	LK53LYH	32334	HG	LK53LYU	32339	HG	LK53LYZ	32344	HG	LK53LZE
32329	LH	LK53LYJ	32335	HG	LK53LYV	32340	HG	LK53LZA	32345	HG	LK53LZF
32330	LH	LK53LYO	32336	HG	LK53LYW	32341	HG	LK53LZB	32346	HG	LK53LZG
32331	HG	LK53LYP	32337	HG	LK53LYX	32342	HG	LK53LZC	32347	HG	LK53LZH
32332	HG	LK53LYR	32338	HG	LK53LYY	32343	HG	LK53LZD	32348	BL	LK53LZL
32333	HG	LK53LYT									

32349-32360 — Volvo B7TL 10.1m — Wrightbus Eclipse Gemini — N38/24F — 2004

32349	BA	LK53LZM	32352	BA	LK53LZP	32355	LH	LK53LZU	32358	LH	LK53LZX
32350	BA	LK53LZN	32353	BA	LK53LZR	32356	LH	LK53LZV	32359	LH	LK53MBF
32351	BA	LK53LZO	32354	BA	LK53LZT	32357	LH	LK53LZW	32360	LH	LK04HYP

32431-32473 — Volvo B7TL 10.1m — Wrightbus Eclipse Gemini — N45/29F — 2004

32431	BM	YW04VAU	32440	BM	YJ04FYL	32449	BM	YJ04FYW	32465	BM	YJ04FZP
32432	BM	YJ04FYB	32441	BM	YJ04FYM	32450	BM	YJ04FYX	32466	BM	YJ04FZR
32433	BM	YJ04FYC	32442	BM	YJ04FYN	32451	BM	YJ04FYY	32467	BM	YJ04FZS
32434	BM	YJ04FYD	32443	BM	YJ04FYP	32452	BM	YJ04FYZ	32468	BM	YJ04FZT
32435	BM	YJ04FYE	32444	BM	YJ04FYR	32460	HP	YJ04FZH	32469	BM	YJ04FZU
32436	BM	YJ04FYF	32445	BM	YJ04FYS	32461	BM	YJ04FZK	32470	BM	YJ04FZV
32437	BM	YJ04FYG	32446	BM	YJ04FYT	32462	BM	YJ04FZL	32471	BM	YJ04FZX
32438	BM	YJ04FYH	32447	BM	YJ04FYU	32463	BM	YJ04FZM	32472	BM	YJ04FZY
32439	BM	YJ04FYK	32448	BM	YJ04FYV	32464	BM	YJ04FZN	32473	BM	YJ04FZZ

32475-32494 — Volvo B7TL 10.7m — TransBus ALX400 4.3m — N49/29F — 2003

32475	CO	AU53HJJ	32480	CO	AU53HJX	32485	CO	AU53HKC	32490	IP	AU53HKH
32476	CO	AU53HJK	32481	CO	AU53HJY	32486	IP	AU53HKD	32491	IP	AU53HKJ
32477	CO	AU53HJN	32482	CO	AU53HJZ	32487	IP	AU53HKE	32492	IP	AU53HKK
32478	CO	AU53HJO	32483	CO	AU53HKA	32488	IP	AU53HKF	32493	IP	AU53HKL
32479	IP	AU53HJV	32484	CO	AU53HKB	32489	IP	AU53HKG	32494	IP	AU53HKM

32503-32542   Volvo B7TL 10.7m   Wrightbus Eclipse Gemini   N45/29F   2004-05

32503	HU	YJ54XTO	32513	HU	YJ54XUB	32523	HX	YJ54XUO	32533	BD	YJ54XVA
32504	HU	YJ54XTP	32514	HU	YJ54XUC	32524	HX	YJ54XUP	32534	BD	YJ54XVB
32505	HU	YJ54XTR	32515	HU	YJ54XUD	32525	HX	YJ54XUR	32535	BD	YJ54XVC
32506	HU	YJ54XTT	32516	HU	YJ54XUE	32526	HX	YJ54XUT	32536	BD	YJ54XVD
32507	HU	YJ54XTU	32517	HU	YJ54XUF	32527	HX	YJ54XUU	32537	BD	YJ05VUX
32508	HU	YJ54XTV	32518	HU	YJ54XUG	32528	BD	YJ54XUV	32538	BD	YJ05VUW
32509	HU	YJ54XTW	32519	HU	YJ54XUH	32529	BD	YJ54XUW	32539	HX	YJ05VWG
32510	HU	YJ54XTX	32520	HX	YJ54XUK	32530	HX	YJ54XUX	32540	HX	YJ05VWE
32511	HU	YJ54XTZ	32521	HX	YJ54XUM	32531	HX	YJ54XUY	32541	HX	YJ05VWF
32512	HU	YJ54XUA	32522	HX	YJ54XUN	32532	HX	YJ05VUY	32542	HX	YJ05VWH

32543-32626   Volvo B7TL 10.7m   Wrightbus Eclipse Gemini   N45/29F   2004-05

32543	CA	SF54OSD	32564	CA	SF54OTE	32585	PH	SF54OUE	32606	CA	SF54TKJ
32544	CA	SF54OSE	32565	CA	SF54OTG	32586	SN	SF54OUG	32607	CA	SF54TKK
32545	SN	SF54OSG	32566	PH	SF54OTH	32587	PH	SF54OUH	32608	CA	SF54TKO
32546	CA	SF54OSJ	32567	PH	SF54OTJ	32588	SN	SF54OUJ	32609	B	SF54TKN
32547	CA	SF54OSK	32568	CA	SF54OTK	32589	PH	SF54OUK	32610	CA	SF54TKT
32548	CA	SF54OSL	32569	CA	SF54OTL	32590	SN	SF54OUL	32611	CA	SF54TKU
32549	CA	SF54OSM	32570	CA	SF54OTM	32591	SN	SF54OUM	32612	CA	SF54TKV
32550	CA	SF54OSN	32571	CA	SF54OTN	32592	SN	SF54OUN	32613	PH	SF54TKX
32551	CA	SF54OSO	32572	CA	SF54OTP	32593	SN	SF54THV	32614	CA	SF54TKY
32552	CA	SF54OSP	32573	CA	SF54OTR	32594	SN	SF54THX	32615	PH	SF54TKZ
32553	CA	SF54OSR	32574	CA	SF54OTT	32595	SN	SF54THZ	32616	PH	SF54TLJ
32554	CA	SF54OSU	32575	CA	SF54OTU	32596	SN	SF54TJO	32617	PH	SF54TLK
32555	SN	SF54OSV	32576	SN	SF54OTV	32597	SN	SF54TJU	32618	PH	SF54TLN
32556	PH	SF54OSW	32577	PH	SF54OTW	32598	CA	SF54TJV	32619	PH	SF54TLO
32557	PH	SF54OSX	32578	PH	SF54OTX	32599	CA	SF54TJX	32620	PH	SF54TLU
32558	PH	SF54OSY	32579	PH	SF54OTY	32600	CA	SF54TJY	32621	PH	SF54TLX
32559	PH	SF54OSZ	32580	CA	SF54OTZ	32601	CA	SF54TJZ	32622	CA	SF54TLY
32560	PH	SF54OTA	32581	CA	SF54OUA	32602	CA	SF54TKA	32623	CA	SF54TLZ
32561	CA	SF54OTB	32582	SN	SF54OUB	32603	CA	SF54TKC	32624	CA	SF54TMO
32562	CA	SF54OTC	32583	CA	SF54OUC	32604	CA	SF54TKD	32625	CA	SF54TMU
32563	CA	SF54OTD	32584	CA	SF54OUD	32605	CA	SF54TKE	32626	CA	SF54TMV

32627-32650   Volvo B7TL 10.7m   Wrightbus Eclipse Gemini   N45/29F   2005

32627	AG	KP54KAO	32633	AG	KP54LAE	32639	AG	KP54AZA	32645	LE	KP54AZJ
32628	BS	KP54KAU	32634	AG	KP54LAO	32640	BS	KP54AZB	32646	LE	KP54AZL
32629	YA	KP54KAX	32635	AG	KX05MGV	32641	BS	KP54AZC	32647	LE	KP54AZN
32630	AG	KP54KBE	32636	HG	WX05UAF	32642	BS	KP54AZD	32648	LE	KP54KBK
32631	BS	KP54KBF	32637	HG	WX05UAG	32643	LE	KP54AZF	32649	LE	KP54KBN
32632	AG	KP54KBJ	32638	HG	WX05UAH	32644	LE	KP54AZG	32650	LE	KP54KBO

32651-32656   Volvo B7TL 10.7m   ADL ALX400   N49/27F   2005

32651	CO	AU05MUO	32653	IP	AU05MUV	32655	IP	AU05MUY	32656	IP	AU05MVA
32652	CO	AU05MUP	32654	CO	AU05MUW						

32657   CA   LK55ACO   Volvo B7TL 10.7m   Wrightbus Eclipse Gemini   N41/25F   2005

32669-32683   Volvo B7TL 10.7m   Wrightbus Eclipse Gemini   N45/29F   2005

32669	GS	SN55HDZ	32673	LV	SN55HFA	32677	LV	SN55HFE	32681	LV	SN55HFJ
32670	GS	SN55HEJ	32674	LV	SN55HFB	32678	LT	SN55HFF	32682	LV	SN55HFK
32671	GS	SN55HEU	32675	LV	SN55HFC	32679	LT	SN55HFG	32683	LV	SN55HFL
32672	GS	SN55HEV	32676	GS	SN55HFD	32680	LV	SN55HFH			

32684-32691   Volvo B7TL 10.7m   Wrightbus Eclipse Gemini   N45/27F   2006

32684	MS	WX56HJZ	32686	MS	WX56HKB	32688	MS	WX56HKD	32690	MS	WX56HKF
32685	MS	WX56HKA	32687	MS	WX56HKC	32689	MS	WX56HKE	32691	MS	WX56HKG

32692-32697   Volvo B7TL 10.7m   Wrightbus Eclipse Gemini   N45/29F   2006

32692	HX	YJ06XLK	32694	HX	YJ06XLM	32696	HX	YJ06XLO	32697	HPu	YJ06XLP
32693	HX	YJ06XLL	32695	HX	YJ06XLN						

32701-32717   Dennis Trident   East Lancs Lolyne   N49/30F   2000

32701	WH	V701FFB	32705	SO	W705PHT	32709	PL	W709RHT	32714	PL	W714RHT
32702	WH	W702PHT	32706	SO	W706PHT	32711	PL	W711RHT	32715	PL	W715RHT
32703	HO	W703PHT	32707	HO	W707PHT	32712	PL	W712RHT	32716	PL	W716RHT
32704	SO	W704PHT	32708	HO	W708PHT	32713	PL	W713RHT	32717	PL	W717RHT

To celebrate the eightieth anniversary of Western National, East Lancs-bodied Trident 32716, W716RHT, was repainted into that operator's traditional colours. It was pictured in November 2013 in Plymouth, while operating route 7 which at that time went to Eberton. *Mark Lyons*

32751-32754   Dennis Trident   East Lancs Lolyne   N49/30F   2000

32751	PL	X501BFJ	32752	PL	X502BFJ	32753	PL	X503BFJ	32754	PL	X504BFJ

32755	PL	WK52SYE	TransBus Trident East Lancs Myllennium Lolyne N49/30F 2002

32756-32768   ADL Trident 9.9m   East Lancs Myllennium Lolyne NC49/31F   2005

32756	PL	WA54OLO	32760	PL	WA54OLR	32763	WH	WJ55CSF	32766	WH	WJ55CSV
32757	PL	WA54OLP	32761	PL	WJ55CRX	32764	HO	WJ55CSO	32767	WH	WJ55CTE
32758	PL	WA54OLT	32762	PL	WJ55CRZ	32765	WH	WJ55CSU	32768	HO	WJ55CTF
32759	PL	WA54OLN									

32801-32821   Dennis Trident 9.9m   Plaxton President 4.4m   N39/24F   1999

32801	BS	T801LLC	32806	CMt	T806LLC	32811	LVu	T811LLC	32818	BS	T818LLC
32802	PL	T802LLC	32808	PL	T808LLC	32813	LVu	T813LLC	32819	PL	T819LLC
32803	PL	T803LLC	32809	BS	T809LLC	32814	LVu	T814LLC	32821	LTu	T821LLC
32804	BS	T804LLC	32810	BR	T810LLC	32817	PL	T817LLC			

32823-32853   Dennis Trident 9.9m   Plaxton President 4.4m   N39/27F   1999

32823	LT	T823LLC	32838	LT	T838LLC	32844	BW	MIG3844	32850	BS	T850LLC
32830	LT	T830LLC	32840	LT	T840LLC	32845	AB	T845LLC	32851	PL	HIG1519
32831	LT	T831LLC	32841	LT	T841LLC	32846	PL	T846LLC	32852	WR	T852LLC
32834	LT	T834LLC	32842	LT	T842LLC	32847	BS	T847LLC	32853	PL	HIG1512
32837	GS	T837LLC	32843	BW	MIG3842	32849	BS	T849LLC			

Heading for Bobblestock, located just outside Hereford on route 72 is Plaxton President 33042, LN51DWG, now converted to single door. Hereford depot has just two double-deck buses in its twenty-four vehicle allocation. *Bill Potter*

32854-32887

			Dennis Trident 9.9m			Plaxton President 4.4m		N39/24F	1999		
32854	WR	T854KLF	32863	BS	V863HBY	32870	MU	T870KLF	32878	CE	HIG1531
32855	BS	V855HBY	32864	BS	T864KLF	32872	BW	HIG1521	32879	CE	HIG1533
32856	BR	V856HBY	32865	AB	T865KLF	32873	BW	HIG1523	32880	CE	HIG1538
32858	PL	HIG1528	32866	BWu	MIG3859	32874	BW	HIG1524	32883	BS	T883KLF
32859	BS	V859HBY	32867	OX	V867HBY	32875	CE	HIG1526	32887	BS	V887HBY
32861	CE	HIG1540	32869	OX	V869HBY	32876	CE	HIG1527			

32889-32930

			Dennis Trident 9.9m			Plaxton President 4.4m		N43/27F	2000		
32889	LT	V889HLH	32905	BS	W905VLN	32913	OX	W913VLN	32922	LT	W922VLN
32892	LW	V892HLH	32906	OXu	W906VLN	32914	LT	W914VLN	32923	LT	W923VLN
32893	LT	V893HLH	32907	LT	W907VLN	32915	OX	W915VLN	32924	LT	W924VLN
32895	LT	V895HLH	32908	OX	W908VLN	32916	OX	W916VLN	32925	SN	W898VLN
32896	LT	V896HLH	32909	LT	W909VLN	32917	LT	W917VLN	32926	OX	W926VLN
32897	LT	V897HLH	32910	LT	W895VLN	32918	LW	W918VLN	32927	Bu	W927VLN
32898	LT	V898HLH	32911	OX	W896VLN	32919	LT	W919VLN	32928	AB	W928VLN
32899	OX	V899HLH	32912	OX	W912VLN	32921	LW	W921VLN	32930	BW	MIG4760
32904	LT	W904VLN									

32931-32951

			Dennis Trident 9.9m			Alexander ALX400 4.4m		N45/27F	2000		
32931	HG	W931ULL	32937	HG	W937ULL	32942	HG	W942ULL	32949	LW	W949ULL
32934	LT	W934ULL	32939	HG	W939ULL	32946	HG	W946ULL	32950	HG	W132VLO
32935	BW	MIG6219	32940	HG	W840VLO	32947	BW	MIG8433	32951	LT	W951ULL
32936	BW	MIG6096	32941	HG	W941ULL	32948	LW	W948ULL			

32954-32983

			Dennis Trident 9.9m			Plaxton President 4.4m		N39/23F	2001		
32954	BW	MIG9615	32961	BW	MIG4761	32970	AB	X613HLT	32977	B	X977HLT
32955	OG	X611HLT	32962	AB	X962HLT	32971	AB	X971HLT	32978	PH	X978HLT
32956	SN	X956HLT	32964	PH	X964HLT	32972	OX	X972HLT	32979	SN	Y224NLF
32957	OG	X957HLT	32965	PHu	X965HLT	32973	AB	X973HLT	32980	PH	X614HLT
32958	AB	X958HLT	32967	LT	X967HLT	32974	AB	X974HLT	32981	SN	X981HLT
32959	OX	X959HLT	32968	LT	X968HLT	32975	AB	X975HLT	32982	B	Y346NLF
32960	B	X612HLT	32969	SN	X969HLT	32976	AB	Y223NLF	32983	B	Y344NLF

Recent changes at Leicester have seen double-deck buses transfer to Bristol in exchange for single-decks. Currently remaining in the city is 33507, LK08FKZ, which is emblazoned with vinyls for route 54.
Dave Heath

32984-33000   Dennis Trident 9.9m   Plaxton President 4.4m   N39/20F   2001

32984	B	Y984NLP	**32989**	B	Y989NLP	**32993**	SN	Y993NLP	**32997**	B	Y997NLP
32985	SN	Y985NLP	**32990**	B	Y932NLP	**32994**	Bu	Y994NLP	**32998**	PH	Y998NLP
32986	SN	Y986NLP	**32991**	B	Y991NLP	**32995**	MU	Y995NLP	**32999**	B	Y933NLP
32987	B	Y987NLP	**32992**	B	Y992NLP	**32996**	PH	Y996NLP	**33000**	PH	Y934NLP
32988	B	Y988NLP									

33001-33035   Dennis Trident 10.5m   Plaxton President 4.4m   N42/25F   2001

33001	BS	LK51UZO	**33012**	CA	LK51UZL	**33020**	PH	LK51UYX	**33028**	PH	LK51UYJ
33002	BS	LK51UZP	**33013**	CA	LK51UZM	**33021**	PH	LK51UYY	**33029**	MU	LK51UYL
33003	VN	LK51UZS	**33014**	CA	LK51UZN	**33022**	PH	LK51UYZ	**33030**	LT	LK51UYM
33004	VN	LK51UZT	**33015**	CA	LK51UYS	**33023**	PH	LK51UZA	**33031**	OG	LK51UYN
33007	VN	LK51UZE	**33016**	CA	LK51UYT	**33024**	PH	LK51UZB	**33032**	OG	LK51UYO
33008	CA	LK51UZF	**33017**	CA	LK51UYU	**33025**	PH	LK51UYF	**33033**	PH	LK51UYP
33009	CA	LK51UZG	**33018**	CA	LK51UYV	**33026**	PH	LK51UYG	**33034**	PH	LK51UYR
33010	CA	LK51UZH	**33019**	CA	LK51UYW	**33027**	PH	LK51UYH	**33035**	PH	LK51UYD
33011	CA	LK51UZJ									

33037-33071   Dennis Trident 9.9m   Plaxton President 4.4m   N39/20F   2001

33037	MU	LN51DWA	**33046**	CA	LN51DVL	**33057**	VN	LN51GJJ	**33065**	OG	LN51GKZ
33039	WR	LN51DWD	**33047**	BS	LN51DVM	**33058**	VN	LN51GJK	**33066**	CE	LN51GLF
33040	CA	LN51DWE	**33050**	MU	LN51GKF	**33059**	MU	LN51GJO	**33067**	CE	LN51GLJ
33041	OG	LN51DWF	**33052**	CA	LN51GKJ	**33060**	VN	LN51GJU	**33068**	CE	LN51GLK
33042	HD	LN51DWG	**33053**	CA	LN51GKK	**33061**	OG	LN51GKU	**33069**	OG	LN51GLV
33043	HD	LN51DVG	**33054**	CA	LN51GKL	**33062**	OG	LN51GKV	**33070**	OG	LN51GLY
33044	BR	LN51DVH	**33055**	VN	LN51GKO	**33063**	OG	LN51GKX	**33071**	OG	LN51GKA
33045	BR	LN51DVK	**33056**	VN	LN51GKP	**33064**	OG	LN51GKY			

33072-33099   Dennis Trident 10.5m   Plaxton President 4.4m   N44/25F   2002

33072	HH	LN51GOC	**33081**	HH	LN51GNU	**33088**	BR	LN51GMU	**33094**	CA	LN51NRK
33073	HH	LN51GOE	**33082**	OG	LN51GNV	**33089**	CA	LN51GMV	**33095**	HH	LN51NRL
33074	HH	LN51GOH	**33083**	OG	LN51GNX	**33090**	HH	LN51GMX	**33096**	CA	LN51GNY
33077	BS	LN51GNF	**33084**	OG	LN51GME	**33091**	CA	LN51GMY	**33097**	CA	LN51GNZ
33078	BR	LN51GNJ	**33086**	BR	LN51GMG	**33092**	CA	LN51GMZ	**33098**	HH	LN51GOA
33079	OG	LN51GNK	**33087**	BR	LN51GMO	**33093**	MU	LN51NRJ	**33099**	OG	LN51GLZ
33080	BR	LN51GNP									

| 33111 | CE | PJ02PZP | Dennis Trident 9.9m | | | Plaxton President | | N39/23F | 2002 | Fal River Buses, 2015 |
| 33112 | CE | PJ02PZY | Dennis Trident 9.9m | | | Plaxton President | | N39/23F | 2002 | Fal River Buses, 2015 |

33113-33129

Dennis Trident 9.9m — Plaxton President 4.4m — N39/23F — 2002

33113	VN	LT02NVX	33117	CA	LT02NVZ	33121	CA	LT02NWD	33126	VN	LT02NVO
33114	CA	LT02NVW	33118	CA	LT02NWA	33122	B	LT02NVL	33127	OG	LT02NVP
33115	CA	LT02NVV	33119	CA	LT02NWB	33124	OG	LT02NVM	33128	OG	LT02NVR
33116	CA	LT02NVU	33120	CA	LT02NWC	33125	OG	LT02NVN	33129	OG	LT02NVS

33131-33140

Dennis Trident 10.5m — Plaxton President 4.4m — N42/26F — 2002

33131	MU	LT02ZBX	33134	HH	LT02ZCA	33137	MU	LT02ZFJ	33139	MU	LT02ZFL
33132	HH	LT02ZBY	33135	MU	LT02ZCE	33138	MU	LT02ZFK	33140	MU	LT02ZFM
33133	HH	LT02ZBZ	33136	HH	LT02ZCF						

33141-33154

Dennis Trident 9.9m — Plaxton President 4.4m — N39/23F — 2002

33141	BL	LR02LWW	33145	BL	LR02LXA	33149	VN	LR02LXH	33152	VN	LR02LXL
33142	BL	LR02LWX	33146	VN	LR02LXB	33150	VN	LR02LXJ	33153	BL	LR02LXM
33143	BL	LR02LWY	33147	BL	LR02LXC	33151	VN	LR02LXK	33154	VN	LR02LXN
33144	BL	LR02LWZ	33148	BL	LR02LXG						

33155-33196

Dennis Trident 9.9m — Plaxton President 4.4m — N39/23F — 2002

33155	VN	LR02LXO	33165	VN	LR02LYC	33175	PL	LR02LYU	33186	BR	LT52WVB
33156	VN	LR02LXP	33166	VN	LR02LYD	33176	PL	LR02LYV	33188	BS	LT52WVD
33157	VN	LR02LXS	33167	VN	LR02LYF	33177	PL	LR02LYW	33189	HH	LT52WVE
33158	VN	LR02LXT	33168	VN	LR02LYG	33178	BS	LR02LYX	33190	BR	LT52XAA
33159	VN	LR02LXU	33169	VN	LR02LYJ	33179	BL	LR02LYY	33191	HH	LT52XAB
33160	VN	LR02LXV	33170	VN	LR02LYK	33180	BL	LR02LYZ	33192	BS	LT52XAC
33161	VN	LR02LXW	33171	VN	LR02LYO	33181	BL	LR02LZA	33194	BS	LT52XAE
33162	VN	LR02LXX	33172	PL	LR02LYP	33182	BL	LR02LZB	33195	BR	LT52XAF
33163	VN	LR02LXZ	33173	PL	LR02LYS	33183	BL	LR02LZC	33196	BR	LT52XAG
33164	VN	LR02LYA	33174	PL	LR02LYT	33184	BR	LR02LZD			

33229-33248

Dennis Trident 9.9m — Plaxton President 4.4m — N39/23F — 2002-03

33229	HH	LT52WXG	33235	VN	LT52WWY	33239	VN	LT52WVH	33245	VN	LT52WUW
33230	OG	LT52WXH	33236	VN	LT52WWZ	33240	VN	LT52WVJ	33246	VN	LT52WUX
33232	HH	LT52WXK	33237	VN	LT52WVF	33242	VN	LT52WVL	33247	VN	LT52WUY
33233	VN	LT52WWV	33238	VN	LT52WVG	33244	VN	LT52WUV	33248	VN	LT52WVA
33234	VN	LT52WWX									

33343-33386

TransBus Trident 10.5m — TransBus ALX400 4.4m — N42/24F — 2003

33343	PH	LK53EZV	33354	PH	LK53FDA	33365	PH	LK53EYF	33376	HH	LK53EYV
33344	PH	LK53EZW	33355	PH	LK53EXT	33366	PH	LK53EYG	33377	TN	LK53EYW
33345	PH	LK53EZX	33356	PH	LK53EXU	33367	PH	LK53EYH	33378	TN	LK53EYX
33346	PH	LK53EZZ	33357	PH	LK53EXV	33368	PH	LK53EYJ	33379	TN	LK53EYY
33347	PH	LK53FCF	33358	PH	LK53EXW	33369	PH	LK53EYL	33380	TN	LK53EYZ
33348	PH	LK53FCG	33359	PH	LK53EXX	33370	PH	LK53EYM	33381	TN	LK53EZA
33349	PH	LK53FCJ	33360	PH	LK53EXZ	33371	PH	LK53EYO	33382	TN	LK53EZB
33350	PH	LK53FCL	33361	PH	LK53EYA	33372	PH	LK53EYP	33383	HH	LK53EZC
33351	PH	LK53FCX	33362	PH	LK53EYB	33373	HH	LK53EYR	33384	HH	LK53EZD
33352	PH	LK53FCY	33363	PH	LK53EYC	33374	PH	LK53EYT	33385	HH	LK53EZE
33353	PH	LK53FCZ	33364	PH	LK53EYD	33375	PH	LK53EYU	33386	PH	LK53EZF

33401-33405

TransBus Trident 10.7m — TransBus ALX400 4.4m — N47/27F — 2004

| 33401 | WR | VX54MTV | 33403 | WR | VX54MTZ | 33404 | WR | VX54MUA | 33405 | WR | VX54MUB |
| 33402 | WR | VX54MTY | | | | | | | | | |

33411-33419

ADL Trident 2 11m — ADL Enviro 400 — NC39/32F — 2006

33411	WS	WA56FUB	33414	WS	WA56FTK	33416	WS	WA56FTO	33418	WS	WA56FTT
33412	MS	WA56FUD	33415	WS	WA56FTN	33417	WS	WA56FTP	33419	MS	WA56FTU
33413	MS	WA56FUE									

33420	PL	WA08MVE	ADL Trident 2 11m	ADL Enviro 400	NC41/27F	2008	
33421	PL	WA08MVF	ADL Trident 2 11m	ADL Enviro 400	NC41/27F	2008	
33422	PL	WA08MVG	ADL Trident 2 11m	ADL Enviro 400	NC41/27F	2008	
33423	YA	SN60CAA	ADL Trident 2 11m	ADL Enviro 400	NC41/27F	2010	Connex, Jersey, 2013
33424	BS	VT59JPT	ADL Trident 2 11m	ADL Enviro 400	N41/27F	2010	JPT, Middleton, 2013
33425	BS	SN59AWV	ADL Trident 2 11m	ADL Enviro 400	NC41/26F	2010	Ensign Bus, 2013

33504-33508

ADL Trident 2 11m — ADL Enviro 400 — N41/30F — 2008

| 33504 | LE | LK08FLX | 33506 | HG | LK08FKY | 33507 | LE | LK08FKZ | 33508 | HG | LK08FLA |

33544-33553 — ADL Trident 2 11m — ADL Enviro 400 — N41/30F — 2008

33544	LE	SN58CFK	33547	HG	SN58CFO	33550	HG	SN58CFV	
33545	LE	SN58CFL	33548	LE	SN58CFP	33551	LE	SN58CFX	
33546	LE	SN58CFM	33549	LE	SN58CFU				
33552	LE	SN58CFY							
33553	LE	SN58CFZ							

33554-33574 — ADL Trident 2 10.8m — ADL Enviro 400 — N41/30F — 2008

33554	HG	SN58CGE	33560	HG	SN58CGV	33565	HG	SN58CHD
33555	LE	SN58CGF	33561	LE	SN58CGX	33566	HG	SN58CHF
33556	HG	SN58CGG	33562	LE	SN58CGY	33567	LE	SN58CHG
33557	LE	SN58CGK	33563	LE	SN58CGZ	33568	LE	SN58CHH
33558	LE	SN58CGO	33564	HG	SN58CHC	33569	HG	SN58CHJ
33559	LE	SN58CGU						
33570	LE	SN58CHK						
33571	HG	SN58CHL						
33572	LE	SN58CHO						
33573	LE	SN58ENR						
33574	LE	SN58ENT						

33656-33755 — ADL E40D — ADL Enviro 400 — N45/29F — 2012

33656	OX	SN12ADU	33681	OM	SN12AFF	33706	OM	SN12AHP
33657	BN	SN12ADV	33682	OM	SN12AFJ	33707	BN	SN12AHU
33658	CE	SN12ADX	33683	OM	SN12AFK	33708	OM	SN12AHV
33659	CE	SN12ADZ	33684	OM	SN12AFO	33709	BN	SN12AHX
33660	CE	SN12AEA	33685	OM	SN12AFU	33710	BN	SN12AHY
33661	CE	SN12AEB	33686	OM	SN12AFV	33711	BN	SN12AHZ
33662	CE	SN12AED	33687	OM	SN12AFX	33712	BN	SN12AJO
33663	OM	SN12AEE	33688	OM	SN12AFY	33713	BN	SN12AJU
33664	CE	SN12AEF	33689	OM	SN12AFZ	33714	BN	SN12AJV
33665	CE	SN12AEG	33690	OM	SN12AGO	33715	BN	SN12AJX
33666	CE	SN12AEJ	33691	BN	SN12AGU	33716	BN	SN12AJY
33667	CE	SN12AEK	33692	OM	SN12AGV	33717	BN	SN12AKF
33668	OX	SN12AEL	33693	BN	SN12AGX	33718	BN	SN12AKG
33669	OX	SN12AEM	33694	OM	SN12AGY	33719	BN	SN12AKJ
33670	OM	SN12AEO	33695	BN	SN12AGZ	33720	BN	SN12AKK
33671	OM	SN12AEP	33696	BN	SN12AHA	33721	BN	SN12AKO
33672	OM	SN12AET	33697	BN	SN12AHC	33722	BN	SN12AKP
33673	BN	SN12AEU	33698	OM	SN12AHD	33723	OM	SN12AKU
33674	OM	SN12AEV	33699	BN	SN12AHE	33724	BN	SN12AKV
33675	OM	SN12AEW	33700	BN	SN12AHF	33725	BN	SN12AKX
33676	OM	SN12AEX	33701	OM	SN12AHG	33726	BN	SN12AKY
33677	BN	SN12AEY	33702	OM	SN12AHJ	33727	BN	SN12AKZ
33678	OM	SN12AEZ	33703	OM	SN12AHK	33728	BN	SN12ALO
33679	OM	SN12AFA	33704	BN	SN12AHL	33729	BN	SN12ALU
33680	OM	SN12AFE	33705	BN	SN12AHO	33730	BN	SN12AMK
33731	BN	SN12AMO						
33732	BN	SN12AMU						
33733	BN	SN12AMV						
33734	BN	SN12AMX						
33735	BN	SN12ANF						
33736	BN	SN12ANP						
33737	BN	SN12ANR						
33738	OM	SN12ANU						
33739	BN	SN12ANV						
33740	BN	SN12ANX						
33741	OM	SN12AOA						
33742	BN	SN12AOB						
33743	BN	SN12AOC						
33744	OM	SN12AOD						
33745	OM	SN12AOE						
33746	OM	SN12AOF						
33747	OM	SN12AOG						
33748	OM	SN12AOH						
33749	BN	SN12AOJ						
33750	OM	SN12AOK						
33751	OM	SN12AOL						
33752	OM	SN12AOM						
33753	BN	SN12AOO						
33754	OM	SN12AOP						
33755	OM	SN12AOR						

Bradshaw Gate in Bolton is the location for this view of 33736, SN12ANP, representing the large batch comprising one hundred of the E40D version Enviro 400 that entered service in 2012.
Alan Blagburn

Twenty-three low-height Enviro 400s were placed in service in Glasgow during 2011 and being the hybrid model, they feature a silver-based livery. Currently allocated to the recently opened Caledonia depot that has replaced the Larkfield facility, 33913, SN61BDX, is seen with route 6 lettering. *Mark Lyons*

33803-33824

			ADL E40D			ADL Enviro 400			NC41/26F	2013	
33803	KL	YX63LJF	33809	KL	YX63LJU	33815	KL	YX63LKD	33820	LO	YX63LKK
33804	KL	YX63LJJ	33810	KL	YX63LJV	33816	KL	YX63LKE	33821	LO	YX63LKL
33805	KL	YX63LJK	33811	KL	YX63LJY	33817	KL	YX63LKF	33822	LO	YX63LKM
33806	KL	YX63LJL	33812	KL	YX63LJZ	33818	LO	YX63LKG	33823	LO	YX63LKN
33807	KL	YX63LJN	33813	KL	YX63LKA	33819	LO	YX63LKJ	33824	LO	YX63LKO
33808	KL	YX63LJO	33814	KL	YX63LKC						

33825-33830

			ADL E40D			ADL Enviro 400			N45/29F	2013	
33825	WS	SN63MYH	33827	WS	SN63MYK	33829	WS	SN63MYM	33830	WS	SN63MYO
33826	WS	SN63MYJ	33828	WS	SN63MYL						

33831-33872

			ADL E40D			ADL Enviro 400			N45/29F	2014	
33831	OX	SK14CTV	33842	OX	SN14TTF	33853	OX	SN14TUJ	33863	OG	SL14LMF
33832	OX	SK14CTX	33843	OX	SN14TTJ	33854	OX	SN14TUO	33864	OG	SL14LMJ
33833	OX	SK14CTY	33844	OX	SN14TTK	33855	OX	SN14TUP	33865	OG	SL14LMK
33834	OX	SN14TRZ	33845	OX	SN14TTO	33856	OX	SN14TUV	33866	OG	SL14LMM
33835	OX	SN14TSO	33846	OX	SN14TTU	33857	OX	SN14TUW	33867	OG	SL14LMO
33836	OX	SN14TSU	33847	OX	SN14TTV	33858	OG	SL14DFD	33868	OG	SL14LMU
33837	OX	SN14TSX	33848	OX	SN14TTX	33859	OG	SL14DFE	33869	OG	SL14LMV
33838	OX	SN14TSX	33849	OX	SN14TTY	33860	OG	SL14DFF	33870	OG	SL14LMY
33839	OX	SN14TSY	33850	OX	SN14TTZ	33861	OG	SL14DFG	33871	OG	SL14LNA
33840	OX	SN14TSZ	33851	OX	SN14TUA	33862	OG	SL14DFK	33872	OG	SL14LNC
33841	OX	SN14TTE	33852	OX	SN14TUH						

33873-33890

			ADL E40D			ADL Enviro 400			NC45/29F	2014	
33873	BM	SN14TUY	33878	BM	SN14TVF	33883	BM	SN14TVO	33887	BM	SN14TVV
33874	BM	SN14TVA	33879	BM	SN14TVJ	33884	BM	SN14TVP	33888	BM	SL14DBO
33875	BM	SN14TVC	33880	BM	SN14TVK	33885	BM	SN14TVT	33889	BM	SL14DBU
33876	BM	SN14TVD	33881	BM	SN14TVL	33886	BM	SN14TVU	33890	BM	SL14DBV
33877	BM	SN14TVE	33882	BM	SN14TVM						

33895	HO	SN14TPZ	ADL E40D	ADL Enviro 400	N45/29F	2014
33896	HO	SN14TRV	ADL E40D	ADL Enviro 400	N45/29F	2014
33897	HO	SN14TRX	ADL E40D	ADL Enviro 400	N45/29F	2014
33900	QS	-	ADL E40D	ADL Enviro 400 MMC	N--/--F	2015

33901-33923 — ADL Trident 2 11m Hybrid — ADL Enviro 400 low-height — N47/29F — 2011

33901	SN	SN11FOJ	33907	CA	SN11FOV	33913	CA	SN61BDX	33919	CA	SN61BEY
33902	SN	SN11FOK	33908	CA	SN11FPA	33914	CA	SN61BDY	33920	CA	SN61BFA
33903	SN	SN11FOM	33909	CA	SN11FPC	33915	CA	SN61BDZ	33921	CA	SN61BFE
33904	CA	SN11FOP	33910	CA	SN11FPD	33916	CA	SN61BEJ	33922	CA	SN61BFF
33905	CA	SN11FOT	33911	CA	SN61BDU	33917	CA	SN61BEO	33923	CA	SN61BFJ
33906	CA	SN11FOU	33912	CA	SN61BDV	33918	CA	SN61BEU			

33951-33999 — ADL Trident 2 — ADL Enviro 400 MMC — N47/29F — 2015

33951	LH	-	33963	LH	-	33977	CA	-	33989	CA	-
33952	LH	-	33964	LH	-	33978	CA	-	33990	CA	-
33953	LH	-	33965	LH	-	33979	CA	-	33991	CA	-
33954	LH	-	33966	LH	-	33980	CA	-	33992	CA	-
33955	LH	-	33967	LH	-	33981	CA	-	33993	CA	-
33956	LH	-	33968	LH	-	33982	CA	-	33994	CA	-
33957	LH	-	33969	LH	-	33983	CA	-	33995	CA	-
33958	LH	-	33970	LH	-	33984	CA	-	33996	CA	-
33959	LH	-	33972	LH	-	33985	CA	-	33997	CA	-
33960	LH	-	33973	LH	-	33986	CA	-	33998	CA	-
33961	LH	-	33974	LH	-	33987	CA	-	33999	CA	-
33962	LH	-	33976	CA	-	33988	CA	-			

34003	PL	K803ORL	Volvo Olympian	Northern Counties Palatine	BC39/30F	1993	
34015	BK	P535EFL	Volvo Olympian	Northern Counties Palatine	B49/33F	1996	Stagecoach, 2003
34016	HO	P536EFL	Volvo Olympian	Northern Counties Palatine	B49/33F	1996	Stagecoach, 2003
34017	HO	P540EFL	Volvo Olympian	Northern Counties Palatine	B49/33F	1996	Stagecoach, 2003

34041-34052 — Volvo Olympian — Northern Counties Palatine II — B43/27F — 1996

34041	CE	P241UCW	34048	GS	P248UCW	34050	CE	P250UCW	34052	CE	P252UCW
34044	WH	P244UCW	34049	CE	P249UCW	34051	CE	P251UCW			

34059-34079 — Volvo Olympian — Northern Counties Palatine — B49/33F — 1996 — Stagecoach, 2003

34059	HOu	P559EFL	34064	TNu	P564EFL	34075	BK	P575EFL	34079	SO	P579EFL

34089-34107 — Volvo Olympian — Northern Counties Palatine — B47/31F — 1999

34089	TEu	T889KLF	34093	CE	T893KLF	34098	CE	T898KLF	34104	CE	T904KLF
34090	OGu	T890KLF	34096	CE	T896KLF	34099	CE	T899KLF	34105	BNu	T905KLF
34091	CE	T891KLF	34097	CE	T897KLF	34102	OMu	T902KLF	34107	HX	T907KLF
34092	PL	T892KLF									

34108-34114 — Volvo Olympian — Alexander Royale — BC43/29F — 2000 — Blazefield, 2005-06

34108	YA	W435CWX	34110	YAu	W437CWX	34112	YAu	W432CWX	34114	YA	W434CWX
34109	YA	W436CWX	34111	YA	W431CWX	34113	YAu	W433CWX			

34116	CE	L816CFJ	Volvo Olympian	Northern Counties Palatine	B47/29F	1993
34137	CEu	L637SEU	Volvo Olympian	Northern Counties Palatine II	O47/29F	1993
34138	CE	L638SEU	Volvo Olympian	Northern Counties Palatine II	B47/29F	1993
34162	CE	R662NHY	Volvo Olympian	Northern Counties Palatine II	B43/29F	1997

34165-34186 — Volvo Olympian — Northern Counties Palatine II — B43/29F — 1998

34165	WH	S665AAE	34173	CE	S673AAE	34179	BW	S679AAE	34184	CE	S684AAE
34167	WH	S667AAE	34176	BW	S676AAE	34181	CE	S681AAE	34185	CE	S685AAE
34168	WH	S668AAE	34177	CE	S677AAE	34182	CE	S682AAE	34186	YA	S686AAE
34172	CE	S672AAE	34178	BW	S678AAE	34183	CE	S683AAE			

34189	BWu	S689AAE	Volvo Olympian	Northern Counties Palatine II	BC47/29F	1998

34192-34200 — Volvo Olympian — Alexander Royale — BC43/22F — 1995 — National Express, 2004

34192	CE	530OHU	34195	CEu	TJI4838	34197	CE	HVJ716	34199	CE	NER621
34193	CEu	VJT738	34196	CE	OWB243	34198	CE	UKT552	34200	CE	VOO273
34194	CE	481FPO									

34206	BYu	S206LLO	Volvo Olympian	Northern Counties Palatine	B47/31F	1998
34211	HX	S211LLO	Volvo Olympian	Northern Counties Palatine	B47/31F	1998

34258	WH	N526LHG	Volvo Olympian	Northern Counties Palatine	B47/30F	1995	Go-Ahead London, 2004
34259	CE	N533LHG	Volvo Olympian	Northern Counties Palatine	B47/27D	1995	Go-Ahead London, 2004
34261	CE	N542LHG	Volvo Olympian	Northern Counties Palatine	B47/27D	1995	Go-Ahead London, 2005
34290	BK	P191TGD	Volvo Olympian	Alexander RL	B47/32F	1996	
34295	HO	P295KPX	Volvo Olympian	Northern Counties Palatine	B47/30F	1996	
34305	CM	L305PWR	Volvo Olympian	Northern Counties Palatine	B47/29F	1994	
34311	NE	L311PWR	Volvo Olympian	Northern Counties Palatine	B47/29F	1994	
34615	CE	K615LAE	Leyland Olympian ON2R56C16Z4	Northern Counties Palatine	B47/30F	1993	
34626	CEu	K626LAE	Leyland Olympian ON2R56C16Z4	Northern Counties Palatine	O47/32F	1993	
34629	CE	K629LAE	Leyland Olympian ON2R56C16Z4	Northern Counties Palatine	B47/30F	1993	

35101	RO	SN64CSF	Wrightbus Streetdeck	Wrightbus	N--/--F	2014	
35102	OM	SN64CSO	Wrightbus Streetdeck	Wrightbus	N--/--F	2015	

35103-35141

Wrightbus Streetdeck · Wrightbus · N--/--F · 2015

35103	HG	-	35113	HG	-	35123	RO	-	35133	RO	-
35104	HG	-	35114	HG	-	35124	RO	-	35134	RO	-
35105	HG	-	35115	HG	-	35125	RO	-	35135	RO	-
35106	HG	-	35116	HG	-	35126	RO	-	35136	RO	-
35107	HG	-	35117	RO	-	35127	RO	-	35137	RO	-
35108	HG	-	35118	RO	-	35128	RO	-	35138	RO	-
35109	HG	-	35119	RO	-	35129	RO	-	35139	HG	-
35110	HG	-	35120	RO	-	35130	RO	-	35140	HG	-
35111	HG	-	35121	RO	-	35131	RO	-	35141	HG	-
35112	HG	-	35122	RO	-	35132	RO	-			

35142-35167

Wrightbus Streetdeck · Wrightbus · N--/--F · 2015

35142	HG	-	35149	HG	-	35156	LE	-	35162	WS	-
35143	HG	-	35150	HG	-	35157	LE	-	35163	WS	-
35144	HG	-	35151	LE	-	35158	LE	-	35164	WS	-
35145	HG	-	35152	LE	-	35159	LE	-	35165	WS	-
35146	HG	-	35153	LE	-	35160	WS	-	35166	WS	-
35147	HG	-	35154	LE	-	35161	WS	-	35167	WS	-
35148	HG	-	35155	LE	-						

36001-36006

Scania N94UD · East Lancs OmniDekka · NC43/26F · 2004-05

36001	WH	YN04GNV	36003	WH	YN04GNY	36005	WH	YN04GLV	36006	WH	YN05HGA
36002	WH	YN04GNX	36004	WH	YN04GNZ						

36007-36030

Scania N94UD · East Lancs OmniDekka · N47/33F · 2005

36007	BK	SN05HWW	36013	BK	SN05HWL	36019	BK	SN05HWH	36025	BK	SN05HWS
36008	BK	SN05HWX	36014	LV	SN05HWK	36020	BF	SN05HWF	36026	BK	SN05HWU
36009	LV	SN05HWY	36015	BF	SN05HWO	36021	BK	SN05HWP	36027	BK	SN05HWV
36010	BK	SN05HWZ	36016	BF	SN05HWM	36022	BF	SN05HWE	36028	BK	SN05HWT
36011	BK	SN05HXA	36017	BF	SN05HWJ	36023	BK	SN05HWD	36029	BK	SN55KKE
36012	LV	SN05HXB	36018	BK	SN05HWG	36024	LV	SN05HWR	36030	MU	SN55KKF

Representing the Scania N94 OmniDekka is Wessex 36005, YN04GLV, one of six fitted with high-back seating allocated to Weymouth which is seen climbing White Hill at Abbotsbury.
Steve Rice

First continues to evaluate suppliers' new models and currently at Oldham depot is a Wrightbus StreetDeck, 35102, which is working alongside the latest model from Volvo, the B5TL pictured leaving Manchester en route for Sholver. On loan to First it is numbered 36300, BF63HDC. *John Birtwistle*

36166-36180

Volvo B9TL · Wrightbus Eclipse Gemini 2 · N45/29F · 2011

36166	VN	BD11CFK	36170	VN	BD11CFP	36174	VN	BD11CFY	36178	VN	BD11CDX
36167	VN	BD11CFM	36171	VN	BD11CFU	36175	VN	BD11CFZ	36179	VN	BD11CDY
36168	VN	BD11CFN	36172	VN	BD11CFV	36176	VN	BD11CGE	36180	VN	BD11CDZ
36169	VN	BD11CFO	36173	VN	BD11CFX	36177	VN	BD11CGF			

36181-36280

Volvo B9TL · Wrightbus Eclipse Gemini 2 · N45/27F · 2012

36181	HP	BF12KXU	36206	HP	BN12WOM	36231	HP	BD12TBZ	36256	HP	BG12YJN
36182	HP	BF12KXV	36207	HP	BJ12VWO	36232	HP	BD12TCV	36257	HP	BG12YJO
36183	HP	BN12JYF	36208	HP	BJ12VWP	36233	HP	BD12TCU	36258	HP	BG12YJP
36184	HP	BN12JYG	36209	HP	BJ12VWR	36234	HP	BD12TCY	36259	HP	BG12YJR
36185	HP	BN12JYH	36210	HP	BJ12VWS	36235	HP	BD12TCX	36260	HP	BG12YJS
36186	HP	BN12JYJ	36211	HP	BJ12VWT	36236	HP	BN12WOR	36261	HP	BG12YJT
36187	HP	BN12JYK	36212	HP	BJ12VWU	36237	HP	BN12WOU	36262	HP	BG12YJU
36188	HP	BN12JYL	36213	HP	BJ12VWV	36238	HP	BN12WOV	36263	HP	BG12YJV
36189	HP	BN12JYO	36214	HP	BJ12VWW	36239	HP	BN12WOX	36264	HP	BG12YJW
36190	HP	BN12JYP	36215	HP	BJ12VWX	36240	HP	BN12WOY	36265	HP	BG12YJX
36191	HP	BN12JYR	36216	HP	BJ12VWY	36241	HP	BN12WPA	36266	HP	BG12YJY
36192	HP	BN12JYS	36217	HP	BJ12VXA	36242	HP	BN12WPD	36267	HP	BG12YJZ
36193	HP	BN12JYT	36218	HP	BJ12VXB	36243	HP	BN12WPE	36268	HP	BG12YKA
36194	HP	BN12JYU	36219	HP	BJ12VXC	36244	HP	BN12WPF	36269	HP	BG12YKB
36195	HP	BN12JYV	36220	HP	BJ12VXD	36245	HP	BN12WPJ	36270	HP	BG12YKC
36196	HP	BN12JYW	36221	HP	BJ12VXE	36246	HP	BJ12VNR	36271	HP	BG12YKD
36197	HP	BN12WNX	36222	HP	BD12SZY	36247	HP	BJ12PNS	36272	HP	BG12YKE
36198	HP	BN12WNY	36223	HP	BD12SZZ	36248	HP	BG12UKM	36273	HP	BG12YKF
36199	HP	BN12WNZ	36224	HP	BD12TAO	36249	HP	BF12KWU	36274	HP	BD12TDV
36200	HP	BN12WOA	36225	HP	BD12TAV	36250	HP	BG12YJF	36275	HP	BD12TCO
36201	HP	BN12WOB	36226	HP	BD12TBO	36251	HP	BG12YJH	36276	HP	BD12TCK
36202	HP	BN12WOC	36227	HP	BD12TBU	36252	HP	BG12YJJ	36277	HP	BD12TDO
36203	HP	BN12WOD	36228	HP	BD12TBV	36253	HP	BG12YJK	36278	HP	BD12TCZ
36204	HP	BN12WOH	36229	HP	BD12TBX	36254	HP	BG12YJL	36279	OM	BD12TDU
36205	HP	BN12WOJ	36230	HP	BD12TBY	36255	HP	BG12YJM	36280	OM	BD12TCJ

36300	TN	BF63HDC	Volvo B5TL		Wrightbus Eclipse Gemini 3	N45/29F	2014	On loan from Volvo

37001-37020
Volvo B7TL — Wrightbus Eclipse Gemini — N45/29F — 2005

Fleet		Reg	Fleet		Reg	Fleet		Reg	Fleet		Reg
37001	HG	WX55VHK	37006	MS	WX55VHP	37011	LH	WX55VHW	37016	HG	WX55VJD
37002	HG	WX55VHL	37007	LH	WX55VHR	37012	LH	WX55VHY	37017	HG	WX55VJE
37003	MS	WX55VHM	37008	HG	WX55VHT	37013	LH	WX55VHZ	37018	HG	WX55VJF
37004	MS	WX55VHN	37009	HG	WX55VHU	37014	LH	WX55VJA	37019	HG	WX55VJG
37005	MS	WX55VHO	37010	HG	WX55VHV	37015	HG	WX55VJC	37020	HG	WX55VJJ

37021-37062
Volvo B7TL — Wrightbus Eclipse Gemini — N45/29F — 2006

Fleet		Reg	Fleet		Reg	Fleet		Reg	Fleet		Reg
37021	OG	YJ06XKK	37032	OG	YJ06XKX	37043	HP	YJ06XLT	37053	HX	YJ06XMD
37022	OG	YJ06XKL	37033	OG	YJ06XKY	37044	HP	YJ06XLU	37054	HX	YJ06XME
37023	OG	YJ06XKM	37034	OG	YJ06XKZ	37045	YK	YJ06XLV	37055	BD	YJ06XMF
37024	OG	YJ06XKN	37035	OG	YJ06XLA	37046	HX	YJ06XLW	37056	BD	YJ06XMG
37025	OG	YJ06XKO	37036	HP	YJ06XLB	37047	HX	YJ06XLX	37057	BD	YJ06XMH
37026	OG	YJ06XKP	37037	HP	YJ06XLC	37048	HX	YJ06XLY	37058	BD	YJ06XMK
37027	OG	YJ06XKS	37038	HP	YJ06XLD	37049	HX	YJ06XLZ	37059	BD	YJ06XML
37028	OG	YJ06XKT	37039	HP	YJ06XLE	37050	HX	YJ06XMA	37060	HP	YJ06XMM
37029	OG	YJ06XKU	37040	HP	YJ06XLF	37051	HX	YJ06XMB	37061	HP	YJ06XMO
37030	OG	YJ06XKV	37041	HP	YJ06XLG	37052	HX	YJ06XMC	37062	HP	YJ06XMP
37031	OG	YJ06XKW	37042	HP	YJ06XLH						

37063-37132
Volvo B9TL — Wrightbus Eclipse Gemini — N45/29F — 2007-08

Fleet		Reg	Fleet		Reg	Fleet		Reg	Fleet		Reg
37063	BM	YK57EZS	37081	BD	YJ08GVT	37099	BD	YJ08GWP	37116	OG	YK07AYP
37064	BM	YK57EZT	37082	BD	YJ08GVU	37100	BD	YJ08GWU	37117	OG	YK07AYS
37065	BD	YK57EZU	37083	BD	YJ08GVV	37101	BD	YJ08GWV	37118	OG	YK07AYT
37066	BD	YK57EZV	37084	BD	YJ08GVW	37102	BD	YJ08GWW	37119	OG	YK07AYU
37067	BD	YK57EZW	37085	BD	YJ08GVX	37103	OG	YK07AYA	37120	OG	YK07AYV
37068	BD	YK57EZX	37086	BD	YJ08GVY	37104	OG	YK07AYB	37121	OG	YK07AYW
37069	BD	YK57EZZ	37087	BD	YJ08GVZ	37105	OG	YK07AYC	37122	OG	YK07AYX
37070	BD	YK57FAA	37088	BD	YJ08GWA	37106	OG	YK07AYD	37123	HP	YK07AYY
37071	BD	YJ08GVE	37089	BD	YJ08GWC	37107	OG	YK07AYE	37124	HP	YK07AYZ
37072	BD	YJ08GVF	37090	BD	YJ08GWD	37108	OG	YK07AYF	37125	HP	YK57CJF
37073	BD	YJ08GVG	37091	BD	YJ08GWE	37109	OG	YK07AYG	37126	HP	YK57CJJ
37074	BD	YJ08GVK	37092	BD	YJ08GWF	37110	OG	YK07AYH	37127	HP	YK57CJO
37075	BD	YJ08GVL	37093	BD	YJ08GWG	37111	OG	YK07AYJ	37128	HP	YK57CJU
37076	BD	YJ08GVM	37094	BD	YJ08GWK	37112	OG	YK07AYL	37129	HP	YK57CJV
37077	BD	YJ08GVN	37095	BD	YJ08GWL	37113	OG	YK07AYM	37130	HP	YK57CJX
37078	BD	YJ08GVO	37096	BD	YJ08GWM	37114	OG	YK07AYN	37131	HP	YK57CJY
37079	BD	YJ08GVP	37097	BD	YJ08GWN	37115	OG	YK07AYO	37132	HP	YK57CJZ
37080	BD	YJ08GVR	37098	BD	YJ08GWO						

37133-37145
Volvo B9TL — Wrightbus Eclipse Gemini — N45/29F — 2007

Fleet		Reg	Fleet		Reg	Fleet		Reg	Fleet		Reg
37133	GS	SN57HDH	37137	LV	SN57HCV	37140	LV	SN57HCZ	37143	LV	SN57HDD
37134	GS	SN57HDJ	37138	GS	SN57HCX	37141	LV	SN57HDA	37144	LV	SN57HDE
37135	GS	SN57HCP	37139	GS	SN57HCY	37142	LV	SN57HDC	37145	LV	SN57HDF
37136	GS	SN57HCU									

37146-37155
Volvo B7TL — Wrightbus Eclipse Gemini — N45/29F — 2006

Fleet		Reg	Fleet		Reg	Fleet		Reg	Fleet		Reg
37146	AG	YN06UPZ	37149	PH	YN06URC	37152	PH	YN06URF	37154	PH	YN06URH
37147	PH	YN06URA	37150	PH	YN06URD	37153	PH	YN06URG	37155	PH	YN06URJ
37148	PH	YN06URB	37151	PH	YN06URE						

37156-37165
Volvo B7TL — Wrightbus Eclipse Gemini — N45/29F — 2007

Fleet		Reg	Fleet		Reg	Fleet		Reg	Fleet		Reg
37156	NE	AU07DXS	37159	NE	AU07DXW	37162	SO	HY07FSV	37164	SO	HY07FSU
37157	NE	AU07DXT	37160	AG	AU07DXX	37163	SO	HY07FSZ	37165	SO	HY07FSX
37158	NE	AU07DXV	37161	HO	HY07FTA						

37166-37185
Volvo B7TL — Wrightbus Eclipse Gemini — N45/29F — 2007

Fleet		Reg	Fleet		Reg	Fleet		Reg	Fleet		Reg
37166	B	SF07FCP	37171	B	SF07FDA	37176	CA	SF07FDJ	37181	B	SF07FDO
37167	B	SF07FCV	37172	CA	SF07FDC	37177	CA	SF07FDK	37182	B	SF07FDP
37168	B	SF07FCX	37173	CA	SF07FDD	37178	CA	SF07FDL	37183	B	SF07FDU
37169	B	SF07FCY	37174	CA	SF07FDE	37179	CA	SF07FDM	37184	B	SF07FDV
37170	B	SF07FCZ	37175	CA	SF07FDG	37180	B	SF07FDN	37185	B	SF07FDX

Following the sale of First's London operation, the Bracknell and Reading services joined those on the south coast to form the Hampshire and Berkshire division. Nine Volvo B9TLs carry the Greenline livery as illustrated by 37274, LK58EDF. *Dave Heath*

37186-37227

			Volvo B9TL						Wrightbus Eclipse Gemini			N45/29F	2007		
37186	CA	SF07FDY	37197	CA	SF07FEM	37208	CA	SF57MKG	37218	DU	SF57MKX
37187	CA	SF07FDZ	37198	CA	SF07FEO	37209	CA	SF57MKJ	37219	DU	SF57MKZ
37188	CA	SF07FCC	37199	CA	SF07FCL	37210	CA	SF57MKK	37220	DU	SF57MLE
37189	CA	SF07FCD	37200	CA	SF07FEP	37211	CA	SF57MKL	37221	DU	SF57MLJ
37190	CA	SF07FCE	37201	CA	SF07FCM	37212	CA	SF57MKM	37222	DU	SF57MLK
37191	CA	SF07FCG	37202	CA	SF07FCO	37213	CA	SF57MKN	37223	DU	SF57MLL
37192	CA	SF07FCJ	37203	CA	SF07FET	37214	CA	SF57MKO	37224	DU	SF57MLN
37193	CA	SF07FEG	37204	CA	SF07FEU	37215	SN	SF57MKP	37225	DU	SF57MLO
37194	CA	SF07FEH	37205	CA	SF57MKA	37216	SN	SF57MKU	37226	DU	SF57MLU
37195	CA	SF07FEJ	37206	CA	SF57MKC	37217	SN	SF57MKV	37227	DU	SF57MLV
37196	CA	SF07FEK	37207	CA	SF57MKD						

37228-37265

			Volvo B9TL						Wrightbus Eclipse Gemini			N45/29F	2007-08		
37228	DN	YN57RJU	37238	B	YN08LCT	37247	YK	YN07MKE	37256	YK	YN07MKV
37229	OG	3910WE	37239	B	YN08LCU	37248	YK	YN07MKF	37257	DN	YN07MKX
37230	DN	YN08LCK	37240	B	YN08LCV	37249	YK	YN07MKG	37258	RO	YN07MKZ
37231	RO	YN08LCL	37241	B	YN08LCW	37250	YK	YN07MKJ	37259	RO	YN07MLE
37232	DN	YN57RJZ	37242	B	YN08LCY	37251	YK	YN07MKK	37261	RO	YN07MLJ
37233	DN	YN57RKA	37243	B	YN08LCZ	37252	YK	YN07MKL	37262	RO	YN07MLK
37234	DN	YN08LCM	37244	B	YN08LDA	37253	YK	YN07MKM	37263	RO	YN07MLL
37235	DN	YN08LCO	37245	B	YN08LDC	37254	YK	YN07MKO	37264	RO	YN07MLO
37236	DN	YN57RKJ	37246	YK	YN07MKD	37255	YK	YN07MKP	37265	RO	YN07MLU
37237	DN	YN08LCP									

37266-37278

			Volvo B9TL						Wrightbus Eclipse Gemini			N45/29F	2008	*37274-6 are NC39/26F	
37266	LV	SN57HDG	37269	LV	SN57JBE	37272	LV	SN57JBV	37275	BL	LK58EDJ
37267	LV	SN57JAO	37270	LV	SN57JBO	37273	LV	SN57JBX	37276	BL	LK58EDL
37268	LV	SN57JAU	37271	LV	SN57JBU	37274	BL	LK58EDF	37278	B	YN08LDD

37279-37304

			Volvo B9TL						Wrightbus Eclipse Gemini			N45/29F	2007		
37279	QS	MX07BPY	37286	QS	MX07BSV	37293	BY	MX07BTV	37299	BY	MX07BUH
37280	QS	MX07BPZ	37287	QS	MX07BSY	37294	BY	MX07BTY	37300	BY	MX07BUJ
37281	QS	MX07BRF	37288	QS	MX07BSZ	37295	BY	MX07BTZ	37301	QS	MX57HDZ
37282	QS	MX07BRV	37289	QS	MX07BTE	37296	BY	MX07BUA	37302	BY	MX57HEJ
37283	QS	MX07BRZ	37290	QS	MX07BTF	37297	BY	MX07BUE	37303	QS	MX07BUU
37284	QS	MX07BSO	37291	BY	MX07BTO	37298	BY	MX07BUF	37304	QS	MX07BUV
37285	QS	MX07BSU	37292	BY	MX07BTU						

First continues to celebrate former liveries when appropriate. Based at Olive Grove depot in Sheffield and now resplendent in the former South Yorkshire Transport scheme is 37524, YN58ETR, a Volvo B7TL.
John Birtwistle

37315-37359   Volvo B9TL   Wrightbus Eclipse Gemini   N45/29F   2007

37315	HG	WX57HJO	37327	LH	WX57HKH	37338	LH	WX57HKW	37349	LH	WX57HLK
37316	HG	WX57HJU	37328	LH	WX57HKJ	37339	LH	WX57HKY	37350	LH	WX57HLM
37317	HG	WX57HJV	37329	LH	WX57HKK	37340	LH	WX57HKZ	37351	HG	WX57HLN
37318	HG	WX57HJY	37330	LH	WX57HKL	37341	LH	WX57HLA	37352	LH	WX57HLO
37319	LH	WX57HJZ	37331	LH	WX57HKM	37342	LH	WX57HLC	37353	LH	WX57HLP
37320	LH	WX57HKA	37332	LH	WX57HKN	37343	LH	WX57HLD	37354	LH	WX57HLR
37321	LH	WX57HKB	37333	LH	WX57HKO	37344	LH	WX57HLE	37355	LH	WX57HLU
37322	LH	WX57HKC	37334	LH	WX57HKP	37345	LH	WX57HLF	37356	LH	WX57HLV
37323	LH	WX57HKD	37335	LH	WX57HKT	37346	LH	WX57HLG	37357	LH	WX57HLW
37324	LH	WX57HKE	37336	LH	WX57HKU	37347	LH	WX57HLH	37358	BA	WX57HLY
37325	LH	WX57HKF	37337	LH	WX57HKV	37348	LH	WX57HLJ	37359	YK	WX57HLZ
37326	LH	WX57HKG									

37360-37440   Volvo B9TL   Wrightbus Eclipse Gemini   N45/29F   2008-09

37360	BD	YJ58GNP	37381	QS	MX58DWM	37401	BY	MX58DXM	37421	BY	MX58DYP
37361	BD	YJ58GMO	37382	QS	MX58DWN	37402	BN	MX58DXO	37422	BY	MX58DYS
37362	BD	YJ58GNU	37383	OM	MX58DWO	37403	BY	MX58DXP	37423	BY	MX58DYT
37363	BD	YJ58GMU	37384	QS	MX58DWP	37404	BY	MX58DXR	37424	BY	MX58DYU
37364	BD	YJ58GNV	37385	QS	MX58DWU	37405	BN	MX58DXS	37425	BY	MX58DYV
37365	BD	YJ58GMV	37386	OM	MX58DWV	37406	BY	MX58DXT	37426	BY	MX58DYW
37366	BD	YJ58GNX	37387	OM	MX58DWW	37407	BN	MX58DXU	37427	BY	MX58DYY
37367	QS	MX58DVU	37388	OM	MX58DWY	37408	BN	MX58DXV	37428	BY	MX58DZA
37368	QS	MX58DVV	37389	QS	MX58DWZ	37409	BN	MX58DXW	37429	BY	MX58DZB
37369	QS	MX58DVW	37390	QS	MX58DXA	37410	BN	MX58DXZ	37430	BN	MX58DZC
37370	QS	MX58DVY	37391	BY	MX58DXB	37411	QS	MX58DYA	37431	BY	MX58DZD
37371	QS	MX58DVZ	37392	BY	MX58DXC	37412	OM	MX58DYC	37432	OM	MX58DZE
37372	QS	MX58DWA	37393	BY	MX58DXD	37413	QS	MX58DYD	37433	OM	MX58DZF
37373	QS	MX58DWC	37394	QS	MX58DXE	37414	QS	MX58DYF	37434	BN	MX58DZG
37374	QS	MX58DWD	37395	QS	MX58DXF	37415	BN	MX58DYG	37435	BN	MX58DZH
37375	QS	MX58DWE	37396	QS	MX58DXG	37416	BN	MX58DYH	37436	OM	MX58DZJ
37376	QS	MX58DWF	37397	BN	MX58DXH	37417	BY	MX58DYJ	37437	OM	MX58DZK
37377	QS	MX58DWG	37398	BY	MX58DXJ	37418	BY	MX58DYM	37438	OM	MX58DZL
37378	QS	MX58DWJ	37399	BY	MX58DXK	37419	BY	MX58DYN	37439	OM	MX58DZN
37379	QS	MX58DWK	37400	BY	MX58DXL	37420	BY	MX58DYO	37440	QS	MX58DZO
37380	QS	MX58DWL									

Lancashire United Transport was founded in 1905 as Lancashire United Tramways Ltd to assume operation of the South Lancashire Tramways tram system. The company continued to operate routes in South Lancashire until purchased by Greater Manchester PTE in 1976. Currently allocated to Bolton, 37430, MX58DZC, can frequently be found on the routes previously served by LUT. *Alan Blagburn*

37441-37471

Volvo B9TL — Wrightbus Eclipse Gemini — N45/29F — 2008-09

37441	OM	MX58DZP	37449	OM	MX58DZZ	37457	OM	MX58EAO	37465	TE	MX58EBK
37442	QS	MX58DZR	37450	OM	MX58EAA	37458	OM	MX58EAP	37466	TE	MX58EBL
37443	OM	MX58DZS	37451	OM	MX58EAC	37459	OM	MX58EAY	37467	OM	MX58EBM
37444	OM	MX58DZT	37452	QS	MX58EAF	37460	OM	MX58EBA	37468	OM	MX58EBN
37445	OM	MX58DZU	37453	OM	MX58EAG	37461	OM	MX58EBC	37469	OM	MX09GXY
37446	OM	MX58DZV	37454	OM	MX58EAJ	37462	OM	MX58EBD	37470	OM	MX09GXZ
37447	OM	MX58DZW	37455	OM	MX58EAK	37463	OM	MX58EBF	37471	BY	MX09GYG
37448	OM	MX58DZY	37456	BN	MX58EAM	37464	TE	MX58EBG			

37472-37529

Volvo B9TL — Wrightbus Eclipse Gemini — N45/29F — 2008

37472	OG	YN08NLL	37487	RO	YN08NMK	37502	DN	YN08PMV	37516	OG	YN58ETA
37473	OG	YN08NLM	37488	RO	YN08NMM	37503	DN	YN08PMX	37517	OG	YN58ETD
37474	OG	YN08NLO	37489	RO	YN08NMU	37504	DN	YN08PMY	37518	OG	YN58ETE
37475	OG	YN08NLP	37490	RO	YN08NMV	37505	DN	YN08PNE	37519	OG	YN58ETF
37476	OG	YN08NLR	37491	RO	YN08NMX	37506	DN	YN08PNF	37520	OG	YN58ETJ
37477	OG	YN08NLT	37492	RO	YN08NMY	37507	DN	YN08PNJ	37521	OG	YN58ETK
37478	OG	YN08NLU	37493	RO	YN08PLF	37508	DN	YN08PNK	37522	OG	YN58ETL
37479	OG	YN08NLV	37494	RO	YN58ERX	37509	RO	YN58ERZ	37523	OG	YN58ETO
37480	OG	YN08NLX	37495	RO	YN08PLO	37510	RO	YN58ESF	37524	OG	YN58ETR
37481	OG	YN08NLY	37496	RO	YN08PLU	37511	OG	YN58ESG	37525	DN	YN58ETT
37482	OG	YN08NLZ	37497	RO	YN58ERY	37512	OG	YN58ESO	37526	OG	YN58ETU
37483	OG	YN08NMA	37498	RO	YN08PLX	37513	OG	YN58ESU	37527	OG	YN58ETV
37484	OG	YN08NME	37499	RO	YN08PLZ	37514	OG	YN58ESV	37528	OG	YN58ETX
37485	OG	YN08NMF	37500	DN	YN08PMO	37515	OG	YN58ESY	37529	OG	YN58ETY
37486	OG	YN08NMJ	37501	DN	YN08PMU						

37530-37544

Volvo B9TL — Wrightbus Eclipse Gemini — N45/29F — 2008

37530	CA	SF08SMU	37534	CA	SF08SNK	37538	CA	SF08SNX	37542	CA	SF58ATZ
37531	CA	SF08SMV	37535	CA	SF08SNN	37539	CA	SF08SNY	37543	CA	SF58AUA
37532	CA	SF08SMX	37536	CA	SF08SNU	37540	CA	SF08SNZ	37544	CA	SF58AUC
37533	CA	SF08SNJ	37537	CA	SF08SNV	37541	CA	SF58ATY			

One of a pair of Volvo B9TL buses that carry the Long Ashton Park and Ride livery is 37606, WX58JXP, pictured on Broad Quay in Bristol while heading out of the city. *Mark Lyons*

37545-37561		Volvo B9TL			Wrightbus Eclipse Gemini			N45/29F	2009		
37545	OM	MX09GYE	37550	OM	MX09GYD	37554	BY	MX09GYH	37558	OM	MX09HUU
37546	OM	MX09GYJ	37551	BY	MX09HUK	37555	OM	MX09LMK	37559	OM	MX09HUP
37547	OM	MX09GYK	37552	OM	MX09GYB	37556	OM	MX09LML	37560	OM	MX09LMF
37548	OM	MX09GYC	37553	OM	MX09GYF	37557	OM	MX09HUO	37561	OM	MX09LMJ
37549	OM	MX09GYA									

37562	VN	FJ08FYN	Volvo B9TL			Wrightbus Eclipse Gemini			N45/29F	2008		Beestons, Hadleigh, 2013

37563-37579		Volvo B9TL			Wrightbus Eclipse Gemini			NC45/26F	2008		
37563	LO	AU58ECA	37568	LO	AU58ECJ	37572	LO	AU58ECW	37576	YA	AU58EDC
37564	LO	AU58ECC	37569	LO	AU58ECN	37573	YA	AU58ECX	37577	YA	AU58EDF
37565	LO	AU58ECD	37570	LO	AU58ECT	37574	YA	AU58ECY	37578	YA	AU58EDJ
37566	LO	AU58ECE	37571	LO	AU58ECV	37575	YA	AU58ECZ	37579	YA	AU58EDK
37567	LO	AU58ECF									

37580-37586		Volvo B9TL			Wrightbus Eclipse Gemini			NC43/27F	2008		
37580	WH	HX08DHL	37582	WH	HX08DHK	37584	WH	HX08DHG	37586	WH	HX08DHJ
37581	WH	HX08DHF	37583	WH	HX08DHE	37585	WH	HX08DHY			

37587-37632		Volvo B9TL			Wrightbus Eclipse Gemini			N45/29F	2008		
37587	HG	WX58JWU	37599	HG	WX58JXH	37611	HG	WX58JXV	37622	LH	WX58JYH
37588	HG	WX58JWV	37600	HG	WX58JXJ	37612	HG	WX58JXW	37623	LH	WX58JYJ
37589	HG	WX58JWW	37601	HG	WX58JXK	37613	LH	WX58JXY	37624	LH	WX58JYK
37590	HG	WX58JWY	37602	HG	WX58JXL	37614	LH	WX58JXZ	37625	LH	WX58JYL
37591	HG	WX58JWZ	37603	HG	WX58JXM	37615	LH	WX58JYA	37626	LH	WX58JYN
37592	HG	WX58JXA	37604	HG	WX58JXN	37616	LH	WX58JYB	37627	LH	WX58JYO
37593	HG	WX58JXB	37605	HG	WX58JXO	37617	LH	WX58JYC	37628	LH	WX58JYP
37594	HG	WX58JXC	37606	HG	WX58JXP	37618	LH	WX58JYD	37629	LH	WX58JYR
37595	HG	WX58JXD	37607	LH	WX58JXR	37619	LH	WX58JYE	37630	LH	WX58JYS
37596	HG	WX58JXE	37608	LH	WX58JXS	37620	LH	WX58JYF	37631	LH	WX58JYT
37597	HG	WX58JXF	37609	HG	WX58JXT	37621	LH	WX58JYG	37632	LH	WX58JYU
37598	HG	WX58JXG	37610	HG	WX58JXU						

37633-37644 — Volvo B9TL — Wrightbus Eclipse Gemini — N45/29F — 2008

Fleet	Dep	Reg	Fleet	Dep	Reg	Fleet	Dep	Reg	Fleet	Dep	Reg
37633	AB	SV08FXP	37636	AB	SV08FXT	37639	AB	SV08FXX	37642	AB	SV08FYA
37634	AB	SV08FXR	37637	AB	SV08FXU	37640	AB	SV08FXY	37643	AB	SV08FYB
37635	AB	SV08FXS	37638	AB	SV08FXW	37641	AB	SV08FXZ	37644	AB	SV08FYC

37645-37685 — Volvo B9TL — Wrightbus Eclipse Gemini — NC45/29F — 2009

Fleet	Dep	Reg	Fleet	Dep	Reg	Fleet	Dep	Reg	Fleet	Dep	Reg
37645	BM	YJ58RNN	37656	BM	YJ58RPV	37666	BM	YJ58RSO	37676	HP	YJ09FVG
37646	BM	YJ58RNO	37657	BM	YJ58RPX	37667	HP	YJ58RSU	37677	HP	YJ09FVH
37647	BM	YJ58RNU	37658	BM	YJ58RPY	37668	HP	YJ58RSV	37678	HP	YJ09FVK
37648	BM	YJ58RNV	37659	BM	YJ58RPZ	37669	HP	YJ58RSX	37679	HP	YJ09FVL
37649	BM	YJ58RNX	37660	BM	YJ58RRO	37670	HP	YJ58RSY	37680	BM	YJ09FVM
37650	BM	YJ58RNY	37661	BM	YJ58RRU	37671	HP	YJ58RSZ	37681	HP	YJ09FVN
37651	BM	YJ58RNZ	37662	BM	YJ58RRV	37672	HP	YJ58RTO	37682	HP	YJ09FVO
37652	BM	YJ58ROH	37663	BM	YJ58RRX	37673	HP	YJ58RTU	37683	HP	YJ09FVP
37653	BM	YJ58ROU	37664	BM	YJ58RRY	37674	HP	YJ58RTV	37684	HP	YJ09FVE
37654	BM	YJ58RPO	37665	BM	YJ58RRZ	37675	HP	YJ58RTX	37685	HP	YJ09FVF
37655	BM	YJ58RPU									

37686-37772 — Volvo B9TL — Wrightbus Eclipse Gemini — N45/29F — 2009

Fleet	Dep	Reg	Fleet	Dep	Reg	Fleet	Dep	Reg	Fleet	Dep	Reg
37686	HP	YJ09NZY	37708	BM	YJ09OBC	37730	BM	YJ09OCB	37752	BM	YJ59KSO
37687	BM	YJ09OAA	37709	BM	YJ09OBD	37731	BM	YJ09OCC	37753	BM	YJ59KSU
37688	BM	YJ09OAB	37710	BM	YJ09OBE	37732	BD	YJ09OCD	37754	BM	YJ59KSV
37689	BM	YJ09OAC	37711	BM	YJ09OBF	37733	BD	YJ09OCE	37755	BM	YJ59KSY
37690	HP	YJ09OAD	37712	BM	YJ09OBG	37734	BD	YJ09OCF	37756	BM	YJ59KSZ
37691	HP	YJ09OAE	37713	BM	YJ09OBH	37735	BD	YJ09OCG	37757	LH	WX09KBK
37692	HP	YJ09OAG	37714	BM	YJ09OBK	37736	CA	SF09LDD	37758	LH	WX09KBN
37693	HP	YJ09OAH	37715	BM	YJ09OBL	37737	CA	SF09LDE	37759	LH	WX09KBO
37694	HP	YJ09OAL	37716	BM	YJ09OBM	37738	CA	SF09LDJ	37760	LH	WX09KBP
37695	HP	YJ09OAM	37717	BM	YJ09OBN	37739	CA	SF09LDK	37761	LH	WX09KBU
37696	HP	YJ09OAN	37718	BM	YJ09OBO	37740	CA	SF09LDL	37762	LH	WX09KBV
37697	HP	YJ09OAO	37719	BM	YJ09OBP	37741	CA	SF09LDN	37763	LH	WX09KBY
37698	HP	YJ09OAP	37720	BM	YJ09OBR	37742	CA	SF09LDO	37764	LH	WX09KBZ
37699	HP	YJ09OAS	37721	BM	YJ09OBS	37743	CA	SF09LDU	37765	LH	WX09KCA
37700	HP	YJ09OAU	37722	BM	YJ09OBT	37744	CA	SF09LDV	37766	LH	WX09KCC
37701	HP	YJ09OAV	37723	BM	YJ09OBU	37745	CA	SF09LDX	37767	LH	WX09KCE
37702	HP	YJ09OAW	37724	BM	YJ09OBV	37746	CA	SF09LDY	37768	LH	WX09KCF
37703	HP	YJ09OAX	37725	BM	YJ09OBW	37747	CA	SF09LDZ	37769	LH	WX09KCG
37704	HP	YJ09OAY	37726	BM	YJ09OBX	37748	CA	SF09LEJ	37770	LH	WX09KCJ
37705	HP	YJ09OAZ	37727	BM	YJ09OBY	37749	CA	SF09LEU	37771	LH	WX09KCK
37706	BM	YJ09OBA	37728	BM	YJ09OBZ	37750	CA	SF09LFA	37772	LH	WX09KCN
37707	BM	YJ09OBB	37729	BM	YJ09OCA	37751	CA	SF09LFB			

Fleet	Dep	Reg	Chassis	Body	Seats	Year
37985	BL	BJ11XGY	Volvo B9TL	Wrightbus Eclipse Gemini 2	NC39/26F	2011
37986	BL	BJ11ECY	Volvo B9TL	Wrightbus Eclipse Gemini 2	NC39/26F	2011
37987	BL	BJ11ECX	Volvo B9TL	Wrightbus Eclipse Gemini 2	NC39/26F	2011
37997	BL	BF63HDV	Volvo B9TL	Wrightbus Eclipse Gemini 2	NC39/26F	2013
37998	BL	BF63HDX	Volvo B9TL	Wrightbus Eclipse Gemini 2	NC39/26F	2013
37999	BL	BF63HDY	Volvo B9TL	Wrightbus Eclipse Gemini 2	NC39/26F	2013

38000-38006 — Volvo Citybus B10M-50 — Alexander RV — O47/35F — 1987

Fleet	Dep	Reg	Fleet	Dep	Reg	Fleet	Dep	Reg	Fleet	Dep	Reg
38000	CEu	D700GHY	38002	CEu	D702GHY	38005	CEu	D705GHY	38006	CEu	D706GHY
38001	CEu	D701GHY	38004	CEu	D704GHY						

Fleet	Dep	Reg	Chassis	Body	Seats	Year
38125	WRu	K125URP	Volvo Citybus B10M-50	Alexander RV	BC47/35F	1992

38201-38225 — ADL Trident 2 3-axle — ADL Enviro 500 — N53/29F — 2009

Fleet	Dep	Reg	Fleet	Dep	Reg	Fleet	Dep	Reg	Fleet	Dep	Reg
38201	CA	SN09CAU	38208	CA	SN09CBX	38214	CA	SN09CCJ	38220	CA	SN09CCY
38202	CA	SN09CAV	38209	CA	SN09CBY	38215	CA	SN09CCK	38221	CA	SN09CCZ
38203	CA	SN09CAX	38210	CA	SN09CCA	38216	CA	SN09CCO	38222	CA	SN09CDE
38204	CA	SN09CBF	38211	CA	SN09CCD	38217	CA	SN09CCU	38223	CA	SN09CDF
38205	CA	SN09CBO	38212	CA	SN09CCE	38218	CA	SN09CCV	38224	CA	SN09CDK
38206	CA	SN09CBU	38213	CA	SN09CCF	38219	CA	SN09CCX	38225	CAu	SN09CDO
38207	CA	SN09CBV									

Fleet	Dep	Reg	Chassis	Body	Seats	Year
38706	CEu	AFJ706T	Bristol VRT/SL3/6LXB	Eastern Coach Works	H43/31F	1979

39001-39005 — VDL Bus Hybrid HEV — Wrightbus Gemini 2 — N41/27F — 2008

Fleet	Dep	Reg	Fleet	Dep	Reg	Fleet	Dep	Reg	Fleet	Dep	Reg
39001	YK	LK58ECV	39003	YK	LK58ECX	39004	YK	LK58ECY	39005	BA	LK58ECZ
39002	YK	LK58ECW									

39101-39110   ADL E400H   ADL Enviro 400   NC45/30F   2011

39101	SN	SN61BFK	39104	SN	SN61BFO	39107	SN	SN61BFV	39109	SN	SN61BFY
39102	SN	SN61BFL	39105	SN	SN61BFP	39108	SN	SN61BFX	39110	SN	SN61BFZ
39103	SN	SN61BFM	39106	SN	SN61BFU						

39133-39141   ADL E40H   ADL Enviro 400   N45/29F   2012

39133	BA	SN62AWA	39135	BA	SN62AWG	39138	BA	SN62AWR	39140	BA	SN62AXB
39134	BA	SN62AWF	39137	BA	SN62AWO	39139	BA	SN62AWY	39141	BA	SN62AXC

39191	LH	-	ADL E400VE	ADL Enviro 400 VE	N--/--D	On order
39192	LH	-	ADL E400VE	ADL Enviro 400 VE	N--/--D	On order

39201-39206   Volvo B5LH   Wrightbus Gemini 2   N41/23F   2011

39201	HP	BJ60BZA	39203	HP	BJ60BZC	39205	HP	BJ60BZE	39206	HP	BJ60BZF
39202	HP	BJ60BZB	39204	HP	BJ60BZD						

39207-39220   Volvo B5LH   Wrightbus Gemini 2   NC41/23F   2011

39207	QS	BN61MWE	39211	QS	BN61MWK	39215	QS	BN61MWP	39218	QS	BN61MWW
39208	QS	BN61MWF	39212	QS	BN61MWL	39216	QS	BN61MWU	39219	QS	BN61MWX
39209	QS	BN61MWG	39213	QS	BN61MWM	39217	QS	BN61MWV	39220	QS	BN61MWY
39210	QS	BN61MWJ	39214	QS	BN61MWO						

39221-39236   Volvo B5LH   Wrightbus Gemini 2   N41/23F   2011

39221	HP	BP11JWA	39225	HP	BP11JWF	39229	HP	BP11JWN	39233	HP	BP11JWU
39222	HP	BP11JWD	39226	HP	BP11JWG	39230	HP	BP11JWJ	39234	HP	BP11JWV
39223	HP	BP11JWC	39227	HP	BP11JWL	39231	HP	BP11JWK	39235	HP	BP11JWX
39224	HP	BP11JWE	39228	HP	BP11JWM	39232	HP	BP11JWO	39236	HP	BP11JWW

39237-39256   Volvo B5LH   Wrightbus Gemini 3   N41/23F   2015

39237	BN	-	39242	BN	-	39247	BN	-	39252	BN	-
39238	BN	-	39243	BN	-	39248	BN	-	39253	BN	-
39239	BN	-	39244	BN	-	39249	BN	-	39254	BN	-
39240	BN	-	39245	BN	-	39250	BN	-	39255	BN	-
39241	BN	-	39246	BN	-	39251	BN	-	39256	BN	-

39301-39305   ADL Enviro 400 GKN Flywheel   ADL Enviro 400 MMC   N45/29F   2015

39301	BK	-	39303	BK	-	39304	BK	-	39305	BK	-
39302	BK	-									

Volvo B5LH hybrid 39205, BJ60BZE, is seen arriving in Leeds from Alwoodley Avenue on route 7A. A further twenty of the model are on order for routes centred on Bolton.
Terry O'Neill

Based in the city of Stoke-on-Trent the Potteries operation uses two depots located at Newcastle and Adderley Green, not to be confused with Baddeley Green, where Optare Solo 40009, T162BBF was heading on route 3. *Mark Doggett*

39480	YAs	JJD480D	AEC Routemaster R2RH1	Park Royal		B40/32R	1966			
39623	YAs	NML623E	AEC Routemaster R2RH1	Park Royal		B40/32R	1967			
39735	BLs	SMK735F	AEC Routemaster R2RH1	Park Royal		B40/32R	1967			
39810	BLs	510CLT	AEC Routemaster R2RH	Park Royal		O32/25R	1962		London Buses, 2004	
39920	WH	L650SEU	Volvo Olympian	Northern Counties Palatine II		O47/29F	1993			
40002	PL	S764RNE	Dennis Dart SLF 8.8m	Plaxton Pointer MPD		N28F	1999		Springfield Cs, Wigan, 2001	

40009-40019

Optare Solo M850 — Optare — N27F — 1999-2000

40009	AG	T162BBF	40015	NE	W474SVT	40016	NE	W475SVT	40019	NE	W478SVT
40010	NEu	T163BBF									

40020-40029

Optare Solo M850 — Optare — N27F — 2000

40020	NE	X289FFA	40023	AG	X293FFA	40026	AG	X296FFA	40028	AG	X298FFA
40021	AG	X291FFA	40024	AG	X294FFA	40027	AG	X297FFA	40029	AG	X299FFA
40022	AG	X292FFA	40025	AG	X295FFA						

40033-40037

Dennis Dart SLF 10.2m — Plaxton Pointer 2 — N41F — 1998-99 — New World First Bus, 2001

40033	PL	S343SUX	40035	PL	S375SUX	40036	PL	S376SUX	40037	PL	S377SUX
40034	PL	S374SUX									

40155	AG	T372NUA	Dennis Dart SLF	Alexander ALX200	N37F	1999	
40173	AG	P126NLW	Dennis Dart SLF	Marshall Capital	N31F	1997	
40175	AG	S247CSF	Dennis Dart SLF	Plaxton Pointer 2	N31F	1998	
40304	AG	V71GEH	Optare Solo M850	Optare	N24F	1999	
40313	OMu	X616OBN	Optare Solo M850	Optare	N28F	2000	
40315	OMu	X618OBN	Optare Solo M850	Optare	N28F	2000	
40317	OMu	X627OBN	Optare Solo M850	Optare	N28F	2000	

40318-40322 — Optare Solo M920 — Optare — N28F — 2001

40318	OM	Y901KNB	40320	OMu	Y903KNB	40321	OMu	Y904KNB	40322	OM	Y905KNB
40319	OM	Y902KNB									

40323-40326 — Optare Solo M850 — Optare — N24F — 2001

40323	OM	MA51AET	40324	TE	MA51AEU	40325	TE	MA51AEV	40326	TE	MA51AEW

40327-40336 — Optare Solo M920 — Optare — N28F — 2002

40327	TE	ML02OFW	40330	OM	ML02OFZ	40333	OM	ML02OGC	40335	OM	ML02OGE
40328	OM	ML02OFX	40331	OM	ML02OGA	40334	OM	ML02OGD	40336	OM	ML02OGF
40329	OM	ML02OFY	40332	OM	ML02OGB						

40367-40378 — Dennis Dart SLF — Plaxton Pointer 2 — N37F — 1997

40367	AG	R241SBA	40373	AG	R247SBA	40375	AG	R249SBA	40378	AG	R252SBA

40437-40444 — Volvo B6BLE — Wright Crusader 2 — N36F — 1999

40437	QS	T701PND	40439	QSu	T703PND	40441	QSu	T705PND	40444	QSu	T708PND
40438	QSu	T702PND	40440	QSu	T704PND	40443	QSu	T707PND			

40566	BM	T315VYG	Volvo B6BLE	Wright Crusader 2	N36F	1999

40570-40599 — Volvo B6BLE — Wrightbus Crusader 2 — N38F — 2001-02

40570	BW	MIG9616	40577	BM	YJ51RHO	40585	BW	WSV409	40593	BW	YG02DHY
40571	YK	YJ51RKO	40578	BM	YJ51RHU	40586	BW	OIG1796	40594	BW	YG02DLK
40572	YK	YJ51RKU	40579	BM	YJ51RHV	40587	BM	YJ51RFZ	40595	DN	YG02DLF
40573	YK	YJ51RKV	40581	TN	XFF283	40588	BW	YJ51RGO	40596	DN	YG02DLE
40574	YK	YJ51RSV	40582	TN	UHW661	40590	BW	YJ51RGV	40597	DN	YG02DKY
40575	YK	YJ51RSX	40583	TN	260ERY	40591	BW	YJ51RGX	40598	DN	YG02DKX
40576	BM	YJ51RSY	40584	BW	HIG8790	40592	BW	YG02DHP	40599	DN	YG02DHX

40683	OMu	T167BBF	Optare Solo M850	Optare	N27F	1999	
40721	SH	T375NUA	Dennis Dart SLF 10.8m	Alexander ALX200	N37F	1999	
40795	BG	R299GHS	Dennis Dart SLF	Plaxton Pointer 2	N37F	1998	
40805	AG	R312GHS	Dennis Dart SLF	Plaxton Pointer 2	N37F	1998	
40827	HI	R647DUS	Dennis Dart SLF	Plaxton Pointer 2	N37F	1998	
40835	BA	R672DUS	Dennis Dart SLF	Plaxton Pointer 2	N37F	1998	
40956	HG	S344SUX	Dennis Dart SLF 10.7m	Plaxton Pointer 2	N41F	1998	New World First Bus, 2001
40957	HI	S372SUX	Dennis Dart SLF 10.7m	Plaxton Pointer 2	N41F	1998	New World First Bus, 2001
40960	PLu	S338TJX	Dennis Dart SLF 10.7m	Plaxton Pointer 2	N36F	1998	New World First Bus, 2001
40965	SN	SJ03DNY	Optare Solo M920	Optare	N30F	2003	
40966	SN	SJ03DOA	Optare Solo M920	Optare	N30F	2003	

40973-40976 — TransBus Dart SLF — Transbus Pointer — N37F — 2003

40973	DN	YV03UOY	40974	DN	YV03UOX	40975	DN	YV03UOW	40976	DN	YV03UOU

41070	AG	V370KLG	Dennis Dart SLF	Marshall Capital	N37F	1999	Chester Bus, 2007
41132	CE	P132NLW	Dennis Dart SLF	Marshall Capital	N31F	1997	
41144	PT	P144NLW	Dennis Dart SLF	Marshall Capital	N31F	1997	
41162	HG	R162TLM	Dennis Dart SLF 9.3m	Marshall Capital	N31F	1998	
41230	BG	R230TLM	Dennis Dart SLF 9.3m	Marshall Capital	N26F	1998	
41265	BG	T265JLD	Dennis Dart SLF 9.3m	Marshall Capital	N26D	1999	
41282	HXu	T282JLD	Dennis Dart SLF 9.3m	Marshall Capital	N26D	1999	
41283	HXu	T283JLD	Dennis Dart SLF 9.3m	Marshall Capital	N26D	1999	
41311	SN	V311GBY	Dennis Dart SLF 10.2m	Marshall Capital	N28D	1999	
41314	SN	V314GBY	Dennis Dart SLF 10.2m	Marshall Capital	N28D	1999	
41336	SH	T336ALR	Dennis Dart SLF 10.2m	Marshall Capital	N35F	1999	

41343-41348 — Dennis Dart SLF 8.9m — Marshall Capital — N25F — 1999

41343	PTu	T343ALR	41346	HI	V346DLH	41347	BGu	V347DLH	41348	HI	V348DLH

Joining the fleet in 2006, Alexander Dennis Pointer 42962, WX06OMU, carries additional branding for the express service that links Portishead with Bristol. It is seen arriving in the city. *Dave Heath*

42892	NE	VX54MUU	ADL Dart 10.7m		ADL Pointer		N37F	2004	
42893	NE	VX54MUV	ADL Dart 10.7m		ADL Pointer		N37F	2004	
42894	NE	VX05JWW	ADL Dart 10.7m		ADL Pointer		N37F	2005	

42895-42916   ADL Dart 10.7m   ADL Pointer   N37F   2005

42895	LH	WX05RUW	42901	LH	WX05RVJ	42907	BA	WX05RVP	42912	RA	WX05RVW
42896	MS	WX05RUY	42902	BA	WX05RVK	42908	BA	WX05RVR	42913	RA	WX05RVX
42897	MS	WX05RVA	42903	BA	WX05RVL	42909	BA	WX05RVT	42914	BA	WX05RVZ
42898	MS	WX05RVC	42904	BA	WX05RVM	42910	BA	WX05RVU	42915	BA	WX05RWE
42899	MS	WX05RVE	42905	BA	WX05RVN	42911	BA	WX05RVV	42916	BA	WX05RWF
42900	LH	WX05RVF	42906	BA	WX05RVO						

42918-42939   ADL Dart 10.7m   ADL Pointer   N37F*   2005   *42918-23 are N34F

42918	CN	EU05AUK	42924	PL	SN05EAA	42930	BR	SN05EAM	42935	CM	SN05DZR
42919	YA	EU05AUL	42925	BA	SN05EAC	42931	BR	SN05EAO	42936	BR	SN05DZS
42920	YA	EU05AUM	42926	BA	SN05EAE	42932	BR	SN05EAP	42937	CN	SN05DZT
42921	VN	EU05AUN	42927	HH	SN05EAF	42933	BS	SN05DZO	42938	BA	WX05SVD
42922	HH	EU05AUO	42928	HH	SN05EAG	42934	BS	SN05DZP	42939	BA	WX05SVE
42923	HH	EU05AUP	42929	YA	SN05EAJ						

42940-42969   ADL Dart 10.7m   ADL Pointer   N37F   2006

42940	TE	MX56HXZ	42948	MS	WA56FTY	42956	HG	WX06OMO	42963	MS	WX06OMW
42941	TE	WA56OAO	42949	SO	WX06OMF	42957	HG	WX06OMP	42964	MS	WX06OMY
42942	CE	WA56OAP	42950	SO	WX06OMG	42958	HG	WX06OMR	42965	MS	WX06OMZ
42943	CE	WA56OAS	42951	SO	WX06OMH	42959	HG	WX06OMS	42966	MS	WX06ONA
42944	TE	WA56OAU	42952	SO	WX06OMJ	42960	HG	WX06OMT	42967	HG	WX06ONB
42945	TE	WA56OAV	42953	SO	WX06OMK	42961	HG	WX06OMV	42968	LH	WX06ONC
42946	PL	WA56FTV	42954	SO	WX06OML	42962	MS	WX06OMU	42969	MS	WA56FTZ
42947	MS	WA56FTX	42955	HG	WX06OMM						

43356-43360   Dennis Dart SLF 8.8m   Plaxton Pointer MPD   N29F   1999

43356	CM	V356DVG	43357	BSw	V357DVG	43359	BS	V359DVG	43360	CM	V360DVG

43448	BRu	P448NEX	Dennis Dart SLF 10.7m	Plaxton Pointer	N40F	1997
43466	LO	R466CAH	Dennis Dart SLF 10.7m	Plaxton Pointer 2	N37F	1998

43480-43485 — Dennis Dart SLF 10.7m — Plaxton Pointer 2 — N34F — 1998

43480	BS	R680DPW	43481	LOu	R681DPW	43483	BR	R683DPW	43485	BR	R685DPW

43584	PT	R584SWN	Dennis Dart SLF 9m	Plaxton Pointer 2	N29F	1998
43679	BR	R679MEW	Dennis Dart SLF 9.3m	Marshall Capital	N31F	1998

43714-43721 — Dennis Dart SLF 10.7m — Plaxton Pointer 2 — N37F — 1998

43714	CN	R714DJN	43717	BS	R717DJN	43719	CN	R719DJN	43721	HH	R721DJN

43731-43736 — Dennis Dart SLF 10.7m — Plaxton Pointer 2 — N37F — 1998

43731	CM	S731TWC	43734	CM	S734TWC	43735	CN	S735TWC	43736	BSu	S737TWC
43733	BS	S733TWC									

43801	CM	AO02ODM	Dennis Dart SLF 8.8m	Plaxton Pointer MPD	N29F	2002	
43802	CM	AO02ODN	Dennis Dart SLF 8.8m	Plaxton Pointer MPD	N29F	2002	
43809	PL	S549SCV	Dennis Dart SLF 8.8m	Plaxton Pointer MPD	N29F	1998	Truronian, 2008
43810	PL	KU52RXJ	TransBus Dart SLF 8.8m	TransBus Mini Pointer	N29F	2003	Truronian, 2008
43811	TN	MIG5685	TransBus Dart SLF 8.8m	TransBus Mini Pointer	N29F	2003	
43812	CE	T12TRU	Dennis Dart SLF 8.8m	Plaxton Pointer MPD	N26F	1999	Truronian, 2008
43821	TN	MIG3863	Dennis Dart SLF 8.8m	Plaxton Pointer MPD	N29F	2000	
43822	TN	MIG3864	Dennis Dart SLF 8.8m	Plaxton Pointer MPD	N29F	2000	
43823	TN	MIG3865	Dennis Dart SLF 8.8m	Plaxton Pointer MPD	N29F	2000	

43836-43841 — TransBus Dart 8.8m — TransBus Mini Pointer — N26F — 2003

43836	PT	SN53ESV	43838	PT	SN53ESY	43840	RA	SN53ETE	43841	RA	SN53ETF
43837	RA	SN53ESU	43839	RA	SN53ETD						

43842	LT	SN04EFX	TransBus Dart 8.8m	TransBus Mini Pointer	N29F	2004
43844	LT	SN04EFZ	TransBus Dart 8.8m	TransBus Mini Pointer	N29F	2004

43845-43849 — ADL Dart 8.8m — ADL Mini Pointer — N29F — 2005

43845	CM	SN55CXH	43847	BS	SN55CXJ	43848	BS	SN55CXE	43849	MS	SN05HEJ
43846	CM	SN55CXF									

43850-43853 — ADL Dart 8.9m — ADL Mini Pointer — N29F — 2006 — Truronian, 2008

43850	RA	WK06AEE	43851	RA	WK06AEF	43852	PT	WK06AFU	43853	PT	WK06AFV

43854-43874 — Dennis Dart 8.8m — Caetano Nimbus — N29F — 2002 — Connex, Jersey, 2013

43854	CN	EG52FFZ	43860	LO	EG52FGF	43865	LO	EG52FGU	43870	HD	EG52FFT
43855	CN	EG52FGC	43861	LO	EG52FGJ	43866	LO	EG52FGV	43871	HD	EG52FFV
43856	CN	EG52FGD	43862	LO	EG52FGK	43867		EG52FHC	43872	HD	EG52FFU
43857	CN	EG52FGE	43863	LO	EG52FFK	43868	LO	EG52FGX	43873	WR	EG52FFJ
43859	LO	EG52FHD	43864	LO	EG52FGA	43869	HD	EG52FFL	43874	WR	EG52FFY

43875	NE	MX56HYO	ADL Dart 8.9m	ADL Pointer MPD	N29F	2006	Centrebus, 2013
43876	NE	MX56HYP	ADL Dart 8.8m	ADL Pointer MPD	N29F	2006	Centrebus, 2013
43877	NE	EU06KDK	ADL Dart 8.8m	Caetano Nimbus	N28F	2006	Poppletons, Pontefract, '13
43901	RA	SN03LGG	TransBus Dart 11.3m	TransBus Super Pointer	N41F	2003	
43902	RA	SN03LGJ	TransBus Dart 11.3m	TransBus Super Pointer	N41F	2003	
43903	RA	SN03LGK	TransBus Dart 11.3m	TransBus Super Pointer	N41F	2003	

44001-44006 — ADL Dart 4 10.2m — ADL Enviro 200 — N32F — 2008

44001	HH	LK57EJD	44003	HH	LK57EJF	44005	HH	LK57EJJ	44006	HH	LK57EJL
44002	HH	LK57EJE	44004	HH	LK57EJG						

44076-44081 — ADL Dart 4 10.2m — ADL Enviro 200 — N32F — 2009

44076	HH	YX58HVF	44078	HH	YX58HVH	44080	HH	YX58HVK	44081	HH	YX58HVL
44077	HH	YX58HVG	44079	HH	YX58HVJ						

44500	RA	WK56ABZ	ADL Dart 4 10.8m	ADL Enviro 200	N38F	2006	Truronian, 2008

44501-44506 — ADL Dart 4 10.8m — ADL Enviro 200 — N35F — 2008

44501	RA	CU08ACY	44503	BL	CU08ADO	44505	BL	CU08ADX	44506	SO	CU08ADZ
44502	BL	CU08ACZ	44504	BL	CU08ADV						

44507-44510 — ADL Dart 4 10.8m — ADL Enviro 200 — N36F — 2009

44507	SO	YX58HWF	44508	SO	YX58HWG	44509	SO	YX58HWH	44510	SO	YX58HWJ

First operates a number of the 8.8 metre Mini Pointer Dart although the majority of twenty-nine seat capacity buses are Optare Solos. Carrying 'Somerset' livery is 43823, X203HAE, pictured in Corporation Street, Taunton. *Mark Lyons*

44511-44514
			ADL Dart 4	10.8m			ADL Enviro 200		N36F	2007	Townlynx, Holywell, 2012
44511	HD	DK57SPZ	44512	WR	DK57SXF	44513	LO	DK57SXG	44514	HD	MX07OZD

44515	HD	MX10DXU	ADL Dart 4	10.8m			ADL Enviro 200		N36F	2010	Premiere, Nottingham, '13

44516-44519
			ADL Dart 4	10.8m			ADL Enviro 200		N28F	2009	
44516	IP	YX09ACV	44517	IP	YX09ACY	44518	IP	YX09ACZ	44519	IP	YX09ADO

44520-44526
			ADL E20D	10.8m			ADL Enviro 200		N33F	2012	
44520	BA	YX62DVM	44522	BA	YX62DWM	44524	BA	YX62DXC	44526	BA	YX62DXH
44521	BA	YX62DWG	44523	BA	YX62DWO	44525	BA	YX62DXF			

44527-44536
			ADL E20D	10.8m			ADL Enviro 200		N39F	2012	
44527	SO	SN62AYV	44530	SO	SN62AZB	44533	SO	SN62DBV	44535	SO	SN62DCY
44528	SO	SN62AYZ	44531	SO	SN62AZW	44534	SO	SN62DCX	44536	SO	SN62DCZ
44529	SO	SN62AZA	44532	SO	SN62DBO						

44537-44559
			ADL E20D	10.8m			ADL Enviro 200		N39F	2013	*44552-9 are N33F
44537	CM	YX13AEF	44543	CM	YX13AHZ	44549	CM	YX13AKO	44555	RA	YX13AEZ
44538	CM	YX13AHN	44544	CM	YX13AKF	44550	CM	YX13AKP	44556	RA	YX13AFA
44539	CM	YX13AHO	44545	CM	YX13AKG	44551	CM	YX13AKY	44557	RA	YX13AFE
44540	CM	YX13AHP	44546	CM	YX13AKJ	44552	RA	YX13AEV	44558	RA	YX13AKU
44541	CM	YX13AHU	44547	CM	YX13AKK	44553	RA	YX13AEW	44559	RA	YX13AKV
44542	CM	YX13AHV	44548	CM	YX13AKN	44554	RA	YX13AEY			

44560-44570
			ADL E20D	10.8m			ADL Enviro 200		N33F	2013	
44560	BL	YX63LKV	44563	SH	YX63LLC	44566	SH	YX63LLF	44569	SH	YX63LHR
44561	BL	YX63LKY	44564	SH	YX63LLD	44567	SH	YX63LLG	44570	BG	YX63LKU
44562	BL	YX63LKZ	44565	SH	YX63LLE	44568	BG	YX63LLJ			

44573-44581 ADL E20D 9.6m ADL Enviro 200 N31F 2013

44573	RA	YX13BNA	44576	RA	YX13BNE	44578	RA	YX13BNJ	44580	RA	YX13BNL
44574	RA	YX13BNB	44577	RA	YX13BNF	44579	RA	YX13BNK	44581	RA	YX13BNN
44575	RA	YX13BND									

44582-44595 ADL E20D 10.8m ADL Enviro 200 N39F 2013-14

44582	BG	YX63ZUD	44586	BG	YX63ZVD	44590	BG	YX63ZVH	44593	BG	YX63LHM
44583	BG	YX63ZVA	44587	PT	YX63ZVE	44591	BG	YX63LHK	44594	RA	YX14RWN
44584	BG	YX63ZVB	44588	PT	YX63ZVF	44592	BG	YX63LHL	44595	RA	YX14RWO
44585	BG	YX63ZVC	44589	PT	YX63ZVG						

44596	CN	EU60LFS	ADL Dart 4 10.8m	ADL Enviro 200	N37F	2010	Connex, Jersey, 2013
44597	CN	FJ58YSL	ADL Dart 4 10.8m	ADL Enviro 200	N36F	2008	Premiere, Nottingham, 2013
44598	CN	KX57BWF	ADL Dart 4 10.8m	ADL Enviro 200	N37F	2008	Townlynx, Holywell, 2013
44599	CN	YX08HJF	ADL Dart 4 10.8m	ADL Enviro 200	N37F	2008	Arriva Yorkshire, 2013

44602-44636 ADL E20D 10.8m ADL Enviro 200 N39F 2014

44602	PT	YX14RUC	44611	RA	YX14RVA	44620	RA	YX14RVO	44629	RA	YX14RWE
44603	RA	YX14RUH	44612	RA	YX14RVC	44621	RA	YX14RVP	44630	RA	YX14RWF
44604	RA	YX14RUJ	44613	RA	YX14RVE	44622	RA	YX14RVR	44631	RA	YX14RWJ
44605	RA	YX14RUO	44614	RA	YX14RVF	44623	RA	YX14RVT	44632	RA	YX14RWK
44606	RA	YX14RUR	44615	RA	YX14RVJ	44624	RA	YX14RVU	44633	RA	YX64VPJ
44607	RA	YX14RUU	44616	RA	YX14RVK	44625	RA	YX14RVV	44634	RA	YX64VPK
44608	RA	YX14RUV	44617	RA	YX14RVL	44626	RA	YX14RVW	44635	RA	YX64VPL
44609	RA	YX14RUW	44618	RA	YX14RVM	44627	RA	YX14RVY	44636	RA	YX64VPM
44610	RA	YX14RUY	44619	RA	YX14RVN	44628	RA	YX14RVZ			

44651-44658 ADL E20D 10.8m ADL Enviro 200 MMC N-F 2015

44651	B	-	44653	B	-	44655	B	-	44657	B	-
44652	B	-	44654	B	-	44656	B	-	44658	B	-

44900	CM	AY08EKT	ADL Dart 4 8.9m	ADL Enviro 200	N29F	2008	Carter, Chapel St Mary, 2013
44902	BA	WX08LNN	ADL Dart 4 8.9m	ADL Enviro 200	N29F	2008	Operated for Wessex Water
44903	BA	WX08LNO	ADL Dart 4 8.9m	ADL Enviro 200	N29F	2008	Operated for Wessex Water
44904	BA	WX08LNP	ADL Dart 4 8.9m	ADL Enviro 200	N29F	2008	Operated for Wessex Water

44905-44924 ADL Dart 4 8.9m ADL Enviro 200 N28F 2009

44905	WS	YX09AFN	44910	WS	YX09AFZ	44915	BA	YX09AHA	44920	BA	YX09AHG
44906	WS	YX09AFO	44911	WS	YX09AGO	44916	BA	YX09AHC	44921	BA	YX09ADU
44907	WS	YX09AFU	44912	WS	YX09AGU	44917	BA	YX09AHD	44922	TN	YX09ADV
44908	WS	YX09AFV	44913	BA	YX09AGV	44918	BA	YX09AHE	44923	TN	YX09ADZ
44909	WS	YX09AFY	44914	BA	YX09AGZ	44919	BA	YX09AHF	44924	TN	YX09AHK

44925	DN	YX11HNW	ADL Dart 4 8.9m	ADL Enviro 200	N29F	2011	
44926	DN	YX11HNY	ADL Dart 4 8.9m	ADL Enviro 200	N29F	2011	
44927	DN	YX11HNZ	ADL Dart 4 8.9m	ADL Enviro 200	N29F	2011	
44928	VN	EU08FHB	ADL Dart 4 8.9m	ADL Enviro 200	N28F	2008	Olympus, Harlow, 2012

45111-45115 ADL Dart 4 8.9m ADL Enviro 200 N28F 2008

45111	TN	YX58FRJ	45113	TN	YX58FRL	45114	TN	YX58FRN	45115	TN	YX58FRP
45112	TN	YX58FRK									

45116-45119 ADL Dart 4 8.9m ADL Enviro 200 N28F 2009 JP Travel, Middleton, 2012

45116	VN	VT09JPT	45117	VN	ST58JPT	45118	VN	ST09JPT	45119	VN	RT09JPT

46264	LH	P264PAE	Dennis Dart SLF 10.2m	Plaxton Pointer	N39F	1996
46324	SO	N324ECR	Dennis Dart 9m	Plaxton Pointer	B35F	1995
46325	SO	N325ECR	Dennis Dart 9m	Plaxton Pointer	B35F	1995

The Wrightbus StreetLite is produced in five lengths ranging from 8.8 and 9.5 metres in the wheel forward (WF) version and 10.2, 10.8 and 11.5 metres in the door forward (DF) variant. First have numbered their shorter DF models in the 47xxx range with the longer, 11.5 (Max) version in the 63xxx range. Based in Bristol, 47439, SK63KNM, heads for Aston Vale. *Dave Heath*

47405-47434

			Wrightbus StreetLite DF			Wrightbus			N37F	2013	
47405	WH	SK63KLE	47413	HI	SK63KLU	47421	HI	SK63KMJ	47428	SO	SK63KMZ
47406	WH	SK63KLF	47414	HI	SK63KLV	47422	SO	SK63KMM	47429	SO	SK63KNA
47407	WH	SK63KLJ	47415	HI	SK63KLX	47423	SO	SK63KMO	47430	SO	SK63KNB
47408	WH	SK63KLL	47416	HI	SK63KLZ	47424	SO	SK63KMU	47431	HI	SK63KNC
47409	WH	SK63KLM	47417	HI	SK63KMA	47425	SO	SK63KMV	47432	HI	SK63KND
47410	WH	SK63KLO	47418	HI	SK63KME	47426	SO	SK63KMX	47433	HI	SK63KNE
47411	HI	SK63KLP	47419	HI	SK63KMF	47427	SO	SK63KMY	47434	HI	SK63KNF
47412	HI	SK63KLS	47420	HI	SK63KMG						

47435-47465

			Wrightbus StreetLite DF			Wrightbus			N37F	2013	
47435	HG	SK63KNG	47443	HG	SK63KNR	47451	HG	SK63KKM	47459	HG	SK63KKW
47436	HG	SK63KNH	47444	HG	SK63KNS	47452	HG	SK63KKN	47460	HG	SK63KKX
47437	HG	SK63KNJ	47445	HG	SK63KNU	47453	HG	SK63KKO	47461	HG	SK63KKY
47438	HG	SK63KNL	47446	HG	SK63KNV	47454	HG	SK63KKP	47462	HG	SK63KKZ
47439	HG	SK63KNM	47447	HG	SK63KNX	47455	HG	SK63KKR	47463	HG	SK63KLA
47440	HG	SK63KNN	47448	HG	SK63KNY	47456	HG	SK63KKS	47464	HG	SK63KLC
47441	HG	SK63KNO	47449	HG	SK63KKJ	47457	HG	SK63KKU	47465	HG	SK63KLD
47442	HG	SK63KNP	47450	HG	SK63KKL	47458	HG	SK63KKV			

47466-47500

			Wrightbus StreetLite DF			Wrightbus			N37F	2014	
47466	OM	SN14DZM	47475	TE	SN14EAM	47484	DN	SN64CNV	47493	HU	SN64CHF
47467	OM	SN14DZO	47476	TE	SN14EAO	47485	DN	SN64CNX	47494	HU	SN64CHG
47468	TE	SN14DZP	47477	TE	SN14EAP	47486	DN	SN64CNY	47495	HU	SN64CHH
47469	TE	SN14EAA	47478	TE	SN14EAW	47487	DN	SN64CNZ	47496	HU	SN64CHJ
47470	TE	SN14EAC	47479	TE	SN14EAX	47488	DN	SN64COA	47497	HU	SN64CHK
47471	OM	SN14EAE	47480	TE	SN14EAY	47489	DN	SN64COH	47498	HU	SN64CHL
47472	OM	SN14EAF	47481	OM	SN14EBA	47490	DN	SN64COJ	47499	HU	SN64CHO
47473	TE	SN14EAG	47482	DN	SN64CNO	47491	HU	SN64CHC	47500	HU	SN64CHV
47474	OM	SN14EAJ	47483	DN	SN64CNU	47492	HU	SN64CHD			

47501-47571 — Wrightbus StreetLite DF — Wrightbus — N37F — 2014

47501	YA	SN64CPU	47518	WR	SN64CFX	47535	TN	MK63XAM	47556	MS	SN14FGJ
47502	YA	SN64CPV	47519	WR	SN64CFY	47536	TN	MK63XAN	47557	MS	SN14FGK
47503	YA	SN64CPX	47520	WR	SN64CFZ	47537	TN	MK63XAO	47558	MS	SN14FGM
47504	YA	SN64CPY	47521	HH	SN64CMV	47538	TN	MK63XAP	47559	LH	SN64CLF
47505	YA	SN64CPZ	47522	HH	SN64CMX	47544	BA	SN14FFU	47560	LH	SN64CLJ
47506	YA	SN64CRF	47523	HH	SN64CMY	47545	BA	SN14FFV	47561	LH	SN64CLO
47507	VN	SN64CRJ	47524	HH	SN64CMZ	47546	BA	SN14FFW	47562	LH	SN64CLU
47508	VN	SN64CRK	47525	HH	SN64CNA	47547	BA	SN14FFX	47563	LH	SN64CLV
47509	VN	SN64CRU	47526	HH	SN64CNC	47548	BA	SN14FFY	47564	LH	SN64CLX
47510	VN	SN64CRV	47527	HH	SN64CNE	47549	BA	SN14FFZ	47565	LH	SN64CLY
47511	VN	SN64CRX	47528	HH	SN64CNF	47550	BA	SN14FGA	47566	LH	SN64CLZ
47512	VN	SN64CRZ	47529	HH	SN64CNJ	47551	MS	SN14FGC	47567	HG	SN64CME
47513	WR	SN64CFM	47530	HH	SN64CNK	47552	MS	SN14FGD	47568	HG	SN64CMF
47514	WR	SN64CFO	47531	LT	SN64CJY	47553	MS	SN14FGE	47569	HG	SN64CMK
47515	WR	SN64CFP	47532	LT	SN64CJZ	47554	MS	SN14FGF	47570	HG	SN64CMO
47516	WR	SN64CFU	47533	LT	SN64CKA	47555	MS	SN14FGG	47571	HG	SN64CMU
47517	WR	SN64CFV	47534	LT	SN64CKC						

47573-47628 — Wrightbus StreetLite DF — Wrightbus — N37F — 2014

47573	HO	SN14EBG	47587	HO	SN14ECE	47601	SO	SN14FFE	47615	LT	SN64CKV
47574	HO	SN14EBJ	47588	HO	SN14ECF	47602	SO	SN14FFG	47616	LT	SN64CKX
47575	HO	SN14EBK	47589	HO	SN14ECJ	47603	SO	SN14FFH	47617	LT	SN64CKY
47576	HO	SN14EBL	47590	HO	SN14ECT	47604	SO	SN14FFJ	47618	PH	SN14DZA
47577	HO	SN14EBM	47591	HO	SN14ECV	47605	SO	SN14FFK	47619	PH	SN14DZB
47578	HO	SN14EBO	47592	HO	SN14ECW	47606	SO	SN14FFL	47620	PH	SN14DZC
47579	HO	SN14EBP	47593	HO	SN14ECX	47607	SO	SN14FFM	47621	PH	SN14DZD
47580	HO	SN14EBU	47594	HO	SN14ECY	47608	SO	SN14FFO	47622	PH	SN14DZE
47581	HO	SN14EBV	47595	SO	SN14FEU	47609	SO	SN14FFP	47623	PH	SN14DZF
47582	HO	SN14EBX	47596	SO	SN14FEV	47610	SO	SN14FFR	47624	PH	SN14DZG
47583	HO	SN14EBZ	47597	SO	SN14FEX	47611	SO	SN14FFS	47625	PH	SN14DZH
47584	HO	SN14ECA	47598	SO	SN14FFA	47612	SO	SN14FFT	47626	PH	SN14DZJ
47585	HO	SN14ECC	47599	SO	SN14FFC	47613	LT	SN64CKD	47627	PH	SN14DZK
47586	HO	SN14ECD	47600	SO	SN14FFD	47614	LT	SN64CKU	47628	PH	SN14DZL

47629-47658 — Wrightbus StreetLite DF — Wrightbus — N37F — 2015

47629	PT	SN15ADO	47637	PT	SN15AED	47645	HH	SN15AFE	47652	BS	SN15AEP
47630	PT	SN15ADU	47638	PT	SN15AEE	47646	HH	SN15AFF	47653	BS	SN15AET
47631	PT	SN15ADV	47639	PT	SN15AEF	47647	HH	SN15AFJ	47654	BS	SN15AEU
47632	PT	SN15ADX	47640	PT	SN15AEG	47648	HH	SN15AFK	47655	BS	SN15AEV
47633	PT	SN15ADZ	47641	PT	SN15AEJ	47649	HH	SN15AFL	47656	BS	SN15AEW
47634	PT	SN15AEA	47642	PT	SN15AEK	47650	BS	SN15AEM	47657	CO	SN15AEX
47635	PT	SN15AEB	47643	HH	SN15AEZ	47651	BS	SN15AEO	47658	CO	SN15AEY
47636	PT	SN15AEC	47644	HH	SN15AFA						

47659-47695 — Wrightbus StreetLite DF — Wrightbus — N37F — 2015

47659	RA	-	47669	SH	SN15ACV	47678	RA	SL15RVV	47687	SO	-
47660	RA	-	47670	WH	SN15ACX	47679	RA	SL15RVW	47688	SO	-
47661	PT	SN15ABK	47671	WH	SN15ACY	47680	RA	SL15RVX	47689	SO	-
47662	PT	SN15ABO	47672	WH	SN15ACZ	47681	RA	SL15RVY	47690	SO	-
47663	PT	SN15ABU	47673	PT	SL15RVO	47682	PT	SL15RWX	47691	SO	-
47664	PT	SN15ABV	47674	PT	SL15RVP	47683	PT	SL15XWY	47692	SO	-
47665	SH	SN15ACF	47675	PT	SL15RVR	47684	PT	SL15XWZ	47693	SO	-
47666	SH	SN15ACJ	47676	PT	SL15RVT	47685	PT	SL15XZA	47694	SO	-
47667	SH	SN15ACO	47677	RA	SL15RVU	47686	SO	-	47695	SO	-
47668	SH	SN15ACU									

Operated on behalf of Transport for Greater Manchester (TfGM) is Optare Versa 49115, YJ61JHO, one of three from the batch allocated to Tameside depot. It is seen in Stockport while working service 381 from Bredbury. *John Birtwistle*

48045	CAs	N345CJA	Volvo B6 9.9m	Alexander Dash	B36F	1996		
48201	PL	T801RHW	Volvo B6BLE	Wright Crusader 2	N36F	1999		
48208	WH	V808EFB	Volvo B6BLE	Wright Crusader 2	N36F	1999		
48210	PL	V810EFB	Volvo B6BLE	Wright Crusader 2	N36F	1999		

48211-48234
Volvo B6BLE — Wright Crusader 2 — N36F — 2000

48211	PL	W811PFB	48218	HGu	W818PFB	48224	HGu	W824PFB	48229	PL	W829PFB
48212	HG	W812PFB	48219	HGu	W819PFB	48225	PL	W825PFB	48231	PL	W831PFB
48213	HG	W813PFB	48221	PL	W821PFB	48226	PL	W826PFB	48232	PL	W832PFB
48214	HG	W814PFB	48222	HGu	W822PFB	48227	PL	W827PFB	48233	PL	W833PFB
48216	HGu	W816PFB	48223	WS	W823PFB	48228	PL	W828PFB	48234	PL	W834PFB
48217	WS	W817PFB									

48261-48269
Volvo B6BLE — Wright Crusader 2 — N37F — 2000

48261	PL	W601PAF	48263	PL	W603PAF	48265	PL	W605PAF	48267	PL	W607PAF
48262	PL	W602PAF	48264	PL	W604PAF	48266	PL	W606PAF	48269	PL	W609PAF

48270-48273
Volvo B6BLE — Wrightbus Crusader 2 — N38F — 2002

48270	WH	WK02TYD	48271	TN	WK02TYF	48272	WH	WK02TYH	48273	WH	YG02DLV

49002-49010
Optare Versa V1080 — Optare — N36F — 2013

49002	BG	YJ13HMD	49005	BG	YJ13HMG	49007	BG	YJ13HMK	49009	BG	YJ13HMV
49003	BG	YJ13HME	49006	BG	YJ13HMH	49008	BG	YJ13HMU	49010	BG	YJ13HMX
49004	BG	YJ13HMF									

49101-49119
Optare Versa V1100 Hybrid — Optare — N27F — 2010-12 — *Operated for TfGM*

49101	QS	YJ60KCU	49108	QS	YJ60KDN	49112	QS	YJ60KDX	49116	BN	YJ61JHU
49102	QS	YJ60KCV	49109	QS	YJ60KDO	49113	TE	YJ61JHK	49117	BN	YJ61JFU
49106	QS	YJ60KDF	49110	QS	YJ60KDU	49114	TE	YJ61JHL	49118	QS	YJ61JFV
49107	QS	YJ60KDK	49111	QS	YJ60KDV	49115	TE	YJ61JHO	49119	QS	YJ61JFX

Wood Street in Cardiff and Optare Versa 49302, YJ13HLU arrives from Porthcawl. Note the Welsh dragon feature applied within the gold band on this livery. First Cymru carries around 21 million passengers a year on a network of routes in South and West Wales, serving Bridgend County, Neath, Port Talbot, Swansea, Llanelli, Carmarthen, Haverfordwest and South Pembrokeshire. *Richard Godfrey*

49202-49222

Optare Versa V1200 Hybrid | Optare | S57F | 2012 | *Operated for TfGM*

49202	OM	YJ12MYF	49208	QS	YJ12MYN	49213	QS	YJ12MYT	49217	BN	YJ12MYX
49203	OM	YJ12MYG	49209	OM	YJ12MYO	49214	BN	YJ12MYU	49218	QS	YJ12MYY
49204	QS	YJ12MYH	49210	OM	YJ12MYP	49215	OM	YJ12MYV	49220	QS	YJ12MZD
49205	OM	YJ12MYK	49211	BN	YJ12MYR	49216	OM	YJ12MYW	49222	OM	YJ12MZF
49206	OM	YJ12MYL	49212	OM	YJ12MYS						

| 49227 | BN | YJ12GXZ | Optare Versa V1200 Hybrid | Optare | S57F | 2012 | *Operated for TfGM* |
| 49228 | BN | YJ12GXV | Optare Versa V1200 Hybrid | Optare | S57F | 2012 | *Operated for TfGM* |

49230-49233

Optare Versa V1200 Hybrid | Optare | S57F | 2014 | *Operated for TfGM*

| 49230 | QS | YJ14BPO | 49231 | QS | YJ14BPK | 49232 | QS | YJ14BPF | 49233 | BN | YJ64DYX |

49301-49309

Optare Versa V1170 | Optare | NC40F | 2013

49301	PT	YJ13HLR	49304	PT	YJ13HLW	49306	PT	YJ13HLY	49308	PT	YJ13HMA
49302	PT	YJ13HLU	49305	PT	YJ13HLX	49307	PT	YJ13HLZ	49309	PT	YJ13HMC
49303	PT	YJ13HLV									

49901-49912

Optare Versa V1100 EV | Optare | NC36F | 2014-15

49901	YK	YJ14BHA	49904	YK	YJ14BHF	49907	YK	YJ15AYK	49910	YK	YJ15AYN
49902	YK	YJ14BHD	49905	YK	YJ14BHK	49908	YK	YJ15AYL	49911	YK	YJ15AYO
49903	YK	YJ14BHE	49906	YK	YJ14BHL	49909	YK	YJ15AYM	49912	YK	YJ15AYP

49921	QS	YJ14BJX	Optare Versa V1100 EV	Optare	N28F	2014	*Operated for TfGM*
49922	QS	YJ14BJZ	Optare Versa V1100 EV	Optare	N28F	2014	*Operated for TfGM*
49923	QS	YJ14BJY	Optare Versa V1100 EV	Optare	N28F	2014	*Operated for TfGM*

Taking a break outside the Angel Centre in Worcester is Optare Solo 53043, VU03YJV, one of twelve of the 8.5 metre model supplied to the Midlands operation in 2002-03. *Mark Lyons*

50232-50239 — Optare Solo M850 — Optare — N26F — 2001-02

50232	LT	Y251HHL	50234	GS	Y253HHL	50236	HX	Y256HHL	50238	BD	YT51EZX
50233	BF	Y252HHL	50235	HX	Y254HHL	50237	BD	YT51EZW	50239	BD	YR02UVU

50276-50296 — Optare Solo M850 — Optare — N27F — 2000

50276	CE	W307DWX	50279	PL	W329DWX	50285	CE	W336DWX	50292	CE	W337DWX
50277	PL	W308DWX	50281	AG	W312DWX	50290	CE	W331DWX	50296	AG	W327DWX
50278	CE	W309DWX	50284	CE	W315DWX	50291	PL	W322DWX			

50318	BA	YN53ELO	Optare Solo M850	Optare	N27F	2003
50319	HX	YN53ELJ	Optare Solo M850	Optare	N27F	2003
50407	HX	YN03ZVX	Optare Solo M850	Optare	N27F	2003

50460-50468 — Optare Solo M850 — Optare — N27F — 2003

50460	GS	SJ03DOH	50463	SN	SJ03DPN	50465	SN	SJ03DPV	50467	WH	SJ03DPY
50461	SN	SJ03DPE	50464	SN	SJ03DPU	50466	WH	SJ03DPX	50468	LT	SJ03DPZ
50462	SN	SJ03DPF									

52526	CEu	S526RWP	Mercedes-Benz Vario O814	Plaxton Beaver 2	B22F	1998
52554	CEu	S554RWP	Mercedes-Benz Vario O814	Plaxton Beaver 2	B22F	1998

53001-53015 — Optare Solo M850 — Optare — N27F — 1999-2000

53001	TN	V801KAF	53009	CE	W809PAF	53012	CE	W812PAF	53014	PL	W814PAF
53007	CE	W807PAF	53011	PL	W811PAF	53013	CE	W813PAF	53015	CE	W815PAF
53008	CM	W808PAF									

53034	BD	Y546XNW	Optare Solo M850	Optare	N29F	2001	Clarkson, S Emsall, 2003
53035	BD	Y547XNW	Optare Solo M850	Optare	N29F	2001	Clarkson, S Emsall, 2003

53040-53051 — Optare Solo M850 — Optare — N22F — 2002-03

53040	CE	VU02PKX	53043	WR	VU03YJV	53046	WR	VU03YJY	53049	WR	VU03YKC
53041	HD	VU02PKY	53044	WR	VU03YJW	53047	WR	VU03YJZ	53050	WR	VU03YKD
53042	HD	VU03YJT	53045	WR	VU03YJX	53048	WR	VU03YKB	53051	WR	VU03YKE

53052-53057 — Optare Solo M850 — Optare — N22F — 2004

53052	SH	LK53MBX	53055	SH	LK53MDF	53056	SH	LK53MDJ	53057	SH	LK53PNO
53054	SH	LK53MDE									

53058-53064 — Optare Solo M850 — Optare — N22F — 2004

53058	HD	VX53OEV	53060	HD	VX53OEO	53062	WR	VX53OER	53064	HD	VX53OEU
53059	HD	VX53OEN	53061	WR	VX53OEP	53063	HD	VX53OET			

53065	BL	YJ58CEV	Optare Solo M850	Optare	N28F	2008

53101-53111 — Optare Solo M850 — Optare — N26F — 2002

53101	BD	EO02FLA	53104	BD	EO02FLD	53108	CE	EO02FLH	53110	WH	EO02FLK
53102	BA	EO02FLB	53107	CE	EO02FLG	53109	WH	EO02FLJ	53111	WH	EO02FKZ
53103	BA	EO02FLC									

53112-53137 — Optare Solo M920 — Optare — N30F — 2002

53112	CM	EO02NDX	53119	NE	EO02NEY	53126	CM	EO02NFH	53132	CM	EO02NFP
53113	CM	EO02NDY	53120	AG	EO02NFA	53127	CM	EO02NFJ	53133	CM	EO02NFR
53114	CM	EO02NDZ	53121	CM	EO02NFC	53128	CM	EO02NFK	53134	CM	EO02NFT
53115	CM	EO02NEF	53122	AG	EO02NFD	53129	CM	EO02NFL	53135	CM	EO02NFU
53116	CM	EO02NEJ	53123	AG	EO02NFE	53130	CM	EO02NFM	53136	CM	EO02NFV
53117	CM	EO02NEN	53124	AG	EO02NFF	53131	CM	EO02NFN	53137	CM	EO02NFX
53118	AG	EO02NEU	53125	CM	EO02NFG						

53138	CM	EU54BNK	Optare Solo M920	Optare	N33F	2004
53139	CM	EU54BNJ	Optare Solo M920	Optare	N33F	2004
53140	HI	YJ05XOP	Optare Solo M920	Optare	N33F	2005

53143-53150 — Optare Solo M920 — Optare — N30F — 2004

53143	OM	MX54GZA	53145	OM	MX54GZC	53147	OM	MX54GZE	53149	QSu	MX54GZG
53144	OM	MX54GZB	53146	OM	MX54GZD	53148	TE	MX54GZF	53150	QSu	MX54GZH

53151	HI	YN03ZVW	Optare Solo M850	Optare	N27F	2003	
53154	PL	HIG8433	Optare Solo M920	Optare	N29F	2005	Truronian, 2008
53155	AG	CN06BXH	Optare Solo M920	Optare	N31F	2006	Veolia, 2012
53201	SN	YJ54BSV	Optare Solo M950	Optare	N30F	2004	
53202	SN	SF05KUJ	Optare Solo M950	Optare	N28F	2005	
53203	SN	SF05KUK	Optare Solo M950	Optare	N28F	2005	
53204	BA	TU04TRU	Optare Solo M950	Optare	N33F	2004	Truronian, 2008
53205	PL	HIG8434	Optare Solo M950	Optare	N33F	2005	Truronian, 2008
53206	HI	T77TRU	Optare Solo M950	Optare	N33F	2004	Truronian, 2008
53207	AG	CN07KZK	Optare Solo M950 SL	Optare	N29F	2007	Veolia, 2012
53208	AG	CN07KZL	Optare Solo M950 SL	Optare	N29F	2007	Veolia, 2012
53209	AG	CN07KZM	Optare Solo M950 SL	Optare	N29F	2007	Veolia, 2012
53301	HX	YJ54BVA	Optare Solo M1020	Optare	N34F	2004	Addison, Steeton, 2013
53302	HX	YJ54BVB	Optare Solo M1020	Optare	N34F	2004	Addison, Steeton, 2013
53303	HX	YJ54BVC	Optare Solo M1020	Optare	N34F	2004	Addison, Steeton, 2013

53401-53404 — Optare Solo M880 — Optare — N29F — 2004 — 53403/4 *operated for Cornwall*

53401	BA	TO54TRU	53402	CE	T20TVL	53403	CE	TL54TVL	53404	CE	TT54TVL

53405	AG	VX57CYO	Optare Solo M880 SL	Optare	N28F	2007	Veolia, 2012
53503	CE	YX06YSK	Optare Solo M880	Optare	N28F	2006	Regal Busways, 2015
53504	CE	YJ56AOT	Optare Solo M880	Optare	N28F	2006	Regal Busways, 2015
53505	CE	YJ56AOU	Optare Solo M880	Optare	N28F	2006	Regal Busways, 2015

53601-53615 — Optare Solo M880 SR — Optare — N28F — 2014

53601	HO	YJ14BKA	53605	HO	YJ14BKG	53609	HO	YJ14BKO	53613	WH	YJ14BVD
53602	BW	YJ14BKD	53606	HO	YJ14BKK	53610	WH	YJ14BVA	53614	WH	YJ14BVE
53603	HO	YJ14BKE	53607	HO	YJ14BKL	53611	WH	YJ14BVB	53615	WH	YJ14BVF
53604	HO	YJ14BKF	53608	HO	YJ14BKN	53612	WH	YJ14BVC			

53701-53706 — Optare Solo M780 SL — Optare — N21F — 2005

53701	CE	LK05DYO	53703	LT	LK05DXR	53705	BF	LK05DXT	53706	LT	LK05DXU
53702	LT	LK05DXP	53704	BF	LK05DXS						

Recent Optare Solo arrivals comprise a batch of fifteen 8.8 metre that feature the SR styling now applied to all models. Representing these vehicles is 53609, YJ14BKO, which is based at Fareham. *Mark Lyons*

53707	RA	MX58KZA	Optare Solo M780 SL	Optare	N23F	2008	*Operated for Carmarthenshire CC*
53708	RA	MX58KZB	Optare Solo M780 SL	Optare	N23F	2008	*Operated for Carmarthenshire CC*
53709	CE	MX59AVP	Optare Solo M780 SL	Optare	N27F	2009	*TM Travel, 2014*

53751-53754

Optare Solo M790 SE-R — Optare — N26F — 2015

53751	CA	YJ15AOW	53752	CA	YJ15AOX	53753	CA	YJ15AOY	53754	CA	YJ15AOZ

53801	CE	YK04KWR	Optare Solo M850 SL	Optare	N22F	2004	

53802-53820

Optare Solo M850 SL — Optare — N26F — 2005

53802	RA	WX05RRV	53807	BA	WX05RSV	53812	BA	WX05RTV	53817	BA	WX05RUO
53803	CE	WX05RRY	53808	BA	WX05RSY	53813	BA	WX05RTZ	53818	BA	WX05RUR
53804	RA	WX05RRZ	53809	BA	WX05RSZ	53814	BA	WX05RUA	53819	BA	WX05RUU
53805	CE	WX05RSO	53810	BA	WX05RTO	53815	BA	WX05RUC	53820	BA	WX05RUV
53806	BA	WX05RSU	53811	BA	WX05RTU	53816	BA	WX05RUJ			

53826	CE	YK05CDN	Optare Solo M780 SL	Optare	N24F	2005	Truronian, 2008
53827	PL	YK05CDO	Optare Solo M780 SL	Optare	N26F	2005	Truronian, 2008
53828	AG	MX56NLJ	Optare Solo M850 SL	Optare	N28F	2006	Veolia, 2012
53829	AG	MX56NLK	Optare Solo M850 SL	Optare	N28F	2006	Veolia, 2012
53830	AG	CN06BXF	Optare Solo M850 SL	Optare	N27F	2006	Veolia, 2012

53904-53909

Optare Solo M920 SL — Optare — N32F — 2005-08 — *Operated for Metro, WYPTE*

53904	HP	YJ55ENR	53906	HP	YJ55ENN	53907	HP	YJ07EHO	53909	HP	YJ07EHR
53905	HP	YJ55ENM									

54302	B	YX10AXP	Volkswagen Transporter	Bluebird Tucana	N14F	2010	*Operated for Strathclyde PT*
54304	B	YX10AYL	Volkswagen Transporter	Bluebird Tucana	N14F	2010	*Operated for Strathclyde PT*
54307	B	YX10AXT	Volkswagen Transporter	Bluebird Tucana	N14F	2010	*Operated for Strathclyde PT*
54401	O	YX12CHK	Fiat Ducato	Bluebird Orion	N14F	2012	*Operated for Strathclyde PT*
54402	O	YX12CHL	Fiat Ducato	Bluebird Orion	N16F	2012	*Operated for Strathclyde PT*
54403	B	YX12CHO	Fiat Ducato	Bluebird Orion	N16F	2012	*Operated for Strathclyde PT*
54404	CA	YX12CJF	Fiat Ducato	Bluebird Orion	N16F	2012	*Operated for Strathclyde PT*
54405	CA	YX12CJJ	Fiat Ducato	Bluebird Orion	N16F	2012	*Operated for Strathclyde PT*

Above: **Four wheel-forward Wrightbus Steetlites entered service in Taunton during 2014, all latterly in the Mistral hire fleet. Illustrating the model is 55102, MX12DZA.** *Steve Rice*

Below: **An interesting mini-coach based at Aberdeen is Mercedes-Benz Atego 56501, FSU382, which features a Ferqui Solera body imported by Optare. When pictured it was undertaking golf duties for the Ryder Cup team.** *Mark Doggett*

54406	CA	YX12CJO	Fiat Ducato	Bluebird Orion	N16F	2012	*Operated for Strathclyde PT*
54407	CA	YX12CJU	Fiat Ducato	Bluebird Orion	N16F	2012	*Operated for Strathclyde PT*
54601	WSs	RA04YGX	Ford Transit	Ford	M16	2004	Truronian, 2008
54602	BW	OIG1799	Ford Transit	Ford	M16	2004	Truronian, 2008

55101-55104 — Wrightbus Streetlite WF — Wrightbus — N35F — 2011-12 — Mistral, 2014

55101	TN	MX61BCF	**55102**	TN	MX12DZA	**55103**	TN	MX12JXV	**55104**	TN	MX61BBZ

56000	TN	W4TRU	Mercedes-Benz Vario 0814	Plaxton Cheetah	C27F	2000	Truronian, 2008

56001-56009 — Mercedes-Benz Vario 0814 — Plaxton Cheetah — C29F — 2003-04

56001	TN	YN53VBT	**56004**	MU	EY54BPX	**56006**	AB	EY54BRF	**56008**	AB	EY54BRX
56002	MU	YN53VBU	**56005**	AB	EY54BPZ	**56007**	AB	EY54BRV	**56009**	AB	EY54BRZ
56003	GS	YN53VBV								

56501	AB	FSU382	Mercedes-Benz Atego O1120L	Optare/Ferqui Solera	C29F	2005	
57000	BA	MX06AEB	Enterprise Plasma EB01	Plaxton Primo	N28F	2006	Truronian, 2008
57001	LT	YN56NHE	Enterprise Plasma EB01	Plaxton Primo	N28F	2006	
57002	LT	YN56NHF	Enterprise Plasma EB01	Plaxton Primo	N28F	2006	

59001-59008 — Optare Solo M820 SR Hybrid — Optare — N23F — 2010 — *Operated for TfGM*

59001	QS	YJ60KCA	**59003**	QS	YJ60KCE	**59005**	QS	YJ60KCG	**59007**	QS	YJ60KCN
59002	QS	YJ60KCC	**59004**	QS	YJ60KCF	**59006**	QS	YJ60KCK	**59008**	QS	YJ60KCO

59009-59013 — Optare Solo M820 SR Hybrid — Optare — N28F — 2012 — *Operated for TfGM*

59009	TE	YJ61JDO	**59012**	QS	YJ61JDZ	**59013**	QS	YJ61JEO		

60006	AG	S350MFP	Scania L113CRL	Wright Axcess-ultralow	N40F	1998
60011	AGu	R346SUT	Scania L113CRL	Wright Axcess-ultralow	N40F	1998
60012	AGu	S348MFP	Scania L113CRL	Wright Axcess-ultralow	N40F	1998
60013	AG	S103TNB	Scania L94UB	Wright Axcess Floline	N40F	1998
60015	AG	S106TNB	Scania L94UB	Wright Axcess Floline	N40F	1998
60057	AGu	S815AEH	Scania L113CRL	Wright Axcess-ultralow	N40F	1998

60065-60074 — Scania L94UB — Wright Axcess Floline — N43F* — 1999 — *60065/6 are N37F

60065	BM	T823SFS	**60067**	HP	T825SFS	**60069**	NE	T827SFS	**60073**	NE	V831GBF
60066	BM	T824SFS	**60068**	NE	T826SFS	**60072**	NE	V830GBF	**60074**	AG	V832GBF

60075	AG	R438ALS	Scania L113CRL	Wright Axcess-ultralow	N49F	1998
60081	AGu	S101TNB	Scania L94UB	Wright Axcess Floline	N40F	1998
60128	AG	S105TNB	Scania L94UB	Wright Axcess Floline	N40F	1998
60135	CMt	R177GSX	Scania L113CRL	Wright Axcess-ultralow	tv	1998

60163-60168 — Scania L94UB — Wright Axcess Floline — N40F — 1998

60163	BF	S110TNB	**60165**	BK	S112TNB	**60166**	BK	S113TNB	**60168**	LT	S115TNB

60171-60193 — Scania L94UB — Wright Axcess Floline — N42F* — 1999-2000 *60171/2 are N40F

60171	AG	T918SSF	**60174**	AG	V122DND	**60180**	LVu	V128DND	**60189**	AG	V137DND
60172	HP	T919SSF	**60175**	AG	V330DBU	**60181**	OMt	V129DND	**60193**	NE	V141DND
60173	AGu	V142DND	**60176**	AG	V124DND	**60188**	OMt	V136DND		

60195-60214 — Scania L94UB — Wright Axcess Floline — N43F — 2001

60195	LT	Y343XBN	**60199**	MU	X256USH	**60204**	LVt	X272USH	**60212**	HP	Y633RTD
60196	AG	X253USH	**60201**	AG	X257USH	**60205**	NE	X261USH	**60213**	BM	X269USH
60197	BK	Y597KNE	**60202**	NE	Y346XBN	**60206**	CO	Y598KNE	**60214**	BM	Y634RTD
60198	LT	Y344XBN	**60203**	LVt	Y632RTD	**60208**	NE	Y347XBN		

60217	HP	T563BSS	Scania L94UB	Wright Axcess Floline	N40F	1998
60220	BK	T566BSS	Scania L94UB	Wright Axcess Floline	N40F	1999
60221	BKu	T567BSS	Scania L94UB	Wright Axcess Floline	N40F	1999

The large batch of Mercedes-Benz Citaro buses remains divided between Oldham and Bury depots in Greater Manchester. Pictured arriving in Bolton on route 510 from Bury is 60270, W348RJA, which carries the latest fleet livery. *Alan Blagburn,*

60223-60282
Mercedes-Benz O530 Citaro   Mercedes-Benz   N38F   2000

60223	OMu	W301JND	60240	OMu	W338JND	60254	BY	W332RJA	60270	BY	W348RJA
60224	OM	W302JND	60241	BY	W319JND	60255	BY	W363RJA	60271	BY	W349RJA
60225	OMu	W303JND	60242	BY	W337JND	60256	BY	W334RJA	60272	BY	W362RJA
60226	BYu	W304JND	60243	BY	W341JND	60257	BY	W335RJA	60273	BY	W351RJA
60229	OMu	W307JND	60244	OMu	W322JND	60258	BY	W336RJA	60274	BY	W352RJA
60230	OMu	W308JND	60245	BY	W339JND	60259	BY	W337RJA	60275	BY	W353RJA
60233	BY	W311JND	60247	BY	W378JNE	60260	BY	W338RJA	60276	BY	W354RJA
60234	OMu	W312JND	60248	OM	W326JND	60261	BY	W339RJA	60277	BY	W366RJA
60235	BY	W313JND	60249	BY	W327JND	60262	BY	W361RJA	60278	BY	W356RJA
60236	OMu	W314JND	60250	BY	W379JNE	60264	BY	W342RJA	60279	BY	W357RJA
60237	BY	W315JND	60251	BY	W329JND	60267	BY	W365RJA	60280	BY	W358RJA
60238	BY	W334JND	60252	BY	W331JND	60268	BY	W346RJA	60281	BYu	W359RJA
60239	BY	W317JND	60253	BY	W331RJA	60269	BY	W347RJA	60282	BY	W364RJA

60283	BY	W179BVP	Mercedes-Benz O530 Citaro	Mercedes-Benz	N38F	2000	Evobus demonstrator, 2001

60299-60340
Volvo B10B   Wright Endurance   tv   1994-96

60299	HOt	M504PNA	60303	OMt	M508PNA	60316	AGt	N521WVR	60337	HOt	N542WVR
60301	BYt	M506PNA	60304	CMt	M509PNA	60317	AGt	N522WVR	60340	WRt	N545WVR
60302	BNu	M507PNA	60311	WRt	M516PNA	60322	BNt	N527WVR			

60361	ROt	R571YNC	Volvo B10BLE	Wright Renown	N41F	1997
60368	ROt	R578SBA	Volvo B10BLE	Wright Renown	N41F	1997
60371	QSu	R581SBA	Volvo B10BLE	Wright Renown	N41F	1997
60374	LEt	J461OVU	Volvo B10M-50	Northern Counties Paladin	tv	1991

60376-60386
Volvo B10BLE   Wright Renown   N41F   1998

60376	BNt	R621CVR	60380	BNu	R625CVR	60381	BNu	R626CVR	60386	QSu	R631CVR
60379	QSu	R624CVR									

From 1997 First's intake of Volvo B10BLEs and Scania L94s provided the main source of single-deck buses, all with similar but corresponding named bodywork from Wrights, the Renown and Axcess Flowline. Allocated to Great Yarmouth, Volvo B10BLE 60618, R781WKW is seen shortly after its repaint. *Mark Doggett*

| 60405 | BN | X699ADK | Volvo B10BLE | | | Wright Renown | | N41F | 2000 | |
| 60406 | DN | Y774TNC | Volvo B7L | | | Wrightbus Eclipse | | N41F | 2001 | |

60458-60486			Volvo B10M-55			Alexander PS		tv	1990	
60458	ROt	G603NWA	60464	CAt	G609NWA	60467	BMu	G622NWA	60472	BMt	G627NWA
60460	LEt	G605NWA	60466	CAt	G613NWA	60468	BMt	G623NWA	60486	OGt	G641NWA

60618-60627			Volvo B10BLE			Wright Renown		N44F	1997-98	
60618	YA	R781WKW	60622	YA	R785WKW	60626	RA	R789WKW	60627	DNu	R790WKW
60621	RA	R784WKW									

| **60630-60632** | | | Volvo B10BLE | | | Wright Renown | | N41F | 1998 | |
| 60630 | OG | S812RWG | 60631 | OG | S813RWG | 60632 | ROt | S814RWG | | | |

60633-60682			Volvo B10BLE			Wright Renown		N41F	1999	
60633	ROu	T815MAK	60646	OGu	T828MAK	60659	OGu	T841MAK	60672	RO	T854MAK
60634	ROu	T816MAK	60647	OGu	T829MAK	60660	QSt	T842MAK	60673	RO	T855MAK
60635	RO	T817MAK	60648	OG	T830MAK	60661	OG	T843MAK	60674	ROu	T856MAK
60636	ROu	T818MAK	60649	OGu	T831MAK	60662	OG	T844MAK	60675	RO	T857MAK
60637	BDt	T819MAK	60650	OG	T832MAK	60663	BNt	T86045MAK	60676	RO	T858MAK
60638	BMt	T820MAK	60651	BNt	T833MAK	60664	ROu	T846MAK	60677	RO	T859MAK
60639	ROu	T821MAK	60653	OGu	T835MAK	60665	HDt	T847MAK	60678	RO	T860MAK
60640	BYt	T822MAK	60654	OGu	T836MAK	60666	RO	T848MAK	60679	RO	T861MAK
60641	OGu	T823MAK	60655	OG	T837MAK	60668	BMt	T850MAK	60680	RO	T862MAK
60642	OG	T824MAK	60656	OG	T838MAK	60669	ROu	T851MAK	60681	ROt	T863MAK
60643	OGu	T825MAK	60657	QSt	T839MAK	60670	RO	T852MAK	60682	RO	T864MAK
60644	OG	T826MAK	60658	BMt	T840MAK	60671	ROu	T853MAK			

60683-60702 — Volvo B10BLE — Wright Renown — N41F — 1999

60683	RO	T865ODT	60688	OG	T870ODT	60693	OG	T875ODT	60698	OG	T880ODT
60684	OG	T866ODT	60689	OG	T871ODT	60694	OG	T876ODT	60699	OG	T881ODT
60685	OG	T867ODT	60690	OG	T872ODT	60695	OGu	T877ODT	60700	OG	T882ODT
60686	OGu	T868ODT	60691	OGu	T873ODT	60696	OG	T878ODT	60701	OG	T883ODT
60687	OG	T869ODT	60692	OG	T874ODT	60697	OG	T879ODT	60702	OG	T884ODT

60703	OG	Y661UKU

Volvo B7L — Wrightbus Eclipse — N41F — 2001

60704-60745 — Volvo B7L — Wrightbus Eclipse — N41F — 2002

60704	RO	MV02VAA	60714	OG	MV02VBF	60725	OG	MV02VCE	60736	OG	MV02VDK
60705	RO	MV02VAD	60715	OG	MV02VBG	60726	RO	MV02VCF	60737	OG	MV02VDL
60706	RO	MV02VAE	60716	OG	MV02VBJ	60727	RO	MV02VCG	60738	RO	MV02VDM
60707	OG	MV02VAF	60717	OG	MV02VBK	60728	RO	MV02VCJ	60739	RO	MV02VDN
60708	OG	MV02VAH	60718	DN	MV02VBL	60729	RO	MV02VCK	60740	RO	MV02VDO
60709	OG	MV02VAJ	60719	OG	MV02VBM	60730	RO	MV02VCL	60741	RO	MV02VDP
60710	OG	MV02VAK	60720	RO	MV02VBN	60731	RO	MV02VDD	60742	RO	MV02VDR
60711	OG	MV02VAM	60721	RO	MV02VBO	60733	RO	MV02VDF	60743	RO	MV02VDT
60712	OG	MV02VAO	60722	RO	MV02VBP	60734	RO	MV02VDG	60744	RO	MV02VDX
60713	OG	MV02VAU	60724	RO	MV02VCD	60735	RO	MV02VDJ	60745	OG	MV02VDY

60807-60820 — Volvo B10BLE — Wright Renown — N41F — 1998

60807	VNt	S658RNA	60813	TN	S664RNA	60814	TN	S665RNA	60820	HX	S677SVU
60808	VNt	S659RNA									

60821-60825 — Volvo B10BLE — Wright Renown — N44F — 1999

60821	BD	T154OUB	60823	BD	T156OUB	60824	BD	T157OUB	60825	BD	T158OUB
60822	BD	T255GUG									

60826-60840 — Volvo B10BLE — Wright Renown — N44F — 2000

60826	BD	V759UVY	60830	BD	V763UVY	60834	BD	V767UVY	60838	BD	V771UVY
60827	HX	V760UVY	60831	BD	V764UVY	60835	BD	V768UVY	60839	BD	V772UVY
60828	BD	V721UVY	60832	BD	V765UVY	60836	BD	V769UVY	60840	BD	V773UVY
60829	BD	V762UVY	60833	BD	W766HBT	60837	BD	V770UVY			

60841-60855 — Volvo B10BLE — Wright Renown — N44F — 2000

60841	HX	W801DWX	60845	HX	W805DWX	60849	HX	W809DWX	60853	BD	W814DWX
60842	HX	W802DWX	60846	HX	W806DWX	60850	HX	W811DWX	60854	BD	W815DWX
60843	HX	W803DWX	60847	HX	W807DWX	60851	HX	W812DWX	60855	BD	W816DWX
60844	HX	W804DWX	60848	HX	W808DWX	60852	BD	W813DWX			

60876-60928 — Volvo B7L — Wrightbus Eclipse — N41F — 2001-02

60876	YK	Y445CUB	60890	OG	YJ51RHK	60903	BD	YG02DHM	60916	PL	YG02DKU
60877	BD	Y446CUB	60891	OG	YJ51RGZ	60904	BD	YG02DHL	60917	PL	YG02DKV
60878	BD	Y447CUB	60892	OG	YJ51RHF	60905	BD	YG02DHO	60918	PL	YG02DLJ
60880	YK	Y449CUB	60893	OG	YJ51RGY	60906	BD	YG02DHN	60919	YK	YG02DLX
60881	YK	Y451CUB	60894	OG	YJ51REU	60907	BD	YG02DHV	60920	YK	YG02DLU
60882	YK	YJ51PZT	60895	PL	YJ51RFE	60908	BD	YG02DHA	60921	YK	YG02DLN
60883	YK	YJ51PZU	60896	YK	YJ51RFF	60909	YK	YG02DGZ	60922	YK	YG02DHJ
60884	YK	YJ51PZV	60897	YK	YJ51RFY	60910	PL	YJ51RFK	60923	BD	YG02DHF
60885	OG	YJ51PZW	60898	YK	YJ51RFX	60911	TN	YG02DLO	60924	BD	YG02DHE
60886	OG	YJ51PZX	60899	YK	YJ51RFL	60912	BA	YG02DLD	60925	BD	YG02DHD
60887	OG	YJ51PZY	60900	YK	YJ51RFN	60913	BA	YG02DLY	60926	YK	YG02DGY
60888	DN	YJ51RDZ	60901	YK	YJ51RFO	60914	BA	YG02DKO	60927	YK	YG02DHC
60889	DN	YJ51RHE	60902	YK	YG02DHK	60915	PL	YG02DLZ	60928	YK	YG02DHU

Scania L113 61235, S680BFS, is heading towards Longton in the Potteries. Initially entering service with First Glasgow it is one of nine now allocated to Stoke. *Mark Doggett*

60944	BMt	M406VWW	Dennis Lance 11m			Plaxton Verde		tv	1995		

61022-61041			Scania L94 UB			Wright Axcess Floline		N43F*	1999		*61037-42 are N37F
61022	CA	T421GUG	61029	BM	T428GUG	61034	HP	V133ESC	61038	BM	V137ESC
61025	CAu	T424GUG	61030	HP	T429GUG	61035	HP	V134ESC	61039	BM	V138ESC
61027	DUu	T426GUG	61031	HP	T430GUG	61036	HP	V135ESC	61040	BM	V139ESC
61028	CAt	T427GUG	61032	HP	T431GUG	61037	HP	V136ESC	61041	BM	V140ESC

61057	CN	R437GSF	Scania L113 CRL	Wright Axcess-ultralow	N40F	1997
61071	BMu	R457JFS	Scania L113 CRL	Wright Axcess-ultralow	N40F	1998
61072	BMu	R458JFS	Scania L113 CRL	Wright Axcess-ultralow	N40F	1998
61074	BM	R460JFS	Scania L113 CRL	Wright Axcess-ultralow	N40F	1998
61135	BL	YS51JVA	Bluebird A3 RE	Bluebird	S60F	2002
61136	BL	YS51JVK	Bluebird A3 RE	Bluebird	S60F	2002
61143	AGu	S361MFP	Scania L94 UB	Wright Axcess Floline	N40F	1998
61145	AGu	S690BFS	Scania L113 CRL	Wright Axcess-ultralow	N40F	1998
61148	VN	MV02VBU	Volvo B7L	Wrightbus Eclipse	N41F	2002

61192-61211			Volvo B7L			Wrightbus Eclipse		N41F	2002		
61192	DN	YU52VXH	61197	DN	YU52VXN	61202	DN	YU52VXT	61208	DN	JDZ2340
61193	DN	YU52VXJ	61198	DN	YU52VXO	61203	DN	YU52VXV	61209	DN	JDZ2391
61194	DN	YU52VXK	61199	DN	YU52VXP	61204	DN	YU52VXW	61210	DN	NDZ3162
61195	DN	YU52VXL	61200	DN	YU52VXR	61206	DN	YU52VXY	61211	DN	NDZ3164
61196	DN	YU52VXM	61201	DN	YU52VXS	61207	DN	JDZ2339			

Now located in Scotland are twenty Wrightbus Solar-bodied Scania L94s from 2003. Allocated to Musselburgh, 61227, YM52UWD, was pictured having arrived in Edinburgh. *Terry O'Neill*

61214-61233 — Scania L94 UB — Wrightbus Solar — N43F — 2003

61214	BK	YM52UVK	61219	GS	YM52UVR	61224	MU	YM52UVZ	61229	LT	YM52UWG
61215	BF	YM52UVL	61220	BF	YM52UVS	61225	BK	YM52UWA	61230	GS	YM52UWH
61216	BF	YM52UVN	61221	BKu	YM52UVT	61226	MU	YM52UWB	61231	LT	YM52UWJ
61217	BK	YM52UVO	61222	LT	YM52UVU	61227	MU	YM52UWD	61232	MU	YM52UWK
61218	BF	YM52UVP	61223	LT	YM52UVW	61228	MU	YM52UWF	61233	LT	YM52UWN

61235	AG	S680BFS	Scania L113 CRL	Wright Axcess-ultralow	N40F	1998
61237	AG	S681BFS	Scania L113 CRL	Wright Axcess-ultralow	N40F	1998
61240	OMt	R340GHS	Volvo B10BLE	Wright Renown	N43F	1998
61241	QSu	R339GHS	Volvo B10BLE	Wright Renown	N43F	1998
61245	AGu	R127GSF	Scania L113 CRL	Wright Axcess-ultralow	N40F	1997
61256	CAt	G601NWA	Volvo B10M-55	Alexander PS	B51F	1990
61289	HX	S809RWG	Volvo B10BLE	Wright Renown	N41F	1998
61306	PH	SJ51DJZ	Volvo B7L	Wrightbus Eclipse	N42F	2001
61351	BYtu	L204KSX	Volvo B10B	Alexander Strider	tv	1993
61356	OMt	L209KSX	Volvo B10B	Alexander Strider	tv	1993
61359	QStu	L212KSX	Volvo B10B	Alexander Strider	tv	1993
61363	BMt	L304VSU	Volvo B10B	Alexander Strider	B51F	1993
61366	OMt	L307VSU	Volvo B10B	Alexander Strider	B51F	1993
61478	CAt	P106MFS	Scania L113C RL	Wright Axcess-ultralow	N47F	1996

61587-61596 — Volvo B7L — Wrightbus Eclipse — N40F — 2002

61587	PH	SA02BZD	61590	PH	SA02BZG	61593	PH	SA02BZK	61595	PH	SA02BZM
61588	PH	SA02BZE	61591	PH	SA02BZH	61594	CE	SA02BZL	61596	PH	SA02BZN
61589	PH	SA02BZF	61592	PH	SA02BZJ						

Blantyre's allocation includes sixteen Volvo B10BLE, one of which, 61606, SF51YAV, is seen operating service 267 linking Newmains, West Crindledyke with Hamilton. *Mark Doggett*

61597-61614   Volvo B10BLE   Wrightbus Renown   N42F   2001

61597	B	SF51YAA	61602	B	SF51YAJ	61607	B	SF51YAW	61611	O	SF51YBB
61598	B	SF51YAD	61603	B	SF51YAK	61608	B	SF51YAX	61612	O	SF51YBC
61599	B	SF51YAE	61604	B	SF51YAO	61609	B	SF51YAY	61613	O	SF51YBD
61600	B	SF51YAG	61605	B	SF51YAU	61610	B	SF51YBA	61614	O	SF51YBE
61601	B	SF51YAH	61606	B	SF51YAV						

61615	PH	SF51YBG	Volvo B7L	Wrightbus Eclipse	N42F	2001

61616-61626   Volvo B10BLE   Wrightbus Renown   N42F   2001

61616	O	SF51YBH	61619	O	SF51YBL	61622	O	SF51YBO	61625	O	SF51YBS
61617	O	SF51YBJ	61620	O	SF51YBM	61623	O	SF51YBP	61626	O	SF51YBT
61618	O	SF51YBK	61621	O	SF51YBN	61624	O	SF51YBR			

61627-61635   Volvo B7L   Wrightbus Eclipse   N42F   2001

61627	PH	SH51MHY	61630	PH	SH51MJF	61632	PH	SH51MKG	61634	PH	SH51MKK
61628	PH	SH51MHZ	61631	OG	SH51MKF	61633	OG	SH51MKJ	61635	PH	SH51MKL
61629	PH	SH51MJE									

61636-61651   Volvo B7L   Wrightbus Eclipse   N40F   2001

61636	OG	SJ51DHD	61640	CA	SJ51DHK	61644	CA	SJ51DHO	61648	CA	SJ51DHZ
61637	CA	SJ51DHE	61641	CA	SJ51DHL	61645	CA	SJ51DHP	61649	CA	SJ51DJD
61638	OG	SJ51DHF	61642	CA	SJ51DHM	61646	CA	SJ51DHV	61650	CA	SJ51DJE
61639	OG	SJ51DHG	61643	CA	SJ51DHN	61647	CA	SJ51DHX	61651	CA	SJ51DJF

61652	O	SJ51DJK	Volvo B10BLE	Wrightbus Renown	N42F	2001
61653	O	SJ51DJO	Volvo B10BLE	Wrightbus Renown	N42F	2001
61654	O	SJ51DJU	Volvo B10BLE	Wrightbus Renown	N42F	2001

61656-61664 — Volvo B7L — Wrightbus Eclipse — N40F — 2001

61656	PH	SJ51DJX	61659	PH	SJ51DKD	61661	PH	SJ51DKF	61663	CA	SJ51DKL
61657	PH	SJ51DJY	61660	PH	SJ51DKE	61662	OG	SJ51DKK	61664	CA	SJ51DKN
61658	PH	SJ51DKA									

61669	CAt	V118FSF	Scania L94UB	Wright Axcess Floline	N40F	1999

61675-61704 — Scania L94UB — Wright Axcess Floline — N43F — 2000

61675	CAu	X424UMS	61682	Bt	X433UMS	61690	CA	X442UMS	61698	DU	X452UMS
61676	Bt	X425UMS	61683	DU	X434UMS	61691	CA	X443UMS	61699	DU	X453UMS
61677	CAt	X426UMS	61685	DU	X436UMS	61693	DU	X446UMS	61700	DU	X454UMS
61679	CAu	X429UMS	61686	CA	X437UMS	61695	DU	X448UMS	61701	DU	X457UMS
61680	CA	X431UMS	61688	CA	X439UMS	61696	DU	X449UMS	61702	DU	X458UMS
61681	CAu	X432UMS	61689	CA	X441UMS	61697	DU	X451UMS	61704	DU	X461UMS

61705-61710 — Volvo B10BLE — Wrightbus Renown — N42F — 2001

61705	O	Y301RTD	61707	O	Y303RTD	61709	O	Y307RTD	61710	O	Y949RTD
61706	O	Y302RTD	61708	O	Y304RTD						

62120	ABs	HSO61N	Leyland Leopard PSU4C/4R	Alexander AYS	BC41F	1975	*Grampian Transport*
62121	ABs	RG1173	Albion PMA28	Walker	B31R	1930	*Aberdeen Corporation*

62122-62141 — Volvo B10BLE — Wright Renown — N43F — 2000

62122	AB	X601NSS	62127	BK	X606NSS	62132	AB	X611NSS	62137	AB	X616NSS
62123	LT	X602NSS	62128	BK	X607NSS	62133	AB	X612NSS	62138	TN	OIG1788
62124	LT	X603NSS	62129	O	X608NSS	62134	AB	X613NSS	62139	BR	X618NSS
62125	BK	X604NSS	62130	O	X609NSS	62135	BK	X614NSS	62140	AB	X619NSS
62126	LT	X605NSS	62131	LT	X69NSS	62136	BK	X615NSS	62141	AB	X944NSO

62143	LO	R589SBA	Volvo B10BLE	Wright Renown	N40F	1998

62149-62169 — Volvo B10BLE — Wright Renown — N43F — 1998-2001

62149	AB	X621NSS	62153	AB	X477NSS	62159	O	R334GHS	62166	AB	Y631RSA
62150	AB	X622NSS	62154	AB	Y626RSA	62163	AB	Y628RSA	62167	AB	Y632RSA
62151	AB	X623NSS	62155	AB	Y627RSA	62164	AB	Y629RSA	62168	AB	Y633RSA
62152	AB	X624NSS	62157	BH	R331GHS	62165	AB	Y701RSA	62169	AB	Y634RSA

62170-62176 — Volvo B10BLE — Alexander ALX300 — N40F — 2000

62170	AB	W577RFS	62172	AB	W579RFS	62174	AB	W582RFS	62176	AB	W584RFS
62171	AB	W578RFS	62173	AB	W581RFS	62175	AB	W583RFS			

62177-62183 — Volvo B10BLE — Wright Renown — N44F — 2000-01

62177	AB	Y635RSA	62179	AB	Y637RSA	62181	AB	Y639RSA	62183	PL	X684ADK
62178	AB	Y636RSA	62180	AB	Y638RSA	62182	BK	X683ADK			

62184-62190 — Volvo B10BLE — Alexander ALX300 — N40F — 2000

62184	GS	W585RFS	62186	LT	W587RFS	62188	BF	W589RFS	62190	LT	W592RFS
62185	LH	W586RFS	62187	GS	W588RFS	62189	LH	W591RFS			

62191-62204 — Volvo B10BLE — Wright Renown — N43F — 2000

62191	PL	OIG1791	62195	BR	X689ADK	62199	LH	X694ADK	62202	AB	X697ADK
62192	PL	OIG1792	62196	AB	X691ADK	62200	LH	X695ADK	62203	LT	X698ADK
62193	TN	OIG1793	62197	BR	X692ADK	62201	AB	X696ADK	62204	BF	W681RNA
62194	CE	OIG1794	62198	LH	X693ADK						

62205-62211 — Volvo B10BLE — Alexander ALX300 — N40F — 2000

62205	LT	W593RFS	62207	LT	W595RFS	62209	LH	W597RFS	62211	BF	W599RFS
62206	BF	W594RFS	62208	LH	W596RFS	62210	LH	W598RFS			

62212-62217 — Volvo B10BLE — Wright Renown — N43F — 1998-2000

62212	BK	W682RNA	62214	BN	S673SVU	62216	QSu	R585SBA	62217	QSu	R586SBA
62213	BF	W683RNA									

Bolton's depot in Weston Street has replaced the former central depot built by GMT which itself replaced three depots that were housing the fleet in Bolton Corporation days. Route 572 passes the former Bridgeman Street site with 62236, Y944CSF, shown heading in the direction of Great Lever. *Alan Blagburn*

62219-62227
		Volvo B10BLE			Alexander ALX300		N40F	2000		
62219	LH	W601RFS	62222	GS	W604RFS	62224	LT	X606RFS	62226	LT	W608RFS
62220	BF	W602RFS	62223	GS	W605RFS	62225	LH	W607RFS	62227	GS	W609RFS
62221	BA	W603RFS								

62228	AB	YS51JVD	Blue Bird AARE			Blue Bird		S60F	2002		

62231-62245
		Volvo B10BLE			Wrightbus Renown		N44F	2001		
62231	BN	Y941CSF	62235	OG	Y946CSF	62239	OG	Y948CSF	62243	OG	Y953CSF
62232	OG	Y937CSF	62236	BN	Y944CSF	62240	OG	Y949CSF	62244	OG	Y952CSF
62233	BN	Y942CSF	62237	OG	Y945CSF	62241	BN	Y951CSF	62245	TN	OIG1795
62234	OG	Y943CSF	62238	BA	Y947CSF	62242	BA	Y939CSF		

62355-62358
		Scania L94UB			Wrightbus Solar		NC43F	2001		
62355	BK	SN51MSV	62356	MU	SN51MSU	62357	BK	SN51MSY	62358	MU	SN51MSX

62385-62392
		Scania L94UB			Wright Access Floline		N43F	1999		
62385	BK	V527ESH	62387	BK	V529ESH	62389	LVu	V531ESH	62392	LVu	V35ESC
62386	BK	V528ESH	62388	LVu	V530ESH	62390	BKu	V532ESH		

62406-62410
		Scania L94UB			Wrightbus Solar		N44F	2003		
62406	CO	YS03ZKA	62408	CO	YS03ZKE	62409	CO	YS03ZKD	62410	CO	YS03ZKF
62407	CO	YS03ZKB								

62411	LT	SN03WMJ	TransBus E300		TransBus Enviro 300		N44F	2003	
62412	LT	SN03WMU	TransBus E300		TransBus Enviro 300		N44F	2003	

Wrightbus Streetlite is now the vehicle of choice for the 2014 deliveries with 63083, SN14DUH illustrating the model and Cymru Clipper livery. *Terry O'Neill*

63001-63041

Wrightbus StreetLite Max DF — Wrightbus — N41F — 2013

63001	OG	SM13NDJ	63012	OG	SM13NEJ	63022	OG	SK63KGY	63032	OG	SK63KHJ
63002	OG	SM13NDK	63013	OG	SM13NEN	63023	OG	SK63KGZ	63033	OG	SK63KHL
63003	OG	SM13NDL	63014	OG	SM13NEO	63024	OG	SK63KHA	63034	OG	SK63KHM
63004	OG	SM13NDN	63015	OG	SM13NEU	63025	OG	SK63KHB	63035	OG	SK63KHO
63005	OG	SM13NDO	63016	OG	SM13NEY	63026	OG	SK63KHC	63036	OG	SK63KHP
63006	OG	SM13NDU	63017	OG	SK63KGO	63027	OG	SK63KHD	63037	OG	SK63KHR
63007	OG	SM13NDV	63018	OG	SK63KGP	63028	OG	SK63KHE	63038	RO	LK62HJD
63008	OG	SM13NDX	63019	OG	SK63KGU	63029	OG	SK63KHF	63039	RO	LK62FUJ
63009	OG	SM13NDY	63020	OG	SK63KGV	63030	OG	SK63KHG	63040	RO	LK62HKG
63010	OG	SM13NDZ	63021	OG	SK63KGX	63031	OG	SK63KHH	63041	RO	LK62HJX
63011	OG	SM13NEF									

63042-63067

Wrightbus StreetLite Max DF — Wrightbus — N41F — 2013

63042	HI	SK63KHT	63049	HI	SK63KJA	63056	HI	SK63KJV	63062	HI	SK63KKC
63043	HI	SK63KHU	63050	HI	SK63KJE	63057	HI	SK63KJX	63063	HI	SK63KKD
63044	HI	SK63KHV	63051	HI	SK63KJF	63058	HI	SK63KJY	63064	HI	SK63KKE
63045	HI	SK63KHW	63052	HI	SK63KJJ	63059	HI	SK63KJZ	63065	HI	SK63KKF
63046	HI	SK63KHX	63053	HI	SK63KJN	63060	HI	SK63KKA	63066	HI	SK63KKG
63047	HI	SK63KHY	63054	HI	SK63KJO	63061	HI	SK63KKB	63067	HI	SK63KKH
63048	HI	SK63KHZ	63055	HI	SK63KJU						

63068-63078

Wrightbus StreetLite Max DF — Wrightbus — NC41F — 2013

63068	BA	SM13NAE	63071	BA	SM13NBB	63074	BA	SM13NBF	63077	BA	SM13NBK
63069	BA	SM13NAO	63072	BA	SM13NBD	63075	BA	SM13NBG	63078	BA	SM13NBL
63070	BA	SM13NBA	63073	BA	SM13NBE	63076	BA	SM13NBJ			

63079-63095

Wrightbus StreetLite Max DF — Wrightbus — N41F — 2014

63079	PT	SN14DTX	63084	PT	SN14DUJ	63088	PT	SN14DVB	63092	PT	SN14DVH
63080	PT	SN14DTY	63085	PT	SN14DUU	63089	PT	SN14DVC	63093	PT	SN14DVJ
63081	PT	SN14DTZ	63086	PT	SN14DUV	63090	PT	SN14DVF	63094	PT	SN14DVK
63082	PT	SN14DUA	63087	PT	SN14DUY	63091	PT	SN14DVG	63095	PT	SN14DVL
63083	PT	SN14DUH									

63096-63118

Wrightbus StreetLite Max DF — Wrightbus — N41F — 2013

63096	QS	SM13NBN	63102	QS	SM13NCC	63108	QS	SM13NCO	63114	OX	SK63KGE
63097	QS	SM13NBO	63103	QS	SM13NCD	63109	QS	SM13NCU	63115	OX	SK63KGF
63098	QS	SM13NBX	63104	QS	SM13NCE	63110	QS	SM13NCV	63116	OX	SK63KGG
63099	QS	SM13NBY	63105	QS	SM13NCF	63111	QS	SK63KFY	63117	OX	SK63KGJ
63100	QS	SM13NBZ	63106	QS	SM13NCJ	63112	QS	SK63KFZ	63118	OX	SK63KGN
63101	QS	SM13NCA	63107	QS	SM13NCN	63113	OX	SK63KGA			

Following First's acquisition of Finglands in South Manchester, both First and Stagecoach have increased the number of cross-city services. Seventeen Wrightbus Steetlites are now allocated to the Fallowfield Depot (code OX for Oxford Road), including 63146, SN14DXK, seen on route 42 to East Didsbury.
John Birtwistle

63119-63170

				Wrightbus StreetLite Max DF		Wrightbus		N41F		2014	
63119	OG	SN14DVM	63132	OG	SN14DWE	63145	OG	SN14DWY	63158	LV	SN64CKF
63120	OG	SN14DVO	63133	OG	SN14DWF	63146	OX	SN14DXK	63159	LV	SN64CKG
63121	OG	SN14DVP	63134	OG	SN14DWG	63147	OX	SN14DXL	63160	LV	SN64CKJ
63122	OG	SN14DVR	63135	OG	SN14DWJ	63148	OX	SN14DXM	63161	HH	SN64CHX
63123	OG	SN14DVT	63136	OG	SN14DWK	63149	OX	SN14DXO	63162	HH	SN64CHY
63124	OG	SN14DVU	63137	OG	SN14DWL	63150	OX	SN14DXP	63163	HH	SN64CHZ
63125	OG	SN14DVV	63138	OG	SN14DWM	63151	OX	SN14DXR	63164	HH	SN64CJE
63126	OG	SN14DVW	63139	OG	SN14DWO	63152	OX	SN14DXS	63165	HH	SN64CJF
63127	OG	SN14DVX	63140	OG	SN14DWP	63153	OX	SN14DXT	63166	HH	SN64CJJ
63128	OG	SN14DVY	63141	OG	SN14DWU	63154	OX	SN14DXU	63167	HH	SN64CJO
63129	OG	SN14DVZ	63142	OG	SN14DWV	63155	OX	SN14DXV	63168	HH	SN64CJU
63130	OG	SN14DWC	63143	OG	SN14DWW	63156	OX	SN14DXJ	63169	HH	SN64CJV
63131	OG	SN14DWD	63144	OG	SN14DWX	63157	LV	SN64CKE	63170	HH	SN64CJX

63171-63240

				Wrightbus StreetLite Max DF		Wrightbus		N41F		2014	
63171	AG	SN64CGE	63189	WH	SN14DXH	63207	AB	SN14FEF	63224	B	SN14DYB
63172	AG	SN64CGF	63190	SH	SN14EBC	63208	AB	SN14FEG	63225	B	SN14DYC
63173	AG	SN64CGG	63191	SH	SN14EBD	63209	AB	SN14FEH	63226	B	SN14DYD
63174	AG	SN64CGK	63192	SH	SN14EBF	63210	AB	SN14FEJ	63227	B	SN14DYF
63175	AG	SN64CGO	63193	AB	SN14ECZ	63211	AB	SN14FEK	63228	B	SN14DYG
63176	AG	SN64CGU	63194	AB	SN14EDC	63212	AB	SN14EDR	63229	B	SN14DYH
63177	AG	SN64CGV	63195	AB	SN14EDF	63213	AB	SN14EDU	63230	B	SN14DYJ
63178	AG	SN64CGX	63196	AB	SN14EDJ	63214	AB	SN14EDV	63231	B	SN14DYM
63179	AG	SN64CGY	63197	AB	SN14EDK	63215	AB	SN14FEM	63232	B	SN14DYO
63180*	AG	DRZ9713	63198	AB	SN14EDL	63216	AB	SN14FEO	63233	B	SN14DYP
63181	WH	SN14DWZ	63199	AB	SN14EDO	63217	AB	SN14FEP	63234	B	SN14DYS
63182	WH	SN14DXA	63200	AB	SN14EDP	63218	AB	SN14FET	63235	B	SN14DYT
63183	WH	SN14DXB	63201	AB	SN14FDP	63219	LV	SN14DXW	63236	B	SN14DYU
63184	WH	SN14DXC	63202	AB	SN14FDU	63220	LV	SN14DXX	63237	B	SN14DYV
63185	WH	SN14DXD	63203	AB	SN14FDV	63221	LV	SN14DXY	63238	B	SN14DYW
63186	WH	SN14DXE	63204	AB	SN14FDX	63222	LV	SN14DXZ	63239	B	SN14DYX
63187	WH	SN14DXF	63205	AB	SN14FDY	63223	LV	SN14DYA	63240	B	SN14DYY
63188	WH	SN14DXG	63206	AB	SN14FDZ						

63241-63249 — Wrightbus StreetLite Max DF — Wrightbus — N41F — 2014

63241	LV	SN64CKK	63244	LV	SN64CKP	63246	LV	SN64CPE	63248	LV	SN64CPK
63242	LV	SN64CKL	63245	LV	SN64COU	63247	LV	SN64CPF	63249	LV	SN64CPO
63243	LV	SN64CKO									

63250	AG	SN15ABF	Wrightbus StreetLite DF Euro 6	Wrightbus	N41F	2015	

63251-63295 — Wrightbus StreetLite Max DF — Wrightbus — N41F — 2015

63251	LV	-	63263	LT	-	63274	LT	-	63285	BD	-
63252	LV	-	63264	LT	-	63275	LT	-	63286	BD	-
63253	LT	-	63265	LT	-	63276	LT	-	63287	BD	-
63254	LT	-	63266	LT	-	63277	BD	-	63288	BD	-
63255	LT	-	63267	LT	-	63278	BD	-	63289	HX	-
63256	LT	-	63268	LT	-	63279	BD	-	63290	HX	-
63257	LT	-	63269	LT	-	63280	BD	-	63291	HX	-
63258	LT	-	63270	LT	-	63281	BD	-	63292	HX	-
63259	LT	-	63271	LT	-	63282	BD	-	63293	HX	-
63260	LT	-	63272	LT	-	63283	BD	-	63294	HX	-
63261	LT	-	63273	LT	-	63284	BD	-	63295	HX	-
63262	LT	-									

63296-63366 — Wrightbus StreetLite Max DF — Wrightbus — N41F — 2015

63296	HO	-	63314	SH	-	63332	CO	-	63350	WR	-
63297	HO	-	63315	SH	-	63333	CO	-	63351	WR	-
63298	HO	-	63316	SH	-	63334	CO	-	63352	WR	-
63299	HO	-	63317	-	-	63335	CO	-	63353	WR	-
63300	HO	-	63318	-	-	63336	CO	-	63354	WR	-
63301	HO	-	63319	-	-	63337	CO	-	63355	WR	-
63302	HO	-	63320	-	-	63338	CO	-	63356	WR	-
63303	HO	-	63321	-	-	63339	CO	-	63357	WR	-
63304	HO	-	63322	-	-	63340	CO	-	63358	LE	-
63305	HO	-	63323	-	-	63341	CO	-	63359	LE	-
63306	HO	-	63324	-	-	63342	CO	-	63360	LE	-
63307	HO	-	63325	-	-	63343	CO	-	63361	LE	-
63308	HO	-	63326	-	-	63344	CO	-	63362	LE	-
63309	HO	-	63327	-	-	63345	WR	-	63363	LE	-
63310	HO	-	63328	CO	-	63346	WR	-	63364	LE	-
63311	HO	-	63329	CO	-	63347	WR	-	63365	LE	-
63312	HO	-	63330	CO	-	63348	WR	-	63366	LE	-
63313	SH	-	63331	CO	-	63349	WR	-			

64000	D	02D78371	Mercedes-Benz O530 Citaro	Mercedes-Benz Citaro	N38D	2002	TfL, 2005

64001-64011 — Mercedes-Benz O530 Citaro — Mercedes-Benz — N36D* — 2002 — *64001/2/5 are N40F

64001	BL	LT02NTV	64004	LV	LT02NUA	64007	LV	LT02NUE	64010	LV	LT02NUJ
64002	SH	LT02NTX	64005	BL	LT02NUB	64008	LV	LT02NUF	64011	LV	LT02NVY
64003	LV	LT02NTY									

64012-64019 — Mercedes-Benz O530 Citaro — Mercedes-Benz — N40F — 2003

64012	BL	LT52WXA	64014	BL	LT52WXL	64016	BL	LT52WXO	64018	BL	LK03LNE
64013	BL	LT52WXB	64015	BL	LT52WXN	64017	BL	LT52WXP	64019	BL	LK03LNF

64020	BL	BU04EZF	Mercedes-Benz O530 Citaro	Mercedes-Benz	N40F	2004
64021	BL	BU04EZG	Mercedes-Benz O530 Citaro	Mercedes-Benz	N40F	2004
64029	BY	BX02CMK	Mercedes-Benz O530 Citaro	Mercedes-Benz	N38F	2002	Evobus demonstrator, 2004

64030-64042 — Mercedes-Benz O530 Citaro — Mercedes-Benz — N40F — 2007-08

64030	BL	LK07CCA	64033	SH	LK07CCF	64036	SH	LK07CCO	64039	SH	LK07CCX
64031	BL	LK07CCD	64034	SH	LK07CCJ	64037	SH	LK07CCU	64042	SH	LK08FNL
64032	SH	LK07CCE	64035	SH	LK07CCN	64038	SH	LK07CCV			

64051-64057 — Mercedes-Benz O295 Citaro — Mercedes-Benz — N40F — 2015

640351	CE	WK15DLZ	640353	CE	WK15DMF	640351	CE	WK15DMU	640351	CE	WK15DMX
640352	CE	WK15DME	640354	CE	WK15DMO	640351	CE	WK15DMV			

Scania OmniCity integral buses are based at Stoke, Chelmsford and Fareham. From Fareham's allocation 65023, YN54NZX, is pictured with Solent Ranger lettering, in Portsmouth's Queen Street while heading out for Southampton. *Mark Lyons*

64043-64048

						Mercedes-Benz O530 Citaro	Mercedes-Benz	N38F	2008	
64043	SH	LK08FMC	64045	SH	LK08FME	**64047**	SH	LK08FMG	**64048**	SH	LK08FMJ
64044	SH	LK08FMD	64046	SH	LK08FMF						

64049	CE	WK08ESV	Mercedes-Benz O530 Citaro	Mercedes-Benz	N38F	2008	Western Greyhound, 2013
64050	CE	WK10AZU	Mercedes-Benz O530 Citaro	Mercedes-Benz	N38F	2010	Western Greyhound, 2013
64818	HIt	M818PGM	Scania L113 CRL	Northern Counties Paladin	B51F	1995	
64994	AB	SV14FYR	Van Hool A330 fuel cell 13.1m	Van Hool	N42F	2014	
64995	AB	SV14FYS	Van Hool A330 fuel cell 13.1m	Van Hool	N42F	2014	
64996	AB	SV14FZD	Van Hool A330 fuel cell 13.1m	Van Hool	N42F	2014	
64997	AB	SV14FZC	Van Hool A330 fuel cell 13.1m	Van Hool	N42F	2014	

65001-65005

						Scania OmniCity CN94UB	Scania	N42F	2004	
65001	AG	YN04YJC	**65003**	AG	YN04YJE	**65004**	AG	YN04YJF	**65005**	AG	YN04YJG
65002	AG	YN04YJD									

65006-65025

						Scania OmniCity CN94UB	Scania	N44F	2004	
65006	HO	YN54NZA	65011	HO	YN54NZG	**65016**	HO	YN54NZO	**65021**	HO	YN54NZV
65007	HO	YN54NZC	65012	HO	YN54NZH	65017	HO	YN54NZP	65022	HO	YN54NZW
65008	HO	YN54NZD	65013	HO	YN54NZJ	65018	HO	YN54NZR	65023	HO	YN54NZX
65009	HO	YN54NZE	65014	HO	YN54NZK	65019	HO	YN54NZT	65024	HO	YN54NZY
65010	HO	YN54NZF	65015	HO	YN54NZM	65020	HO	YN54NZU	65025	HO	YN54NZZ

65026-65042

						Scania OmniCity CN94UB	Scania	N44F*	2005-06	*65028-32 are NC41F
65026	AG	YN54OCK	65031	CM	YN06TDX	65035	AG	YN06WMG	65039	AG	YN06WMM
65027	AG	YN05HCL	65032	CM	YN06TDZ	65036	AG	YN06WMJ	65040	AG	YN06WMO
65028	CM	YN06TDO	65033	AG	YN06WME	65037	AG	YN06WMK	65041	AG	YN06WMP
65029	CM	YN06TDU	65034	AG	YN06WMF	65038	AG	YN06WML	65042	AG	YN06WMT
65030	CM	YN06TDV									

65527-65564 — Scania L113CRL — Wright Axcess-ultralow — N40F — 1997-98

65527	CN	R147GSF	65556	CN	R556CNG	65561	AG	R261DVF	65564	AG	R264DVF

65565-65579 — Scania L94UB — Wright Axcess Floline — N40F — 1999

65565	CO	S565TPW	65568	AG	S568TPW	65574	CO	S574TPW	65578	AG	T578JNG
65566	CO	S566TPW	65572	AG	S572TPW	65576	COu	T576JNG	65579	CE	T579JNG
65567	AG	S567TPW	65573	CO	S573TPW						

65586-65601 — Scania L94UB — Wright Axcess Floline — N40F — 1999-2000

65586	CO	V586DVF	65590	IPu	V590DVF	65595	BK	W595SNG	65598	LT	W598SNG
65587	CO	V587DVF	65591	CAu	W591SNG	65596	CA	W596SNG	65599	LT	W599SNG
65588	VN	V588DVF	65593	CA	W593SNG	65597	BK	W597SNG	65601	BK	W601SNG
65589	CO	V589DVF	65594	BK	W594SNG						

65621	BLu	T821JBL	Scania L94UB	Wright Axcess Floline	N40F	1999
65622	BLu	T822JBL	Scania L94UB	Wright Axcess Floline	N40F	1999

65626-65632 — Scania L94UB — Wright Axcess Floline — N43F — 2000

65626	CO	V826FSC	65630	CO	V830FSC	65631	CO	V831FSC	65632	IPu	V832FSC
65627	CO	V827FSC									

65650-65654 — Scania L94UB — Wright Axcess Floline — N43F — 1999

65650	CO	T650SSF	65652	COu	T652SSF	65653	CO	T653SSF	65654	CO	T654SSF
65651	COu	T651SSF									

65662	BK	V362CNH	Scania L94UB	Wright Axcess Floline	N43F	1999
65663	BK	V363CNH	Scania L94UB	Wright Axcess Floline	N43F	1999
65664	LT	V364CNH	Scania L94UB	Wright Axcess Floline	N43F	1999

65665-65677 — Scania L94UB — Wrightbus Solar — N43F — 2001

65665	CN	SN51UXX	65669	CO	SN51UYB	65672	CO	SN51UYE	65675	CO	SN51UYJ
65666	CO	SN51UXY	65670	CN	SN51UYC	65673	CO	SN51UYG	65676	CN	SN51UYK
65667	CN	SN51UXZ	65671	CN	SN51UYD	65674	CO	SN51UYH	65677	CO	SN51UYL
65668	CN	SN51UYA									

65678-65692 — Scania L94UB — Wrightbus Solar — N44F — 2002-03

65678	CO	YP02ABN	65682	CO	YR52VEP	65686	CO	YS03ZKC	65690	CN	YS03ZKK
65679	CO	YR52VEH	65683	CO	YR52VEU	65687	CO	YS03ZKG	65691	CN	YS03ZKL
65680	CO	YR52VEK	65684	CO	YR52VEY	65688	CO	YS03ZKH	65692	CN	YS03ZKM
65681	CO	YR52VEL	65685	CO	YR52VFO	65689	CO	YS03ZKJ			

65693-65699 — Scania L94UB — Wrightbus Solar — N43F — 2003

65693	CA	SN53KHH	65695	BK	SN53KHK	65697	CA	SN53KHM	65699	LT	SN53KHP
65694	BK	SN53KHJ	65696	CA	SN53KHL	65698	LT	SN53KHO			

65700-65706 — Scania L94UB — Wrightbus Solar — N43F — 2004

65700	MU	SN04CKY	65702	BK	SN04CLF	65705	NE	YN04GME	65706	NE	YN04GMF
65701	MU	SN04CKX	65703	MU	SN04CNK						

65708-65723 — Scania L94UB — Wrightbus Solar — N43F — 2004-05

65708	BF	SN54KDF	65712	BK	SN54KDU	65716	MU	SN54KEJ	65720	BK	SN54KFC
65709	BK	SN54KDJ	65713	BK	SN54KDV	65717	MU	SN54KEK	65721	BK	SN54KFD
65710	BK	SN54KDK	65714	BK	SN54KDX	65718	MU	SN54KEU	65722	BK	SN54KFE
65711	BK	SN54KDO	65715	BK	SN54KDZ	65719	BK	SN54KFA	65723	BK	SN54KFF

65724-65733 — Scania L94UB — Wrightbus Solar — N43F — 2005

65724	SH	LK55ABZ	65727	NE	YN05HCO	65730	NE	YN05HCV	65732	NE	YN05HCY
65725	SH	LK55ACF	65728	NE	YN05HCP	65731	NE	YN05HCX	65733	NE	YN05HCZ
65726	SH	LK55ACJ	65729	NE	YN05HCU						

65742-65754 — Scania L94UB — Wrightbus Solar — N43F — 2005-06

65742	GS	SN55JVG	65746	GS	SN55JVL	65749	GS	SN55JVP	65752	LT	SN55JVD
65743	GS	SN55JVH	65747	GS	SN55JVM	65750	GS	SN55JVA	65753	LT	SN55JVE
65744	GS	SN55JVJ	65748	GS	SN55JVO	65751	MU	SN55JVC	65754	LT	SN06AHK
65745	GS	SN55JVK									

65755	CA	SK02ZYG	Scania L94UB	Wrightbus Solar	N43F	2002	Hutchison, Overtown, 2007
65756	CA	SK02ZYH	Scania L94UB	Wrightbus Solar	N43F	2002	Hutchison, Overtown, 2007

Several vehicles in the Potteries fleet have gained a modified livery incorporating red fronts. Illustrating the scheme is 65705, YN04GME, currently allocated to Newcastle. *Mark Doggett*

65757	CA	SN03CLX		Scania L94UB		Wrightbus Solar		N43F	2003	Hutchison, Overtown, 2007
65758	CA	SN03CLY		Scania L94UB		Wrightbus Solar		N43F	2003	Hutchison, Overtown, 2007

65759-65764

				Scania L94UB		Wrightbus Solar		N44F	2005-06	Reading Buses, 2013-14
65759	CE	YN05GXF	65761	CE	YN06NXP	65763	CE	YN05GXM	65764	CE	YN05GXO
65760	CE	YN05GXR	65762	CE	YN06NXW						

66100	WS	R460VOP		Volvo B10BLE		Wright Renown		N44F	1997	Volvo demonstrator, 1999

66101-66120

Volvo B10BLE   Wright Renown   N47F   1998

66101	HU	R901BOU	66106	WS	R906BOU	66110	LH	R910BOU	66117	MS	R917BOU
66102	LH	R902BOU	66107	WS	R907BOU	66112	LO	R912BOU	66118	MS	R918BOU
66104	LH	R904BOU	66108	WS	R908BOU	66115	MS	R915BOU	66120	MS	R920COU
66105	LH	R905BOU	66109	LH	R909BOU	66116	MS	R916BOU			

66121-66130

Volvo B10BLE   Wright Renown   N41F   1998-99

66121	HOu	S121JTP	66126	CE	S116JTP	66128	HO	S118JTP	66130	HO	S120JTP
66122	HO	S122UOT	66127	CE	S117JTP						

66151-66163

Volvo B10BLE   Wright Renown   N44F   1998-99

66151	HO	S351NPO	66154	HO	S354NPO	66158	HO	S358XCR	66161	MS	S361XCR
66152	HO	S352NPO	66156	SO	S356XCR	66159	MS	S359XCR	66162	MS	S362XCR
66153	HO	S353NPO	66157	SO	S357XCR	66160	WS	S360XCR	66163	BA	S363XCR

66164-66181

Volvo B10BLE   Wright Renown   N44F   2000

66164	HO	W364EOW	66168	BR	W368EOW	66174	WS	W374EOW	66178	MS	W378EOW
66165	BR	W365EOW	66169	BR	W369EOW	66176	HO	W376EOW	66179	CO	W379EOW
66166	MS	W366EOW	66171	WS	W371EOW	66177	CO	W377EOW	66181	HO	W381EOW
66167	MS	W367EOW	66173	LH	W373EOW						

66191-66207 Volvo B10BLE Wright Renown N41F 1998

66191	QSu	S791RWG	66195	QSu	S795RWG	66201	HO	S801RWG	66205	HO	S805RWG
66192	QSu	S792RWG	66196	HO	S796RWG	66202	HO	S802RWG	66206	WS	S806RWG
66193	QSt	S793RWG	66197	HO	S797RWG	66203	HO	S803RWG	66207	WS	S807RWG
66194	BN	S794RWG	66198	HO	S798RWG	66204	HO	S804RWG			

66233	B	X303JGE	Volvo B10BLE	Alexander ALX300	N44F	2000	Hutchison, Overtown, 2007
66281	O	Y181BGB	Volvo B10BLE	Wrightbus Renown	N44F	2001	Hutchison, Overtown, 2007
66282	O	Y182BGB	Volvo B10BLE	Wrightbus Renown	N44F	2001	Hutchison, Overtown, 2007

66301-66348 Volvo B7L Wrightbus Eclipse N41F 2002

66301	VN	KV02VVC	66313	NE	KV02VVP	66325	VN	MV02VAY	66338	VN	MV02VCN
66302	NE	KV02VVD	66314	NE	KV02VVR	66326	VN	MV02VBA	66339	VN	MV02VCO
66303	NE	KV02VVE	66315	LE	KV02VVS	66327	VN	MV02VBB	66340	VN	MV02VCP
66304	NE	KV02VVF	66316	LE	KV02VVT	66328	VN	MV02VBC	66341	YA	MV02VCT
66305	NE	KV02VVG	66317	LE	KV02VVU	66329	VN	MV02VBD	66342	VN	MV02VCU
66306	NE	KV02VVH	66318	LE	KV02VVW	66330	VN	MV02VBE	66343	VN	MV02VCW
66307	NE	KV02VVJ	66319	LE	KV02VVX	66332	VN	MV02VBX	66344	YA	MV02VCX
66308	NE	KV02VVK	66320	LE	KV02VVY	66333	VN	MV02VBY	66345	VN	MV02VCY
66309	NE	KV02VVL	66321	LE	KV02VVZ	66334	YA	MV02VBZ	66346	VN	MV02VCZ
66310	NE	KV02VVM	66322	LE	KV02VWA	66335	VN	MV02VCA	66347	VN	MV02VDA
66311	NE	KV02VVN	66323	LE	KV02VWB	66336	VN	MV02VCC	66348	VN	MV02VDC
66312	NE	KV02VVO	66324	VN	MV02VAX	66337	VN	MV02VCM			

66349-66356 Volvo B7L Wrightbus Eclipse N41F 2002

66349	PH	MV02VDZ	66351	BA	MV02VEB	66353	BA	MV02VEH	66355	BA	MV02VEL
66350	BA	MV02VEA	66352	BA	MV02VEF	66354	BA	MV02VEK	66356	BA	MV02VEM

66651	BDtu	K114PRV	Volvo B10B	Northern Counties Paladin	tv	1993	
66652	BDt	M967GDU	Volvo B10B	Plaxton Verde	tv	1994	Plaxton demonstrator, 1995
66691	WR	CN07HVG	Volvo B7RLE	Plaxton Centro	N45F	2007	Veolia, 2012

66692-66699 Volvo B7RLE Plaxton Centro N45F* 2007 Veolia, 2011 *66697 is NC45F

66692	WR	CN07HVH	66694	WR	CN07HVJ	66696	WR	CN57EFE	66698	WR	CN07HVL
66693	WR	CN07HVK	66695	WR	CN57EFB	66697	WR	CN57EFF	66699	HD	CN07HVM

66707-66715 Volvo B7RLE Wrightbus Eclipse Urban N43F 2003-04

66707	HX	YK53GXR	66710	HX	YK53GXV	66712	HX	YK04EZL	66714	HU	YK04EZM
66708	HX	YK53GXT	66711	HX	YK04EZJ	66713	HX	YK04EZG	66715	BD	YK04EZH
66709	HX	YK53GXU									

66716-66737 Volvo B7RLE Wrightbus Eclipse Urban NC43F 2004

66716	RA	WX54XDA	66722	WS	WX54XDL	66728	MS	WX54XCN	66733	BA	WX54XCU
66717	RA	WX54XDD	66723	WS	WX54XDH	66729	MS	WX54XCO	66734	BA	WX54XCV
66718	RA	WX54XDB	66724	WS	WX54XDG	66730	BA	WX54XCP	66735	B	WX54XCW
66719	BA	WX54XDC	66725	WS	WX54XDJ	66731	BA	WX54XCR	66736	B	WX54XCY
66720	WS	WX54XDF	66726	WS	WX54XDK	66732	BA	WX54XCT	66737	B	WX54XCZ
66721	WS	WX54XDE	66727	WS	WX54XCM						

66738-66758 Volvo B7RLE Wrightbus Eclipse Urban N43F 2005

66738	HX	YJ54XVM	66744	HX	YJ54XVU	66749	HX	YJ54XWA	66754	YK	YJ05KNV
66739	HX	YJ54XVN	66745	TN	YJ54XVW	66750	HX	YJ05KOB	66755	YK	YJ05KNW
66740	HX	YJ54XVO	66746	HX	YJ54XVX	66751	HX	YJ05KOD	66756	YK	YJ05KNX
66741	HX	YJ54XVP	66747	HX	YJ54XVY	66752	HX	YJ05KOE	66757	YK	YJ05KNY
66742	HX	YJ54XVR	66748	HX	YJ54XVZ	66753	HU	YJ05KOH	66758	YK	YJ05KNZ
66743	HX	YJ54XVT									

66759-66792 Volvo B7RLE Wrightbus Eclipse Urban N43F 2005

66759	YK	YJ05VVA	66768	BM	YJ05VVL	66777	HX	YJ05VVW	66785	HU	YK05FPA
66760	YK	YJ05VVB	66769	BM	YJ05VVM	66778	HX	YJ05VVX	66786	HU	YK05FLC
66761	YK	YJ05VVC	66770	B	YJ05VVN	66779	HX	YJ05VVY	66787	HU	YK05FOV
66762	YK	YJ05VVD	66771	B	YJ05VVO	66780	HX	YJ05VVZ	66788	HU	YK05FOU
66763	YK	YJ05VVE	66772	BM	YJ05VVP	66781	HX	YK05FJJ	66789	HX	YK05FOT
66764	YK	YJ05VVF	66773	HU	YJ05VVR	66782	HX	YK05FLB	66790	HX	YA05SOU
66765	HX	YJ05VVG	66774	HU	YJ05VVS	66783	HX	YK05FJF	66791	HU	YK05FOP
66766	BM	YJ05VVH	66775	HU	YJ05VVT	66784	HU	YK05FJE	66792	HU	YA05SOJ
66767	BM	YJ05VVK	66776	HX	YJ05VVU						

First operates eight hundred and fifty Volvo B7RLEs, making the model the most common in use. Leaving Taunton for Minehead is 66745, YJ54XVM, the exception from a batch that otherwise are all based in Yorkshire. *Steve Rice*

66794-66933 Volvo B7RLE Wrightbus Eclipse Urban N43F 2005

66794	CM	MX05CBF	66826	BS	MX05CFA	66858	OM	MX05CHO	66896	BN	MX55FFG
66795	CM	MX05CBU	66827	BS	MX05CFD	66859	OM	MX05CHV	66897	BY	MX55FFH
66796	CM	MX05CBV	66828	CO	MX05CFE	66860	OM	MX05CHY	66898	QS	MX55FFJ
66797	CM	MX05CBY	66829	CM	MX05CFG	66861	BN	MX05CHZ	66899	BN	MX55FFK
66798	CO	MX05CCA	66830	CM	MX05CFJ	66862	OM	MX05CJE	66900	BY	MX55FFL
66799	CM	MX05CCD	66831	QS	MX05CFK	66863	OM	MX05CJF	66901	BN	MX55FFM
66800	CO	MX05CCF	66832	QS	MX05CFL	66864	OM	MX05CJJ	66902	QS	MX55FFO
66801	CO	MX05CCJ	66833	QS	MX05CFM	66865	OM	MX05CJO	66903	BN	MX55FFP
66802	CM	MX05CCK	66834	QS	MX05CFN	66866	OM	MX05CJU	66904	BN	MX55FFR
66803	CO	MX05CCN	66835	QS	MX05CFO	66867	BN	MX05CJV	66905	BN	MX55FFS
66804	CO	MX05CCO	66836	BY	MX05CFP	66868	OM	MX05CJY	66906	BN	MX55FFT
66805	BS	MX05CCU	66837	CM	MX05CFU	66869	OM	MX05CJZ	66907	BN	MX55FFU
66806	BS	MX05CCV	66838	NE	MX05CFV	66870	BN	MX05CKA	66908	QS	MX55FFV
66807	CO	MX05CCY	66839	NE	MX05CFY	66871	OM	MX05CKC	66909	BY	MX55FFW
66808	CM	MX05CCZ	66840	NE	MX05CGE	66872	BY	MX05CKD	66910	QS	MX55FFY
66809	CO	MX05CDE	66841	NE	MX05CGF	66873	BY	MX05CKE	66911	QS	MX55FFZ
66810	CO	MX05CDF	66842	LE	MX05CGG	66874	QS	MX05CKF	66912	QS	MX55FGA
66811	CM	MX05CDK	66843	NE	MX05CGK	66875	QS	MX55NWE	66913	BY	MX55FGC
66812	CM	MX05CDN	66844	BY	MX05CGO	66876	BN	MX05CKJ	66914	BY	MX55FGE
66813	BS	MX05CDO	66845	NE	MX05CGU	66880	BY	MX05CKO	66915	BY	MX55FGF
66814	CM	MX05CDU	66846	BY	MX05CGV	66881	SO	MX05CKP	66916	BY	MX55FGG
66815	CM	MX05CDV	66847	NE	MX05CGY	66882	SO	MX55HHR	66917	BY	MX55FGJ
66816	CO	MX05CDY	66848	OM	MX05CGZ	66883	SO	MX55HHP	66918	BY	MX55FGK
66817	CM	MX05CDZ	66849	NE	MX05CHC	66884	SO	MX55HHO	66919	BY	MX55FGM
66818	CM	MX05CEA	66850	IP	MX05CHD	66885	SO	MX05CLF	66920	QS	MX55FGN
66819	BS	MX05CEF	66851	NE	MX05CHF	66886	SO	MX55LHL	66922	QS	MX55FGP
66820	BS	MX05CEJ	66852	NE	MX05CHG	66890	QS	MX55NWH	66923	QS	MX55FGU
66821	BS	MX05CEK	66853	BY	MX05CHH	66891	QS	MX55UAA	66928	QS	MX55FHC
66822	BS	MX05CEO	66854	OM	MX05CHJ	66892	QS	MX55LDJ	66929	QS	MX55FHD
66823	BS	MX05CEU	66855	BY	MX05CHK	66893	QS	MX55LDK	66930	BY	MX55FHE
66824	BS	MX05CEV	66856	OM	MX05CHL	66894	BN	MX55FFD	66931	BN	MX55FHF
66825	BS	MX05CEY	66857	OM	MX05CHN	66895	BN	MX55FFE	66933	QS	MX55FHH

Unusual in First's provincial fleet is dual-doored 66992, RKZ4761, seen here in Bath. *Dave Heath*

66934-66961

Volvo B7RLE — Wrightbus Eclipse Urban — N43F — 2005

66934	WS	WX55UAA	66941	BA	WX55TZC	66948	B	WX55TZK	66955	O	WX55TZS
66935	WS	WX55UAB	66942	BA	WX55TZD	66949	B	WX55TZL	66956	WS	WX55TZT
66936	WS	WX55UAC	66943	BA	WX55TZE	66950	IP	WX55TZM	66957	IP	WX55TZU
66937	BA	WX55UAD	66944	SO	WX55TZF	66951	B	WX55TZN	66958	PT	WX55TZV
66938	BA	WX55TYZ	66945	SO	WX55TZG	66952	O	WX55TZO	66959	IP	WX55TZW
66939	BA	WX55TZA	66946	B	WX55TZH	66953	SO	WX55TZP	66960	PT	WX55TZY
66940	BA	WX55TZB	66947	B	WX55TZJ	66954	O	WX55TZR	66961	PT	WX55TZZ

66962-66987

Volvo B7RLE — Wrightbus Eclipse Urban — N43F — 2005

66962	NE	KX05MHY	66969	LE	KX05MJU	66976	IP	KX05MGZ	66982	IP	KX05MHL
66963	NE	KX05MHZ	66970	LE	KX05MJV	66977	IP	KX05MHA	66983	IP	KX05MHM
66964	NE	KX05MJE	66971	LE	KX05MJY	66978	IP	KX05MHE	66984	IP	KX05MHN
66965	LE	KX05MJF	66972	LE	KX05AOC	66979	IP	KX05MHF	66985	IP	KX05MHO
66966	LE	KX05MJJ	66973	LE	KX05AOD	66980	IP	KX05MHJ	66986	IP	KX05MHU
66967	LE	KX05MJK	66974	LE	KX05AOE	66981	IP	KX05MHK	66987	IP	KX05MHV
66968	LE	KX05MJO	66975	LE	KX05MGY						

66988-66999

Volvo B7RLE — Wrightbus Eclipse Urban — N43F — 2006-07 — *66992-4 N34D

66988	B	SF56GYP	66991	B	SF56GYT	66994	D	06D85192	66997	HP	YJ07LWE
66989	B	SF56GYR	66992	BA	RKZ4761	66995	BM	YJ07LWC	66998	HP	YJ07LWF
66990	B	SF56GYS	66993	BA	RKZ4760	66996	BM	YJ07LWD	66999	BD	YK57FCL

67041-67095

ADL E20D — ADL Enviro 200 MMC — N41F — 2015

67041	B	-	67055	O	-	67069	PH	-	67083	PH	-
67042	B	-	67056	O	-	67070	PH	-	67084	AB	-
67043	B	-	67057	O	-	67071	PH	-	67085	AB	-
67044	B	-	67058	O	-	67072	PH	-	67086	AB	-
67045	B	-	67059	O	-	67073	PH	-	67087	AB	-
67046	B	-	67060	O	-	67074	PH	-	67088	AB	-
67047	B	-	67061	O	-	67075	PH	-	67089	AB	-
67048	B	-	67062	O	-	67076	PH	-	67090	AB	-
67049	O	-	67063	O	-	67077	PH	-	67091	RA	-
67050	O	-	67064	O	-	67078	PH	-	67092	RA	-
67051	O	-	67065	PH	-	67079	PH	-	67093	RA	-
67052	O	-	67066	PH	-	67080	PH	-	67094	RA	-
67053	O	-	67067	PH	-	67081	PH	-	67095	RA	-
67054	O	-	67068	PH	-	67082	PH	-			

Swansea's Park & Ride service gained new vehicles for the start of the 2014 season and these feature the orange and red livery shown on 67436, SL63GBY. *Steve Rice*

667401-67430			ADL E30D			ADL Enviro 300			N41F	2013		
67401	BN	SN13CJV	67409	BN	SN13CKF	67417	OM	SN13CKV	67424	OM	SN13CLV
67402	BN	SN13CJX	67410	BN	SN13CKG	67418	OM	SN13CKX	67425	OM	SN13CLX
67403	BN	SN13CJY	67411	BN	SN13CKJ	67419	OM	SN13CKY	67426	OM	SN13CLY
67404	BN	SN13CJZ	67412	BN	SN13CKK	67420	OM	SN13CLF	67427	OM	SN13CLZ
67405	BN	SN13CKA	67413	OM	SN13CKL	67421	OM	SN13CLJ	67428	OM	SN13CME
67406	BN	SN13CKC	67414	OM	SN13CKO	67422	OM	SN13CLO	67429	OM	SN13CMF
67407	BN	SN13CKD	67415	OM	SN13CKP	67423	OM	SN13CLU	67430	OM	SN13CMK
67408	BN	SN13CKE	67416	OM	SN13CKU						

67431-67439			ADL E30D			ADL Enviro 300			N44F	2013-14		
67431	RA	SL63GBF	67434	RA	SL63GBV	67436	RA	SL63GBY	67438	RA	SL63GCF
67432	RA	SL63GBO	67435	RA	SL63GBX	67437	RA	SL63GBZ	67439	RA	SL63GCK
67433	RA	SL63GBU									

67600	WS	SN53KKY	TransBus Enviro 300			TransBus Enviro 300			N47F	2003		

67601-67604			TransBus Enviro 300			TransBus Enviro 300			N44F	2004		
67601	WR	VX53VJV	67602	WR	VX53VJZ	67603	WR	VX53VKA	67604	WR	VX53VKB

67631-67651			ADL E30D			ADL Enviro 300			N43F	2005		
67631	WR	VX54MOV	67636	WR	VX54MPV	67641	WR	VX54MRV	67648	WR	VX54MTJ
67632	WR	VX54MPE	67637	WR	VX54MPY	67642	WR	VX54MRY	67649	WR	VX54MTK
67633	WR	VX54MPF	67638	WR	VX54MPZ	67643	WR	VX54MSO	67650	WR	VX54MTO
67634	WR	VX54MPO	67639	WR	VX54MRO	67647	WR	VX54MTF	67651	WR	VX54MTU
67635	WR	VX54MPU	67640	WR	VX54MRU						

67652-67664			ADL E30D			ADL Enviro 300			N44F	2005		
67652	WR	VX05LVS	67656	WR	VX05LVW	67659	WR	VX05LWC	67662	WR	VX05LWF
67653	WR	VX05LVT	67657	WR	VX05LVY	67660	WR	VX05LWD	67663	WR	VX05LWG
67654	WR	VX05LVU	67658	WR	VX05LVZ	67661	WR	VX05LWE	67664	WR	VX05LWH
67655	WR	VX05LVV									

Since 2012 the Alexander Dennis Enviro 300 model has featured in First's orders, particularly for the Scottish-based operations. Lettered for Glasgow's One network, and from an allocation of forty at Dumbarton, 67723, SN62AEU, is seen heading towards Helensburgh. *Mark Lyons*

| 67665 | WR | FN08AZZ | ADL E300 | | | ADL Enviro 300 | N44F | 2008 | Premiere, Nottingham, '13 |
| 67699 | WR | PT59JPT | ADL E300 | | | ADL Enviro 300 | N44F | 2010 | JP Travel, Middleton, 2013 |

67701-67710 ADL E300 — ADL Enviro 300 — NC37F — 2010

67701	CA	SN60EAA	67704	CA	SN60EAF	67707	CA	SN60EAM	67709	CA	SN60EAP
67702	CA	SN60EAC	67705	CA	SN60EAG	67708	CA	SN60EAO	67710	CA	SN60EAW
67703	CA	SN60EAE	67706	CA	SN60EAJ						

67711-67750 ADL E30D — ADL Enviro 300 — N41F — 2012

67711	DU	SN62ABU	67721	DU	SN62AEK	67731	DU	SN62AGV	67741	SN	SN62AKJ
67712	DU	SN62ABV	67722	DU	SN62AET	67732	DU	SN62AGY	67742	SN	SN62AKO
67713	DU	SN62ABX	67723	DU	SN62AEU	67733	DU	SN62AHD	67743	SN	SN62AKP
67714	DU	SN62ABZ	67724	DU	SN62AEY	67734	DU	SN62AHF	67744	SN	SN62AMV
67715	DU	SN62ACX	67725	DU	SN62AFE	67735	DU	SN62AHL	67745	SN	SN62ANR
67716	DU	SN62ACZ	67726	DU	SN62AFJ	67736	DU	SN62AHV	67746	SN	SN62ANU
67717	DU	SN62ADU	67727	DU	SN62AFK	67737	DU	SN62AHX	67747	SN	SN62AOA
67718	DU	SN62ADV	67728	DU	SN62AFU	67738	DU	SN62AJU	67748	SN	SN62AOC
67719	DU	SN62AEA	67729	DU	SN62AFY	67739	DU	SN62AJV	67749	SN	SN62AOF
67720	DU	SN62AEF	67730	DU	SN62AFZ	67740	DU	SN62AKG	67750	SN	SN62AOG

67751-67772 ADL E30D — ADL Enviro 300 — N41F — 2013

67751	PH	SN62AOZ	67757	PH	SN62ASX	67763	PH	SN62AUK	67768	PH	SN13CGK
67752	PH	SN62APF	67758	PH	SN62ASZ	67764	PH	SN62AUU	67769	PH	SN13CGO
67753	PH	SN62APO	67759	PH	SN62ATZ	67765	PH	SN62AUW	67770	PH	SN13CGU
67754	PH	SN62APZ	67760	PH	SN62AUC	67766	PH	SN13CGF	67771	PH	SN13CGV
67755	PH	SN62ASO	67761	PH	SN62AUH	67767	PH	SN13CGG	67772	PH	SN13CGX
67756	PH	SN62ASU	67762	PH	SN62AUJ						

67773-67782 ADL E30D — ADL Enviro 300 — NC41F — 2013

67773	GS	SN62AXH	67776	GS	SN62AXU	67779	GS	SN62AXZ	67781	GS	SN62AYB
67774	GS	SN62AXK	67777	GS	SN62AXW	67780	GS	SN62AYA	67782	GS	SN62AYJ
67775	GS	SN62AXO	67778	GS	SN62AXY						

Trongate in Glasgow and Enviro 300 67842, SN13EDV, heads south-east on the twenty-seven kilometre trip towards Motherwell. *Mark Lyons*

67783-67805

			ADL E30D			ADL Enviro 300			N41F	2013			
67783	AB	SN13CMO	67789	AB	SN13CNA	67795	AB	SN13CNO	67801	AB	SN13COA
67784	AB	SN13CMU	67790	AB	SN13CNC	67796	AB	SN13CNU	67802	AB	SN13COH
67785	AB	SN13CMV	67791	AB	SN13CNE	67797	AB	SN13CNV	67803	AB	SN13COJ
67786	AB	SN13CMX	67792	AB	SN13CNF	67798	AB	SN13CNX	67804	AB	SN13COU
67787	AB	SN13CMY	67793	AB	SN13CNJ	67799	AB	SN13CNY	67805	AB	SN13CPE
67788	AB	SN13CMZ	67794	AB	SN13CNK	67800	AB	SN13CNZ			

67806-67894

			ADL E30D			ADL Enviro 300			N41F	2013			
67806	SN	SN13EAY	67829	SN	SN13ECW	67851	B	SN13EES	67873	SN	SN63MYT
67807	SN	SN13EBA	67830	SN	SN13ECX	67852	B	SN13EET	67874	SN	SN63MYU
67808	SN	SN13EBC	67831	SN	SN13ECY	67853	B	SN13EEU	67875	SN	SN63MYV
67809	SN	SN13EBD	67832	SN	SN13ECZ	67854	B	SN13EEV	67876	SN	SN63MYW
67810	SN	SN13EBF	67833	B	SN13EDC	67855	B	SN13EEW	67877	SN	SN63MYX
67811	SN	SN13EBG	67834	B	SN13EDF	67856	B	SN13EEX	67878	SN	SN63MYY
67812	SN	SN13EBJ	67835	B	SN13EDJ	67857	B	SN13EEY	67879	SN	SN63MYZ
67813	SN	SN13EBK	67836	B	SN13EDK	67858	B	SN13EEZ	67880	SN	SN63MZD
67814	SN	SN13EBL	67837	B	SN13EDL	67859	B	SN13EFA	67881	SN	SN63MZE
67815	SN	SN13EBM	67838	B	SN13EDO	67860	B	SN13EFB	67882	SN	SN63MZF
67816	SN	SN13EBO	67839	B	SN13EDP	67861	B	SN13EFC	67883	SN	SN63MZG
67817	SN	SN13EBP	67840	B	SN13EDR	67862	B	SN13EFD	67884	SN	SK63ATY
67818	SN	SN13EBU	67841	B	SN13EDU	67863	B	SN13EFE	67885	SN	SK63ATZ
67819	SN	SN13EBV	67842	B	SN13EDV	67864	SN	SN13EFF	67886	SN	SK63AUA
67820	SN	SN13EBX	67843	B	SN13EDX	67865	SN	SN13EFG	67887	SN	SK63AUC
67821	SN	SN13EBZ	67844	B	SN13EEF	67866	SN	SN13EFH	67888	SN	SK63AUE
67822	SN	SN13ECA	67845	B	SN13EEG	67867	SN	SN13EFJ	67889	SN	SK63AUF
67823	SN	SN13ECC	67846	B	SN13EEH	67868	SN	SN13EFK	67890	SN	SK63AUH
67824	SN	SN13ECD	67847	B	SN13EEJ	67869	SN	SN13EFL	67891	SN	SK63AUJ
67825	SN	SN13ECF	67848	B	SN13EEM	67870	SN	SN63MYP	67892	SN	SK63AUL
67826	SN	SN13ECJ	67849	B	SN13EEO	67871	SN	SN63MYR	67893	SN	SK63AUM
67827	SN	SN13ECT	67850	B	SN13EEP	67872	SN	SN63MYS	67894	SN	SK63AUN
67828	SN	SN13ECV									

Four Hybrid Enviro 350s operate from Chelmsford depot, The Alexander Dennis Enviro35OH is a nineteen tonne hybrid-electric bus chassis using hybrid technology that promised fuel savings, CO2 reductions of between 30% and 40% and reduced maintenance. 67902, SN13CHV, is shown. *Steve Rice*

67901-67904

			ADL E35H			ADL Enviro 350		N41F	2013		
67901	CM	SN13CHO		67902	CM	SN13CHV		67903	CM	SN13CHX	67904	CM	SN13CHY

| 68000 | ABt | Q275LBA | Blue Bird | | | Blue Bird | | B60F | 1999 | | |

68001-68006

			Blue Bird AARE			Blue Bird		S60F	2002		
68001	BL	RD51FKV	68003	BL	RD51FKZ	68005	BL	YS51JVE	68006	BL	YS51JVH
68002	BL	RD51FKW	68004	BL	RD51FLA						

68225-68229

			Irisbus Scolabus 24			Vehixel		S63F	2005	Operated for GMPTE	
68225	BN	FJ55KNB	68227	OM	FJ55KMY	68228	OM	FJ55KMZ	68229	BN	FN55EDV
68226	QS	FJ55KMO									

| 68301 | SO | BX55NZV | Autosan Eagle A1012T | | | Autosan | | S67D | 2006 | Truronian, 2008 |
| 68302 | SO | BX06NZT | Autosan Eagle A1012T | | | Autosan | | S67D | 2006 | Truronian, 2008 |

68503-68548

			BMC 1100FE Student			BMC		S60F	2004-05	*68515/6/27-30/45-8 WYPTE	
68503	PT	BX54VUN	68512	SO	RX54AOY	68522	SO	RX54OGZ	68534	CM	LK54FNL
68504	MU	CU54CYX	68513	WSt	CU54DCE	68527	HX	YA54WBL	68535	CM	EU05DXR
68505	WSt	CU54CYY	68514	BF	CU54DCF	68528	HX	YA54WBK	68536	SO	LK54FNF
68506	RA	CU54CYZ	68515	HX	YJ54YCO	68529	HX	YA54WBO	68537	SO	LK54FNH
68507	WR	KX54AHP	68516	HX	YJ54YCP	68530	HX	YA54WBN	68545	HX	YJ05VWA
68508	BR	KX54AHU	68518	AB	SV54CFY	68531	CM	LK54FNC	68546	HX	YJ55CAO
68509	CM	KX54AHY	68519	AB	SV54CFZ	68532	CM	LK54FNE	68547	HX	YJ55CAV
68510	CM	KX54ANR	68520	BR	KP54AZU	68533	SO	LK54FNJ	68548	HX	YJ55CAU
68511	SO	RX54AOV	68521	CM	KP54AZV						

68550-68566

			BMC 1100FE Student			BMC		S55F	2005-06		
68550	SO	HX05BUO	68555	CM	MX55NWS	68559	WR	LK55ABV	68563	HOt	HX55AOK
68551	CM	EU05DXS	68556	LT	MX55NWC	68560	LT	LK55ABX	68564	SO	SF55TXA
68552	CM	EU05DXT	68557	SO	MX55NWD	68561	LT	HX55AOJ	68565	SO	SF55TXB
68553	SO	HX05BUJ	68558	GS	LK55ABU	68562	HOt	HX55AOH	68566	GS	SF55TXC
68554	SO	LK05FCE									

68567-68571

			BMC 1100FE Student			BMC		S55F	2007-08		
68567	WSt	BV57MSO	68569	RAt	BV57MSX	68570	WSt	BV57MSY	68571	PLt	BG57ZGJ
68568	RAt	BV57MSU									

68603-68648

										BMC Condor 220		BMC		NC57F	2005-06		*Operated for Metro WYPTE*

68603	BD	YK55AAJ	68616	HU	YK55AUH	68628	BD	YJ06WTV	68640	BD	YJ06XEK
68606	BD	YK55AUP	68621	BD	YK55AVF	68630	BD	YJ06WTZ	68641	HX	YJ06XEL
68608	HX	YJ06XFR	68622	BD	YK55AVG	68631	BD	YJ06WUA	68642	HX	YK06ATO
68609	HX	YK55AUU	68623	BD	YK55AVJ	68635	HX	YK06DYJ	68643	HX	YK06CZZ
68610	HX	YK55AAN	68625	HX	YK55AVM	68638	HX	YK06DNN	68646	BD	YK06DAA
68614	HU	YK55AUE	68626	BD	YJ06WTX	68639	BD	YK06DTZ	68648	BD	YK06EHE
68615	HX	YK55AUF									

68651-68683

BMC Condor 220   BMC   NC57F   2006-07   *Operated for Metro WYPTE*

68651	BD	YJ56LJE	68659	HX	YJ56LLN	68668	HX	YJ56LKD	68675	HX	YJ56ZMU
68652	BD	YJ56LJF	68660	HX	YJ56LLO	68669	HX	YJ56LMX	68676	HX	YK07FTU
68653	BD	YJ56LJK	68662	HX	YJ56LNA	68670	HX	YJ56LRU	68677	HX	YK07FUD
68654	HX	YJ56LJN	68663	HX	YJ56LKE	68671	HX	YJ56LRN	68680	HX	YK07FUA
68655	HX	YJ56LJL	68664	HX	YJ56LJY	68672	BD	YJ56LRL	68682	HX	YK07FTP
68656	HX	YJ56LLG	68667	HX	YJ56LKC	68674	HX	YJ56WGA	68683	HX	YK07FTT
68657	HX	YJ56LLK									

68684-68700

BMC Condor 225   BMC   NC57F   2007-08   *Operated for Metro WYPTE*

68684	HU	YJ57VYX	68689	HU	YJ08XCR	68693	HU	YJ08XCS	68697	BD	YJ07XMB
68685	HU	YJ57VTV	68690	HU	YJ08XCO	68694	HU	YK07BJX	68698	BD	YJ07XWG
68686	HU	YJ57VVA	68691	HU	YJ08XCP	68695	HU	YK07BJY	68699	HU	YK07FTX
68687	HU	YJ57VYY	68692	HU	YJ08XCN	68696	HU	YK07BJZ	68700	BD	YJ07WBL

68701-68708

BMC Condor 220   BMC   NC57F   2005-07   *Operated for Metro WYPTE*

68701	HX	YK55JCN	68703	HX	YK06EFS	68705	HX	YJ57NFF	68707	HX	YJ57WKB
68702	HX	YK06EFR	68704	HX	YJ56ZTM	68706	HX	YJ57WKC	68708	HX	YJ07XND

68709	BD	YJ07FLP	BMC Condor 225	BMC	NC57F	2007	*Operated for Metro WYPTE*
68710	BD	YJ07XWF	BMC Condor 225	BMC	NC57F	2007	*Operated for Metro WYPTE*
68711	BD	YJ07WBK	BMC Condor 225	BMC	NC57F	2007	*Operated for Metro WYPTE*

69000-69011

Volvo B7RLE   Wrightbus Eclipse Urban   N43F*   2005   *69000-4 are N40F

69000	BM	YK54ENP	69003	YK	YK54ENN	69006	IP	AU05DMF	69009	IP	AU05DMX
69001	YK	YK54ENL	69004	YK	YK54ENO	69007	IP	AU05DMO	69010	IP	AU05DMY
69002	YK	YK54ENM	69005	IP	AU05DME	69008	IP	AU05DMV	69011	IP	AU05DMZ

69012-69134

Volvo B7RLE   Wrightbus Eclipse Urban   N43F   2006-07

69012	TN	SF55UAD	69043	RO	SF55UBC	69074	SN	SF06GXX	69105	SN	SF06GZP
69013	TN	SF55UAE	69044	RO	SF55UBD	69075	SN	SF06GXY	69106	SN	SF06GZR
69014	O	SF55UAG	69045	RO	SF55UBE	69076	O	SF06GXZ	69107	SN	SF06GZS
69015	O	SF55UAH	69046	RO	SF55UBG	69077	O	SF06GYA	69108	SN	SF06GZT
69016	O	SF55UAJ	69047	RO	SF55UBH	69078	O	SF06GYJ	69109	SN	SF06GZV
69017	TN	SF55UAK	69048	RO	SF55UBJ	69079	O	SF06GYK	69110	AB	SV06GRF
69018	TN	SF55UAL	69049	RO	SF55UBK	69080	O	SF06GYN	69111	CA	SF06GZX
69019	O	SF55UAM	69050	RO	SF55UBL	69081	O	SF06GYO	69112	CA	SF06GZY
69020	RO	SF55UAN	69051	RO	SF55UBM	69082	O	SF06GYP	69113	CA	SF06GZZ
69021	O	SF55UAO	69052	RO	SF55UBN	69083	O	SF06GYR	69114	CA	SF06HAA
69022	RO	SF55UAP	69053	RO	SF55UBO	69084	O	SF06GYS	69115	CA	SF06HAE
69023	RO	SF55UAR	69054	RO	SF55UBP	69085	SN	SF06GYT	69116	CA	SF06HAO
69024	RO	SF55UAS	69055	RO	SF55UBR	69086	SN	SF06GYU	69117	CA	SF06HAU
69025	RO	SF55UAT	69056	RO	SF55UBS	69087	SN	SF06GYV	69118	CA	SF06HAX
69026	RO	SF55UAU	69057	CA	SF06GXM	69088	SN	SF06GYW	69119	CA	SF06HBA
69027	SN	SF55UAV	69058	CA	SF06GXN	69089	SN	SF06GYX	69120	CA	SF06HBB
69028	RO	SF55UAW	69059	CA	SF06GXH	69090	SN	SF06GYY	69121	CA	SF06HBC
69029	RO	SF55UAX	69060	CA	SF06GXO	69091	SN	SF06GYZ	69122	AB	SV06GRK
69030	RO	SF55UAY	69061	CA	SF06GXP	69092	SN	SF06GZA	69123	AB	SV06GRU
69031	RO	SF55UAZ	69062	CA	SF06GXR	69093	O	SF06GZB	69124	AB	SV06GRX
69032	RO	SF55UBA	69063	CA	SF06GXS	69094	SN	SF06GZC	69125	AB	SV07EHB
69033	RO	SF55UBT	69064	CA	SF06GXT	69095	SN	SF06GZD	69126	AB	SV07EHC
69034	O	SF55UBU	69065	CA	SF06GXU	69096	SN	SF06GZE	69127	AB	SV07EHD
69035	O	SF55UBV	69066	CA	SF06GYB	69097	SN	SF06GZG	69128	AB	SV07EHE
69036	O	SF55UBW	69067	CA	SF06GYC	69098	SN	SF06GZH	69129	AB	SV07EHF
69037	O	SF55UBX	69068	CA	SF06GYD	69099	SN	SF06GZJ	69130	AB	SV07EHG
69038	O	SF06GXJ	69069	CA	SF06GYE	69100	SN	SF06GZK	69131	AB	SV07EHH
69039	O	SF06GXG	69070	CA	SF06GYG	69101	SN	SF06GZL	69132	AB	SV07EHJ
69040	O	SF06GXK	69071	CA	SF06GYH	69102	SN	SF06GZM	69133	AB	SV07EHK
69041	B	SF06GXL	69072	SN	SF06GXV	69103	SN	SF06GZN	69134	AB	SV07EHL
69042	CA	SF55UBB	69073	SN	SF06GXW	69104	SN	SF06GZO			

69135-69244   Volvo B7RLE   Wrightbus Eclipse Urban   N43F   2006

69135	BY	MV06CZS	69164	BN	MX06VNV	69191	B	MX56ADZ	69218	CE	MX56AEG
69136	BY	MV06CZG	69165	BY	MX06VMW	69192	B	MX56AEA	69219	CE	MX56AEJ
69137	BY	MV06CZT	69166	BY	MX06VMZ	69193	B	MX56AEB	69220	CE	MX56AEK
69138	BY	MV06CXB	69167	BY	MX06VNB	69194	B	MX56AEC	69221	CE	MX56AEL
69139	BN	MX06VOP	69168	BN	MX06VNC	69195	QS	MX06VPR	69222	CE	MX56AEM
69141	BN	MX06VOU	69169	BN	MX06VND	69196	QS	MX06VPT	69223	CE	MX56AEN
69142	BN	MX06VOV	69170	BN	MX06VNE	69197	QS	MX06VPU	69224	CE	MX56AEO
69143	BN	MX06VOY	69171	BN	MX06VNF	69198	QS	MX06VPV	69225	CE	MX56AEP
69144	BN	MX06VPA	69172	BN	MV06CZJ	69199	QS	MX06VPW	69226	CE	MX56AET
69145	BN	MX06VNW	69173	BN	MV06DWZ	69200	OM	MX06VPY	69227	CE	MX56AEU
69146	BN	MX06VNY	69174	BN	MX06VNK	69201	BN	MX06VPZ	69228	CE	MX56AEV
69147	BN	MX06VNZ	69175	BN	MX06VPO	69202	OM	MX06VRC	69229	CE	MX56AEW
69148	BN	MX06VOA	69176	QS	MX06VPP	69203	QS	MX06VPC	69230	CE	MX56AEY
69149	BN	MX06VOB	69177	OM	MX06YXJ	69204	OM	MX06VPD	69231	PT	MX56AEZ
69150	BN	MX06VOC	69178	BY	MX06YXK	69205	OM	MX06VPE	69232	PT	MX56AFA
69151	BN	MX06VOD	69179	QS	MX06YXL	69206	TN	MV06DYU	69233	PT	MX56AFE
69152	BN	MX06VOF	69180	QS	MX06YXM	69207	TN	MX06VPG	69234	PT	MX56AFF
69153	BN	MX06VOG	69181	CA	MX06YXN	69208	TN	MX06VPJ	69235	PT	MX56AFJ
69154	BN	MX06VOH	69182	CA	MX06YXO	69209	CE	MX06VPK	69236	PT	MX56AFK
69155	BN	MX06VNL	69183	CA	MX06YXP	69210	WH	MX06VPL	69237	PT	MX56AFN
69156	BN	MX06VNM	69184	CA	MX06YXR	69211	WH	MX06VPM	69238	PT	MX56AFO
69157	BN	MX06VNN	69185	QS	MX56ACV	69212	WH	MX06VPN	69239	RA	MX56AFU
69158	BN	MX06VNO	69186	BY	MX56ACY	69213	WH	MX06YXS	69240	RA	MX56AFV
69159	BN	MX06VNP	69187	CA	MX56ACZ	69214	WH	MX06YXT	69241	RA	MX56AFY
69160	BN	MX06VNR	69188	CA	MX56ADO	69215	WH	MX56AED	69242	RA	MX56AFZ
69161	BN	MX06VNS	69189	CA	MX56ADU	69216	SO	MX56AEE	69243	RA	MX56AGO
69162	BN	MX06VNT	69190	B	MX56ADV	69217	WH	MX56AEF	69244	RA	MX56AGU
69163	BN	MX06VNU									

69245-69294   Volvo B7RLE   Wrightbus Eclipse Urban   N43F   2007

69245	SO	YJ07WFM	69258	LT	SK57ADU	69271	BD	YJ07WFX	69283	LT	SN57JCO
69246	SO	YJ07WFN	69259	LT	SK57ADV	69272	BD	YJ07WFY	69284	LT	SN57JCU
69247	SO	YJ07WFO	69260	LT	SK57ADX	69273	BD	YJ07WFZ	69285	LT	SN57JCV
69248	SO	YJ07WFP	69261	LT	SK57ADZ	69274	BD	YJ07WGA	69286	LT	SN57JCX
69249	RA	YJ07WFR	69262	LT	SK57AEA	69275	YK	YJ57YSN	69287	LT	SN57JCY
69250	RA	YJ07WFS	69263	LT	SK57AEB	69276	YK	YJ57YSM	69288	LT	SN57JCZ
69251	RA	YJ07WFT	69264	LT	SK57AEC	69277	YK	YJ57YSO	69289	LT	SN57JDF
69252	RA	YJ07WFU	69265	AB	SV57EYH	69278	YK	YJ57YSP	69290	LT	SN57JDJ
69253	BA	YJ07WFV	69266	AB	SV57EYJ	69279	YK	YJ57YSR	69291	LT	SN57JDK
69254	LT	SK07JVN	69267	AB	SV57EYK	69280	LT	SN57MSU	69292	LT	SN57HZX
69255	LT	SK07JVO	69268	BM	YJ57YSK	69281	LT	SN57JBZ	69293	LT	SN57HZY
69256	LT	SK07JVP	69269	BM	YJ57YSL	69282	LT	SN57JCJ	69294	LT	SN57HZZ
69257	LT	SK57ADO	69270	BD	YJ07WFW						

Volvo B7RLE 69017, SF55UAK, in Somerset colours is seen in Taunton. *Steve Rice*

York's allocation of forty-two Volvo B7RLEs includes 69359, YJ08ZGM, which along with several others at this depot features roof level advertising boards. *Tony Wilson*

69295-69298
Volvo B7RLE — Wrightbus Eclipse Urban — N38F — 2004 — Hutchison, Overtown, 2007

69295	O	SF04HXW	69296	O	SF04HXX	69297	O	SF04ZPE	69298	O	SF04ZPG

69299-69328
Volvo B7RLE — Wrightbus Eclipse Urban — N43F — 2008-09

69299	BD	YJ08GWX	69305	RA	CU08AHX	69317	BD	YJ09FWM	69323	HU	YJ09FWT
69300	BD	YJ08GWY	69306	YK	YJ09FWA	69318	BD	YJ09FWN	69324	HU	YJ09FWU
69301	RA	CU08AHN	69307	HU	YJ09FWB	69319	BD	YJ09FWO	69325	QS	YJ09FWV
69302	RA	CU08AHO	69308	HU	YJ09FWC	69320	BD	YJ09FWP	69326	QS	YJ09FWW
69303	RA	CU08AHP	69315	BD	YJ58RVA	69321	BD	YJ09FWR	69327	QS	YJ09FWX
69304	RA	CU08AHV	69316	BD	YJ09FWL	69322	BD	YJ09FWS	69328	OM	YJ09FWY

69329-69350
Volvo B7RLE — Wrightbus Eclipse Urban — N43F — 2008

69329	HU	YJ08CDE	69335	BM	YJ08CDV	69341	BM	YJ08CEK	69346	BM	YJ08CEX
69330	HU	YJ08CDF	69336	BM	YJ08CDX	69342	BM	YJ08CEN	69347	BM	YJ08CEY
69331	BM	YJ08CDK	69337	BM	YJ08CDY	69343	BM	YJ08CEO	69348	BM	YJ08CFA
69332	BM	YJ08CDN	69338	BM	YJ08CDZ	69344	BM	YJ08CEU	69349	BM	YJ08CFD
69333	BM	YJ08CDO	69339	BM	YJ08CEA	69345	BM	YJ08CEV	69350	BM	YJ08CFE
69334	BM	YJ08CDU	69340	BM	YJ08CEF						

69351-69379
Volvo B7RLE — Wrightbus Eclipse Urban — N43F — 2008

69351	AB	SV08FHA	69359	YK	YJ08ZGM	69366	YK	YJ08XYE	69373	YK	YJ08XYN
69352	AB	SV08FHB	69360	YK	YJ08ZGN	69367	YK	YJ08XYF	69374	YK	YJ08XYO
69353	AB	SV08FHC	69361	YK	YJ08ZGO	69368	YK	YJ08XYG	69375	YK	YJ08XYP
69354	AB	SV08FHD	69362	YK	YJ08ZGP	69369	YK	YJ08XYH	69376	YK	YJ08XYR
69355	AB	SV08FHE	69363	YK	YJ08XYB	69370	YK	YJ08XYK	69377	YK	YJ08XYS
69356	AB	SV08FHF	69364	YK	YJ08XYC	69371	YK	YJ08XYL	69378	YK	YJ08XYT
69357	AB	SV08FHG	69365	YK	YJ08XYD	69372	YK	YJ08XYM	69379	YK	YJ08XXW
69358	YK	YJ08ZGL									

69380-69401 — Volvo B7RLE — Wrightbus Eclipse Urban — N38F — 2009

69380	RA	HY09AJX	69386	SO	HY09AZB	69392	SO	HY09AOR	69397	SO	HY09AZL
69381	RA	HY09AKG	69387	SO	HY09AUW	69393	SO	HY09AZD	69398	SO	HY09AUX
69382	RA	HY09AOU	69388	SO	HY09AOT	69394	SO	HY09AZC	69399	SO	HY09AZN
69383	RA	HY09AZA	69389	SO	HY09AUO	69395	SO	HY09AZF	69400	SO	HY09AZJ
69384	RA	HY09AKF	69390	SO	HY09AOS	69396	SO	HY09AZO	69401	SO	HY09AZG
69385	SO	HY09AJV	69391	SO	HY09AUV						

69402-69420 — Volvo B7RLE — Wrightbus Eclipse Urban — N43F — 2009

69402	LT	SN09EZW	69407	LT	SN09FBC	69413	HP	YJ09FXA	69417	HP	YJ09FXE
69403	LT	SN09EZX	69408	LT	SN09FBD	69414	HP	YJ09FXB	69418	HP	YJ09FXF
69404	LT	SN09FAU	69409	LT	SN09FBE	69415	HP	YJ09FXC	69419	HU	YJ09FXG
69405	LT	SN09FBA	69410	LT	SN09FBF	69416	HP	YJ09FXD	69420	OM	YJ09FXH
69406	LT	SN09FBB	69412	HP	YJ09FWZ						

69421-69434 — Volvo B7RLE — Wrightbus Eclipse Urban — N43F — 2009

69421	CO	AU58FFH	69425	IP	AU58FFM	69429	CO	AU58FFR	69432	CO	AU58FFV
69422	IP	AU58FFJ	69426	IP	AU58FFN	69430	CO	AU58FFS	69433	CO	AU58FFW
69423	IP	AU58FFK	69427	IP	AU58FFO	69431	CO	AU58FFT	69434	CO	EU58JWZ
69424	IP	AU58FFL	69428	IP	AU58FFP						

69435-69460 — Volvo B7RLE — Wrightbus Eclipse Urban 2 — NC43F — 2009

69435	LE	WX59BYM	69442	WS	WX59BYU	69449	LE	WX59BZC	69455	LE	WX59BZJ
69436	LE	WX59BYN	69443	WS	WX59BYV	69450	LE	WX59BZD	69456	LE	WX59BZK
69437	BA	WX59BYO	69444	WS	WX59BYW	69451	LE	WX59BZE	69457	LH	WX59BZL
69438	WS	WX59BYP	69445	WS	WX59BYY	69452	LE	WX59BZF	69458	HG	WX59BZM
69439	WS	WX59BYR	69446	WS	WX59BYZ	69453	LE	WX59BZG	69459	LE	WX59BZN
69440	WS	WX59BYS	69447	WS	WX59BZA	69454	LE	WX59BZH	69460	LE	WX59BZO
69441	WS	WX59BYT	69448	WS	WX59BZB						

69461-69485 — Volvo B7RLE — Wrightbus Eclipse Urban — N43F — 2009

69461	DN	YN09HFH	69468	BD	YJ09NYC	69474	BD	YJ09NYM	69480	BD	YJ09NYT
69462	DN	YN09HFJ	69469	BD	YJ09NYD	69475	BD	YJ09NYN	69481	BD	YJ09NYU
69463	DN	YN09HFK	69470	BD	YJ09NYF	69476	BD	YJ09NYO	69482	BD	YJ09NYV
69464	DN	YN09HFL	69471	BD	YJ09NYG	69477	BD	YJ09NYP	69483	BD	YJ09NYW
69465	DN	YN09HFM	69472	BD	YJ09NYH	69478	BD	YJ09NYR	69484	BD	YJ09NYX
69466	BD	YJ09NYA	69473	BD	YJ09NYK	69479	BD	YJ09NYS	69485	BD	YJ09NYY
69467	BD	YJ09NYB									

69500-69531 — Volvo B7RLE — Wrightbus Eclipse Urban 2 — NC37F — 2010-11

69500	HG	BJ10VGA	69508	HG	BJ11EBX	69516	CM	BJ11ECE	69524	BN	BD11CEV
69501	HG	BJ10VGD	69509	HG	BJ11XHZ	69517	CM	BJ11ECD	69525	BN	BD11CFA
69502	HG	BJ10VGC	69510	HG	BJ11EBU	69518	CM	BJ11ECT	69526	BN	BD11CEY
69503	HG	BJ10VGE	69511	HG	BJ11EBZ	69519	CM	BJ11ECV	69527	BN	BD11CEX
69504	HG	BJ10VGF	69512	CM	BJ11ECA	69520	CM	BJ11ECW	69528	BN	BD11CFG
69505	HG	BJ10VGG	69513	CM	BJ11ECC	69521	BN	BD11CEN	69529	BN	BD11CFJ
69506	HG	BJ11XHY	69514	CM	BJ11ECF	69522	BN	BD11CEU	69530	BN	BD11CFF
69507	HG	BJ11EBV	69515	CM	BJ11ECN	69523	BN	BD11CEO	69531	BN	BD11CFE

69532	CM	PL05UBR	Volvo B7RLE	Wrightbus Eclipse Urban	NC43F	2005	Transdev, Harrogate, 2013
69533	CM	PL05UBS	Volvo B7RLE	Wrightbus Eclipse Urban	NC43F	2005	Transdev, Harrogate, 2013

69537-69555 — Volvo B7RLE — Wrightbus Eclipse Urban 2 — NC42F — 2012-13

69537	HO	BF63HDN	69544	HO	BF12KWD	69548	HO	BF12KWJ	69552	HO	BF12KWP
69538	HO	BF63HDU	69545	HO	BF12KWC	69549	HO	BF12KWK	69553	HO	BF12KWM
69539	HO	BF63HDO	69546	HO	BF12KWL	69550	HO	BF12KWO	69554	HO	BF12KWS
69542	HO	BF12KWE	69547	HO	BF12KWH	69551	HO	BF12KWN	69555	HO	BF12KWR
69543	HO	BF12KWG									

69556-69587 — Volvo B7RLE — Wrightbus Eclipse Urban 2 — N43F — 2013

69556	HU	BV13ZDH	69564	HU	BD13NFK	69572	BD	BD13OHL	69580	HX	BT13YVW
69557	HU	BV13ZDJ	69565	HU	BD13NFO	69573	BD	BD13OHN	69581	HX	BT13YVX
69558	HU	BV13ZDK	69566	BD	BD13NFP	69574	BD	BD13OHO	69582	HX	BT13YVY
69559	HU	BV13YZZ	69567	BD	BD13NFM	69575	BD	BD13OHP	69583	HX	BT13YVZ
69560	HU	BG13VUD	69568	BD	BD13NFN	69576	BD	BD13OHN	69584	HX	BT13YWA
69561	HU	BG13VUC	69569	BD	BD13NFR	69577	BD	BD13OHS	69585	HX	BT13YWB
69562	HU	BG13VUE	69570	BD	BD13NFV	69578	HX	BD13OHT	69586	HX	BT13YWC
69563	HU	BD13NFL	69571	BD	BD13OHK	69579	HX	BT13YVV	69587	HX	BT13YWD

Volvo 7900 Hybrid buses are gaining popularity particularly in continental Europe and an all-electric version was unveiled during 2014. First operates two batches, one in Berkshire and the other in Essex, where 69910, BV13ZBP was pictured leaving Chelmsford on route 100 to Lakeside. *Mark Lyons*

69901-69919   Volvo 7900 Hybrid   Volvo   N40F   2013

69901	BS	BV13ZBC	69906	BS	BV13ZBJ	69911	BS	BV13ZBR	69916	BS	BV13ZBY
69902	BS	BV13ZBD	69907	BS	BV13ZBL	69912	BS	BV13ZBT	69917	BS	BV13ZBZ
69903	BS	BV13ZBE	69908	BS	BV13ZBN	69913	BS	BV13ZBU	69918	BS	BV13ZCA
69904	BS	BV13ZBF	69909	BS	BV13ZBO	69914	BS	BV13ZBW	69919	BS	BV13ZCE
69905	BS	BV13ZBG	69910	BS	BV13ZBP	69915	BS	BV13ZBX			

69920-69934   Volvo 7900 Hybrid   Volvo   NC37F   2013-14

69920	SH	BV13ZCF	69924	SH	BV13ZCN	69928	SH	BV13ZCX	69932	SH	BJ63UJW
69921	SH	BV13ZCJ	69925	SH	BV13ZCO	69929	SH	BV13ZCY	69933	SH	BJ63UJX
69922	SH	BV13ZCK	69926	SH	BV13ZCT	69930	SH	BJ63UHZ	69934	SH	BJ63UJZ
69923	SH	BV13ZCL	69927	SH	BV13ZCU	69931	SH	BJ63UJV			

90092	ROs	OWJ782A	Leyland Titan PD3	Roe	RV	1963	
90181	CEu	824KDV	Bristol Lodekka FLF6G	Eastern Coach Works	B38/32F	1962	
90489	HUs	RL02FYX	Dennis Dart SLF 10.3m	Marshall Capital 2	N--F	2002	St Helen's College, 2012
90557	SOs	EHO228	Guy Arab I	Weymann	H32/26R	1942	Provincial
90575	HPs	M656VWE	Volvo B10M-62	Plaxton Première 350	C8F	1995	Yorkshire Traction

Allocations - May 2015

Aberdeen

Aberdeen - AB

Volvo B10BLA	10044	10045	10108					
Volvo B7LA	10047	10048	10049	10050	10051	10052	10136	10138
	10141	10144	10148	10154	10155	10156	10157	10158
	10159	10160	10161	10162	10163	10164	10165	10166
	10167	10168	10169	10170	10171	10172	10173	10183
Volvo B12B	20021							
Volvo B12T	20205	20207						
Volvo B7R	20351	20352	20353	20367	20372	20373	20374	
Volvo B12M	20505	20506	20507					
Scania coach	23021	23305	23306	23307	23314	23330	23401	23402
Temsa Safari	29004	29006	29007					
Trident	32845	32865	32928	32958	32962	32970	32971	32973
	32974	32975	32976					
Volvo B9TL	37633	37634	37635	37636	37637	37638	37639	37640
	37641	37642	37643	37644				
Mercedes-Benz Vario	56005	56006	56007	56008	56009			
Mercedes-Benz Atego	56501							
Volvo B10BLE	62123	62132	62133	62134	62137	62140	62141	62149
	62150	62151	62152	62153	62154	62155	62163	62164
	62165	62166	62167	62168	62169	62170	62171	62172
	62173	62174	62175	62176	62177	62178	62179	62180
	62181	62196	62201	62202				
Bluebird Schoolbus	62228							
StreetLite Max	63193	63194	63195	63196	63197	63198	63199	63200
	63201	63202	63203	63204	63205	63206	63207	63208
	63209	63210	63211	63212	63213	63214	63215	63216
	63217	63218						
Van Hool Cellbus	64994	64995	64996	64997				
Enviro 300	67783	67784	67785	67786	67787	67788	67789	67790
	67791	67792	67793	67794	67795	67796	67797	67798
	67799	67800	67801	67802	67803	67804	67805	
BMC Schoolbus	68518	68519						
Volvo B7RLE	69110	69122	69123	69124	69125	69126	69127	69128
	69129	69130	69131	69132	69133	69134	69265	69266
	69267	69351	69352	69353	69354	69355	69356	69357

Ancillary / Reserve / Specials:

Volvo B10BLA	10110	
Atlantean	31528	31577
Daimler CVG6	31529	
Leyland Leopard	62120	
Albion	62121	
Bluebird	68000	

Scotland East

Balfron - BF

Olympian	30560					
Scania N94	36015	36016	36017	36020	36022	
Optare Solo	50233	53704	53705			
Volvo B10BLE	62188	62204	62206	62211	62213	62220
Scania L94	60163	61215	61216	61218	61220	65708
BMC Schoolbus	68514					

Ancillary / Reserve / Specials:

Olympian	30745	30750	30751

Bannockburn - BK

Volvo B7R	20321	20322	20358					
Olympian	31497	34015	34075	34290				
Volvo B7TL	31558	31559	31560	31561	31562	31563		
Scania N94	36007	36008	36010	36011	36013	36018	36019	36021
	36023	36025	36026	36027	36028	36029		
Scania L94 UB	60165	60166	60197	60220	61214	61217	61225	62355
	62357	62385	62386	62387	65594	65595	65597	65601
	65662	65663	65694	65695	65702	65709	65710	65711
	65712	65713	65714	65715	65719	65720	65721	65722
	65723							
Volvo B10BLE	62125	62127	62128	62135	62136	62157	62182	62212

Ancillary / Reserve / Specials:

Scania	60221	61221	62390

Galashiels - GS - *outstations: Hawick, Kelso and Peebles*

Volvo B7R	20300	20301	20326	20327	20368	20370	20371	
Olympian	30744	31684	34048					
Volvo B7TL	31790	31791	31792	32669	32670	32671	32672	32676
Trident	32837							
Volvo B9TL	37133	37134	37135	37136	37138	37139		
Dart	41488	41751	41752	41753	41754	41755	41756	
Optare Solo	50234	50460						
Mercedes-Benz	56003							
Volvo B10BLE	62184	62187	62222	62223	62227			
Scania L94UB	61219	61230	65742	65743	65744	65745	65746	65747
	65748	65749	65750					
Enviro 300	67773	67774	67775	67776	67777	67778	67779	67780
	67781	67782						
BMC Schoolbus	68558	68566						

Larbert - LT

Volvo B7R	20355	20360						
Volvo B7TL	32678	32679						
Trident	32823	32830	32831	32834	32838	32841	32842	32889
	32893	32895	32896	32897	32898	32904	32907	32909
	32910	32914	32917	32919	32922	32923	32924	32951
	32967	32968	33030					
Dart	43842	43844						
StreetLite	47531	47532	47533	47534	47613	47614	47615	47616
	47617							
Optare Solo	50232	50468	53702	53703	53706			
Plaxton Primo	57001	57002						

Scania L94UB	60168	60195	60198	61222	61223	61229	61231	61233
	65598	65599	65664	65698	65699	65752	65753	65754
Volvo B10BLE	62123	62124	62126	62131	62186	62190	62203	62205
	62207	62224	62226					
Enviro 300	62411	62412						
BMC Schoolbus	68556	68560	68561					
Volvo B7RLE	69254	69255	69256	69257	69258	69259	69260	69261
	69262	69263	69264	69280	69281	69282	69283	69284
	69285	69286	69287	69288	69289	69290	69291	69292
	69293	69294	69402	69403	69404	69405	69406	69407
	69408	69409	69410					

Ancillary / Reserve / Specials:

Trident	32821

Linlithgow - LW

Volvo B7R	20302	20307	20354	20351	20363	20365	20369
Olympian	30826	30832	31656				
Trident	32892	32918	32921	32948	32949		

Livingston - LV

Volvo B7R	20356	20359	20362	20364	20366			
Volvo B7TL	32221	32225	32226	32227	32228	32294	32295	32296
	32297	32298	32299	32673	32674	32675	32677	32680
	32681	32682	32683					
Trident	32934							
Scania OmniDekka	36009	36012	36014	36024				
Volvo B9TL	37137	37140	37141	37142	37143	37144	37145	37266
	37267	37268	37269	37270	37271	37272	37273	
StreetLite Max	63157	63158	63159	63160	63219	63220	63221	63222
	63223	63241	63242	63243	63244	63245	63246	63247
	63248	63249						
Mercedes Benz Citaro	64003	64004	64007	64008	64010	64011		

Ancillary / Reserve / Specials:

Trident	32811	32813	32814			
Scania	60180	60203	60204	62388	62389	62392

Musselburgh - MU - *outstation: North Berwick*

Volvo B7R	20357							
Volvo B7TL	32222	32223	32224					
Trident	32870	32995	33029	33037	33050	33059	33093	33131
	33135	33137	33138	33139	33140			
Scania OmniDekka	36030							
Mercedes-Benz	56002	56004						
Scania L94	60199	61224	61226	61227	61228	61232	62356	62358
	65700	65701	65703	65716	65717	65718	65751	
BMC Schoolbus	68504							

Glasgow

Blantyre - B

Volvo B7TL	31787	31788	31789	31793	31794	31795	31796	31797
	31798	31799	31800	31801	31802	31803	31804	32609
	37166	37167	37168	37169	37170	37171	37180	37181
	37182	37183	37184	37185				
Trident	32960	32977	32982	32983	32984	32987	32988	32989
	32990	32991	32992	32997	32999	33122		
Volvo B9TL	37238	37239	37240	37241	37242	37243	37244	37245
	37278							
Dart	41410	41415	41426	41777	41778	41779	42885	42886
	42887	42888						
VW Transporter	54302	54304	54307					
Fiat Ducato	54403							
Volvo B10BLE	61597	61598	61599	61600	61601	61602	61603	61604
	61605	61606	61607	61608	61609	61610	66233	
StreetLite	63224	63225	63226	63227	63228	63229	63230	63231
	63232	63233	63234	63235	63236	63237	63238	63239
	63240							
Volvo B7RLE	66735	66736	66737	66770	66771	66946	66947	66948
	66949	66951	66988	66989	66990	66991	69041	69190
	69191	69192	69193	69194				
Enviro 300	67833	67834	67835	67836	67837	67838	67839	67840
	67841	67842	67843	67844	67845	67846	67847	67848
	67849	67850	67851	67852	67853	67854	67855	67856
	67857	67858	67859	67860	67861	67862	67863	

Ancillary / Reserve / Specials:

Trident	32927	32994
Scania L94	61676	61682

Dumbarton - DU

Volvo B12M	20508	20509						
Volvo B9TL	37218	37219	37220	37221	37222	37223	37224	37225
	37226	37227						
Scania L94 UB	61027	61683	61685	61693	61695	61696	61697	61698
	61699	61700	61701	61702	61704	65596		
Enviro 300	67711	67712	67713	67714	67715	67716	67717	67718
	67719	67720	67721	67722	67723	67724	67725	67726
	67727	67728	67729	67730	67731	67732	67733	67734
	67735	67736	67737	67738	67739	67740		

Ancillary / Reserve / Specials:

Volvo B12M	20503
Scania L94	61027

Glasgow (Caledonia) - CA

Volvo B7TL	32543	32544	32546	32547	32548	32549	32550	32551
	32552	32553	32554	32561	32562	32563	32564	32565
	32568	32569	32570	32571	32572	32573	32574	32575
	32580	32581	32583	32584	32598	32599	32600	32601
	32602	32603	32604	32605	32606	32607	32608	32610
	32611	32612	32614	32622	32623	32624	32625	32626
	32657	37172	37173	37174	37175	37176	37177	37178
	37179							
Trident	33008	33009	33010	33011	33012	33013	33014	33015
	33016	33017	33018	33019	33040	33046	33053	33054
	33089	33091	33092	33094	33096	33097	33114	33115
	33116	33117	33118	33119	33120	33121		

Enviro 400	33904	33905	33906	33907	33908	33909	33910	33911
	33912	33913	33914	33915	33916	33917	33918	33919
	33920	33921	33922	33923				
Volvo B9TL	37186	37187	37188	37189	37190	37191	37192	37193
	37194	37195	37196	37197	37198	37199	37200	37201
	37202	37203	37204	37205	37206	37207	37208	37209
	37210	37211	37212	37213	37214	37530	37531	37532
	37533	37534	37535	37536	37537	37538	37539	37540
	37541	37542	37543	37544	37736	37737	37738	37739
	37740	37741	37742	37743	37744	37745	37746	37747
	37748	37749	37750	37751				
Enviro 500	38201	38202	38203	38204	38205	38206	38207	38208
	38209	38210	38211	38212	38213	38214	38215	38216
	38217	38218	38219	38220	38221	38222	38223	38224
Optare Solo	53751	53752	53753	53754				
Fiat	54404	54405	54406	54407				
Volvo B7L	61637	61640	61641	61642	61643	61644	61645	61646
	61647	61648	61649	61650	61651	61663	61664	
Scania L94UB	61022	61680	61686	61688	61689	61690	61691	65593
	65596	65693	65696	65697	65755	65756	65757	65758
Enviro 300	67701	67702	67703	67704	67705	67706	67707	67708
	67709	67710						
Volvo B7RLE	69042	69057	69058	69059	69060	69061	69062	69063
	69064	69065	69066	69067	69068	69069	69070	69071
	69111	69112	69113	69114	69115	69116	69117	69118
	69119	69120	69121	69181	69182	69183	69184	69187
	69188	69189						

Ancillary / Reserve / Specials:

Enviro 500	38225							
Volvo B6	48045							
Volvo B10M	60464	60466	61256					
Scania L94	61025	61028	61669	61675	61677	61679	61681	65591
Scania L113	61478							

Glasgow (Parkhead) - PH

Volvo B7TL	32556	32557	32558	32559	32560	32566	32567	32577
	32578	32579	32585	32587	32589	32613	32615	32616
	32617	32618	32619	32620	32621	37147	37148	37149
	37150	37151	37152	37153	37154	37155		
Trident	32964	32978	32980	32996	32998	33000	33020	33021
	33022	33023	33024	33025	33026	33027	33028	33033
	33034	33035	33343	33344	33345	33346	33347	33348
	33349	33350	33351	33352	33353	33354	33355	33356
	33357	33358	33359	33360	33361	33362	33363	33364
	33365	33366	33367	33368	33369	33370	33371	33372
	33374	33375	33386					
Dart	41405	41406	41414	41416	41417	41418	41447	
StreetLite	47618	47619	47620	47621	47622	47623	47624	47625
	47626	47627	47628					
Volvo B7L	61306	61587	61588	61589	61590	61591	61592	61593
	61594	61595	61596	61615	61627	61628	61629	61630
	61632	61634	61635	61656	61657	61658	61659	61660
	61661	66349						
Enviro 300	67751	67752	67753	67754	67755	67756	67757	67758
	67759	67760	67761	67762	67763	67764	67765	67766
	67767	67768	67769	67770	67771	67772		

Ancillary / Reserve / Specials:

Trident	32965

A new bus depot called Caledonian (code CA) is claimed to be the biggest bus depot in Britain and is designed to accommodate up to 450 buses. Its initial allocation comprises the recent Larkfield allocation. The location is close to the former Larkfield garage on the edge of the Gorbals area of south Glasgow and is unusual in that it is constructed on both sides of a motorway with a tunnel linking the two sites. First has kindly supplied these two pictures of the property.

Glasgow (Scotstoun) - SN

Volvo B7TL	32300	32301	32302	32303	32304	32305	32545	32555
	32576	32582	32586	32588	32590	32591	32592	32593
	32594	32595	32596	32597				
Trident	32925	32956	32969	32979	32981	32985	32986	32993
Enviro 400	33901	33902	33903					
Volvo B9TL	37215	37216	37217					
Enviro 400 Hybrid	39101	39102	39103	39104	39105	39106	39107	39108
	39109	39110						
Dart	41311	41314	41407	41408	41409	41422	41448	41683
	41684	41685	41775	41776				
Optare Solo	40965	40966	50461	50462	50463	50464	50465	53201
	53202	53203						
Enviro 300	67741	67742	67743	67744	67745	67746	67747	67748
	67749	67750	67806	67807	67808	67809	67810	67811
	67812	67813	67814	67815	67816	67817	67818	67819
	67820	67821	67822	67823	67824	67825	67826	67827
	67828	67829	67830	67831	67832	67864	67865	67866
	67867	67868	67869	67870	67871	67872	67873	67874
	67875	67876	67877	67878	67879	67880	67881	67882
	67883	67884	67885	67886	67887	67888	67889	67890
	67891	67892	67893	67894				
Volvo B7RLE	69027	69072	69073	69074	69075	69085	69086	69087
69088								
	69089	69090	69091	69092	69094	69095	69096	69097
	69098	69099	69100	69101	69102	69103	69104	69105
	69106	69107	69108	69109				

Overtown - O

Dart	41446	41449						
Fiat	54401	54402						
Volvo B10BLE	61611	61612	61613	61614	61616	61617	61618	61619
	61620	61621	61622	61623	61624	61625	61626	61652
	61653	61654	61705	61706	61707	61708	61709	61710
	62129	62130	62159	66281	66282			
Volvo B7RLE	66952	66954	66955	69014	69015	69016	69019	69021
	69034	69035	69036	69037	69038	69039	69040	69076
	69077	69078	69079	69080	69081	69082	69083	69084
	69093	69295	69296	69297	69298			

Scotland East operates from Edinburgh across the English border and into Carlisle. Pictured while setting off on a 'short' return journey north is Enviro 300 67781, SN62AYB. *Steve Rice*

West Yorkshire

Bradford - BD

Olympian	30791	30796	30817	30834	31677	31761	31762	31763
	31764	31765	31766	31767	31768	31769	31770	
Volvo B7TL	30857	30866	30867	30868	30869	30870	30890	30891
	30892	30893	30894	30895	30896	30897	30908	30909
	30910	30911	30912	30913	30914	30915	30922	30939
	30940	32528	32529	32533	32534	32535	32536	32537
	32538	37055	37056	37057	37058	37059		
Volvo B9TL	37065	37066	37067	37068	37069	37070	37071	37072
	37073	37074	37075	37076	37077	37078	37079	37080
	37081	37082	37083	37084	37085	37086	37087	37088
	37089	37090	37091	37092	37093	37094	37095	37096
	37097	37098	37099	37100	37101	37102	37360	37361
	37362	37363	37364	37365	37366	37732	37733	37734
	37735							
Optare Solo	50237	50238	50239	53034	53035	53101	53104	
Volvo B10BLE	60821	60822	60823	60824	60825	60826	60828	60829
	60830	60831	60832	60833	60834	60835	60836	60837
	60838	60839	60840	60852	60853	60854	60855	
Volvo B7L	60877	60878	60903	60904	60905	60906	60907	60908
	60923	60924	60925					
Volvo B7RLE	66715	66999	69270	69271	69272	69273	69274	69299
	69300	69315	69316	69317	69318	69319	69320	69321
	69322	69466	69467	69468	69469	69470	69471	69472
	69473	69474	69475	69476	69477	69478	69479	69480
	69481	69482	69483	69484	69485	69566	69567	69568
	69569	69570	69571	69572	69573	69574	69575	69576
	69577							
BMC Schoolbus	68603	68606	68621	68622	68623	68626	68628	68630
	68631	68639	68640	68646	68648	68651	68652	68653
	68672	68697	68698	68700	68709	68710	68711	

Ancillary / Reserve / Specials:

Olympian	31760	
Volvo B10BLE	60637	
Volvo B10B	66651	66652

Bramley - BM

Volvo B7LA	19001	19002	19003	19004	19005	19006	19007	19008
	19009	19010	19011	19013	19015	19016	19017	19018
	19019	19021	19023	19024	19025	19026	19027	19028
Volvo B7TL	30923	30924	30925	30926	30927	30928	30929	30930
	30931	30932	30933	30934	32431	32432	32433	32434
	32435	32436	32437	32438	32439	32440	32441	32442
	32443	32444	32445	32446	32447	32448	32449	32450
	32451	32452	32461	32462	32463	32464	32465	32466
	32467	32468	32469	32470	32471	32472	32473	
Enviro 400	33873	33874	33875	33876	33877	33878	33879	33880
	33881	33882	33883	33884	33885	33886	33887	33888
	33889	33890						
Volvo B9TL	37063	37064	37645	37646	37647	37648	37649	37650
	37651	37652	37653	37654	37655	37656	37657	37658
	37659	37660	37661	37662	37663	37664	37665	37666
	37680	37682	37687	37688	37689	37706	37707	37708
	37709	37710	37711	37712	37713	37714	37715	37716
	37717	37718	37719	37720	37721	37722	37723	37724
	37725	37726	37727	37728	37729	37730	37731	37752
	37753	37754	37755	37756				
Volvo B6BLE	40566	40576	40577	40578	40579	40587		
Scania L113CRL	61074							
Scania L94UB	60065	60066	60213	60214	61029	61038	61039	61040
	61041							
Volvo B7RLE	66766	66767	66768	66769	66772	66995	66996	69000
	69268	69269	69331	69332	69333	69334	69335	69336
	69337	69338	69339	69340	69341	69342	69343	69344
	69345	69346	69347	69348	69349	69350		

Ancillary / Reserve / Specials:

Volvo B7LA	19012	19014	19020	19022
Olympian	30722			
Volvo B10M	60467	60468	60472	
Volvo B10BLE	60638	60658	60668	
Lance	60944			
Scania	61071	61072		
Volvo B10B	61363			

Halifax - HX - *outstation: Todmorden*

Olympian	30800	30802	30805	30806	30808	30809	30811	30812
	30813	30844	31774	31775	31807	31808	34107	34211
Volvo B7TL	30849	30855	30856	30858	30859	30860	32520	32521
	32522	32523	32524	32525	32526	32527	32530	32531
	32532	32539	32540	32541	32542	32692	32693	32694
	32695	32696	37046	37047	37048	37049	37050	37051
	37052	37053	37054					
Optare Solo	50235	50236	50319	50407	53301	53302	53303	
Volvo B10BLE	60827	60841	60842	60843	60844	60845	60846	60847
	60848	60849	60850	60851	61289			
Volvo B7RLE	66707	66708	66709	66710	66711	66712	66713	66738
	66739	66740	66741	66742	66743	66744	66746	66747
	66748	66749	66750	66751	66752	66764	66765	66776
	66777	66778	66779	66780	66781	66782	66783	66789
	66790	69578	69579	69580	69581	69582	69583	69584
	69585	69586	69587					
BMC Schoolbus	68515	68516	68527	68528	68529	68530	68545	68546
	68547	68548	68608	68609	68610	68615	68625	68635
	68638	68641	68642	68643	68654	68655	68656	68657
	68659	68660	68662	68663	68664	68667	68668	68669
	68670	68671	68574	68675	68676	68677	68680	68682
	68683	68701	68702	68703	68704	68705	68706	68707
	68708							

Ancillary / Reserve / Specials:

Olympian	30845		
Dart	41282	41283	
Volvo B10BLE	60816	60819	60820

Huddersfield - HU

Olympian	30815	30816	30818	30821	30822	30823	30840	30841
	30843							
Volvo B7TL	30847	30848	30850	30851	30852	30853	30854	30863
	30864	30865	30916	30917	30918	30919	30920	30921
	30935	30936	30941	30942	30943	30944	30945	30946
	30947	30948	30949	30950	30951	30952	30953	31143
	31146	31147	32503	32504	32505	32506	32507	32508
	32509	32510	32511	32512	32513	32514	32515	32516
	32517	32518	32519					
StreetLite	47491	47492	47493	47494	47495	47496	47497	47498
	47499	47500						
Volvo B10BLE	66101							
Volvo B7RLE	66714	66753	66773	66774	66775	66784	66785	66786
	66787	66788	66791	66792	69307	69308	69323	69324
	69329	69330	69419	69556	69557	69558	69559	69560
	69561	69562	69563	69564	69565			
BMC Schoolbus	68614	68616	68684	68685	68686	68687	68689	68690
	68691	68692	68693	68694	68695	68696	68699	

Ancillary / Reserve / Specials:

Olympian	30814
Dart	90489

Leeds (Hunslet Park) - HP

Volvo B7LA	10038	10039	10040	10041	10042	10043		
Volvo B7TL	32460	37036	37037	37038	37039	37040	37041	37042
	37043	37044	37060	37061	37062			
Volvo B9TL	36181	36182	36183	36184	36185	36186	36187	36188
	36189	36190	36191	36192	36193	36194	36195	36196
	36197	36198	36199	36200	36201	36202	36203	36204
	36205	36206	36207	36208	36209	36210	36211	36212
	36213	36214	36215	36216	36217	36218	36219	36220
	36221	36222	36223	36224	36225	36226	36227	36228
	36229	36230	36231	36232	36233	36234	36235	36236
	36237	36238	36239	36240	36241	36242	36243	36244
	36245	36246	36247	36248	36249	36250	36251	36252
	36253	36254	36255	36256	36257	36258	36259	36260
	36261	36262	36263	36264	36265	36266	36267	36268
	36269	36270	36271	36272	36273	36274	36275	36276
	36277	36278	37123	37124	37125	37126	37127	37128
	37129	37130	37131	37132	37667	37668	37669	37670
	37671	37672	37673	37674	37675	37676	37677	37678
	37679	37681	37683	37684	37685	37686	37690	37691
	37692	37693	37694	37695	37696	37697	37698	37699
	37700	37701	37702	37703	37704	37705		
Volvo B5LH	39201	39202	39203	39204	39205	39206	39221	39222
	39223	39224	39225	39226	39227	39228	39229	39230
	39231	39232	39233	39234	39235	39236		
Optare Solo	53904	53905	53906	53907	53909			
Scania L94UB	60067	60172	60212	60217	61030	61031	61032	61034
	61035	61036	61037					
Volvo B7RLE	66997	66998	69412	69413	69414	69415	69416	69417
	69418							

Ancillary / Reserve / Specials:
Volvo B7TL	32697
Volvo B10M	90575

York

York - YK

Mercedes-Benz Citaro	11101	11102	11103	11104	11105	11106	11107	11108
	11109	11110	11111	11112	11113	11114	11115	
Volvo B7TL	37045							
Volvo B9TL	37246	37247	37248	37249	37250	37251	37252	37253
	37254	37255	37256	37359				
VDL/Wrightbus Hybrid	39001	39002	39003	39004				
Volvo B6BLE	40571	40572	40573	40574	40575			
Optare Versa	49901	49902	49903	49904	49905	49906	49907	49908
	49909	49910	49911	49912				
Volvo B7L	60876	60880	60881	60882	60883	60884	60896	60897
	60898	60899	60900	60901	60902	60909	60919	60920
	60921	60922	60926	60927	60928			
Volvo B7RLE	66754	66755	66756	66757	66758	66759	66760	66761
	66762	66763	69001	69002	69003	69004	69275	69276
	69277	69278	69279	69306	69358	69359	69360	69361
	69362	69363	69364	69365	69366	69367	69368	69369
	69370	69371	69372	69373	69374	69375	69376	69377
	69378	69379						

South Yorkshire

Doncaster - DN

Volvo B7TL	30881	30882	30883	30884	30885	30898	30899	30904
	30905	30906	30907	31148	31781	31782	31783	31784
	31785	31786	32249	32250	32260	32261	32262	32263
	32264	32265	32266	32267	32268	32269	32270	32271
	32272	32273	32274	32275	32276			
Volvo B9TL	37228	37230	37232	37233	37234	37235	37236	37237
	37257	37500	37501	37502	37503	37504	37505	37506
	37507	37508	37525					
Volvo B6	40595	40596	40597	40598	40599			
Dart	40973	40974	40975	40976				
Enviro 200	44925	44926	44927					
StreetLite	47482	47483	47484	47485	47486	47487	47488	47489
	47490							
Volvo B7L	60406	60718	60888	60889	61192	61193	61194	61195
	61196	61197	61198	61199	61200	61201	61202	61203
	61204	61206	61207	61208	61209	61210	61211	
Volvo B7RLE	69461	69462	69463	69464	69465			

Ancillary / Reserve / Specials:

| Volvo B10BLE | 60627 |

Sheffield - OG

Volvo B7TL	30571	30572	30573	30574	30576	30846	30862	30937
	30938	31129	31130	31131	31132	31133	31134	31135
	31137	31138	31139	31140	31141	31776	31777	31778
	31779	31780	32108	32109	32110	32111	32215	32216
	32217	32218	32219	32220	32308	32309	32310	32311
	32312	37021	37022	37023	37024	37025	37026	37027
	37028	37029	37030	37031	37032	37033	37034	37035
Trident	32955	32957	33031	33032	33041	33052	33061	33062
	33063	33064	33065	33069	33070	33071	33079	33082
	33083	33084	33099	33124	33125	33127	33128	33129
	33230							
Enviro 400	33858	33859	33860	33861	33862	33863	33864	33865
	33866	33867	33868	33869	33870	33871	33872	
Volvo B9TL	37103	37104	37105	37106	37107	37108	37109	37110
	37111	37112	37113	37114	37115	37116	37117	37118
	37119	37120	37121	37122	37229	37472	37473	37474
	37475	37476	37477	37478	37479	37480	37481	37482
	37483	37484	37485	37486	37511	37512	37513	37514
	37515	37516	37517	37518	37519	37520	37521	37522
	37523	37524	37526	37527	37528	37529		
Volvo B10BLE	60630	60631	60642	60644	60648	60650	60655	60656
	60661	60662	60684	60685	60687	60688	60689	60690
	60692	60693	60694	60696	60697	60698	60699	60700
	60701	60702	62232	62234	62235	62237	62239	62240
	62243	62244						
Volvo B7L	60703	60707	60708	60709	60710	60711	60712	60713
	60714	60715	60716	60717	60719	60725	60736	60737
	60745	60885	60886	60887	60890	60891	60892	60893
	60894	61631	61633	61636	61638	61639	61662	
StreetLite Max	63001	63002	63003	63004	63005	63006	63007	63008
	63009	63010	63011	63012	63013	63014	63015	63016
	63017	63018	63019	63020	63021	63022	63023	63024
	63025	63026	63027	63028	63029	63030	63031	63032
	63033	63034	63035	63036	63037	63119	63120	63121
	63122	63123	63124	63125	63126	63127	63128	63129
	63130	63131	63132	63133	63134	63135	63136	63137
	63138	63139	63140	63141	63142	63143	63144	63145

Volvo B7TL	30861							
Olympian	34090							
Volvo B10M	60486							
Volvo B10BLE	60641	60643	60646	60647	60649	60653	60654	60659
	60686	60691	60695					

Rotherham - RO

Volvo B7TL	30561	30562	30563	30564	30565	30567	30568	30569
	30570	30575	30577	30578	31142	31144	31145	
StreetDeck	35101							
Volvo B9TL	37231	37258	37259	37261	37262	37263	37264	37265
	37487	37488	37489	37490	37491	37492	37493	37494
	37495	37496	37497	37498	37499	37509	37510	
Volvo B10BLE	60635	60666	60670	60672	60673	60675	60676	60677
	60678	60679	60680	60682	60683			
Volvo B7L	60704	60705	60706	60720	60721	60722	60724	60726
	60727	60728	60729	60730	60731	60733	60734	60735
	60738	60739	60740	60741	60742	60743	60744	
StreetLite Max	63038	63039	63040	63041				
Volvo B7RLE	69020	69022	69023	69024	69025	69026	69028	69029
	69030	69031	69032	69033	69043	69044	69045	69046
	69047	69048	69049	69050	69051	69052	69053	69054
	69055	69056						

Volvo B10M	60458							
Volvo B10BLE	60361	60368	60632	60633	60634	60636	60639	60664
	60669	60681						
Leyland Titan PD3	90092							

Manchester

Bolton - BN

Volvo B7TL	30874	30875	30878					
Enviro 400	33657	33673	33677	33691	33693	33695	33696	33697
	33699	33700	33704	33705	33707	33709	33710	33711
	33712	33713	33714	33715	33716	33717	33718	33719
	33720	33721	33722	33724	33725	33726	33727	33728
	33729	33730	33731	33732	33733	33734	33735	33736
	33737	33739	33740	33742	33743	33749	33753	
Volvo B9TL	37397	37402	37405	37407	37408	37409	37410	37415
	37416	37430	37434	37435	37456			
Optare Versa hybrid	49116	49117	49211	49214	49217	49227	49228	49233
Volvo B10BLE	60405	62214	62231	62233	62236	62241	66194	
Volvo B7RLE	66861	66867	66870	66876	66894	66895	66896	66899
	66901	66903	66904	66905	66906	66907	66931	69139
	69141	69142	69143	69144	69145	69146	69147	69148
	69149	69150	69151	69152	69153	69154	69155	69156
	69157	69158	69159	69160	69161	69162	69163	69164
	69168	69169	69170	69171	69172	69173	69174	69175
	69201	69521	69522	69523	69524	69525	69526	69527
	69528	69529	69530	69531				
Enviro 300	67401	67402	67403	67404	67405	67406	67407	67408
	67409	67410	67411	67412				
Irisbus Schoolbus	68225	68229						

Olympian	34105					
Volvo B10B	60302	60322				
Volvo B10BLE	60376	60380	60381	60651	60663	

Bury - BY

Scania L94 UA	10017							
Scania OmniCity G	12001	12002	12003	12004	12005	12006	12007	12008
	12009	12010	12011	12012	12013	12014	12015	12016
	12017	12018						
Volvo B7TL	30871	30872	30873	30876	30877	30879	30880	
Volvo B9TL	37291	37292	37293	37294	37295	37296	37297	37298
	37299	37300	37302	37391	37392	37393	37398	37399
	37400	37401	37403	37404	37406	37417	37418	37419
	37420	37421	37422	37423	37424	37425	37426	37427
	37428	37429	37431	37471	37551	37554		
Mercedes-Benz Citaro	60233	60235	60237	60238	60239	60241	60242	60243
	60245	60247	60249	60250	60251	60252	60253	60254
	60255	60256	60257	60258	60259	60260	60261	60262
	60264	60267	60268	60269	60270	60271	60272	60273
	60274	60275	60276	60277	60278	60279	60280	60282
	60283	64029						
Volvo B7RLE	66836	66844	66846	66853	66855	66872	66873	66880
	66892	66897	66900	66909	66914	66915	66916	66917
	66918	66919	66930	69135	69136	69137	69138	69165
	69166	69167	69178	69186				

Ancillary / Reserve / Specials:

Olympian	34206	
Volvo B10B	60301	61351
Volvo B10BLE	60640	
Mercedes-Benz Citaro	60226	60281

Manchester (Fallowfield) - OX

Trident	32867	32869	32899	32908	32911	32912	32913	32915
	32916	32926	32959	32972				
Enviro 400	33656	33668	33669	33831	33832	33833	33834	33835
	33836	33837	33838	33839	33840	33841	33842	33843
	33844	33845	33846	33847	33848	33849	33850	33851
	33852	33853	33854	33855	33856	33857		
StreetLite	63113	63114	63115	63116	63117	63118	63146	63147
	63148	63149	63150	63151	63152	63153	63154	63155
	63156							

Ancillary / Reserve / Specials:

Olympian	34206

Manchester (Queen's Road) - QS

Volvo B9TL	37279	37280	37281	37282	37283	37284	37285	37286
	37287	37288	37289	37290	37301	37303	37304	37367
	37368	37369	37370	37371	37372	37373	37374	37375
	37376	37377	37378	37379	37380	37381	37382	37384
	37385	37386	37389	37390	37394	37395	37396	37411
	37413	37414	37440	37442	37452			
Volvo B5LH	39207	39208	39209	39210	39211	39212	39213	39214
	39215	39216	39217	39218	39219	39220		
Volvo B6	40437							
Optare Versa	49101	49102	49106	49107	49108	49109	49110	49111
	49112	49118	49119	49204	49208	49213	49218	49220
	49230	49231	49232	49921	49922	49923		
Solo Hybrid	59001	59002	59003	59004	59005	59006	59007	59008
	59012	59013						
Volvo B10BLE	60371							
SteetLite	63096	63097	63098	63099	63100	63101	63102	63103
	63104	63105	63106	63107	63108	63109	63110	63111
	63112							
Volvo B7RLE	66831	66832	66833	66834	66835	66874	66875	66890
	66891	66893	66898	66902	66908	66910	66911	66912
	66913	66920	66922	66923	66928	66929	66933	69176
	69179	69180	69185	69195	69196	69197	69198	69199
	69203	69325	69326	69327				

| Irisbus Scolabus | 68226 | | | | | | | |

Ancillary / Reserve / Specials:

Volvo B6	40438	40439	40440	40441	40443	40444		
Optare Solo	53149	53150						
Volvo B10B	61359							
Volvo B10BLE	60371	60379	60386	60657	60660	61241	62216	62217
	66191	66192	66193	66195				

Oldham - OM

Volvo B7TL	30954	30955	30956	30957	30958	30959	30960	30961
	30962	30963						
Enviro 400	33663	33670	33671	33672	33674	33675	33676	33678
	33679	33680	33681	33682	33683	33684	33685	33686
	33687	33688	33689	33690	33692	33694	33698	33701
	33702	33703	33706	33708	33723	33738	33741	33744
	33745	33746	33747	33748	33750	33751	33752	33754
	33755							
Streetdeck	35102							
Volvo B9TL	36279	36280	37383	37387	37388	37412	37432	37433
	37436	37437	37438	37439	37441	37443	37444	37445
	37446	37447	37448	37449	37450	37451	37453	37454
	37455	37457	37458	37459	37460	37461	37462	37463
	37467	37468	37469	37470	37545	37546	37547	37548
	37549	37550	37552	37553	37555	37556	37557	37558
	37559	37560	37561					
Optare Solo	40318	40319	40322	40323	40328	40329	40330	40331
	40332	40333	40334	40335	40336	53143	53144	53145
	53146	53147						
StreetLite	47466	47471	47472	47474	47481			
Optare Versa hybrid	49202	49203	49205	49206	49209	49210	49212	49215
	49216	49222						
Mercedes-Benz	60224	60248						
Volvo B7RLE	66848	66854	66856	66857	66858	66859	66860	66862
	66863	66864	66865	66866	66868	66869	66871	69177
	69200	69202	69204	69205	69328	69420		
Enviro 300	67413	67414	67415	67416	67417	67418	67419	67420
	67421	67422	67423	67424	67425	67426	67427	67428
	67429	67430						
Irisbus Scolabus	68227	68228						

Ancillary / Reserve / Specials:

Olympian	34102						
Dart	41788						
Optare Solo	40313	40315	40317	40320	40321	40683	
Scania	60181	60188					
Mercedes Benz	60223	60225	60229	60230	60234	60236	60240	60244
Volvo B10B	60303	61356	61366				
Volvo B10BLE	61240						

Tameside - TE

Volvo B7TL	30964	30965						
Volvo B9TL	37464	37465	37466					
Dart	41780	41781	41783	41784	41785	41786	41787	42940
	42941	42944	42945					
StreetLite	47467	47468	47469	47470	47473	47475	47476	47477
	47478	47479	47480					
Versa	49113	49114	49115					
Optare Solo	40324	40325	40326	40327	53148			
Optare Solo hybrid	59009							

Ancillary / Reserve / Specials:

| Olympian | 34089 | | | | | | | |

Midlands

Hereford - HD

Trident	33042	33043					
Dart	42351	42352	42354	43869	43870	43871	43872
Enviro 200	44511	44514	44515				
Optare Solo	53041	53042	53058	53059	53060	53063	53064
Volvo B7RLE	66699						

Ancillary / Reserve / Specials:

Dart	42353	42356
Volvo B10BLE	60665	

Leicester - LE

Volvo B7TL	32066	32067	32068	32069	32070	32071	32072	32073
	32074	32075	32076	32077	32078	32079	32080	32081
	32082	32083	32084	32085	32086	32087	32088	32089
	32090	32091	32092	32093	32094	32095	32096	32098
	32099	32277	32643	32644	32645	32646	32647	32648
	32649	32650						
Enviro 400	33504	33507	33544	33545	33546	33548	33549	33551
	33552	33553	33555	33557	33558	33559	33561	33562
	33563	33567	33568	33570	33572	33573	33574	
Volvo B7L	66315	66316	66317	66318	66319	66320	66321	66322
	66323							
Volvo B7RLE	66842	66965	66966	66967	66968	66969	66970	66971
	66972	66973	66974	66975	69435	69436	69449	69450
	69451	69452	69453	69454	69455	69456	69459	69460

Ancillary / Reserve / Specials:

Volvo B10M	60374	60460

Newcastle-under-Lyme - NE

Olympian	34311							
Volvo B7TL	32053	32054	32055	32056	32057	37156	37157	37158
	37159							
Optare Solo	40015	40016	40019	40020	53119			
Dart	41494	41497	41501	41512	42892	42893	42894	43875
	43876	43877						
Scania L94UB	60068	60069	60072	60073	60193	60202	60205	60208
	65705	65706	65727	65728	65729	65730	65731	65732
	65733							
Volvo B7L	66302	66303	66304	66305	66306	66307	66308	66309
	66310	66311	66312	66313	66314			
Volvo B7RLE	66838	66839	66840	66841	66843	66845	66847	66849
	66851	66852	66962	66963	66964			

Ancillary / Reserve / Specials:

Olympian	30031
Optare Solo	40010

Stoke-on-Trent (Adderley Green) - AG

Volvo B7TL	32627	32630	32632	32633	32634	32635	32639	37146
	37160							
Dart	40155	40173	40175	40367	40373	40375	40378	40805
	41070	41492	41493	41495	41496	41498	41499	41500
	41502	41514	41520	41521	41522	41540		

Optare Solo	40009	40021	40022	40023	40024	40025	40026	40027
	40028	40029	40304	50281	50296	53118	53120	53122
	53123	53124	53155	53207	53208	53209	53405	53828
	53829	53830						
Scania L113	60006	60075	61235	61237	65561	65564		
Scania L94	60013	60015	60074	60128	60171	60174	60175	60176
	60189	60196	60201	65567	65568	65572	65578	
StreetLite	63171	63172	63173	63174	63175	63176	63177	63178
	63179	63180	63250					
Scania OmniCity	65001	65002	65003	65004	65005	65026	65027	65033
	65034	65035	65036	65037	65038	65039	65040	65041
	65042							

Ancillary / Reserve / Specials:

Dart	42727				
Scania L113	60011	60012	60057	61145	61245
Scania L94	60081	60173	61143		
Volvo B10B	60316	60317			

Worcester - WR

Volvo B12T	20201	20202						
Trident	32852	32854	33039	33401	33402	33403	33404	33405
Dart	43873	43874						
Enviro 200	44512							
StreetLite	47513	47514	47515	47516	47517	47518	47519	47520
Optare Solo	53043	53044	53045	53046	53047	53048	53049	53050
	53051	53061	53062					
Volvo B7RLE	66691	66692	66693	66694	66695	66696	66697	66698
Enviro 300	67601	67602	67603	67604	67631	67632	67633	67634
	67635	67636	67637	67638	67639	67640	67641	67642
	67643	67647	67648	67649	67650	67651	67652	67653
	67654	67655	67656	67657	67658	67659	67660	67661
	67662	67663	67664	67665	67699			
BMC schoolbus	68507	68559						

Ancillary / Reserve / Specials:

Volvo B10M Citybus	38125	
Volvo B10B	60311	60340

Worcester's 66691, CN07HVG, is one of seven Plaxton-bodied Volvo B7RLEs acquired from Veolia. It is seen on the link to Malvern.
Mark Lyons

Eastern Counties

Great Yarmouth - YA

Olympian	34108	34109	34111	34114	34186			
Volvo B7TL	32058	32059	32061	32062	32063	32064	32065	32200
	32204	32205	32206	32207	32208	32209	32210	32212
	32213	32214	32629					
Enviro 400	33423							
Volvo B9TL	37573	37574	37575	37576	37577	37578	37579	
Dart	42919	42920	42929					
StreetLite	47501	47502	47503	47504	47505	47506		
Volvo B10BLE	60618	60622						
Volvo B7L	66334	66341	66344					

Ancillary / Reserve / Specials:

Olympian	34110	34112	34113
Routemaster	39480	39623	

Ipswich - IP

Volvo B12M	20514	20515						
Volvo B7TL	32479	32486	32487	32488	32489	32490	32491	32492
	32493	32494	32653	32655	32656			
Enviro 200	44516	44517	44518	44519				
Volvo B7RLE	66850	66950	66957	66959	66976	66977	66978	66979
	66980	66981	66982	66983	66984	66985	66986	66987
	69005	69006	69007	69008	69009	69010	69011	69422
	69423	69424	69425	69426	69427	69428		

Ancillary / Reserve / Specials:

Scania	65590	65632

King's Lynn - KL

Enviro 400	33803	33804	33805	33806	33807	33808	33809	33810
	33811	33812	33813	33814	33815	33816	33817	

Carrying the livery latterly applied to the erstwhile Eastern Counties company, Alexander-bodied Volvo B7TL 32479, AU53HJV, is currently allocated to Ipswich.
Mark Doggett

Lowestoft - LO

Volvo B7TL	30886	30888	30889	30900	30901			
Enviro 400	33818	33819	33820	33821	33822	33823	33824	
Volvo B9TL	37563	37564	37565	37566	37567	37568	37569	37570
	37571	37572						
Dart	42358	43466	43859	43860	43861	43862	43863	43864
	43865	43866	43867	43868				
Enviro 200	44513							
Volvo B10BLE	62143	66112						

Ancillary / Reserve / Specials:

| Dart | 43481 |

Norwich - VN

Volvo B7TL	32100	32101	32102	32103	32104	32105	32106	32107
	32112	32201	32202	32203	32211			
Trident	33003	33004	33007	33055	33056	33057	33058	33060
	33113	33126	33146	33149	33150	33151	33152	33154
	33155	33156	33157	33158	33159	33160	33161	33162
	33163	33164	33165	33166	33167	33168	33169	33170
	33171	33233	33234	33235	33236	33237	33238	33239
	33240	33242	33244	33245	33246	33247	33248	
Volvo B9TL	36166	36167	36168	36169	36170	36171	36172	36173
	36174	36175	36176	36177	36178	36179	36180	37562
Dart	42921							
Enviro 200	44928	45116	45117	45118	45119			
StreetLite	47507	47508	47509	47510	47511	47512		
Scania L94	65588							
Volvo B7L	61148	66301	66324	66325	66326	66327	66328	66329
	66330	66332	66333	66335	66336	66337	66338	66339
	66340	66342	66343	66345	66346	66347	66348	

Ancillary / Reserve / Specials:

| Volvo B10M | 20122 | |
| Volvo B10BLE | 60807 | 60808 |

Essex

Basildon - BS

Volvo B7TL	32628	32631	32640	32641	32642			
Trident	32801	32804	32809	32818	32847	32849	32850	32855
	32859	32863	32864	32883	32887	32905	33001	33002
	33047	33077	33178	33188	33192	33194		
Enviro 400	33424	33425						
Dart	41513	41523	41524	41525	41527	41538	41539	41541
	41542	41543	41544	42519	42933	42934	43357	43359
	43480	43717	43733	43847	43848			
StreetLite	47650	47651	47652	47653	47654	47655	47656	
Volvo B7RLE	66805	66806	66813	66819	66820	66821	66822	66823
	66824	66825	66826	66827				
Volvo 9700 Hybrid	69901	69902	69903	69904	69905	69906	69907	69908
	69909	69910	69911	69912	69913	69914	69915	69916
	69917	69918	69919					

Ancillary / Reserve / Specials:

| Dart | 43736 |

Braintree - BR

Volvo B7TL	30903							
Trident	32810	32856	33044	33045	33078	33080	33086	33087
	33088	33184	33186	33190	33195	33196		
Dart	42488	42489	42930	42931	42932	42936	43483	43485
	43679							
Volvo B10BLE	62139	62195	62197	66165	66168	66169		
BMC Schoolbus	68508	68520						

Ancillary / Reserve / Specials:

Dart	43448

Chelmsford - CM

Volvo B10M	20463							
Volvo B12M	20500	20501						
Volvo B9R	20801	20802	20803	20804	20805			
Scania coach	23019	23020						
Olympian	34305							
Dart	42482	42483	42484	42485	42486	42487	42935	43356
	43360	43731	43734	43801	43802	43845	43846	
Enviro 200	44537	44538	44539	44540	44541	44542	44543	44544
	44545	44546	44547	44548	44549	44550	44551	44900
Optare Solo	53008	53112	53113	53114	53115	53116	53117	53121
	53125	53126	53127	53128	53129	53130	53131	53132
	53133	53134	53135	53136	53137	53138	53139	
Scania OmniCity	65028	65029	65030	65031	65032			
Volvo B7RLE	66794	66795	66796	66797	66799	66802	66808	66811
	66812	66814	66815	66817	66818	66829	66830	66837
	69512	69513	69514	69515	69516	69517	69518	69519
	69520	69532	69533					
Enviro 350H	67901	67902	67903	67904				
BMC Schoolbus	689509	68510	68521	68531	68532	68534	68535	68551
	68552	68555						

Ancillary / Reserve / Specials:

Trident	32806
Scania	60135
Volvo B10B	60304

Clacton-on-Sea - CN

Volvo B7TL	30887	30902						
Dart	42918	42937	43714	43719	43735	43854	43855	43856
	43857							
Enviro 200	44596	44597	44598	44599				
Scania L113	61057	65527	65556					
Scania L94	65665	65667	65668	65670	65671	65676	65690	65691
	65692							

Colchester - CO

Volvo B7TL	32475	32476	32477	32478	32480	32481	32482	32483
	32484	32485	32651	32652	32654			
StreetLite	47657	47658						
Scania L94	60206	62406	62407	62408	62409	62410	65565	65566
	65573	65574	65586	65587	65589	65626	65627	65630
	65631	65650	65653	65654	65666	65669	65672	65673
	65674	65675	65677	65678	65679	65680	65681	65682
	65683	65684	65685	65686	65687	65688	65689	
Volvo B10BLE	66177	66179						
Volvo B7RLE	66798	66800	66801	66803	66804	66807	66809	66810
	66816	66828	69421	69429	69430	69431	69432	69433
	69434							

Scania L94   65576   65651   65652

Hadleigh - HH

Trident	33072	33073	33074	33081	33090	33095	33098	33132
	33133	33134	33136	33189	33191	33229	33232	33373
	33376	33383	33384	33385				
Dart	41730	41732	41735	41736	41737	41761	41762	42922
	42923	42927	42928	43357	43721			
Enviro 200	44001	44002	44003	44004	44005	44006	44076	44077
	44078	44079	44080	44081				
StreetLite	47521	47522	47523	47524	47525	47526	47527	47528
	47529	47530	47643	47644	47645	47646	47647	47648
	47649	63161	63162	63163	63164	63165	63166	63167
	63168	63169	63170					

Hampshire, Dorset & Berkshire

Bracknell - BL - *Outstation: Chertsey*

Volvo B7TL	32348							
Trident	33141	33142	33143	33144	33145	33147	33148	33153
	33179	33180	33181	33182	33183			
Volvo B9TL	37274	37275	37276	37985	37986	37987	37997	37998
	37999							
Enviro 200	44502	44503	44504	44505	44560	44561	44562	
Optare Solo	53065							
Mercedes-Benz Citaro	64001	64005	64012	64013	64014	64015	64016	64017
	64018	64019	64020	64021	64030	64031		
Bluebird Schoolbus	61135	61136	68001	68002	68003	68004	68005	68006

Ancillary / Reserve / Specials:

Routemaster	39735	39810
Scania	65621	65622

Hilsea - HI

Dart	40827	40957	41346	41348	42125	42130	42133	42136
	42137	42138	42139	42140	42142	42232	42234	42728
StreetLite DF	47411	47412	47413	47414	47415	47416	47417	47418
	47419	47420	47421	47431	47432	47433	47434	
Optare Solo	53140	53151	53206					
StreetLite Max	63042	63043	63044	63045	63046	63047	63048	63049
	63050	63051	63052	63053	63054	63055	63056	63057
	63058	63059	63060	63061	63062	63063	63064	63065
	63066	63067						

Ancillary / Reserve / Specials:

Scania L113   64818

Hoeford - HO

Volvo B7TL	32032	32033	32035	37161				
Trident	32703	32707	32708	32764	32768			
Enviro 400	33895	33896	33897					
Olympian	34016	34017	34059	34295				
StreetLite DF	47573	47574	47575	47576	47577	47578	47579	47580
	47581	47582	47583	47584	47585	47586	47587	47588
	47589	47590	47591	47592	47593	47594		
Optare Solo	53601	53603	53604	53605	53606	53607	53608	53609

Scania OmniCity	65006	65007	65008	65009	65010	65011	65012	65013
	65014	65015	65016	65017	65018	65019	65020	65021
	65022	65023	65024	65025				
Volvo B10BLE	66122	66128	66130	66151	66152	66153	66154	66158
	66164	66176	66181	66196	66197	66198	66201	66202
	66203	66204	66205					
Volvo B7RLE	69537	69538	69539	69542	69543	69544	69545	69546
	69547	69548	69549	69550	69551	69552	69553	69554
	69555							

Ancillary / Reserve / Specials:

Volvo B10M	20417	20418	20457
Volvo B10B	60299	60337	
Volvo B10BLE	66121		
BMC Schoolbus	68562	68563	

Reading - RG

Volvo B12B	20550	20611	20612	20613		
Volvo B9R	20806	20807	20808	20809	20810	20811
Scania K114IB	23015					

Slough - SH

Dart	40721	41336	42339	42341	42346	42347	42656	42673
Enviro 200	44563	44564	44565	44566	44567	44569		
Optare Solo	53052	53054	53055	53056	53057			
StreetLite	47665	47666	47667	47668	47669	63190	63191	63192
Mercedes-Benz Citaro	64002	64032	64033	64034	64035	64036	64037	64038
	64039	64042	64043	64044	64045	64046	64047	64048
Scania L94	65724	65725	65726					
Volvo 7900 Hybrid	69920	69921	69922	69923	69924	69925	69926	69927
	69928	69929	69930	69931	69932	69933	69934	

Ancillary / Reserve / Specials:

Dart	41403	42344

Southampton - SO

Olympian	34079							
Trident	32704	32705	32706					
Volvo B7TL	32031	32034	32038	37162	37163	37164	37165	
Dart	42949	42950	42951	42952	42953	42954	46324	46325
Enviro 200	44506	44507	44508	44509	44510	44527	44528	44529
	44530	44531	44532	44533	44534	44535	44536	
StreetLite DF	47422	47423	47424	47425	47426	47427	47428	47429
	47430	47595	47596	47597	47598	47599	47600	47601
	47602	47603	47604	47605	47606	47607	47608	47609
	47610	47611	47612					
Volvo B10BLE	66156	66157						
Volvo B7RLE	66881	66882	66883	66884	66885	66886	66944	66945
	66953	69216	69245	69246	69247	69248	69385	69386
	69387	69388	69389	69390	69391	69392	69393	69394
	69395	69396	69397	69398	69399	69400	69401	
Autosan Eagle	68301	68302						
BMC Schoolbus	68511	68512	68522	68533	68536	68537	68550	68553
	68554	68557	68564	68565				

Ancillary / Reserve / Specials:

Volvo B12B	20551
Guy Arab	90557

Weymouth - WH - *Outstations: Bridport, Poole and Yeovil*

Olympian	34044	34165	34167	34168	34258			
Volvo B7TL	32036	32039	32043	32045	32046			
Trident	32701	32702	32763	32765	32766	32767		
Scania OmniDekka	36001	36002	36003	36004	36005	36006		
Volvo B9TL	37580	37581	37582	37583	37584	37585	37586	
Dart	42113	42114	42120	42524	42818	42821	42822	42823
StreetLite	47405	47406	47407	47408	47409	47410	47670	47671
	47672	63181	63182	63183	63184	63185	63186	63187
	63188	63189						
Volvo B6BLE	48208	48270	48272	48273				
Optare Solo	50466	50467	53109	53110	53111	53610	53611	53612
	53613	53614	53615					
Volvo B7RLE	69210	69211	69212	69213	69214	69215	69217	

Ancillary / Reserve / Specials:

Olympian	39920

West of England

Bath - BA - *Outstation: Westbury*

Volvo B7LA	10035	10036	10037	10174	10175	10176	10177	10178
	10179							
Volvo B7TL	32281	32282	32283	32284	32285	32349	32350	32351
	32352	32353	32354					
Volvo B9TL	37358	37359						
VDL/Wrightbus Hybrid	39005							
Enviro 400 Hybrid	39133	39134	39135	39137	39138	39139	39140	39141
Dart	40835	42553	42554	42555	42556	42557	42561	42643
	42754	42824	42902	42903	42904	42905	42906	42907
	42908	42909	42910	42911	42914	42915	42916	42925
	42926	42938	42939					
Enviro 200	44520	44521	44522	44523	44524	44525	44526	44902
	44903	44904	44913	44914	44915	44916	44917	44918
	44919	44920	44921					
StreetLite DF	47544	47545	47546	47547	47548	47549	47550	
Optare Solo	50318	53102	53103	53204	53401	53806	53807	53808
	53809	53810	53811	53812	53813	53814	53815	53816
	53817	53818	53819	53820				
Plaxton Primo	57000							
Volvo B7L	60912	60913	60914	66350	66351	66352	66353	66354
	66355	66356						
Volvo B10BLE	62221	62238	62242	66163				
StreetLite Max	63068	63069	63070	63071	63072	63073	63074	63075
	63076	63077	63078					
Volvo B7RLE	66719	66730	66731	66732	66733	66734	66937	66938
	66939	66940	66941	66942	66943	66992	66993	69253
	69437							

Bristol (Hengrove) - HG

Volvo B7TL	32279	32331	32332	32333	32334	32335	32336	32337
	32338	32339	32340	32341	32342	32343	32344	32345
	32346	32347	32636	32637	32638	37001	37002	37008
	37009	37010	37015	37016	37017	37018	37019	37020
Trident	32931	32937	32939	32940	32941	32942	32946	32950
Enviro 400	33506	33508	33547	33550	33554	33556	33560	33564
	33565	33566	33569	33571				
Volvo B9TL	37315	37316	37317	37318	37351	37587	37588	37589
	37590	37591	37592	37593	37594	37595	37596	37597
	37598	37599	37600	37601	37602	37603	37604	37605
	37606	37608	37609	37610	37611	37612		

Dart	40956	41162	42109	42115	42701	42704	42707	42708
	42709	42710	42711	42712	42718	42723	42732	42733
	42734	42735	42736	42737	42955	42956	42957	42958
	42959	42960	42961	42967				
StreetLite DF	47435	47436	47437	47438	47439	47440	47441	47442
	47443	47444	47445	47446	47447	47448	47449	47450
	47451	47452	47453	47454	47455	47456	47457	47458
	47459	47460	47461	47462	47463	47464	47465	47567
	47568	47569	47570	47571				
Volvo B6BLE	48212	48213	48214					
Volvo B7RLE	69458	69500	69501	69502	69503	69504	69505	69506
	69507	69508	69509	69510	69511			

Ancillary / Reserve / Specials:

| Volvo B6BLE | 48216 | 48218 | 48219 | 48222 | 48224 | | | |

Bristol (Lawrence Hill) - LH

Volvo B7TL	32001	32002	32003	32004	32005	32006	32007	32008
	32009	32011	32012	32013	32014	32015	32016	32017
	32018	32019	32021	32022	32023	32024	32251	32252
	32253	32254	32255	32256	32257	32258	32259	32280
	32286	32287	32288	32289	32290	32291	32292	32328
	32329	32330	32355	32356	32357	32358	32359	32360
	37007	37011	37012	37013	37014			
Volvo B9TL	37319	37320	37321	37322	37323	37324	37325	37326
	37327	37328	37329	37330	37331	37332	37333	37334
	37335	37336	37337	37338	37339	37340	37341	37342
	37343	37344	37345	37346	37347	37348	37349	37350
	37352	37353	37354	37355	37356	37357	37607	37613
	37614	37615	37616	37617	37618	37619	37620	37621
	37622	37623	37624	37625	37626	37627	37628	37629
	37630	37631	37632	37757	37758	37759	37760	37761
	37762	37763	37764	37765	37766	37767	37768	37769
	37770	37771	37772					
Dart	42703	42705	42706	42895	42900	42901	42968	46264
StreetLite	47559	47560	47561	47562	47563	47564	47565	47566
Volvo B10BLE	62185	62189	62198	62199	62200	62208	62209	62210
	62219	62225	66102	66104	66105	66109	66110	66173
Volvo B7RLE	69457							

Cribbs Causeway in June 2014 and Volvo B7TL 32688, WX56HKD, from Marlborough Street depot in Bristol is seen on a return journey from Chepstow.
Steve Rice

Bristol (Marlbrough Street) - MS *- Outstation: Chepstow*

Volvo B7TL	32278	32684	32685	32686	32687	32688	32689	32690
	32691	37003	37004	37005	37006			
Enviro 400	33412	33413	33419					
Dart	42896	42897	42898	42899	42947	42948	42962	42963
	42964	42965	42966	42969	43849			
StreetLite DF	47551	47552	47553	47554	47555	47556	47557	47558
Volvo B10BLE	66115	66116	66117	66118	66120	66159	66161	66162
	66166	66167	66178					
Volvo B7RLE	66728	66729						

Weston-super-Mare - WS *- Outstation: Wells*

Enviro 400	33411	33414	33415	33416	33417	33418	33825	33826
	33827	33828	33829	33830				
Dart	42552	42730	42731	42738				
Enviro 200	44905	44906	44907	44908	44909	44910	44911	44912
Enviro 300	67600							
Volvo B6LE	48217	48223						
Volvo B10BLE	66100	66106	66107	66108	66160	66171	66174	66206
	66207							
Volvo B7RLE	66720	66721	66722	66723	66724	66725	66726	66727
	66934	66935	66936	66956	69438	69439	69440	69441
	69442	69443	69444	69445	69446	69447	69448	

Ancillary / Reserve / Specials:

Volvo B7TL	32052				
Dart	41404	41420	41421	41423	41795
Ford Transit	54601				
BMC Schoolbus	68505	68513	68567	68570	

South West

Bridgwater - BW

Olympian	34176	34178	34179	34189				
Trident	32843	32844	32872	32873	32874	32930	32935	32936
	32947	32954	32961					
Volvo B6BLE	40570	40584	40585	40586	40588	40590	40591	40592
	40593	40594						
Optare Solo	53602							
Ford Transit	54602							

Ancillary / Reserve / Specials:

Trident	32866

Camborne - CE *Outstations: Falmouth, Helston, Newquay, Padstow, Par, Penzance and Truro*

Mercedes-Benz Citaro	11036	11037	11038	11085	11087			
Volvo B12B	20556	20557	20558	20561	23208			
Scania coach	23009	23313	23316	23317				
Olympian	31820	31821	31826	31828	31830	31836	31841	31846
	31877	34041	34049	34050	34051	34052	34091	34093
	34096	34097	34098	34099	34104	34116	34138	34162
	34172	34173	34177	34181	34182	34183	34184	34185
	34192	34194	34196	34197	34198	34199	34200	34259
	34261	34615	34629					
Trident	32861	32875	32876	32878	32879	32880	33066	33067
Volvo B7TL	32097							
Enviro 400	33658	33659	33660	33661	33662	33664	33665	33666
	33667							

Dart	41132	41383	41490	42235	42255	42430	42469	42470
	42471	42472	42473	42474	42475	42476	42477	42511
	42521	42522	42558	42559	42560	42562	42563	42623
	42719	42720	42725	42801	42802	42842	42843	42860
	42871	42872	42873	42874	42875	42876	42942	42943
	43812							
Optare Solo	50276	50278	50284	50285	50290	50292	53007	53009
	53012	53013	53015	53040	53107	53108	53402	53403
	53404	53503	53504	53701	53709	53801	53803	53805
	53826							
Volvo B10BLE	62194	66126	66127					
Mercedes-Benz	64049	64050						
Scania L94	65579	65759	65760	65761	65762	65763	65764	
Volvo B7RLE	69209	69218	69219	69220	69221	69222	69223	69224
	69225	69226	69227	69228	69229	69230		

Ancillary / Reserve / Specials:

Mercedes-Benz Citaro	11086					
Volvo B10M	20412					
Scania	23008	23013				
Olympian	34137	34195	34626			
Volvo Citybus	38000	38001	38002	38004	38005	38006
Bristol VRT	38706					
Mercedes-Benz	52526	52554				
Bristol Lodekka	90181					

Plymouth - PL - *Outstations: Dartmouth; Tavistock and Torpoint*

Olympian	34003	34092						
Trident	32709	32711	32712	32713	32714	32715	32716	32717
	32751	32752	32753	32754	32755	32756	32757	32758
	32759	32760	32761	32762	32802	32803	32808	32817
	32819	32846	32851	32853	32858	33172	33173	33174
	33175	33176	33177					
Enviro 400	33420	33421	33422					
Dart	40002	40033	40034	40035	40036	40037	42463	42724
	42752	42758	42764	42784	42924	42946	43809	43810
Volvo B6LE	48201	48210	48211	48221	48225	48226	48227	48228
	48229	48231	48232	48233	48234	48261	48262	48263
	48264	48265	48266	48267	48269			
Optare Solo	50277	50279	50291	53011	53014	53154	53205	53827
Volvo B7L	60895	60910	60915	60916	60917	60918		
Volvo B10BLE	62183	62191	62192					

Ancillary / Reserve / Specials:

Scania K114	23201	23202	23204	23303
Dart	40960	42252	42777	
BMC Schoolbus	68571			

Taunton -TN - *Outstation: Minehead*

Scania K114	23010	23012	23014					
Trident	33377	33378	33379	33380	33381	33382		
Volvo B5TL	36300							
Volvo B6LE	40581	40582	40583	48271				
Dart	42526	42527	42832	42841	43811	43821	43822	43823
Enviro 200	44922	44923	44924	45111	45112	45113	45114	45115
StreetLite DF	47535	47536	47537	47538				
Optare Solo	53001							
StreetLite	55101	55102	55103	55104				
Mercedes-Benz	56000	56001						
Volvo B7L	60911							
Volvo B10BLE	60813	60814	62193	62245				
Volvo B7RLE	66745	69012	69013	69017	69018	69206	69207	69208

Ancillary / Reserve / Specials:

Scania K114	23011	
Olympian	34064	
Dart	42833	42835

Cymru

Bridgend - BG

Dart	40795	41230	41265	41381	41385	42328	42330	42331
	42569	42620						
Enviro 200	44568	44570	44582	44583	44584	44585	44586	44590
	44591	44592	44593					
Optare Versa	49002	49003	49004	49005	49006	49007	49008	49009
	49010							

Ancillary / Reserve / Specials:

Dart	41347	41390	42327

Haverfordwest - HV - *Outstations: Narberth and Pembroke*

Dart	42682	42861	42862	42869	42878	42879	42880	42881
	42882	42883	42884					

Port Talbot - PT - *Outstation: Maesteg*

Volvo B7TL	32037	32041	32042	32044				
Dart	41144	41386	41391	41398				
	41399	41489	41718	41719	41727	42412	42575	42595
	42631	42689	42690	42691	42721	42722	42845	43584
	43836	43838	43852	43853				
Enviro 200	44587	44588	44589	44602				
StreetLite	47629	47630	47631	47632	47633	47634	47635	47636
	47637	47638	47639	47640	47641	47642	47661	47662
	47663	47664	63079	63080	63081	63082	63083	63084
	63085	63086	63087	63088	63089	63090	63091	63092
	63093	63094	63095					
Optare Versa	49301	49302	49303	49304	49305	49306	49307	49308
	49309							
StreetLite Max								
Volvo B7RLE	66958	66960	66961	69231	69232	69233	69234	69235
	69236	69237	69238					
BMC Schoolbus	68503							

Ancillary / Reserve / Specials:

Dart	41343	41382	41393	41395

Swansea - RA - *Outstations: Aberystwyth, Ammanford, Carmarthen and Llanelli*

Volvo B7LA	19000	19029	19030	19032	19033	19034	19035	19036
	19037	19038						
Volvo B7R	20323	20324	20325					
Scania K114	23320	23321	23322	23323	23324	23325		
Dart	41392	41491	42600	42601	42602	42603	42604	42605
	42606	42607	42608	42609	42610	42611	42612	42613
	42614	42674	42675	42676	42677	42678	42679	42680
	42681	42683	42684	42685	42686	42687	42688	42692
	42693	42694	42863	42864	42865	42866	42867	42868
	42870	42877	42912	42913	43837	43839	43840	43841
	43850	43851	43901	43902	43903			
Enviro 200	44500	44501	44552	44553	44554	44555	44556	44557
	44558	44559	44573	44574	44575	44576	44577	44578
	44579	44580	44581	44594	44595	44603	44604	44605
	44606	44607	44608	44609	44610	44611	44612	44613
	44614	44615	44616	44617	44618	44619	44620	44621
	44622	44623	44624	44625	44626	44627	44628	44629
	44630	44631	44632	44633	44634	44635	44636	

Optare Solo	53707	53708	53802	53804				
Volvo B10BLE	60621	60626						
Enviro 300	67431	67432	67433	67434	67435	67436	67437	67438
	67439							
Volvo B7RLE	66716	66717	66718	69239	69240	69241	69242	69243
	69244	69249	69250	69251	69252	69301	69302	69303
	69304	69305	69380	69381	69382	69383	69384	
BMC Schoolbus	68506							

Ancillary / Reserve / Specials:

Dart	42596		
Scania coach	23315	23318	23319
BMC Schoolbus	68568	68569	

Aircoach

Belfast - BT

| Setra S415 HD | 24032 | 24033 | 24035 | | | | | |

Dublin Airport - D

Mercedes-Benz Citaro	11073	11074	11075	11076	11077	11078	11079	11080
	11081	11082	11083					
Volvo B12BT	20651	20652	20653	20654	20655	20656	20657	20658
	20659	20660	20661	20662	20663	20664	20665	20666
	20667	20668	20669					
Volvo B11R	20901	20902	20903	20904	20905	20906	20907	20908
	20909	20910	20911	20912	20913	20914	20915	20916
Scania	23501	23502	23503	23504				
Setra S315 GT-HD	24000							
Setra S415 HD	24036	24044	24047					
Mercedes-Benz	64000							
Volvo B7RLE	66994							

First operates a selection of historical buses at special events. A Bristol FLF numbered 90181, 824KDV, is retained in the pre-National Bus livery used by Western National. *Steve Rice*

260ERY	40583	Devon & Cornwall	AU58ECJ	37568	East	BD12TBZ	36231	West Yorkshire
3910WE	37229	South Yorkshire	AU58ECN	37569	East	BD12TCJ	36280	Manchester
481FPO	34194	Devon & Cornwall	AU58ECT	37570	East	BD12TCK	36276	West Yorkshire
510CLT	39810	Hampshire & B	AU58ECV	37571	East	BD12TCO	36275	West Yorkshire
530OHU	34192	Devon & Cornwall	AU58ECW	37572	East	BD12TCU	36233	West Yorkshire
824KDV	90181	Devon & Cornwall	AU58ECX	37573	East	BD12TCV	36232	West Yorkshire
AFJ706T	38706	Devon & Cornwall	AU58ECY	37574	East	BD12TCX	36235	West Yorkshire
AN02EDN	10178	West of England	AU58ECZ	37575	East	BD12TCY	36234	West Yorkshire
AO02ODM	43801	Essex	AU58EDC	37576	East	BD12TCZ	36278	West Yorkshire
AO02ODN	43802	Essex	AU58EDF	37577	East	BD12TDO	36277	West Yorkshire
AO02RBX	20500	Essex	AU58EDJ	37578	East	BD12TDU	36279	Manchester
AO02RBY	20501	Essex	AU58EDK	37579	East	BD12TDV	36274	West Yorkshire
AO02RBZ	20502	Glasgow	AU58FFH	69421	Essex	BD13NFK	69564	West Yorkshire
AO02RCF	20503	Glasgow	AU58FFJ	69422	East	BD13NFL	69563	West Yorkshire
AO02RCU	20504	Glasgow	AU58FFK	69423	East	BD13NFM	69568	West Yorkshire
AO02RCV	20505	Aberdeen	AU58FFL	69424	East	BD13NFN	69567	West Yorkshire
AO02RCX	20506	Aberdeen	AU58FFM	69425	East	BD13NFO	69565	West Yorkshire
AO02RCY	20507	Aberdeen	AU58FFN	69426	East	BD13NFP	69566	West Yorkshire
AO02RCZ	20508	Glasgow	AU58FFO	69427	East	BD13NFR	69569	West Yorkshire
AO02RDU	20509	Glasgow	AU58FFP	69428	East	BD13NFV	69570	West Yorkshire
AU05DME	69005	East	AU58FFR	69429	Essex	BD13OHK	69571	West Yorkshire
AU05DMF	69006	East	AU58FFS	69430	Essex	BD13OHL	69572	West Yorkshire
AU05DMO	69007	East	AU58FFT	69431	Essex	BD13OHN	69573	West Yorkshire
AU05DMV	69008	East	AU58FFV	69432	Essex	BD13OHO	69574	West Yorkshire
AU05DMX	69009	East	AU58FFW	69433	East	BD13OHP	69575	West Yorkshire
AU05DMY	69010	East	AY08EKT	44900	Essex	BD13OHR	69576	West Yorkshire
AU05DMZ	69011	East	B46PJA	30722	West Yorkshire	BD13OHS	69577	West Yorkshire
AU05MUO	32651	Essex	B7FTR	19004	West Yorkshire	BD13OHT	69578	West Yorkshire
AU05MUP	32652	Essex	BD11CDX	36178	East	BF12KWC	69545	Hampshire & B
AU05MUV	32653	East	BD11CDY	36179	East	BF12KWD	69544	Hampshire & B
AU05MUW	32654	Essex	BD11CDZ	36180	East	BF12KWE	69542	Hampshire & B
AU05MUY	32655	East	BD11CEN	69521	Manchester	BF12KWG	69543	Hampshire & B
AU05MVA	32656	East	BD11CEO	69523	Manchester	BF12KWH	69547	Hampshire & B
AU07DXS	37156	Midlands	BD11CEU	69522	Manchester	BF12KWJ	69548	Hampshire & B
AU07DXT	37157	Midlands	BD11CEV	69524	Manchester	BF12KWK	69549	Hampshire & B
AU07DXV	37158	Midlands	BD11CEX	69527	Manchester	BF12KWL	69546	Hampshire & B
AU07DXW	37159	Midlands	BD11CEY	69526	Manchester	BF12KWM	69553	Hampshire & B
AU07DXX	37160	Midlands	BD11CFA	69525	Manchester	BF12KWN	69551	Hampshire & B
AU53HJJ	32475	Essex	BD11CFE	69531	Manchester	BF12KWO	69550	Hampshire & B
AU53HJK	32476	Essex	BD11CFF	69530	Manchester	BF12KWP	69552	Hampshire & B
AU53HJN	32477	Essex	BD11CFG	69528	Manchester	BF12KWR	69555	Hampshire & B
AU53HJO	32478	Essex	BD11CFJ	69529	Manchester	BF12KWS	69554	Hampshire & B
AU53HJV	32479	East	BD11CFK	36166	East	BF12KWU	36249	West Yorkshire
AU53HJX	32480	Essex	BD11CFM	36167	East	BF12KXU	36181	West Yorkshire
AU53HJY	32481	Essex	BD11CFN	36168	East	BF12KXV	36182	West Yorkshire
AU53HJZ	32482	Essex	BD11CFO	36169	East	BF63HDN	69537	Hampshire & B
AU53HKA	32483	Essex	BD11CFP	36170	East	BF63HDO	69539	Hampshire & B
AU53HKB	32484	Essex	BD11CFU	36171	East	BF63HDU	69538	Hampshire & B
AU53HKC	32485	Essex	BD11CFV	36172	East	BF63HDV	37997	Hampshire & B
AU53HKD	32486	East	BD11CFX	36173	East	BF63HDX	37998	Hampshire & B
AU53HKE	32487	East	BD11CFY	36174	East	BF63HDY	37999	Hampshire & B
AU53HKF	32488	East	BD11CFZ	36175	East	BG12UKM	36248	West Yorkshire
AU53HKG	32489	East	BD11CGE	36176	East	BG12YJO	36257	West Yorkshire
AU53HKH	32490	East	BD11CGF	36177	East	BG12YJP	36258	West Yorkshire
AU53HKJ	32491	East	BD12SZY	36222	West Yorkshire	BG12YJR	36259	West Yorkshire
AU53HKK	32492	East	BD12SZZ	36223	West Yorkshire	BG12YJS	36260	West Yorkshire
AU53HKL	32493	East	BD12TAO	36224	West Yorkshire	BG12YJT	36261	West Yorkshire
AU53HKM	32494	East	BD12TAV	36225	West Yorkshire	BG12YJU	36262	West Yorkshire
AU58ECA	37563	East	BD12TBO	36226	West Yorkshire	BG12YJV	36263	West Yorkshire
AU58ECC	37564	East	BD12TBU	36227	West Yorkshire	BG12YJW	36264	West Yorkshire
AU58ECD	37565	East	BD12TBV	36228	West Yorkshire	BG12YJX	36265	West Yorkshire
AU58ECE	37566	East	BD12TBX	36229	West Yorkshire	BG12YJY	36266	West Yorkshire
AU58ECF	37567	East	BD12TBY	36230	West Yorkshire	BG12YJZ	36267	West Yorkshire

Reg	No.	Area	Reg	No.	Area	Reg	No.	Area
BG12YKA	36268	West Yorkshire	BJ12YJH	36251	West Yorkshire	BP11JWC	39222	West Yorkshire
BG12YKB	36269	West Yorkshire	BJ12YJJ	36252	West Yorkshire	BP11JWD	39223	West Yorkshire
BG12YKC	36270	West Yorkshire	BJ12YJK	36253	West Yorkshire	BP11JWE	39224	West Yorkshire
BG12YKD	36271	West Yorkshire	BJ12YJL	36254	West Yorkshire	BP11JWF	39225	West Yorkshire
BG12YKE	36272	West Yorkshire	BJ12YJM	36255	West Yorkshire	BP11JWG	39226	West Yorkshire
BG12YKF	36273	West Yorkshire	BJ12YJN	36256	West Yorkshire	BP11JWJ	39230	West Yorkshire
BG13VUD	69560	West Yorkshire	BJ60BZA	39201	West Yorkshire	BP11JWK	39231	West Yorkshire
BG13VUE	69562	West Yorkshire	BJ60BZB	39202	West Yorkshire	BP11JWL	39227	West Yorkshire
BG13VUG	69561	West Yorkshire	BJ60BZC	39203	West Yorkshire	BP11JWM	39228	West Yorkshire
BG57ZGJ	68571	Devon & Cornwall	BJ60BZD	39204	West Yorkshire	BP11JWN	39229	West Yorkshire
BG58OLR	11101	York	BJ60BZE	39205	West Yorkshire	BP11JWO	39232	West Yorkshire
BG58OLT	11102	York	BJ60BZF	39206	West Yorkshire	BP11JWU	39233	West Yorkshire
BG58OLU	11103	York	BJ63UHZ	69930	Hampshire & B	BP11JWV	39234	West Yorkshire
BG58OLV	11104	York	BJ63UJV	69931	Hampshire & B	BP11JWW	39236	West Yorkshire
BG58OLX	11105	York	BJ63UJW	69932	Hampshire & B	BP11JWX	39235	West Yorkshire
BG58OMA	11106	York	BJ63UJX	69933	Hampshire & B	BT13YVV	69579	West Yorkshire
BG58OMB	11107	York	BJ63UJZ	69934	Hampshire & B	BT13YVW	69580	West Yorkshire
BG58OMC	11108	York	BN02EDN	10179	West of England	BT13YVX	69581	West Yorkshire
BG58OMD	11109	York	BN12JYF	36183	West Yorkshire	BT13YVY	69582	West Yorkshire
BG58OME	11110	York	BN12JYG	36184	West Yorkshire	BT13YVZ	69583	West Yorkshire
BG58OMF	11111	York	BN12JYH	36185	West Yorkshire	BT13YWA	69584	West Yorkshire
BG58OMH	11112	York	BN12JYJ	36186	West Yorkshire	BT13YWB	69585	West Yorkshire
BG58OMJ	11113	York	BN12JYK	36187	West Yorkshire	BT13YWC	69586	West Yorkshire
BG58OMK	11114	York	BN12JYL	36188	West Yorkshire	BT13YWD	69587	West Yorkshire
BG58OML	11115	York	BN12JYO	36189	West Yorkshire	BU04EZF	64020	Hampshire & B
BJ10VGA	69500	West of England	BN12JYP	36190	West Yorkshire	BU04EZG	64021	Hampshire & B
BJ10VGC	69502	West of England	BN12JYR	36191	West Yorkshire	BV13YZZ	69559	West of England
BJ10VGD	69501	West of England	BN12JYS	36192	West Yorkshire	BV13ZBC	69901	Essex
BJ10VGE	69503	West of England	BN12JYT	36193	West Yorkshire	BV13ZBD	69902	Essex
BJ10VGF	69504	West of England	BN12JYU	36194	West Yorkshire	BV13ZBE	69903	Essex
BJ10VGG	69505	West of England	BN12JYV	36195	West Yorkshire	BV13ZBF	69904	Essex
BJ11EBU	69510	West of England	BN12JYW	36196	West Yorkshire	BV13ZBG	69905	Essex
BJ11EBV	69507	West of England	BN12WNX	36197	West Yorkshire	BV13ZBJ	69906	Essex
BJ11EBX	69508	West of England	BN12WNY	36198	West Yorkshire	BV13ZBL	69907	Essex
BJ11EBZ	69511	West of England	BN12WNZ	36199	West Yorkshire	BV13ZBN	69908	Essex
BJ11ECA	69512	Essex	BN12WOA	36200	West Yorkshire	BV13ZBO	69909	Essex
BJ11ECC	69513	Essex	BN12WOB	36201	West Yorkshire	BV13ZBP	69910	Essex
BJ11ECD	69514	Essex	BN12WOC	36202	West Yorkshire	BV13ZBR	69911	Essex
BJ11ECE	69515	Essex	BN12WOD	36203	West Yorkshire	BV13ZBT	69912	Essex
BJ11ECF	69516	Essex	BN12WOH	36204	West Yorkshire	BV13ZBU	69913	Essex
BJ11ECN	69517	Essex	BN12WOJ	36205	West Yorkshire	BV13ZBW	69914	Essex
BJ11ECT	69518	Essex	BN12WOM	36206	West Yorkshire	BV13ZBX	69915	Essex
BJ11ECV	69519	Essex	BN12WOR	36236	West Yorkshire	BV13ZBY	69916	Essex
BJ11ECW	69520	Essex	BN12WOU	36237	West Yorkshire	BV13ZBZ	69917	Essex
BJ11ECX	37987	Hampshire & B	BN12WOV	36238	West Yorkshire	BV13ZCA	69918	Essex
BJ11ECY	37986	Hampshire & B	BN12WOX	36239	West Yorkshire	BV13ZCE	69919	Essex
BJ11XGY	37985	Hampshire & B	BN12WOY	36240	West Yorkshire	BV13ZCF	69920	Hampshire & B
BJ11XHY	69506	West of England	BN12WPA	36241	West Yorkshire	BV13ZCJ	69921	Hampshire & B
BJ11XHZ	69509	West of England	BN12WPD	36242	West Yorkshire	BV13ZCK	69922	Hampshire & B
BJ12PNS	36247	West Yorkshire	BN12WPE	36243	West Yorkshire	BV13ZCL	69923	Hampshire & B
BJ12VNR	36246	West Yorkshire	BN12WPF	36244	West Yorkshire	BV13ZCN	69924	Hampshire & B
BJ12VWO	36207	West Yorkshire	BN12WPJ	36245	West Yorkshire	BV13ZCO	69925	Hampshire & B
BJ12VWP	36208	West Yorkshire	BN61MWE	39207	Manchester	BV13ZCT	69926	Hampshire & B
BJ12VWR	36209	West Yorkshire	BN61MWF	39208	Manchester	BV13ZCU	69927	Hampshire & B
BJ12VWS	36210	West Yorkshire	BN61MWG	39209	Manchester	BV13ZCX	69928	Hampshire & B
BJ12VWT	36211	West Yorkshire	BN61MWJ	39210	Manchester	BV13ZCY	69929	Hampshire & B
BJ12VWU	36212	West Yorkshire	BN61MWK	39211	Manchester	BV13ZDH	69556	West Yorkshire
BJ12VWV	36213	West Yorkshire	BN61MWL	39212	Manchester	BV13ZDJ	69557	West Yorkshire
BJ12VWW	36214	West Yorkshire	BN61MWM	39213	Manchester	BV13ZDK	69558	West Yorkshire
BJ12VWX	36215	West Yorkshire	BN61MWO	39214	Manchester	BV57MSO	68567	West of England
BJ12VWY	36216	West Yorkshire	BN61MWP	39215	Manchester	BV57MSU	68568	Cymru
BJ12VXA	36217	West Yorkshire	BN61MWU	39216	Manchester	BV57MSX	68569	Cymru
BJ12VXB	36218	West Yorkshire	BN61MWV	39217	Manchester	BV57MSY	68570	West of England
BJ12VXC	36219	West Yorkshire	BN61MWW	39218	Manchester	BX02CMK	64029	Manchester
BJ12VXD	36220	West Yorkshire	BN61MWX	39219	Manchester	BX06NZT	68302	Hampshire & B
BJ12VXE	36221	West Yorkshire	BN61MWY	39220	Manchester	BX54UDE	11085	Devon & Cornwall
BJ12YJF	36250	West Yorkshire	BP11JWA	39221	West Yorkshire	BX54UDL	11086	Devon & Cornwall

Reg	No	Region	Reg	No	Region	Reg	No	Region
BX54UDU	11087	Devon & Cornwall	CU54DCE	68513	West of England	EO02FKZ	53111	Hampshire & B
BX54VUN	68503	Cymru	CU54DCF	68514	Scotland East	EO02FLA	53101	West Yorkshire
BX55NZV	68301	Hampshire & B	CU54HYK	42600	Cymru	EO02FLB	53102	West of England
CN06BXF	53830	Midlands	CU54HYL	42601	Cymru	EO02FLC	53103	West of England
CN06BXH	53155	Midlands	CU54HYM	42602	Cymru	EO02FLD	53104	West Yorkshire
CN07HVG	66691	Midlands	CU54HYN	42603	Cymru	EO02FLG	53107	Devon & Cornwall
CN07HVH	66692	Midlands	CU54HYO	42604	Cymru	EO02FLH	53108	Devon & Cornwall
CN07HVJ	66694	Midlands	CU54HYP	42605	Cymru	EO02FLJ	53109	Hampshire & B
CN07HVK	66693	Midlands	CU54HYR	42606	Cymru	EO02FLK	53110	Hampshire & B
CN07KZK	53207	Midlands	CU54HYT	42607	Cymru	EO02NDX	53112	Essex
CN07KZL	53208	Midlands	CU54HYV	42608	Cymru	EO02NDY	53113	Essex
CN07KZM	53209	Midlands	CU54HYW	42609	Cymru	EO02NDZ	53114	Essex
CN57EFB	66695	Midlands	CU54HYX	42610	Cymru	EO02NEF	53115	Essex
CN57EFE	66696	Midlands	CU54HYY	42611	Cymru	EO02NEJ	53116	Essex
CN57EFF	66697	Midlands	CU54HYZ	42612	Cymru	EO02NEN	53117	Essex
CN57HVL	66698	Midlands	CU54HZA	42613	Cymru	EO02NEU	53118	East
CN57HVM	66699	Midlands	CU54HZB	42614	Cymru	EO02NEY	53119	East
CRG325C	31529	Aberdeen	CV55ABK	20357	Scotland East	EO02NFA	53120	East
CU03BHV	42693	Cymru	CV55ABN	20356	Scotland East	EO02NFC	53121	Essex
CU03BHW	42694	Cymru	CV55ACO	20358	Scotland East	EO02NFD	53122	East
CU04AYP	20550	Hampshire & B	CV55ACU	20359	Scotland East	EO02NFE	53123	East
CU04AYS	20551	Hampshire & B	CV55ACX	20360	Scotland East	EO02NFF	53124	East
CU05LGJ	20354	Scotland East	CV55ACY	20361	Scotland East	EO02NFG	53125	Essex
CU05LGK	20355	Scotland East	CV55ACZ	20363	Scotland East	EO02NFH	53126	Essex
CU08ACY	44501	Cymru	CV55AFA	20362	Scotland East	EO02NFJ	53127	Essex
CU08ACZ	44502	Hampshire & B	CV55AFE	20364	Scotland East	EO02NFK	53128	Essex
CU08ADO	44503	Hampshire & B	CV55AFF	20366	Scotland East	EO02NFL	53129	Essex
CU08ADV	44504	Hampshire & B	CV55AGX	20367	Aberdeen	EO02NFM	53130	Essex
CU08ADX	44505	Hampshire & B	CV55AGY	20370	Scotland East	EO02NFN	53131	Essex
CU08ADZ	44506	Hampshire & B	CV55AGZ	20368	Scotland East	EO02NFP	53132	Essex
CU08AHN	69301	Cymru	CV55AHA	20365	Scotland East	EO02NFR	53133	Essex
CU08AHO	69302	Cymru	CV55AMU	20369	Scotland East	EO02NFT	53134	Essex
CU08AHP	69303	Cymru	CV55AMX	20371	Scotland East	EO02NFU	53135	Essex
CU08AHV	69304	Cymru	CV55ANF	20372	Aberdeen	EO02NFV	53136	Essex
CU08AHX	69305	Cymru	CV55ANP	20373	Aberdeen	EO02NFX	53137	Essex
CU53APO	42674	Cymru	CV55AOO	20374	Aberdeen	EU05AUK	42918	Essex
CU53APV	42675	Cymru	D700GHY	38000	Devon & Cornwall	EU05AUL	42919	East
CU53APX	42676	Cymru	D701GHY	38001	Devon & Cornwall	EU05AUM	42920	East
CU53APY	42683	Cymru	D702GHY	38002	Devon & Cornwall	EU05AUN	42921	East
CU53APZ	42682	Cymru	D704GHY	38004	Devon & Cornwall	EU05AUO	42922	Essex
CU53ARF	42681	Cymru	D705GHY	38005	Devon & Cornwall	EU05AUP	42923	Essex
CU53ARO	42680	Cymru	D706GHY	38006	Devon & Cornwall	EU05DXR	68535	Essex
CU53ARX	42679	Cymru	DK57SPZ	44511	Midlands	EU05DXS	68551	Essex
CU53ARZ	42678	Cymru	DK57SXF	44512	Midlands	EU05DXT	68552	Essex
CU53ASO	42677	Cymru	DK57SXG	44513	East	EU06KDK	43877	Midlands
CU53AUO	42685	Cymru	DRZ9713	63180	Midlands	EU08FHB	44928	East
CU53AUP	42684	Cymru	EG52FFJ	43873	Midlands	EU54BNJ	53139	Essex
CU53AUT	42686	Cymru	EG52FFK	43863	East	EU54BNK	53138	Essex
CU53AUV	42687	Cymru	EG52FFL	43869	Midlands	EU58JWZ	69434	Essex
CU53AUW	42688	Cymru	EG52FFT	43870	Midlands	EU60LFS	44596	Essex
CU53AUX	42690	Cymru	EG52FFU	43872	Midlands	EY54BPX	56004	Scotland East
CU53AUY	42691	Cymru	EG52FFV	43871	Midlands	EY54BPZ	56006	Aberdeen
CU53AVB	42692	Cymru	EG52FFY	43874	Midlands	EY54BRV	56007	Aberdeen
CU53AVJ	42861	West Yorkshire	EG52FFZ	43854	Essex	EY54BRX	56008	Aberdeen
CU53AVK	42862	West Yorkshire	EG52FGA	43864	East	EY54BRZ	56009	Aberdeen
CU53AVL	42863	Cymru	EG52FGC	43855	Essex	FJ08FYN	37562	East
CU53AVM	42864	Cymru	EG52FGD	43856	Essex	FJ55KMO	68226	Manchester
CU53AVN	42865	Cymru	EG52FGE	43857	Essex	FJ55KMY	68227	Manchester
CU53AVO	42866	Cymru	EG52FGF	43860	East	FJ55KMZ	68228	Manchester
CU53AVP	42868	Cymru	EG52FGJ	43861	East	FJ55KNB	68225	Manchester
CU53AVR	42867	Cymru	EG52FGK	43862	East	FJ58YSL	44597	Essex
CU53AVT	42870	Cymru	EG52FGU	43865	East	FN08AZZ	67665	Midlands
CU53AVV	42869	West Yorkshire	EG52FGV	43866	East	FN55EDV	68229	Manchester
CU53AVW	42689	Cymru	EG52FGX	43868	East	FSU382	56501	Aberdeen
CU54CYX	68504	Scotland East	EG52FHC	43867	East	FV14FYR	64994	Aberdeen
CU54CYY	68505	West of England	EG52FHD	43859	East	FV14FYS	64995	Aberdeen
CU54CYZ	68506	Cymru	EHO228	90557	Hampshire & B	FV14FZC	64996	Aberdeen

Reg	No	Region	Reg	No	Region	Reg	No	Region
FV14FZD	64997	Aberdeen	JDZ2339	61207	South Yorkshire	KP54LAO	32634	Midlands
G601NWA	61256	Glasgow	JDZ2340	61208	South Yorkshire	KU52RXJ	43810	Devon & Cornwall
G603NWA	60458	South Yorkshire	JDZ2391	61209	South Yorkshire	KV02VVC	66301	East
G605NWA	60460	Midlands	JJD480D	39480	East	KV02VVD	66302	Midlands
G609NWA	60464	Glasgow	K114PRV	66651	West Yorkshire	KV02VVE	66303	Midlands
G613NWA	60466	Glasgow	K125URP	38125	Midlands	KV02VVF	66304	Midlands
G622NWA	60467	West Yorkshire	K615LAE	34615	Devon & Cornwall	KV02VVG	66305	Midlands
G623NWA	60468	West Yorkshire	K626LAE	34626	Devon & Cornwall	KV02VVH	66306	Midlands
G627NWA	60472	West Yorkshire	K629LAE	34629	Devon & Cornwall	KV02VVJ	66307	Midlands
G641NWA	60486	West Yorkshire	K803ORL	34003	Devon & Cornwall	KV02VVK	66308	Midlands
G755XRE	30031	Midlands	KDZ5104	32275	South Yorkshire	KV02VVL	66309	Midlands
HIG1512	32853	Devon & Cornwall	KP51VZO	32066	Midlands	KV02VVM	66310	Midlands
HIG1519	32851	Devon & Cornwall	KP51VZR	32067	Midlands	KV02VVN	66311	Midlands
HIG1521	32872	West of England	KP51VZS	32068	Midlands	KV02VVO	66312	Midlands
HIG1523	32873	West of England	KP51VZT	32069	Midlands	KV02VVP	66313	Midlands
HIG1524	32874	West of England	KP51VZW	32070	Midlands	KV02VVR	66314	Midlands
HIG1525	32875	Devon & Cornwall	KP51VZX	32071	Midlands	KV02VVS	66315	Midlands
HIG1527	32876	Devon & Cornwall	KP51VZY	32072	Midlands	KV02VVT	66316	Midlands
HIG1528	32858	Devon & Cornwall	KP51VZZ	32073	Midlands	KV02VVU	66317	Midlands
HIG1531	32878	Devon & Cornwall	KP51WAJ	32074	Midlands	KV02VVW	66318	Midlands
HIG1533	32879	Devon & Cornwall	KP51WAO	32075	Midlands	KV02VVX	66319	Midlands
HIG1538	32880	Devon & Cornwall	KP51WAU	32076	Midlands	KV02VVY	66320	Midlands
HIG1540	32861	Devon & Cornwall	KP51WBD	32077	Midlands	KV02VVZ	66321	Midlands
HIG8433	53154	Devon & Cornwall	KP51WBG	32078	Midlands	KV02VWA	66322	Midlands
HIG8434	53205	Devon & Cornwall	KP51WBJ	32079	Midlands	KV02VWB	66323	Midlands
HIG8790	40584	Devon & Cornwall	KP51WBK	32080	Midlands	KX05AOC	66972	Midlands
HVJ716	34197	Devon & Cornwall	KP51WBL	32081	Midlands	KX05AOD	66973	Midlands
HX05BUJ	68553	Hampshire & B	KP51WBO	32082	Midlands	KX05AOE	66974	Midlands
HX05BUO	68550	Hampshire & B	KP51WBT	32083	Midlands	KX05MGV	32635	Midlands
HX08DHE	37583	Hampshire & B	KP51WBU	32084	Midlands	KX05MGY	66975	Midlands
HX08DHF	37581	Hampshire & B	KP51WBV	32085	Midlands	KX05MGZ	66976	East
HX08DHG	37584	Hampshire & B	KP51WBY	32086	Midlands	KX05MHA	66977	East
HX08DHJ	37586	Hampshire & B	KP51WBZ	32087	Midlands	KX05MHE	66978	East
HX08DHK	37582	Hampshire & B	KP51WCA	32088	Midlands	KX05MHF	66979	East
HX08DHL	37580	Hampshire & B	KP51WCF	32089	Midlands	KX05MHJ	66980	East
HX08DHY	37585	Hampshire & B	KP51WCG	32090	Midlands	KX05MHK	66981	East
HX55AOH	68562	Hampshire & B	KP51WCJ	32091	Midlands	KX05MHL	66982	East
HX55AOJ	68561	Scotland East	KP51WCN	32092	Midlands	KX05MHM	66983	East
HX55AOK	68563	Hampshire & B	KP51WCO	32093	Midlands	KX05MHN	66984	East
HY07FSU	37164	Hampshire & B	KP51WCR	32094	Midlands	KX05MHO	66985	East
HY07FSV	37162	Hampshire & B	KP51WCW	32095	Midlands	KX05MHU	66986	East
HY07FSX	37165	Hampshire & B	KP51WCX	32096	Midlands	KX05MHV	66987	East
HY07FSZ	37163	Hampshire & B	KP51WCY	32097	Midlands	KX05MHY	66962	Midlands
HY07FTA	37161	Hampshire & B	KP51WDD	32098	Midlands	KX05MHZ	66963	Midlands
HY09AJV	69385	Hampshire & B	KP51WDE	32099	Midlands	KX05MJE	66964	Midlands
HY09AJX	69380	Cymru	KP51WDF	32277	Midlands	KX05MJF	66965	Midlands
HY09AKF	69384	Cymru	KP54AZA	32639	East	KX05MJJ	66966	Midlands
HY09AKG	69381	Cymru	KP54AZB	32640	Essex	KX05MJK	66967	Midlands
HY09AOR	69392	Hampshire & B	KP54AZC	32641	Essex	KX05MJO	66968	Midlands
HY09AOS	69390	Hampshire & B	KP54AZD	32642	Essex	KX05MJU	66969	Midlands
HY09AOT	69388	Hampshire & B	KP54AZF	32643	Midlands	KX05MJV	66970	Midlands
HY09AOU	69382	Cymru	KP54AZG	32644	Midlands	KX05MJY	66971	Midlands
HY09AUO	69389	Hampshire & B	KP54AZJ	32645	Midlands	KX54AHP	68507	Midlands
HY09AUV	69391	Hampshire & B	KP54AZL	32646	Midlands	KX54AHU	68508	Essex
HY09AUW	69387	Hampshire & B	KP54AZN	32647	Midlands	KX54AHY	68509	Essex
HY09AUX	69398	Hampshire & B	KP54AZU	68520	Essex	KX54ANR	68510	Essex
HY09AZA	69383	Cymru	KP54AZV	68521	Essex	KX57BWF	44598	Essex
HY09AZB	69386	Hampshire & B	KP54KAO	32627	Midlands	L204KSX	61351	Manchester
HY09AZC	69394	Hampshire & B	KP54KAU	32628	Essex	L209KSX	61356	Manchester
HY09AZD	69393	Hampshire & B	KP54KAX	32629	East	L212KSX	61359	Manchester
HY09AZF	69395	Hampshire & B	KP54KBE	32630	Midlands	L304VSU	61363	West Yorkshire
HY09AZG	69401	Hampshire & B	KP54KBF	32631	Essex	L305PWR	34305	Essex
HY09AZJ	69400	Hampshire & B	KP54KBJ	32632	Midlands	L306VSU	61365	Manchester
HY09AZL	69397	Hampshire & B	KP54KBK	32648	Midlands	L307VSU	61366	Manchester
HY09AZN	69399	Hampshire & B	KP54KBN	32649	Midlands	L311PWR	34311	Midlands
HY09AZO	69396	Hampshire & B	KP54KBO	32650	Midlands	L637SEU	34137	Devon & Cornwall
J461OVU	60374	Midlands	KP54LAE	32633	Midlands	L638SEU	34138	Devon & Cornwall

The 2015 First Bus Handbook

L650SEU	39920	Hampshire & B	LK08FMC	64043	Hampshire & B	LK53EZA	33381	Devon & Cornwall
L816CFJ	34116	Devon & Cornwall	LK08FMD	64044	Hampshire & B	LK53EZB	33382	Devon & Cornwall
LK03LLX	41493	Midlands	LK08FME	64045	Hampshire & B	LK53EZC	33383	Essex
LK03LLZ	41494	Midlands	LK08FMF	64046	Hampshire & B	LK53EZD	33384	Essex
LK03LME	41495	Midlands	LK08FMG	64047	Hampshire & B	LK53EZE	33385	Essex
LK03LMF	41496	Midlands	LK08FMJ	64048	Hampshire & B	LK53EZF	33386	Glasgow
LK03LMJ	41492	Midlands	LK08FNL	64042	Hampshire & B	LK53EZV	33343	Glasgow
LK03LNE	64018	Hampshire & B	LK51JYO	41414	Glasgow	LK53EZW	33344	Glasgow
LK03LNF	64019	Hampshire & B	LK51UYD	33035	Glasgow	LK53EZX	33345	Glasgow
LK03LNU	41497	Midlands	LK51UYF	33025	Glasgow	LK53EZZ	33346	Glasgow
LK03LNV	41499	Midlands	LK51UYG	33026	Glasgow	LK53FCF	33347	Glasgow
LK03LNW	41500	Midlands	LK51UYH	33027	Glasgow	LK53FCG	33348	Glasgow
LK03LNX	41501	Midlands	LK51UYJ	33028	Glasgow	LK53FCJ	33349	Glasgow
LK03NGE	41512	Midlands	LK51UYL	33029	Scotland East	LK53FCL	33350	Glasgow
LK03NGF	41513	Essex	LK51UYM	33030	Scotland East	LK53FCX	33351	Glasgow
LK03NGG	41514	Midlands	LK51UYN	33031	South Yorkshire	LK53FCY	33352	Glasgow
LK03NGJ	32294	Scotland East	LK51UYO	33032	South Yorkshire	LK53FCZ	33353	Glasgow
LK03NGN	32295	Scotland East	LK51UYP	33033	Glasgow	LK53FDA	33354	Glasgow
LK03NGU	32296	Scotland East	LK51UYR	33034	Glasgow	LK53FDD	41527	Essex
LK03NGV	32297	Scotland East	LK51UYS	33015	Glasgow	LK53FDX	41538	Essex
LK03NGX	32298	Scotland East	LK51UYT	33016	Glasgow	LK53FDY	41539	Essex
LK03NGY	32299	Scotland East	LK51UYU	33017	Glasgow	LK53FDZ	41540	Midlands
LK03NGZ	32300	Glasgow	LK51UYV	33018	Glasgow	LK53FEF	41541	Essex
LK03NHA	32301	Glasgow	LK51UYW	33019	Glasgow	LK53FEG	41542	Essex
LK03NHB	32302	Glasgow	LK51UYX	33020	Glasgow	LK53FEH	41543	Essex
LK03NHC	32303	Glasgow	LK51UYY	33021	Glasgow	LK53FEJ	41544	Essex
LK03NHD	32304	Glasgow	LK51UYZ	33022	Glasgow	LK53LYH	32328	West of England
LK03NHE	32305	Glasgow	LK51UZA	33023	Glasgow	LK53LYJ	32329	West of England
LK03NHH	32308	South Yorkshire	LK51UZB	33024	Glasgow	LK53LYO	32330	West of England
LK03NHJ	32309	South Yorkshire	LK51UZE	33007	East	LK53LYP	32331	West of England
LK03NHL	32310	South Yorkshire	LK51UZF	33008	Glasgow	LK53LYR	32332	West of England
LK03NHM	32311	South Yorkshire	LK51UZG	33009	Glasgow	LK53LYT	32333	West of England
LK03NHN	32312	South Yorkshire	LK51UZH	33010	Glasgow	LK53LYU	32334	West of England
LK03NKN	42519	Essex	LK51UZJ	33011	Glasgow	LK53LYV	32335	West of England
LK03NLD	41502	Midlands	LK51UZL	33012	Glasgow	LK53LYW	32336	West of England
LK03NLN	41498	Midlands	LK51UZM	33013	Glasgow	LK53LYX	32337	West of England
LK03UEX	41520	Midlands	LK51UZN	33014	Glasgow	LK53LYY	32338	West of England
LK03UEY	41521	Midlands	LK51UZO	33001	Essex	LK53LYZ	32339	West of England
LK03UEZ	41522	Midlands	LK51UZP	33002	Essex	LK53LZA	32340	West of England
LK03UFA	41523	Essex	LK51UZS	33003	East	LK53LZB	32341	West of England
LK03UFB	41524	Essex	LK51UZT	33004	East	LK53LZC	32342	West of England
LK03UFC	41525	Essex	LK53EXT	33355	Glasgow	LK53LZD	32343	West of England
LK04HYP	32360	West of England	LK53EXU	33356	Glasgow	LK53LZE	32344	West of England
LK05DXP	53702	Scotland East	LK53EXV	33357	Glasgow	LK53LZF	32345	West of England
LK05DXR	53703	Scotland East	LK53EXW	33358	Glasgow	LK53LZG	32346	West of England
LK05DXS	53704	Scotland East	LK53EXX	33359	Glasgow	LK53LZH	32347	West of England
LK05DXT	53705	Scotland East	LK53EXZ	33360	Glasgow	LK53LZL	32348	Hampshire & B
LK05DXU	53706	Scotland East	LK53EYA	33361	Glasgow	LK53LZM	32349	West of England
LK05DYO	53701	Essex	LK53EYB	33362	Glasgow	LK53LZN	32350	West of England
LK05FCE	68554	Hampshire & B	LK53EYC	33363	Glasgow	LK53LZO	32351	West of England
LK07CCA	64030	Hampshire & B	LK53EYD	33364	Glasgow	LK53LZP	32352	West of England
LK07CCD	64031	Hampshire & B	LK53EYF	33365	Glasgow	LK53LZR	32353	West of England
LK07CCE	64032	Hampshire & B	LK53EYG	33366	Glasgow	LK53LZT	32354	West of England
LK07CCF	64033	Hampshire & B	LK53EYH	33367	Glasgow	LK53LZU	32355	West of England
LK07CCJ	64034	Hampshire & B	LK53EYJ	33368	Glasgow	LK53LZV	32356	West of England
LK07CCN	64035	Hampshire & B	LK53EYL	33369	Glasgow	LK53LZW	32357	West of England
LK07CCO	64036	Hampshire & B	LK53EYM	33370	Glasgow	LK53LZX	32358	West of England
LK07CCU	64037	Hampshire & B	LK53EYO	33371	Glasgow	LK53MBF	32359	West of England
LK07CCV	64038	Hampshire & B	LK53EYP	33372	Glasgow	LK53MBX	53052	Hampshire & B
LK07CCX	64039	Hampshire & B	LK53EYR	33373	Glasgow	LK53MDE	53054	Hampshire & B
LK07CDE	20611	Hampshire & B	LK53EYT	33374	Glasgow	LK53MDF	53055	Hampshire & B
LK07CDF	20612	Hampshire & B	LK53EYU	33375	Glasgow	LK53MDJ	53056	Hampshire & B
LK07CDN	20613	Hampshire & B	LK53EYV	33376	Essex	LK53PNO	53057	Hampshire & B
LK08FKY	33506	Midlands	LK53EYW	33377	Devon & Cornwall	LK54FNC	68531	Essex
LK08FKZ	33507	Midlands	LK53EYX	33378	Devon & Cornwall	LK54FNE	68532	Essex
LK08FLA	33508	Midlands	LK53EYY	33379	Devon & Cornwall	LK54FNF	68536	Hampshire & B
LK08FLX	33504	Midlands	LK53EYZ	33380	Devon & Cornwall	LK54FNH	68537	Hampshire & B

LK54FNJ	68533	Hampshire & B	LN51GLJ	33067	South Yorkshire	LR02LYX	33178	Essex
LK54FNL	68534	Essex	LN51GLK	33068	South Yorkshire	LR02LYY	33179	Hampshire & B
LK55ABU	68558	Scotland East	LN51GLV	33069	South Yorkshire	LR02LYZ	33180	Hampshire & B
LK55ABV	68559	Midlands	LN51GLY	33070	South Yorkshire	LR02LZA	33181	Hampshire & B
LK55ABX	68560	Scotland East	LN51GLZ	33099	South Yorkshire	LR02LZB	33182	Hampshire & B
LK55ABZ	65724	Hampshire & B	LN51GME	33084	South Yorkshire	LR02LZC	33183	Hampshire & B
LK55ACF	65725	Hampshire & B	LN51GMG	33086	Essex	LR02LZD	33184	Essex
LK55ACJ	65726	Hampshire & B	LN51GMO	33087	Essex	LSK570	23401	Aberdeen
LK55ACO	32657	Glasgow	LN51GMU	33088	Essex	LSK571	23402	Aberdeen
LK57EJD	44001	Essex	LN51GMV	33089	Glasgow	LT02NTV	64001	Hampshire & B
LK57EJE	44002	Essex	LN51GMX	33090	Essex	LT02NTX	64002	Hampshire & B
LK57EJF	44003	Essex	LN51GMY	33091	Glasgow	LT02NTY	64003	Scotland East
LK57EJG	44004	Essex	LN51GMZ	33092	Glasgow	LT02NUA	64004	Scotland East
LK57EJJ	44005	Essex	LN51GNF	33077	Essex	LT02NUB	64005	Hampshire & B
LK57EJL	44006	Essex	LN51GNJ	33078	Essex	LT02NUE	64007	Scotland East
LK58ECV	39001	York	LN51GNK	33079	South Yorkshire	LT02NUF	64008	Scotland East
LK58ECW	39002	York	LN51GNP	33080	Essex	LT02NUJ	64010	Scotland East
LK58ECX	39003	York	LN51GNU	33081	Essex	LT02NVL	33122	Glasgow
LK58ECY	39004	York	LN51GNV	33082	South Yorkshire	LT02NVM	33124	South Yorkshire
LK58ECZ	39005	York	LN51GNX	33083	South Yorkshire	LT02NVN	33125	South Yorkshire
LK58EDF	37274	Hampshire & B	LN51GNY	33096	Glasgow	LT02NVO	33126	East
LK58EDJ	37275	Hampshire & B	LN51GNZ	33097	Glasgow	LT02NVP	33127	South Yorkshire
LK58EDL	37276	Hampshire & B	LN51GOA	33098	Essex	LT02NVR	33128	South Yorkshire
LK62FUJ	63039	South Yorkshire	LN51GOC	33072	Essex	LT02NVS	33129	South Yorkshire
LK62HJD	63038	South Yorkshire	LN51GOE	33073	Essex	LT02NVU	33116	Glasgow
LK62HJX	63041	South Yorkshire	LN51GOH	33074	Essex	LT02NVV	33115	Glasgow
LK62HKG	63040	South Yorkshire	LN51GOU	41795	West of England	LT02NVW	33114	Glasgow
LN51DUJ	41446	Glasgow	LN51NRJ	33093	Scotland East	LT02NVX	33113	East
LN51DUU	41447	Glasgow	LN51NRK	33094	Glasgow	LT02NVY	64011	Scotland East
LN51DUV	41448	Glasgow	LN51NRL	33095	Essex	LT02NVZ	33117	Glasgow
LN51DUY	41449	Glasgow	LR02LWW	33141	Hampshire & B	LT02NWA	33118	Glasgow
LN51DVG	33043	Midlands	LR02LWX	33142	Hampshire & B	LT02NWB	33119	Glasgow
LN51DVH	33044	Essex	LR02LWY	33143	Hampshire & B	LT02NWC	33120	Glasgow
LN51DVK	33045	Essex	LR02LWZ	33144	Hampshire & B	LT02NWD	33121	Glasgow
LN51DVL	33046	Glasgow	LR02LXA	33145	Hampshire & B	LT02ZBX	33131	Scotland East
LN51DVM	33047	Essex	LR02LXB	33146	East	LT02ZBY	33132	Essex
LN51DWA	33037	Scotland East	LR02LXC	33147	Hampshire & B	LT02ZBZ	33133	Essex
LN51DWD	33039	Midlands	LR02LXG	33148	Hampshire & B	LT02ZCA	33134	Essex
LN51DWE	33040	Glasgow	LR02LXH	33149	East	LT02ZCE	33135	Scotland East
LN51DWF	33041	South Yorkshire	LR02LXJ	33150	East	LT02ZCF	33136	Essex
LN51DWG	33042	Midlands	LR02LXK	33151	East	LT02ZCJ	32100	East
LN51DWK	41426	Glasgow	LR02LXL	33152	East	LT02ZCK	32101	East
LN51DWY	41415	Glasgow	LR02LXM	33153	Hampshire & B	LT02ZCL	32102	East
LN51DWZ	41416	Glasgow	LR02LXN	33154	East	LT02ZCN	32103	East
LN51DXA	41417	Glasgow	LR02LXO	33155	East	LT02ZCO	32104	East
LN51DXB	41418	Glasgow	LR02LXP	33156	East	LT02ZCU	32105	East
LN51DXD	41420	West of England	LR02LXS	33157	East	LT02ZCV	32106	East
LN51DXE	41421	West of England	LR02LXT	33158	East	LT02ZCX	32108	South Yorkshire
LN51DXF	41422	Glasgow	LR02LXU	33159	East	LT02ZCY	32107	East
LN51DXG	41423	West of England	LR02LXV	33160	East	LT02ZDH	32109	South Yorkshire
LN51GJJ	33057	East	LR02LXW	33161	East	LT02ZDJ	32110	South Yorkshire
LN51GJK	33058	East	LR02LXX	33162	East	LT02ZDK	32111	South Yorkshire
LN51GJO	33059	Scotland East	LR02LXZ	33163	East	LT02ZDL	32112	East
LN51GJU	33060	East	LR02LYA	33164	East	LT02ZDZ	41488	Scotland East
LN51GKA	33071	South Yorkshire	LR02LYC	33165	East	LT02ZFA	41489	Cymru
LN51GKF	33050	Scotland East	LR02LYD	33166	East	LT02ZFB	41490	West of England
LN51GKJ	33052	South Yorkshire	LR02LYF	33167	East	LT02ZFC	41491	Cymru
LN51GKK	33053	Glasgow	LR02LYG	33168	East	LT02ZFJ	33137	Scotland East
LN51GKL	33054	Glasgow	LR02LYJ	33169	East	LT02ZFK	33138	Scotland East
LN51GKO	33055	East	LR02LYK	33170	East	LT02ZFL	33139	Scotland East
LN51GKP	33056	East	LR02LYO	33171	East	LT02ZFM	33140	Scotland East
LN51GKU	33061	South Yorkshire	LR02LYP	33172	Devon & Cornwall	LT52WTE	32200	East
LN51GKV	33062	South Yorkshire	LR02LYS	33173	Devon & Cornwall	LT52WTF	32201	East
LN51GKX	33063	South Yorkshire	LR02LYT	33174	Devon & Cornwall	LT52WTG	32202	East
LN51GKY	33064	South Yorkshire	LR02LYU	33175	Devon & Cornwall	LT52WTJ	32203	East
LN51GKZ	33065	South Yorkshire	LR02LYV	33176	Devon & Cornwall	LT52WTK	32204	East
LN51GLF	33066	South Yorkshire	LR02LYW	33177	Devon & Cornwall	LT52WTL	32205	East

LT52WTM	32206	East	LT52WXG	33229	Essex	MV02VBN	60720	South Yorkshire
LT52WTN	32207	East	LT52WXH	33230	South Yorkshire	MV02VBO	60721	South Yorkshire
LT52WTO	32208	East	LT52WXK	33232	Essex	MV02VBP	60722	South Yorkshire
LT52WTP	32209	East	LT52WXL	64014	Hampshire & B	MV02VBU	61148	East
LT52WTR	32210	East	LT52WXN	64015	Hampshire & B	MV02VBX	66332	East
LT52WTU	32211	East	LT52WXO	64016	Hampshire & B	MV02VBY	66333	East
LT52WTV	32212	East	LT52WXP	64017	Hampshire & B	MV02VBZ	66334	East
LT52WTW	32213	East	LT52XAA	33190	Essex	MV02VCA	66335	East
LT52WTX	32214	East	LT52XAB	33191	Essex	MV02VCC	66336	East
LT52WTY	32215	South Yorkshire	LT52XAC	33192	Essex	MV02VCD	60724	South Yorkshire
LT52WTZ	32216	South Yorkshire	LT52XAE	33194	Essex	MV02VCE	60725	South Yorkshire
LT52WUA	32217	South Yorkshire	LT52XAF	33195	Essex	MV02VCF	60726	South Yorkshire
LT52WUB	32218	South Yorkshire	LT52XAG	33196	Essex	MV02VCG	60727	South Yorkshire
LT52WUC	32219	South Yorkshire	LT52XAL	32227	Scotland East	MV02VCJ	60728	South Yorkshire
LT52WUD	32220	South Yorkshire	LT52XAM	32228	Scotland East	MV02VCK	60729	South Yorkshire
LT52WUE	32221	Scotland East	M406VWW	60944	West Yorkshire	MV02VCL	60730	South Yorkshire
LT52WUG	32222	Scotland East	M504PNA	60299	Hampshire & B	MV02VCM	66337	East
LT52WUH	32223	Scotland East	M506PNA	60301	Manchester	MV02VCN	66338	East
LT52WUJ	32224	Scotland East	M507PNA	60302	Manchester	MV02VCO	66339	East
LT52WUK	32225	Scotland East	M508PNA	60303	Manchester	MV02VCP	66340	East
LT52WUL	32226	Scotland East	M509PNA	60304	Essex	MV02VCT	66341	East
LT52WUV	33244	East	M516PNA	60311	Midlands	MV02VCU	66342	East
LT52WUW	33245	East	M818PGM	64818	Hampshire & B	MV02VCW	66343	West of England
LT52WUX	33246	East	M847DUS	31518	Midlands	MV02VCX	66344	West of England
LT52WUY	33247	East	M967GDU	66652	West Yorkshire	MV02VCY	66345	East
LT52WVA	33248	East	MA51AET	40323	Manchester	MV02VCZ	66346	East
LT52WVB	33186	Essex	MA51AEU	40324	Manchester	MV02VDA	66347	East
LT52WVD	33188	Essex	MA51AEV	40325	Manchester	MV02VDC	66348	East
LT52WVE	33189	Essex	MA51AEW	40326	Manchester	MV02VDD	60731	South Yorkshire
LT52WVF	33237	East	MIG9614	23014	Devon & Cornwall	MV02VDF	60733	South Yorkshire
LT52WVG	33238	East	MK63XAM	47535	Devon & Cornwall	MV02VDG	60734	South Yorkshire
LT52WVH	33239	East	MK63XAN	47536	Devon & Cornwall	MV02VDJ	60735	South Yorkshire
LT52WVJ	33240	East	MK63XAO	47537	Devon & Cornwall	MV02VDK	60736	South Yorkshire
LT52WVL	33242	East	MK63XAP	47538	Devon & Cornwall	MV02VDL	60737	South Yorkshire
LT52WVM	32249	South Yorkshire	ML02OFW	40327	Manchester	MV02VDM	60738	South Yorkshire
LT52WVN	32250	South Yorkshire	ML02OFX	40328	Manchester	MV02VDN	60739	South Yorkshire
LT52WVO	32251	West of England	ML02OFY	40329	Manchester	MV02VDO	60740	South Yorkshire
LT52WVP	32252	West of England	ML02OFZ	40330	Manchester	MV02VDP	60741	South Yorkshire
LT52WVY	32253	West of England	ML02OGA	40331	Manchester	MV02VDR	60742	South Yorkshire
LT52WVZ	32254	West of England	ML02OGB	40332	Manchester	MV02VDT	60743	South Yorkshire
LT52WWA	32255	West of England	ML02OGC	40333	Manchester	MV02VDX	60744	South Yorkshire
LT52WWB	32256	West of England	ML02OGD	40334	Manchester	MV02VDY	60745	South Yorkshire
LT52WWC	32257	West of England	ML02OGE	40335	Manchester	MV02VDZ	66349	Glasgow
LT52WWD	32258	West of England	ML02OGF	40336	Manchester	MV02VEA	66350	West of England
LT52WWE	32259	West of England	MV02VAA	60704	South Yorkshire	MV02VEB	66351	West of England
LT52WWF	32260	South Yorkshire	MV02VAD	60705	South Yorkshire	MV02VEF	66352	West of England
LT52WWG	32261	South Yorkshire	MV02VAE	60706	South Yorkshire	MV02VEH	66353	West of England
LT52WWH	32262	South Yorkshire	MV02VAF	60707	South Yorkshire	MV02VEK	66354	West of England
LT52WWJ	32263	South Yorkshire	MV02VAH	60708	South Yorkshire	MV02VEL	66355	West of England
LT52WWK	32264	South Yorkshire	MV02VAJ	60709	South Yorkshire	MV02VEM	66356	West of England
LT52WWL	32265	South Yorkshire	MV02VAK	60710	South Yorkshire	MV06CXB	69138	Manchester
LT52WWM	32266	South Yorkshire	MV02VAM	60711	South Yorkshire	MV06CZG	69172	Manchester
LT52WWN	32267	South Yorkshire	MV02VAO	60712	South Yorkshire	MV06CZS	69135	Manchester
LT52WWO	32268	South Yorkshire	MV02VAU	60713	South Yorkshire	MV06CZT	69137	Manchester
LT52WWP	32269	South Yorkshire	MV02VAX	66324	East	MV06DWZ	69173	Manchester
LT52WWR	32270	South Yorkshire	MV02VAY	66325	East	MV06DYU	69206	Devon & Cornwall
LT52WWS	32271	South Yorkshire	MV02VBA	66326	East	MX05CBF	66794	Essex
LT52WWU	32272	South Yorkshire	MV02VBB	66327	East	MX05CBU	66795	Essex
LT52WWV	33233	East	MV02VBC	66328	East	MX05CBV	66796	Essex
LT52WWX	33234	East	MV02VBD	66329	East	MX05CBY	66797	Essex
LT52WWY	33235	East	MV02VBE	66330	East	MX05CCA	66798	Essex
LT52WWZ	33236	East	MV02VBF	60714	South Yorkshire	MX05CCD	66799	Essex
LT52WXA	64012	Hampshire & B	MV02VBG	60715	South Yorkshire	MX05CCF	66800	Essex
LT52WXB	64013	Hampshire & B	MV02VBJ	60716	South Yorkshire	MX05CCJ	66801	Essex
LT52WXC	32273	South Yorkshire	MV02VBK	60717	South Yorkshire	MX05CCK	66802	Essex
LT52WXD	32274	South Yorkshire	MV02VBL	60718	South Yorkshire	MX05CCN	66803	Essex
LT52WXF	32276	South Yorkshire	MV02VBM	60719	South Yorkshire			

MX05CCO	66804	Essex	MX05CKC	66871	Manchester	MX06YXP	69183	Glasgow
MX05CCU	66805	Essex	MX05CKD	66872	Manchester	MX06YXR	69184	Glasgow
MX05CCV	66806	Essex	MX05CKE	66873	Manchester	MX06YXS	69213	Hampshire & B
MX05CCY	66807	Essex	MX05CKF	66874	Manchester	MX06YXT	69214	Hampshire & B
MX05CCZ	66808	Essex	MX05CKJ	66876	Manchester	MX07BPY	37279	Manchester
MX05CDE	66809	Essex	MX05CKO	66880	Manchester	MX07BPZ	37280	Manchester
MX05CDF	66810	Essex	MX05CKP	66881	Hampshire & B	MX07BRF	37281	Manchester
MX05CDK	66811	Essex	MX05CLF	66885	Hampshire & B	MX07BRV	37282	Manchester
MX05CDN	66812	Essex	MX06AEB	57000	West of England	MX07BRZ	37283	Manchester
MX05CDO	66813	Essex	MX06VMW	69165	Manchester	MX07BSO	37284	Manchester
MX05CDU	66814	Essex	MX06VMZ	69166	Manchester	MX07BSU	37285	Manchester
MX05CDV	66815	Essex	MX06VNB	69167	Manchester	MX07BSV	37286	Manchester
MX05CDY	66816	Essex	MX06VNC	69168	Manchester	MX07BSY	37287	Manchester
MX05CDZ	66817	Essex	MX06VND	69169	Manchester	MX07BSZ	37288	Manchester
MX05CEA	66818	Essex	MX06VNE	69170	Manchester	MX07BTE	37289	Manchester
MX05CEF	66819	Essex	MX06VNF	69171	Manchester	MX07BTF	37290	Manchester
MX05CEJ	66820	Essex	MX06VNK	69174	Manchester	MX07BTO	37291	Manchester
MX05CEK	66821	Essex	MX06VNL	69155	Manchester	MX07BTU	37292	Manchester
MX05CEO	66822	Essex	MX06VNM	69156	Manchester	MX07BTV	37293	Manchester
MX05CEU	66823	Essex	MX06VNN	69157	Manchester	MX07BTY	37294	Manchester
MX05CEV	66824	Essex	MX06VNO	69158	Manchester	MX07BTZ	37295	Manchester
MX05CEY	66825	Essex	MX06VNP	69159	Manchester	MX07BUA	37296	Manchester
MX05CFA	66826	Essex	MX06VNR	69160	Manchester	MX07BUE	37297	Manchester
MX05CFD	66827	Essex	MX06VNS	69161	Manchester	MX07BUF	37298	Manchester
MX05CFE	66828	Essex	MX06VNT	69162	Manchester	MX07BUH	37299	Manchester
MX05CFG	66829	Essex	MX06VNU	69163	Manchester	MX07BUJ	37300	Manchester
MX05CFJ	66830	Essex	MX06VNV	69164	Manchester	MX07BUU	37303	Manchester
MX05CFK	66831	Manchester	MX06VNW	69145	Manchester	MX07BUV	37304	Manchester
MX05CFL	66832	Manchester	MX06VNY	69146	Manchester	MX07OZD	44514	Midlands
MX05CFM	66833	Manchester	MX06VNZ	69147	Manchester	MX09GXY	37469	Manchester
MX05CFN	66834	Manchester	MX06VOA	69148	Manchester	MX09GXZ	37470	Manchester
MX05CFO	66835	Manchester	MX06VOB	69149	Manchester	MX09GYA	37549	Manchester
MX05CFP	66836	Manchester	MX06VOC	69150	Manchester	MX09GYB	37552	Manchester
MX05CFU	66837	Essex	MX06VOD	69151	Manchester	MX09GYC	37548	Manchester
MX05CFV	66838	Midlands	MX06VOF	69152	Manchester	MX09GYD	37550	Manchester
MX05CFY	66839	Midlands	MX06VOG	69153	Manchester	MX09GYE	37545	Manchester
MX05CGE	66840	Midlands	MX06VOH	69154	Manchester	MX09GYF	37553	Manchester
MX05CGF	66841	Midlands	MX06VOP	69139	Manchester	MX09GYG	37471	Manchester
MX05CGG	66842	Midlands	MX06VOU	69141	Manchester	MX09GYH	37554	Manchester
MX05CGK	66843	Midlands	MX06VOV	69142	Manchester	MX09GYJ	37546	Manchester
MX05CGO	66844	Manchester	MX06VOY	69143	Manchester	MX09GYK	37547	Manchester
MX05CGU	66845	Midlands	MX06VPA	69144	Manchester	MX09HUK	37551	Manchester
MX05CGV	66846	Manchester	MX06VPC	69203	Manchester	MX09HUO	37557	Manchester
MX05CGY	66847	Midlands	MX06VPD	69204	Manchester	MX09HUP	37559	Manchester
MX05CGZ	66848	Manchester	MX06VPE	69205	Manchester	MX09HUU	37558	Manchester
MX05CHC	66849	Midlands	MX06VPG	69207	Devon & Cornwall	MX09LMF	37560	Manchester
MX05CHD	66850	East	MX06VPJ	69208	Devon & Cornwall	MX09LMJ	37561	Manchester
MX05CHF	66851	Midlands	MX06VPK	69209	Devon & Cornwall	MX09LMK	37555	Manchester
MX05CHG	66852	Midlands	MX06VPL	69210	Hampshire & B	MX09LML	37556	Manchester
MX05CHH	66853	Manchester	MX06VPM	69211	Hampshire & B	MX10DXU	44515	Midlands
MX05CHJ	66854	Manchester	MX06VPN	69212	Hampshire & B	MX54GZA	53143	Manchester
MX05CHK	66855	Manchester	MX06VPO	69175	Manchester	MX54GZB	53144	Manchester
MX05CHL	66856	Manchester	MX06VPP	69176	Manchester	MX54GZC	53145	Manchester
MX05CHN	66857	Manchester	MX06VPR	69195	Manchester	MX54GZD	53146	Manchester
MX05CHO	66858	Manchester	MX06VPT	69196	Manchester	MX54GZE	53147	Manchester
MX05CHV	66859	Manchester	MX06VPU	69197	Manchester	MX54GZF	53148	Manchester
MX05CHY	66860	Manchester	MX06VPV	69198	Manchester	MX54GZG	53149	Manchester
MX05CHZ	66861	Manchester	MX06VPW	69199	Manchester	MX54GZH	53150	Manchester
MX05CJE	66862	Manchester	MX06VPY	69200	Manchester	MX55FFD	66894	Manchester
MX05CJF	66863	Manchester	MX06VPZ	69201	Manchester	MX55FFE	66895	Manchester
MX05CJJ	66864	Manchester	MX06VRC	69202	Manchester	MX55FFG	66896	Manchester
MX05CJO	66865	Manchester	MX06YXJ	69177	Manchester	MX55FFH	66897	Manchester
MX05CJU	66866	Manchester	MX06YXK	69178	Manchester	MX55FFJ	66898	Manchester
MX05CJV	66867	Manchester	MX06YXL	69179	Manchester	MX55FFK	66899	Manchester
MX05CJY	66868	Manchester	MX06YXM	69180	Manchester	MX55FFL	66900	Manchester
MX05CJZ	66869	Manchester	MX06YXN	69181	Glasgow	MX55FFM	66901	Manchester
MX05CKA	66870	Manchester	MX06YXO	69182	Glasgow	MX55FFO	66902	Manchester

Reg	No.	Location	Reg	No.	Location	Reg	No.	Location
MX55FFP	66903	Manchester	MX56AFJ	69235	Cymru	MX58DYH	37416	Manchester
MX55FFR	66904	Manchester	MX56AFK	69236	Cymru	MX58DYJ	37417	Manchester
MX55FFS	66905	Manchester	MX56AFN	69237	Cymru	MX58DYM	37418	Manchester
MX55FFT	66906	Manchester	MX56AFO	69238	Cymru	MX58DYN	37419	Manchester
MX55FFU	66907	Manchester	MX56AFU	69239	Cymru	MX58DYO	37420	Manchester
MX55FFV	66908	Manchester	MX56AFV	69240	Cymru	MX58DYP	37421	Manchester
MX55FFW	66909	Manchester	MX56AFY	69241	Cymru	MX58DYS	37422	Manchester
MX55FFY	66910	Manchester	MX56AFZ	69242	Cymru	MX58DYT	37423	Manchester
MX55FFZ	66911	Manchester	MX56AGO	69243	Cymru	MX58DYU	37424	Manchester
MX55FGA	66912	Manchester	MX56AGU	69244	Cymru	MX58DYV	37425	Manchester
MX55FGC	66913	Manchester	MX56HXZ	42940	Manchester	MX58DYW	37426	Manchester
MX55FGE	66914	Manchester	MX56HYO	43875	Midlands	MX58DYY	37427	Manchester
MX55FGF	66915	Manchester	MX56HYP	43876	Midlands	MX58DZA	37428	Manchester
MX55FGG	66916	Manchester	MX56NLJ	53828	Midlands	MX58DZB	37429	Manchester
MX55FGJ	66917	Manchester	MX56NLK	53829	Midlands	MX58DZC	37430	Manchester
MX55FGK	66918	Manchester	MX57HDZ	37301	Manchester	MX58DZD	37431	Manchester
MX55FGM	66919	Manchester	MX57HEJ	37302	Manchester	MX58DZE	37432	Manchester
MX55FGN	66920	Manchester	MX58AVP	53709	Devon & Cornwall	MX58DZF	37433	Manchester
MX55FGP	66922	Manchester	MX58DVU	37367	Manchester	MX58DZG	37434	Manchester
MX55FGU	66923	Manchester	MX58DVV	37368	Manchester	MX58DZH	37435	Manchester
MX55FHC	66928	Manchester	MX58DVW	37369	Manchester	MX58DZJ	37436	Manchester
MX55FHD	66929	Manchester	MX58DVY	37370	Manchester	MX58DZK	37437	Manchester
MX55FHE	66930	Manchester	MX58DVZ	37371	Manchester	MX58DZL	37438	Manchester
MX55FHF	66931	Manchester	MX58DWA	37372	Manchester	MX58DZN	37439	Manchester
MX55FHH	66933	Manchester	MX58DWC	37373	Manchester	MX58DZO	37440	Manchester
MX55HHO	66884	Hampshire & B	MX58DWD	37374	Manchester	MX58DZP	37441	Manchester
MX55HHP	66883	Hampshire & B	MX58DWE	37375	Manchester	MX58DZR	37442	Manchester
MX55HHR	66882	Hampshire & B	MX58DWF	37376	Manchester	MX58DZS	37443	Manchester
MX55LDJ	66892	Manchester	MX58DWG	37377	Manchester	MX58DZT	37444	Manchester
MX55LDK	66893	Manchester	MX58DWJ	37378	Manchester	MX58DZU	37445	Manchester
MX55LHL	66886	Hampshire & B	MX58DWK	37379	Manchester	MX58DZV	37446	Manchester
MX55NWC	68556	Scotland East	MX58DWL	37380	Manchester	MX58DZW	37447	Manchester
MX55NWD	68557	Hampshire & B	MX58DWM	37381	Manchester	MX58DZY	37448	Manchester
MX55NWE	66875	Manchester	MX58DWN	37382	Manchester	MX58DZZ	37449	Manchester
MX55NWH	66890	Manchester	MX58DWO	37383	Manchester	MX58EAA	37450	Manchester
MX55NWS	68555	Essex	MX58DWP	37384	Manchester	MX58EAC	37451	Manchester
MX55UAA	66891	Manchester	MX58DWU	37385	Manchester	MX58EAF	37452	Manchester
MX56ACV	69185	Manchester	MX58DWV	37386	Manchester	MX58EAG	37453	Manchester
MX56ACY	69186	Manchester	MX58DWW	37387	Manchester	MX58EAJ	37454	Manchester
MX56ACZ	69187	Glasgow	MX58DWY	37388	Manchester	MX58EAK	37455	Manchester
MX56ADO	69188	Glasgow	MX58DWZ	37389	Manchester	MX58EAM	37456	Manchester
MX56ADU	69189	Glasgow	MX58DXA	37390	Manchester	MX58EAO	37457	Manchester
MX56ADV	69190	Glasgow	MX58DXB	37391	Manchester	MX58EAP	37458	Manchester
MX56ADZ	69191	Glasgow	MX58DXC	37392	Manchester	MX58EAY	37459	Manchester
MX56AEA	69192	Glasgow	MX58DXD	37393	Manchester	MX58EBA	37460	Manchester
MX56AEB	69193	Glasgow	MX58DXE	37394	Manchester	MX58EBC	37461	Manchester
MX56AEC	69194	Glasgow	MX58DXF	37395	Manchester	MX58EBD	37462	Manchester
MX56AED	69215	Hampshire & B	MX58DXG	37396	Manchester	MX58EBF	37463	Manchester
MX56AEE	69216	Hampshire & B	MX58DXH	37397	Manchester	MX58EBG	37464	Manchester
MX56AEF	69217	Hampshire & B	MX58DXJ	37398	Manchester	MX58EBK	37465	Manchester
MX56AEG	69218	Devon & Cornwall	MX58DXK	37399	Manchester	MX58EBL	37466	Manchester
MX56AEJ	69219	Devon & Cornwall	MX58DXL	37400	Manchester	MX58EBM	37467	Manchester
MX56AEK	69220	Devon & Cornwall	MX58DXM	37401	Manchester	MX58EBN	37468	Manchester
MX56AEL	69221	Devon & Cornwall	MX58DXO	37402	Manchester	MX58KZA	53707	Cymru
MX56AEM	69222	Devon & Cornwall	MX58DXP	37403	Manchester	MX58KZB	53708	Cymru
MX56AEN	69223	Devon & Cornwall	MX58DXR	37404	Manchester	N212WRD	42412	Cymru
MX56AEO	69224	Devon & Cornwall	MX58DXS	37405	Manchester	N324ECR	46324	Hampshire & B
MX56AEP	69225	Devon & Cornwall	MX58DXT	37406	Manchester	N325ECR	46325	Hampshire & B
MX56AET	69226	Devon & Cornwall	MX58DXU	37407	Manchester	N345CJA	48045	Glasgow
MX56AEU	69227	Devon & Cornwall	MX58DXV	37408	Manchester	N521WVR	60316	Midlands
MX56AEV	69228	Devon & Cornwall	MX58DXW	37409	Manchester	N522WVR	60317	Midlands
MX56AEW	69229	Devon & Cornwall	MX58DXZ	37410	Manchester	N527WVR	60322	Manchester
MX56AEY	69230	Devon & Cornwall	MX58DYA	37411	Manchester	N528LHG	34258	Hampshire & B
MX56AEZ	69231	Cymru	MX58DYC	37412	Manchester	N533LHG	34259	Devon & Cornwall
MX56AFA	69232	Cymru	MX58DYD	37413	Manchester	N542LHG	34261	Devon & Cornwall
MX56AFE	69233	Cymru	MX58DYF	37414	Manchester	N542WVR	60337	Hampshire & B
MX56AFF	69234	Cymru	MX58DYG	37415	Manchester	N545WVR	60340	Midlands

Reg	No	Location	Reg	No	Location	Reg	No	Location
N946SOS	31435	Glasgow	R127GSF	61245	Midlands	R622CVR	60377	Manchester
NDZ3162	61210	South Yorkshire	R131FUP	42631	Cymru	R622JUB	30802	West Yorkshire
NDZ3164	61211	South Yorkshire	R147GSF	65527	Essex	R624CVR	60379	Manchester
NER621	34199	Devon & Cornwall	R162TLM	41162	West of England	R625CVR	60380	Manchester
NML623E	39623	East	R176HUG	30808	West Yorkshire	R625JUB	30805	West Yorkshire
OIG1788	62138	Devon & Cornwall	R177GSX	60135	Essex	R626CVR	60381	Manchester
OIG1791	62191	Devon & Cornwall	R179GSX	60136	Midlands	R626JUB	30806	West Yorkshire
OIG1792	62192	Devon & Cornwall	R241LGH	31841	Devon & Cornwall	R629JUB	30809	West Yorkshire
OIG1793	62193	West of England	R241SBA	40367	Midlands	R630JUB	30810	West Yorkshire
OIG1795	62245	Devon & Cornwall	R247SBA	40373	Midlands	R631CVR	60386	Manchester
OIG1799	54602	Devon & Cornwall	R249SBA	40375	Midlands	R631JUB	30811	West Yorkshire
OO06FTR	19006	West Yorkshire	R252SBA	40378	Midlands	R632JUB	30812	West Yorkshire
OWB243	34196	Devon & Cornwall	R261DVF	65561	Midlands	R633JUB	30813	West Yorkshire
OWJ782A	90092	South Yorkshire	R264DVF	65564	Midlands	R634JUB	30814	West Yorkshire
P106MFS	61478	Glasgow	R277LGH	31877	Devon & Cornwall	R636HYG	30816	West Yorkshire
P126NLW	40173	Midlands	R277SBA	40403	Manchester	R636JUB	30815	West Yorkshire
P132NLW	41132	Devon & Cornwall	R278LGH	31878	Devon & Cornwall	R637HYG	30817	West Yorkshire
P144NLW	41144	Cymru	R299GHS	40795	Cymru	R638DUS	40820	Glasgow
P176NAK	20418	Hampshire & B	R312GHS	40805	Midlands	R638HYG	30818	West Yorkshire
P177NAK	20417	Hampshire & B	R331GHS	62157	Scotland East	R641HYG	30821	West Yorkshire
P190TGD	30560	Scotland East	R334GHS	62159	Glasgow	R642HYG	30822	West Yorkshire
P191TGD	34290	Scotland East	R336LGH	31836	Devon & Cornwall	R643HYG	30823	West Yorkshire
P196TGD	30744	Scotland East	R339GHS	61241	Manchester	R646HYG	30826	Scotland East
P197TGD	30745	Scotland East	R340GHS	61240	Manchester	R647DUS	40827	Hampshire & B
P203TGD	30750	Scotland East	R346LGH	31846	Devon & Cornwall	R652HYG	30832	Scotland East
P204TGD	30751	Scotland East	R346SUT	60011	Midlands	R655DUS	31497	Scotland East
P241UCW	34041	Devon & Cornwall	R411WPX	42511	Devon & Cornwall	R662NHY	34162	Devon & Cornwall
P244UCW	34044	Hampshire & B	R421WPX	42521	Devon & Cornwall	R672DUS	40835	West of England
P248UCW	34048	Scotland East	R422WPX	42522	Devon & Cornwall	R679MEW	43679	Essex
P249UCW	34049	Devon & Cornwall	R423WPX	42523	Devon & Cornwall	R680DPW	43480	Essex
P250UCW	34050	Devon & Cornwall	R424WPX	42524	Hampshire & B	R683DPW	43483	Essex
P251UCW	34051	Devon & Cornwall	R426WPX	42526	Devon & Cornwall	R685DPW	43485	Essex
P252UCW	34052	Devon & Cornwall	R427WPX	42527	West of England	R701BAE	42701	West of England
P264PAE	46264	West of England	R437GSF	61057	Essex	R703BAE	42703	West of England
P295KPX	34295	Hampshire & B	R438ALS	60075	Midlands	R704BAE	42704	West of England
P430ORL	42430	Devon & Cornwall	R443ULE	31943	Manchester	R705BAE	42705	West of England
P436YSH	61056	West Yorkshire	R447CCV	42447	Essex	R706BAE	42706	West of England
P439ORL	42439	Essex	R451JSG	61065	West Yorkshire	R707BAE	42707	West of England
P448NEX	43448	Essex	R453JFS	61067	West Yorkshire	R708BAE	42708	West of England
P452SCV	42252	Devon & Cornwall	R454JFS	61068	West Yorkshire	R709BAE	42709	West of England
P455SCV	42255	Devon & Cornwall	R457JFS	61071	West Yorkshire	R710BAE	42710	West of England
P535EFL	34015	Scotland East	R458JFS	61072	West Yorkshire	R711BAE	42711	West of England
P536EFL	34016	Hampshire & B	R460JFS	61074	West Yorkshire	R712BAE	42712	West of England
P540EFL	34017	Hampshire & B	R460VOP	66100	West of England	R714DJN	43714	Essex
P559EFL	34059	Hampshire & B	R463CCV	42463	Devon & Cornwall	R717DJN	43717	Essex
P564EFL	34064	Devon & Cornwall	R466CAH	43466	East	R718BAE	42718	West of England
P569BTH	42569	Cymru	R474CAH	43474	Essex	R719DJN	43719	Essex
P575BTH	42575	Cymru	R556CNG	65556	Essex	R719RAD	42719	Devon & Cornwall
P575EFL	34075	Scotland East	R571YNC	60361	South Yorkshire	R721DJN	43721	Essex
P579EFL	34079	Hampshire & B	R578SBA	60368	South Yorkshire	R781WKW	60618	East
P588WSU	31684	Scotland East	R579SBA	60369	Manchester	R784WKW	60621	Cymru
P613WSU	31677	West Yorkshire	R581SBA	60371	Manchester	R785WKW	60622	East
P632CGM	40911	Scotland East	R584SWN	43584	Cymru	R789WKW	60626	Cymru
P732NVG	20122	East	R585SBA	62216	Manchester	R790WKW	60627	South Yorkshire
P908RYO	31828	Devon & Cornwall	R586SBA	62217	Manchester	R813HWS	20457	Hampshire & B
P920RYO	31820	Devon & Cornwall	R589SBA	62143	East	R901BOU	66101	West Yorkshire
P921RYO	31821	Devon & Cornwall	R595SWN	42595	Cymru	R902BOU	66102	West of England
P926RYO	31826	Devon & Cornwall	R596SWN	42596	Cymru	R904BOU	66104	West of England
P930RYO	31830	Devon & Cornwall	R609YCR	42109	West of England	R905BOU	66109	West of England
PL05UBR	69533	Essex	R611JUB	30791	West Yorkshire	R906BOU	66106	West of England
PL05UBS	69532	Essex	R613YCR	42113	Hampshire & B	R907BOU	66107	West of England
PSU628	23305	Aberdeen	R614YCR	42114	West of England	R908BOU	66108	West of England
PSU629	23306	Aberdeen	R615YCR	42115	West of England	R909BOU	66109	West of England
PSU627	23330	Aberdeen	R616JUB	30796	West Yorkshire	R910BOU	66110	West of England
PT59JPT	67699	Midlands	R620JUB	30800	West Yorkshire	R912BOU	66112	East
Q275LBA	68000	Aberdeen	R620YCR	42120	West of England	R915BOU	66115	West of England
R120FUP	42620	Cymru	R621CVR	60376	Manchester	R916BOU	66116	West of England

The 2015 First Bus Handbook

Reg	No	Location	Reg	No	Location	Reg	No	Location
R917BOU	66117	West of England	S30FTR	19034	Cymru	S677AAE	34177	Devon & Cornwall
R918BOU	66118	West of England	S312SCV	20412	Devon & Cornwall	S677SNG	42777	Devon & Cornwall
R920COU	66120	West of England	S338TJX	40960	Devon & Cornwall	S677SVU	60820	West Yorkshire
R921WOE	31760	West Yorkshire	S343EWU	42643	West of England	S678AAE	34178	West of England
R922WOE	31761	West Yorkshire	S343SUX	40033	West of England	S679AAE	34179	West of England
R923WOE	31762	West Yorkshire	S344SUX	40956	West of England	S680BFS	61235	Midlands
R924WOE	31763	West Yorkshire	S348MFP	60012	Midlands	S681AAE	34181	Devon & Cornwall
R925WOE	31764	West Yorkshire	S350MFP	60006	Midlands	S681BFS	61237	Midlands
R926WOE	31765	West Yorkshire	S351NPO	66151	Hampshire & B	S682AAE	34182	Devon & Cornwall
R928WOE	31806	West Yorkshire	S352NPO	66152	Hampshire & B	S683AAE	34183	Devon & Cornwall
R929WOE	31807	West Yorkshire	S353NPO	66153	Hampshire & B	S684AAE	34184	Devon & Cornwall
R930WOE	31766	West Yorkshire	S354NPO	66154	Hampshire & B	S684SNG	42784	Devon & Cornwall
R931WOE	31767	West Yorkshire	S356XCR	66156	Hampshire & B	S685AAE	34185	Devon & Cornwall
R932YOV	31768	West Yorkshire	S357XCR	66157	Hampshire & B	S686AAE	34186	East
R933YOV	31769	West Yorkshire	S358XCR	66158	Hampshire & B	S688AAE	34188	West of England
R934YOV	31770	West Yorkshire	S359XCR	66159	West of England	S689AAE	34189	West of England
R935YOV	31771	West Yorkshire	S360XCR	66160	West of England	S690BFS	61145	Midlands
R936YOV	31808	West Yorkshire	S361MFP	61143	Midlands	S70FTR	19038	Cymru
R938YOV	31773	West Yorkshire	S361XCR	66161	West of England	S720AFB	42720	Devon & Cornwall
R939YOV	31774	West Yorkshire	S362XCR	66162	West of England	S721AFB	42721	Cymru
R940YOV	31775	West Yorkshire	S363XCR	66163	West of England	S722AFB	42722	Cymru
RA04YGX	54601	West of England	S372SUX	40957	Hampshire & B	S723AFB	42723	West of England
RD51FKV	68001	Hampshire & B	S374SUX	40034	Devon & Cornwall	S723KNV	42623	Devon & Cornwall
RD51FKW	68002	Hampshire & B	S375SUX	40035	Devon & Cornwall	S724AFB	42724	Devon & Cornwall
RD51FKZ	68003	Hampshire & B	S376SUX	40036	Devon & Cornwall	S725AFB	42725	Devon & Cornwall
RD51FLA	68004	Hampshire & B	S377SUX	40037	Devon & Cornwall	S731TWC	43731	Essex
RG1173	62121	Aberdeen	S40FTR	19035	Cymru	S733TWC	43733	Essex
RG51FWZ	41403	Hampshire & B	S50FTR	19036	Cymru	S734TWC	43734	Essex
RG51FXA	41404	West of England	S526RWP	52526	Devon & Cornwall	S735TWC	43735	Essex
RG51FXB	41405	Glasgow	S549SCV	43809	Devon & Cornwall	S736TWC	43736	Essex
RG51FXC	41406	Glasgow	S554RWP	52554	Devon & Cornwall	S764RNE	40002	Devon & Cornwall
RG51FXD	41407	Glasgow	S565TPW	65565	Essex	S791RWG	66191	Manchester
RG51FXE	41408	Glasgow	S566TPW	65566	Essex	S792RWG	66192	Manchester
RG51FXF	41409	Glasgow	S567TPW	65567	Midlands	S793RWG	66193	Manchester
RG51FXH	41410	Glasgow	S568TPW	65568	Midlands	S794RWG	66194	Manchester
RKZ4760	66993	West of England	S572TPW	65572	Midlands	S795RWG	66195	Manchester
RKZ4761	66992	West of England	S573TPW	65573	Essex	S796RWG	66196	Hampshire & B
RL02FYX	90489	West Yorkshire	S574TPW	65574	Essex	S797RWG	66197	Hampshire & B
RT09JPT	45119	East	S60FTR	19037	Cymru	S798RWG	66198	Hampshire & B
RX54AOV	68511	Hampshire & B	S625KTP	42125	Hampshire & B	S799RWG	66199	Hampshire & B
RX54AOY	68512	Hampshire & B	S630KTP	42130	Hampshire & B	S801RWG	66201	Hampshire & B
RX54OGZ	68522	Hampshire & B	S633KTP	42133	Hampshire & B	S802RWG	66202	Hampshire & B
S100FTR	19029	Cymru	S636XCR	42136	Hampshire & B	S803RWG	66203	Hampshire & B
S101TNB	60081	Midlands	S637XCR	42137	Hampshire & B	S804RWG	66204	Hampshire & B
S103TNB	60013	Midlands	S638XCR	42138	Hampshire & B	S805RWG	66205	Hampshire & B
S105TNB	60128	Midlands	S639XCR	42139	Hampshire & B	S806RWG	66206	West of England
S106TNB	60015	Midlands	S640XCR	42140	Hampshire & B	S807RWG	66207	West of England
S10FTR	19030	Cymru	S642XCR	42142	Hampshire & B	S809RWG	61289	West Yorkshire
S110TNB	60163	Scotland East	S652SNG	42752	Devon & Cornwall	S80FTR	19033	Cymru
S112TNB	60165	Scotland East	S653SNG	42754	West of England	S810RWG	60628	West Yorkshire
S113TNB	60166	Scotland East	S654FWY	30834	West Yorkshire	S812RWG	60630	South Yorkshire
S115TNB	60168	Scotland East	S658RNA	60807	East	S813RWG	60631	South Yorkshire
S116JTP	66126	Midlands	S658SNG	42758	Devon & Cornwall	S814RWG	60632	South Yorkshire
S117JTP	66127	Devon & Cornwall	S659RNA	60808	East	S815AEH	60057	Midlands
S118JTP	66128	Hampshire & B	S664RNA	60813	East	S817AEH	60059	Midlands
S120JTP	66130	Hampshire & B	S664SNG	42764	Devon & Cornwall	S818KPR	42818	Hampshire & B
S121JTP	66131	Hampshire & B	S665AAE	34165	Hampshire & B	S820AEH	60062	Midlands
S122UOT	66122	Hampshire & B	S665RNA	60814	East	S821AEH	60063	Midlands
S206LLO	34206	Manchester	S667AAE	34167	Devon & Cornwall	S821KPR	42821	Hampshire & B
S209LLO	34209	Manchester	S668AAE	34168	Hampshire & B	S822KPR	42822	Hampshire & B
S20FTR	19032	Cymru	S668RNA	60816	West of England	S823KPR	42823	Hampshire & B
S210LLO	34210	Manchester	S672AAE	34172	Devon & Cornwall	S824WYD	42824	West of England
S211LLO	34211	West Yorkshire	S672SVU	62118	West Yorkshire	S90FTR	19000	Cymru
S214LLO	34214	West Yorkshire	S673AAE	34173	Devon & Cornwall	S925AKS	31656	Scotland East
S244KLM	41244	Glasgow	S673SVU	62214	Manchester	SA02BZD	61587	Glasgow
S247CSF	40175	Midlands	S676AAE	34176	West of England	SA02BZE	61588	Glasgow
S251CSF	40899	Scotland East	S676SVU	60819	West Yorkshire	SA02BZF	61589	Glasgow

SA02BZG	61590	Glasgow	SF06GYB	69066	Glasgow	SF07FDJ	37176	Glasgow
SA02BZH	61591	Glasgow	SF06GYC	69067	Glasgow	SF07FDK	37177	Glasgow
SA02BZJ	61592	Glasgow	SF06GYD	69068	Glasgow	SF07FDL	37178	Glasgow
SA02BZK	61593	Glasgow	SF06GYE	69069	Glasgow	SF07FDM	37179	Glasgow
SA02BZL	61594	Glasgow	SF06GYG	69070	Glasgow	SF07FDN	37180	Glasgow
SA02BZM	61595	Glasgow	SF06GYH	69071	Glasgow	SF07FDO	37181	Glasgow
SA02BZN	61596	Glasgow	SF06GYJ	69078	Glasgow	SF07FDP	37182	Glasgow
SB14EBG	47573	Hampshire & B	SF06GYK	69079	Glasgow	SF07FDU	37183	Glasgow
SB14EBJ	47574	Hampshire & B	SF06GYN	69080	Glasgow	SF07FDV	37184	Glasgow
SB14EBK	47575	Hampshire & B	SF06GYO	69081	Glasgow	SF07FDX	37185	Glasgow
SB14EBL	47576	Hampshire & B	SF06GYP	69082	Glasgow	SF07FDY	37186	Glasgow
SB14EBM	47577	Hampshire & B	SF06GYR	69083	Glasgow	SF07FDZ	37187	Glasgow
SB14EBO	47578	Hampshire & B	SF06GYS	69084	Glasgow	SF07FEG	37193	Glasgow
SB14EBP	47579	Hampshire & B	SF06GYT	69085	Glasgow	SF07FEH	37194	Glasgow
SB14EBU	47580	Hampshire & B	SF06GYU	69086	Glasgow	SF07FEJ	37195	Glasgow
SB14EBV	47581	Hampshire & B	SF06GYV	69087	Glasgow	SF07FEK	37196	Glasgow
SB14EBX	47582	Hampshire & B	SF06GYW	69088	Glasgow	SF07FEM	37197	Glasgow
SB14EBZ	47583	Hampshire & B	SF06GYX	69089	Glasgow	SF07FEO	37198	Glasgow
SB14ECA	47584	Hampshire & B	SF06GYY	69090	Glasgow	SF07FEP	37200	Glasgow
SB14ECC	47585	Hampshire & B	SF06GYZ	69091	Glasgow	SF07FET	37203	Glasgow
SB14ECD	47586	Hampshire & B	SF06GZA	69092	Glasgow	SF07FEU	37204	Glasgow
SB14ECE	47587	Hampshire & B	SF06GZB	69093	Glasgow	SF08SMU	37530	Glasgow
SB14ECF	47588	Hampshire & B	SF06GZC	69094	Glasgow	SF08SMV	37531	Glasgow
SB14ECJ	47589	Hampshire & B	SF06GZD	69095	Glasgow	SF08SMX	37532	Glasgow
SB14ECT	47590	Hampshire & B	SF06GZE	69096	Glasgow	SF08SNJ	37533	Glasgow
SB14ECV	47591	Hampshire & B	SF06GZG	69097	Glasgow	SF08SNK	37534	Glasgow
SB14ECW	47592	Hampshire & B	SF06GZH	69098	Glasgow	SF08SNN	37535	Glasgow
SB14ECX	47593	Hampshire & B	SF06GZJ	69099	Glasgow	SF08SNU	37536	Glasgow
SB14ECY	47594	Hampshire & B	SF06GZK	69100	Glasgow	SF08SNV	37537	Glasgow
SF04HXW	69295	Glasgow	SF06GZL	69101	Glasgow	SF08SNX	37538	Glasgow
SF04HXX	69296	Glasgow	SF06GZM	69102	Glasgow	SF08SNY	37539	Glasgow
SF04ZPE	69297	Glasgow	SF06GZN	69103	Glasgow	SF08SNZ	37540	Glasgow
SF04ZPG	69298	Glasgow	SF06GZO	69104	Glasgow	SF09LDD	37736	Glasgow
SF05KUH	10183	Aberdeen	SF06GZP	69105	Glasgow	SF09LDE	37737	Glasgow
SF05KUJ	53202	Glasgow	SF06GZR	69106	Glasgow	SF09LDJ	37738	Glasgow
SF05KUK	53203	Glasgow	SF06GZS	69107	Glasgow	SF09LDK	37739	Glasgow
SF05KWY	42877	Cymru	SF06GZT	69108	Glasgow	SF09LDL	37740	Glasgow
SF05KWZ	42878	Cymru	SF06GZV	69109	Glasgow	SF09LDN	37741	Glasgow
SF05KXA	42879	West Yorkshire	SF06GZX	69111	Glasgow	SF09LDO	37742	Glasgow
SF05KXB	42880	West Yorkshire	SF06GZY	69112	Glasgow	SF09LDU	37743	Glasgow
SF05KXC	42881	West Yorkshire	SF06GZZ	69113	Glasgow	SF09LDV	37744	Glasgow
SF05KXD	42882	West Yorkshire	SF06HAA	69114	Glasgow	SF09LDX	37745	Glasgow
SF05KXE	42883	West Yorkshire	SF06HAE	69115	Glasgow	SF09LDY	37746	Glasgow
SF05KXH	42884	West Yorkshire	SF06HAO	69116	Glasgow	SF09LDZ	37747	Glasgow
SF05KXJ	42885	Glasgow	SF06HAU	69117	Glasgow	SF09LEJ	37748	Glasgow
SF05KXK	42886	Glasgow	SF06HAX	69118	Glasgow	SF09LEU	37749	Glasgow
SF05KXL	42887	Glasgow	SF06HBA	69119	Glasgow	SF09LFA	37750	Glasgow
SF05KXM	42888	Glasgow	SF06HBB	69120	Glasgow	SF09LFB	37751	Glasgow
SF06GXG	69039	Glasgow	SF06HBC	69121	Glasgow	SF51YAA	61597	Glasgow
SF06GXH	69059	Glasgow	SF07FCC	37188	Glasgow	SF51YAD	61598	Glasgow
SF06GXJ	69038	Glasgow	SF07FCD	37189	Glasgow	SF51YAE	61599	Glasgow
SF06GXK	69040	Glasgow	SF07FCE	37190	Glasgow	SF51YAG	61600	Glasgow
SF06GXL	69041	Glasgow	SF07FCG	37191	Glasgow	SF51YAH	61601	Glasgow
SF06GXM	69057	Glasgow	SF07FCJ	37192	Glasgow	SF51YAJ	61602	Glasgow
SF06GXN	69058	Glasgow	SF07FCL	37199	Glasgow	SF51YAK	61603	Glasgow
SF06GXO	69060	Glasgow	SF07FCM	37201	Glasgow	SF51YAO	61604	Glasgow
SF06GXP	69061	Glasgow	SF07FCO	37202	Glasgow	SF51YAU	61605	Glasgow
SF06GXR	69062	Glasgow	SF07FCP	37166	Glasgow	SF51YAV	61606	Glasgow
SF06GXS	69063	Glasgow	SF07FCV	37167	Glasgow	SF51YAW	61607	Glasgow
SF06GXT	69064	Glasgow	SF07FCX	37168	Glasgow	SF51YAX	61608	Glasgow
SF06GXU	69065	Glasgow	SF07FCY	37169	Glasgow	SF51YAY	61609	Glasgow
SF06GXV	69072	Glasgow	SF07FCZ	37170	Glasgow	SF51YBA	61610	Glasgow
SF06GXW	69073	Glasgow	SF07FDA	37171	Glasgow	SF51YBB	61611	Glasgow
SF06GXX	69074	Glasgow	SF07FDC	37172	Glasgow	SF51YBC	61612	Glasgow
SF06GXY	69075	Glasgow	SF07FDD	37173	Glasgow	SF51YBD	61613	Glasgow
SF06GXZ	69076	Glasgow	SF07FDE	37174	Glasgow	SF51YBE	61614	Glasgow
SF06GYA	69077	Glasgow	SF07FDG	37175	Glasgow	SF51YBG	61615	Glasgow

Reg	No.	Location	Reg	No.	Location	Reg	No.	Location
SF51YBH	61616	Glasgow	SF54TJX	32599	Glasgow	SF55UBT	69033	South Yorkshire
SF51YBJ	61617	Glasgow	SF54TJY	32600	Glasgow	SF55UBU	69034	Glasgow
SF51YBK	61618	Glasgow	SF54TJZ	32601	Glasgow	SF55UBV	69035	Glasgow
SF51YBL	61619	Glasgow	SF54TKA	32602	Glasgow	SF55UBW	69036	Glasgow
SF51YBM	61620	Glasgow	SF54TKC	32603	Glasgow	SF55UBX	69037	Glasgow
SF51YBN	61621	Glasgow	SF54TKD	32604	Glasgow	SF56GYP	66988	Glasgow
SF51YBO	61622	Glasgow	SF54TKE	32605	Glasgow	SF56GYR	66989	Glasgow
SF51YBP	61623	Glasgow	SF54TKJ	32606	Glasgow	SF56GYS	66990	Glasgow
SF51YBR	61624	Glasgow	SF54TKK	32607	Glasgow	SF56GYT	66991	Glasgow
SF51YBS	61625	Glasgow	SF54TKN	32609	Glasgow	SF57MKA	37205	Glasgow
SF51YBT	61626	Glasgow	SF54TKO	32608	Glasgow	SF57MKC	37206	Glasgow
SF54OSD	32543	Glasgow	SF54TKT	32610	Glasgow	SF57MKD	37207	Glasgow
SF54OSE	32544	Glasgow	SF54TKU	32611	Glasgow	SF57MKG	37208	Glasgow
SF54OSG	32545	Glasgow	SF54TKV	32612	Glasgow	SF57MKJ	37209	Glasgow
SF54OSJ	32546	Glasgow	SF54TKX	32613	Glasgow	SF57MKK	37210	Glasgow
SF54OSK	32547	Glasgow	SF54TKY	32614	Glasgow	SF57MKL	37211	Glasgow
SF54OSL	32548	Glasgow	SF54TKZ	32615	Glasgow	SF57MKM	37212	Glasgow
SF54OSM	32549	Glasgow	SF54TLJ	32616	Glasgow	SF57MKN	37213	Glasgow
SF54OSN	32550	Glasgow	SF54TLK	32617	Glasgow	SF57MKO	37214	Glasgow
SF54OSO	32551	Glasgow	SF54TLN	32618	Glasgow	SF57MKP	37215	Glasgow
SF54OSP	32552	Glasgow	SF54TLO	32619	Glasgow	SF57MKU	37216	Glasgow
SF54OSR	32553	Glasgow	SF54TLU	32620	Glasgow	SF57MKV	37217	Glasgow
SF54OSU	32554	Glasgow	SF54TLX	32621	Glasgow	SF57MKX	37218	Glasgow
SF54OSV	32555	Glasgow	SF54TLY	32622	Glasgow	SF57MKZ	37219	Glasgow
SF54OSW	32556	Glasgow	SF54TLZ	32623	Glasgow	SF57MLE	37220	Glasgow
SF54OSX	32557	Glasgow	SF54TMO	32624	Glasgow	SF57MLJ	37221	Glasgow
SF54OSY	32558	Glasgow	SF54TMU	32625	Glasgow	SF57MLK	37222	Glasgow
SF54OSZ	32559	Glasgow	SF54TMV	32626	Glasgow	SF57MLL	37223	Glasgow
SF54OTA	32560	Glasgow	SF55TXA	68564	Hampshire & B	SF57MLN	37224	Glasgow
SF54OTB	32561	Glasgow	SF55TXB	68565	Hampshire & B	SF57MLO	37225	Glasgow
SF54OTC	32562	Glasgow	SF55TXC	68566	Scotland East	SF57MLU	37226	Glasgow
SF54OTD	32563	Glasgow	SF55UAD	69012	Devon & Cornwall	SF57MLV	37227	Glasgow
SF54OTE	32564	Glasgow	SF55UAE	69013	Devon & Cornwall	SF58ATY	37541	Glasgow
SF54OTG	32565	Glasgow	SF55UAG	69014	Glasgow	SF58ATZ	37542	Glasgow
SF54OTH	32566	Glasgow	SF55UAH	69015	Glasgow	SF58AUA	37543	Glasgow
SF54OTJ	32567	Glasgow	SF55UAJ	69016	Glasgow	SF58AUC	37544	Glasgow
SF54OTK	32568	Glasgow	SF55UAK	69017	Devon & Cornwall	SH51MHY	61627	Glasgow
SF54OTL	32569	Glasgow	SF55UAL	69018	Devon & Cornwall	SH51MHZ	61628	Glasgow
SF54OTM	32570	Glasgow	SF55UAM	69019	Glasgow	SH51MJE	61629	Glasgow
SF54OTN	32571	Glasgow	SF55UAN	69020	South Yorkshire	SH51MJF	61630	Glasgow
SF54OTP	32572	Glasgow	SF55UAO	69021	Glasgow	SH51MKF	61631	South Yorkshire
SF54OTR	32573	Glasgow	SF55UAP	69022	South Yorkshire	SH51MKG	61632	Glasgow
SF54OTT	32574	Glasgow	SF55UAR	69023	South Yorkshire	SH51MKJ	61633	South Yorkshire
SF54OTU	32575	Glasgow	SF55UAS	69024	South Yorkshire	SH51MKK	61634	Glasgow
SF54OTV	32576	Glasgow	SF55UAT	69025	South Yorkshire	SH51MKL	61635	Glasgow
SF54OTW	32577	Glasgow	SF55UAU	69026	South Yorkshire	SJ03DNY	40965	Glasgow
SF54OTX	32578	Glasgow	SF55UAV	69027	Glasgow	SJ03DOA	40966	Glasgow
SF54OTY	32579	Glasgow	SF55UAW	69028	South Yorkshire	SJ03DOH	50460	Scotland East
SF54OTZ	32580	Glasgow	SF55UAX	69029	South Yorkshire	SJ03DPE	50461	Glasgow
SF54OUA	32581	Glasgow	SF55UAY	69030	South Yorkshire	SJ03DPF	50462	Glasgow
SF54OUB	32582	Glasgow	SF55UAZ	69031	South Yorkshire	SJ03DPN	50463	Glasgow
SF54OUC	32583	Glasgow	SF55UBA	69032	South Yorkshire	SJ03DPU	50464	Glasgow
SF54OUD	32584	Glasgow	SF55UBB	69042	Glasgow	SJ03DPV	50465	Glasgow
SF54OUE	32585	Glasgow	SF55UBC	69043	South Yorkshire	SJ03DPX	50466	Hampshire & B
SF54OUG	32586	Glasgow	SF55UBD	69044	South Yorkshire	SJ03DPY	50467	Hampshire & B
SF54OUH	32587	Glasgow	SF55UBE	69045	South Yorkshire	SJ03DPZ	50468	Scotland East
SF54OUJ	32588	Glasgow	SF55UBG	69046	South Yorkshire	SJ51DHD	61636	South Yorkshire
SF54OUK	32589	Glasgow	SF55UBH	69047	South Yorkshire	SJ51DHE	61637	Glasgow
SF54OUL	32590	Glasgow	SF55UBJ	69048	South Yorkshire	SJ51DHF	61638	South Yorkshire
SF54OUM	32591	Glasgow	SF55UBK	69049	South Yorkshire	SJ51DHG	61639	South Yorkshire
SF54OUN	32592	Glasgow	SF55UBL	69050	South Yorkshire	SJ51DHK	61640	Glasgow
SF54THV	32593	Glasgow	SF55UBM	69051	South Yorkshire	SJ51DHL	61641	Glasgow
SF54THX	32594	Glasgow	SF55UBN	69052	South Yorkshire	SJ51DHM	61642	Glasgow
SF54THZ	32595	Glasgow	SF55UBO	69053	South Yorkshire	SJ51DHN	61643	Glasgow
SF54TJO	32596	Glasgow	SF55UBP	69054	South Yorkshire	SJ51DHO	61644	Glasgow
SF54TJU	32597	Glasgow	SF55UBR	69055	South Yorkshire	SJ51DHP	61645	Glasgow
SF54TJV	32598	Glasgow	SF55UBS	69056	South Yorkshire	SJ51DHV	61646	Glasgow

SJ51DHX	61647	Glasgow	SK63KHH	63031	South Yorkshire	SK63KMM	47422	Hampshire & B
SJ51DHZ	61648	Glasgow	SK63KHJ	63032	South Yorkshire	SK63KMO	47423	Hampshire & B
SJ51DJD	61649	Glasgow	SK63KHL	63033	South Yorkshire	SK63KMU	47424	Hampshire & B
SJ51DJE	61650	Glasgow	SK63KHM	63034	South Yorkshire	SK63KMV	47425	Hampshire & B
SJ51DJF	61651	Glasgow	SK63KHO	63035	South Yorkshire	SK63KMX	47426	Hampshire & B
SJ51DJK	61652	Glasgow	SK63KHP	63036	South Yorkshire	SK63KMY	47427	Hampshire & B
SJ51DJO	61653	Glasgow	SK63KHR	63037	South Yorkshire	SK63KMZ	47428	Hampshire & B
SJ51DJU	61654	Glasgow	SK63KHT	63042	Hampshire & B	SK63KNA	47429	Hampshire & B
SJ51DJX	61656	Glasgow	SK63KHU	63043	Hampshire & B	SK63KNB	47430	Hampshire & B
SJ51DJY	61657	Glasgow	SK63KHV	63044	Hampshire & B	SK63KNC	47431	Hampshire & B
SJ51DJZ	61306	Glasgow	SK63KHW	63045	Hampshire & B	SK63KND	47432	Hampshire & B
SJ51DKA	61658	Glasgow	SK63KHX	63046	Hampshire & B	SK63KNE	47433	Hampshire & B
SJ51DKD	61659	Glasgow	SK63KHY	63047	Hampshire & B	SK63KNF	47434	Hampshire & B
SJ51DKE	61660	Glasgow	SK63KHZ	63048	Hampshire & B	SK63KNG	47435	West of England
SJ51DKF	61661	Glasgow	SK63KJA	63049	Hampshire & B	SK63KNH	47436	West of England
SJ51DKK	61662	South Yorkshire	SK63KJE	63050	Hampshire & B	SK63KNJ	47437	West of England
SJ51DKL	61663	Glasgow	SK63KJF	63051	Hampshire & B	SK63KNL	47438	West of England
SJ51DKN	61664	Glasgow	SK63KJJ	63052	Hampshire & B	SK63KNM	47439	West of England
SK02ZYG	65755	Glasgow	SK63KJN	63053	Hampshire & B	SK63KNN	47440	West of England
SK02ZYH	65756	Glasgow	SK63KJO	63054	Hampshire & B	SK63KNO	47441	West of England
SK07JVN	69254	Scotland East	SK63KJU	63055	Hampshire & B	SK63KNP	47442	West of England
SK07JVO	69255	Scotland East	SK63KJV	63056	Hampshire & B	SK63KNR	47443	West of England
SK07JVP	69256	Scotland East	SK63KJX	63057	Hampshire & B	SK63KNS	47444	West of England
SK14CTV	33831	Manchester	SK63KJY	63058	Hampshire & B	SK63KNU	47445	West of England
SK14CTX	33832	Manchester	SK63KJZ	63059	Hampshire & B	SK63KNV	47446	West of England
SK14CTY	33833	Manchester	SK63KKA	63060	Hampshire & B	SK63KNX	47447	West of England
SK57ADO	69257	Scotland East	SK63KKB	63061	Hampshire & B	SK63KNY	47448	West of England
SK57ADU	69258	Scotland East	SK63KKC	63062	Hampshire & B	SL14DBO	33888	West Yorkshire
SK57ADV	69259	Scotland East	SK63KKD	63063	Hampshire & B	SL14DBU	33889	West Yorkshire
SK57ADX	69260	Scotland East	SK63KKE	63064	Hampshire & B	SL14DBV	33890	West Yorkshire
SK57ADZ	69261	Scotland East	SK63KKF	63065	Hampshire & B	SL14DFD	33858	South Yorkshire
SK57AEA	69262	Scotland East	SK63KKG	63066	Hampshire & B	SL14DFE	33859	South Yorkshire
SK57AEB	69263	Scotland East	SK63KKH	63067	Hampshire & B	SL14DFF	33860	South Yorkshire
SK57AEC	69264	Scotland East	SK63KKJ	47449	West of England	SL14DFG	33861	South Yorkshire
SK63ATY	67884	Glasgow	SK63KKL	47450	West of England	SL14DFK	33862	South Yorkshire
SK63ATZ	67885	Glasgow	SK63KKM	47451	West of England	SL14LMF	33863	South Yorkshire
SK63AUA	67886	Glasgow	SK63KKN	47452	West of England	SL14LMJ	33864	South Yorkshire
SK63AUC	67887	Glasgow	SK63KKO	47453	West of England	SL14LMK	33865	South Yorkshire
SK63AUE	67888	Glasgow	SK63KKP	47454	West of England	SL14LMM	33866	South Yorkshire
SK63AUF	67889	Glasgow	SK63KKR	47455	West of England	SL14LMO	33867	South Yorkshire
SK63AUH	67890	Glasgow	SK63KKS	47456	West of England	SL14LMU	33868	South Yorkshire
SK63AUJ	67891	Glasgow	SK63KKU	47457	West of England	SL14LMV	33869	South Yorkshire
SK63AUL	67892	Glasgow	SK63KKV	47458	West of England	SL14LMY	33870	South Yorkshire
SK63AUM	67893	Glasgow	SK63KKW	47459	West of England	SL14LNA	33871	South Yorkshire
SK63AUN	67894	Glasgow	SK63KKX	47460	West of England	SL14LNC	33872	South Yorkshire
SK63KFY	63111	Manchester	SK63KKY	47461	West of England	SL63GBF	67431	Cymru
SK63KFZ	63112	Manchester	SK63KKZ	47462	West of England	SL63GBO	67432	Cymru
SK63KGA	63113	Manchester	SK63KLA	47463	West of England	SL63GBU	67433	Cymru
SK63KGE	63114	Manchester	SK63KLC	47464	West of England	SL63GBV	67434	Cymru
SK63KGF	63115	Manchester	SK63KLD	47465	West of England	SL63GBX	67435	Cymru
SK63KGG	63116	Manchester	SK63KLE	47405	Hampshire & B	SL63GBY	67436	Cymru
SK63KGJ	63117	Manchester	SK63KLF	47406	Hampshire & B	SL63GBZ	67437	Cymru
SK63KGN	63118	Manchester	SK63KLJ	47407	Hampshire & B	SL63GCF	67438	Cymru
SK63KGO	63017	South Yorkshire	SK63KLL	47408	Hampshire & B	SL63GCK	67439	Cymru
SK63KGP	63018	South Yorkshire	SK63KLM	47409	Hampshire & B	SM13NAE	63068	West of England
SK63KGU	63019	South Yorkshire	SK63KLO	47410	Hampshire & B	SM13NAO	63069	West of England
SK63KGV	63020	South Yorkshire	SK63KLP	47411	Hampshire & B	SM13NBA	63070	West of England
SK63KGX	63021	South Yorkshire	SK63KLS	47412	Hampshire & B	SM13NBB	63071	West of England
SK63KGY	63022	South Yorkshire	SK63KLU	47413	Hampshire & B	SM13NBD	63072	West of England
SK63KGZ	63023	South Yorkshire	SK63KLV	47414	Hampshire & B	SM13NBE	63073	West of England
SK63KHA	63024	South Yorkshire	SK63KLX	47415	Hampshire & B	SM13NBF	63074	West of England
SK63KHB	63025	South Yorkshire	SK63KLZ	47416	Hampshire & B	SM13NBG	63075	West of England
SK63KHC	63026	South Yorkshire	SK63KMA	47417	Hampshire & B	SM13NBJ	63076	West of England
SK63KHD	63027	South Yorkshire	SK63KME	47418	Hampshire & B	SM13NBK	63077	West of England
SK63KHE	63028	South Yorkshire	SK63KMF	47419	Hampshire & B	SM13NBL	63078	West of England
SK63KHF	63029	South Yorkshire	SK63KMG	47420	Hampshire & B	SM13NBN	63096	Manchester
SK63KHG	63030	South Yorkshire	SK63KMJ	47421	Hampshire & B	SM13NBO	63097	Manchester

SM13NBX	63098	Manchester	SN05EAJ	42929	East	SN11FOU	33906	Glasgow
SM13NBY	63099	Manchester	SN05EAM	42930	Essex	SN11FOV	33907	Glasgow
SM13NBZ	63100	Manchester	SN05EAO	42931	Essex	SN11FPA	33908	Glasgow
SM13NCA	63101	Manchester	SN05EAP	42932	Essex	SN11FPC	33909	Glasgow
SM13NCC	63102	Manchester	SN05HEJ	43849	West of England	SN11FPD	33910	Glasgow
SM13NCD	63103	Manchester	SN05HWD	36023	Scotland East	SN12ADU	33656	Manchester
SM13NCE	63104	Manchester	SN05HWE	36022	Scotland East	SN12ADV	33657	Manchester
SM13NCF	63105	Manchester	SN05HWF	36020	Scotland East	SN12ADX	33658	Devon & Cornwall
SM13NCJ	63106	Manchester	SN05HWG	36018	Scotland East	SN12ADZ	33659	Devon & Cornwall
SM13NCN	63107	Manchester	SN05HWH	36019	Scotland East	SN12AEA	33660	Devon & Cornwall
SM13NCO	63108	Manchester	SN05HWJ	36017	Scotland East	SN12AEB	33661	Devon & Cornwall
SM13NCU	63109	Manchester	SN05HWK	36014	Scotland East	SN12AED	33662	Devon & Cornwall
SM13NCV	63110	Manchester	SN05HWL	36013	Scotland East	SN12AEE	33663	Manchester
SM13NDJ	63001	South Yorkshire	SN05HWM	36016	Scotland East	SN12AEF	33664	Devon & Cornwall
SM13NDK	63002	South Yorkshire	SN05HWO	36015	Scotland East	SN12AEG	33665	Devon & Cornwall
SM13NDL	63003	South Yorkshire	SN05HWP	36021	Scotland East	SN12AEJ	33666	Devon & Cornwall
SM13NDN	63004	South Yorkshire	SN05HWR	36024	Scotland East	SN12AEK	33667	Devon & Cornwall
SM13NDO	63005	South Yorkshire	SN05HWS	36025	Scotland East	SN12AEL	33668	Manchester
SM13NDU	63006	South Yorkshire	SN05HWT	36028	Scotland East	SN12AEM	33669	Manchester
SM13NDV	63007	South Yorkshire	SN05HWU	36026	Scotland East	SN12AEO	33670	Manchester
SM13NDX	63008	South Yorkshire	SN05HWV	36027	Scotland East	SN12AEP	33671	Manchester
SM13NDY	63009	South Yorkshire	SN05HWW	36007	Scotland East	SN12AET	33672	Manchester
SM13NDZ	63010	South Yorkshire	SN05HWX	36008	Scotland East	SN12AEU	33673	Manchester
SM13NEF	63011	South Yorkshire	SN05HWY	36009	Scotland East	SN12AEV	33674	Manchester
SM13NEJ	63012	South Yorkshire	SN05HWZ	36010	Scotland East	SN12AEW	33675	Manchester
SM13NEN	63013	South Yorkshire	SN05HXA	36011	Scotland East	SN12AEX	33676	Manchester
SM13NEO	63014	South Yorkshire	SN05HXB	36012	Scotland East	SN12AEY	33677	Manchester
SM13NEU	63015	South Yorkshire	SN06AHK	65754	Scotland East	SN12AEZ	33678	Manchester
SM13NEY	63016	South Yorkshire	SN09CAU	38201	Glasgow	SN12AFA	33679	Manchester
SMK735F	39735	Hampshire & B	SN09CAV	38202	Glasgow	SN12AFE	33680	Manchester
SN03CLX	65757	Glasgow	SN09CAX	38203	Glasgow	SN12AFF	33681	Manchester
SN03CLY	65758	Glasgow	SN09CBF	38204	Glasgow	SN12AFJ	33682	Manchester
SN03LGG	43901	Cymru	SN09CBO	38205	Glasgow	SN12AFK	33683	Manchester
SN03LGJ	43902	Cymru	SN09CBU	38206	Glasgow	SN12AFO	33684	Manchester
SN03LGK	43903	Cymru	SN09CBV	38207	Glasgow	SN12AFU	33685	Manchester
SN03WLD	42482	Essex	SN09CBX	38208	Glasgow	SN12AFV	33686	Manchester
SN03WLK	42483	Essex	SN09CBY	38209	Glasgow	SN12AFX	33687	Manchester
SN03WLW	42484	Essex	SN09CCA	38210	Glasgow	SN12AFY	33688	Manchester
SN03WME	42487	Essex	SN09CCD	38211	Glasgow	SN12AFZ	33689	Manchester
SN03WMJ	62411	Scotland East	SN09CCE	38212	Glasgow	SN12AGO	33690	Manchester
SN03WMM	42485	Essex	SN09CCF	38213	Glasgow	SN12AGU	33691	Manchester
SN03WMU	62412	Scotland East	SN09CCJ	38214	Glasgow	SN12AGV	33692	Manchester
SN03WMX	42486	Essex	SN09CCK	38215	Glasgow	SN12AGX	33693	Manchester
SN04CKX	65701	Scotland East	SN09CCO	38216	Glasgow	SN12AGY	33694	Manchester
SN04CKY	65700	Scotland East	SN09CCU	38217	Glasgow	SN12AGZ	33695	Manchester
SN04CLF	65702	Scotland East	SN09CCV	38218	Glasgow	SN12AHA	33696	Manchester
SN04CNK	65703	Scotland East	SN09CCX	38219	Glasgow	SN12AHC	33697	Manchester
SN04EFX	43842	Scotland East	SN09CCY	38220	Glasgow	SN12AHD	33698	Manchester
SN04XXY	11037	Devon & Cornwall	SN09CCZ	38221	Glasgow	SN12AHE	33699	Manchester
SN04XXZ	11038	Devon & Cornwall	SN09CDE	38222	Glasgow	SN12AHF	33700	Manchester
SN04XYA	11036	Devon & Cornwall	SN09CDF	38223	Glasgow	SN12AHG	33701	Manchester
SN05DZO	42933	Essex	SN09CDK	38224	Glasgow	SN12AHJ	33702	Manchester
SN05DZP	42934	Essex	SN09CDO	38225	Glasgow	SN12AHK	33703	Manchester
SN05DZR	42935	Essex	SN09EZW	69402	Scotland East	SN12AHL	33704	Manchester
SN05DZS	42936	Essex	SN09EZX	69403	Scotland East	SN12AHO	33705	Manchester
SN05DZT	42937	Essex	SN09FAU	69404	Scotland East	SN12AHP	33706	Manchester
SN05DZU	42558	Devon & Cornwall	SN09FBA	69405	Scotland East	SN12AHU	33707	Manchester
SN05DZV	42559	Devon & Cornwall	SN09FBB	69406	Scotland East	SN12AHU	33714	Manchester
SN05DZW	42560	Devon & Cornwall	SN09FBC	69407	Scotland East	SN12AHV	33713	Manchester
SN05DZX	42561	West of England	SN09FBD	69408	Scotland East	SN12AHV	33708	Manchester
SN05DZY	42562	Devon & Cornwall	SN09FBE	69409	Scotland East	SN12AHX	33709	Manchester
SN05DZZ	42563	Devon & Cornwall	SN09FBF	69410	Scotland East	SN12AHX	33715	Manchester
SN05EAA	42924	Devon & Cornwall	SN11FOJ	33901	Glasgow	SN12AHY	33710	Manchester
SN05EAC	42925	West of England	SN11FOK	33902	Glasgow	SN12AHZ	33711	Manchester
SN05EAE	42926	West of England	SN11FOM	33903	Glasgow	SN12AJO	33712	Manchester
SN05EAF	42927	Essex	SN11FOP	33904	Glasgow	SN12AJY	33716	Manchester
SN05EAG	42928	Essex	SN11FOT	33905	Glasgow	SN12AKF	33717	Manchester

SN12AKG	33718	Manchester	SN13CKP	67415	Manchester	SN13EDF	67834	Glasgow
SN12AKJ	33719	Manchester	SN13CKU	67416	Manchester	SN13EDJ	67835	Glasgow
SN12AKK	33720	Manchester	SN13CKV	67417	Manchester	SN13EDK	67836	Glasgow
SN12AKO	33721	Manchester	SN13CKX	67418	Manchester	SN13EDL	67837	Glasgow
SN12AKP	33722	Manchester	SN13CKY	67419	Manchester	SN13EDO	67838	Glasgow
SN12AKU	33723	Manchester	SN13CLF	67420	Manchester	SN13EDP	67839	Glasgow
SN12AKV	33724	Manchester	SN13CLJ	67421	Manchester	SN13EDR	67840	Glasgow
SN12AKX	33725	Manchester	SN13CLO	67422	Manchester	SN13EDU	67841	Glasgow
SN12AKY	33726	Manchester	SN13CLU	67423	Manchester	SN13EDV	67842	Glasgow
SN12AKZ	33727	Manchester	SN13CLV	67424	Manchester	SN13EDX	67843	Glasgow
SN12ALO	33728	Manchester	SN13CLX	67425	Manchester	SN13EEF	67844	Glasgow
SN12ALU	33729	Manchester	SN13CLY	67426	Manchester	SN13EEG	67845	Glasgow
SN12AMK	33730	Manchester	SN13CLZ	67427	Manchester	SN13EEH	67846	Glasgow
SN12AMO	33731	Manchester	SN13CME	67428	Manchester	SN13EEJ	67847	Glasgow
SN12AMU	33732	Manchester	SN13CMF	67429	Manchester	SN13EEM	67848	Glasgow
SN12AMV	33733	Manchester	SN13CMK	67430	Manchester	SN13EEO	67849	Glasgow
SN12AMX	33734	Manchester	SN13CMO	67783	Aberdeen	SN13EEP	67850	Glasgow
SN12ANF	33735	Manchester	SN13CMU	67784	Aberdeen	SN13EES	67851	Glasgow
SN12ANP	33736	Manchester	SN13CMV	67785	Aberdeen	SN13EET	67852	Glasgow
SN12ANR	33737	Manchester	SN13CMX	67786	Aberdeen	SN13EEU	67853	Glasgow
SN12ANU	33738	Manchester	SN13CMY	67787	Aberdeen	SN13EEV	67854	Glasgow
SN12ANV	33739	Manchester	SN13CMZ	67788	Aberdeen	SN13EEW	67855	Glasgow
SN12ANX	33740	Manchester	SN13CNA	67789	Aberdeen	SN13EEX	67856	Glasgow
SN12AOA	33741	Manchester	SN13CNC	67790	Aberdeen	SN13EEY	67857	Glasgow
SN12AOB	33742	Manchester	SN13CNE	67791	Aberdeen	SN13EEZ	67858	Glasgow
SN12AOC	33743	Manchester	SN13CNF	67792	Aberdeen	SN13EFA	67859	Glasgow
SN12AOD	33744	Manchester	SN13CNJ	67793	Aberdeen	SN13EFB	67860	Glasgow
SN12AOE	33745	Manchester	SN13CNK	67794	Aberdeen	SN13EFC	67861	Glasgow
SN12AOF	33746	Manchester	SN13CNO	67795	Aberdeen	SN13EFD	67862	Glasgow
SN12AOG	33747	Manchester	SN13CNU	67796	Aberdeen	SN13EFE	67863	Glasgow
SN12AOH	33748	Manchester	SN13CNV	67797	Aberdeen	SN13EFF	67864	Glasgow
SN12AOJ	33749	Manchester	SN13CNX	67798	Aberdeen	SN13EFG	67865	Glasgow
SN12AOK	33750	Manchester	SN13CNY	67799	Aberdeen	SN13EFH	67866	Glasgow
SN12AOL	33751	Manchester	SN13CNZ	67800	Aberdeen	SN13EFJ	67867	Glasgow
SN12AOM	33752	Manchester	SN13COA	67801	Aberdeen	SN13EFK	67868	Glasgow
SN12AOO	33753	Manchester	SN13COH	67802	Aberdeen	SN13EFL	67869	Glasgow
SN12AOP	33754	Manchester	SN13COJ	67803	Aberdeen	SN14DTX	63079	Cymru
SN12AOR	33755	Manchester	SN13COU	67804	Aberdeen	SN14DTY	63080	Cymru
SN12AOZ	67751	Glasgow	SN13CPE	67805	Aberdeen	SN14DTZ	63081	Cymru
SN12AP0	67753	Glasgow	SN13EAY	67806	Glasgow	SN14DUA	63082	Cymru
SN12APF	67752	Glasgow	SN13EBA	67807	Glasgow	SN14DUH	63083	Cymru
SN12APZ	67754	Glasgow	SN13EBC	67808	Glasgow	SN14DUJ	63084	Cymru
SN13CGF	67766	Glasgow	SN13EBD	67809	Glasgow	SN14DUU	63085	Cymru
SN13CGG	67767	Glasgow	SN13EBF	67810	Glasgow	SN14DUV	63086	Cymru
SN13CGK	67768	Glasgow	SN13EBG	67811	Glasgow	SN14DUY	63087	Cymru
SN13CGO	67769	Glasgow	SN13EBJ	67812	Glasgow	SN14DVB	63088	Cymru
SN13CGU	67770	Glasgow	SN13EBK	67813	Glasgow	SN14DVC	63089	Cymru
SN13CGV	67771	Glasgow	SN13EBL	67814	Glasgow	SN14DVF	63090	Cymru
SN13CGX	67772	Glasgow	SN13EBM	67815	Glasgow	SN14DVG	63091	Cymru
SN13CHO	67901	Essex	SN13EBO	67816	Glasgow	SN14DVH	63092	Cymru
SN13CHV	67902	Essex	SN13EBP	67817	Glasgow	SN14DVJ	63093	Cymru
SN13CHX	67903	Essex	SN13EBU	67818	Glasgow	SN14DVK	63094	Cymru
SN13CHY	67904	Essex	SN13EBV	67819	Glasgow	SN14DVL	63095	Cymru
SN13CJV	67401	Manchester	SN13EBX	67820	Glasgow	SN14DVM	63119	South Yorkshire
SN13CJX	67402	Manchester	SN13EBZ	67821	Glasgow	SN14DVO	63120	South Yorkshire
SN13CJY	67403	Manchester	SN13ECA	67822	Glasgow	SN14DVP	63121	South Yorkshire
SN13CJZ	67404	Manchester	SN13ECC	67823	Glasgow	SN14DVR	63122	South Yorkshire
SN13CKA	67405	Manchester	SN13ECD	67824	Glasgow	SN14DVT	63123	South Yorkshire
SN13CKC	67406	Manchester	SN13ECF	67825	Glasgow	SN14DVU	63124	South Yorkshire
SN13CKD	67407	Manchester	SN13ECJ	67826	Glasgow	SN14DVV	63125	South Yorkshire
SN13CKE	67408	Manchester	SN13ECT	67827	Glasgow	SN14DVW	63126	South Yorkshire
SN13CKF	67409	Manchester	SN13ECV	67828	Glasgow	SN14DVX	63127	South Yorkshire
SN13CKG	67410	Manchester	SN13ECW	67829	Glasgow	SN14DVY	63128	South Yorkshire
SN13CKJ	67411	Manchester	SN13ECX	67830	Glasgow	SN14DVZ	63129	South Yorkshire
SN13CKK	67412	Manchester	SN13ECY	67831	Glasgow	SN14DWC	63130	South Yorkshire
SN13CKL	67413	Manchester	SN13ECZ	67832	Glasgow	SN14DWD	63131	South Yorkshire
SN13CKO	67414	Manchester	SN13EDC	67833	Glasgow	SN14DWE	63132	South Yorkshire

Reg	Fleet	Depot	Reg	Fleet	Depot	Reg	Fleet	Depot
SN14DWF	63133	South Yorkshire	SN14DZO	47467	Manchester	SN14FFZ	47549	West of England
SN14DWG	63134	South Yorkshire	SN14DZP	47468	Manchester	SN14FGA	47550	West of England
SN14DWJ	63135	South Yorkshire	SN14EAA	47469	Manchester	SN14FGC	47551	West of England
SN14DWK	63136	South Yorkshire	SN14EAC	47470	Manchester	SN14FGD	47552	West of England
SN14DWL	63137	South Yorkshire	SN14EAE	47471	Manchester	SN14FGE	47553	West of England
SN14DWM	63138	South Yorkshire	SN14EAF	47472	Manchester	SN14FGF	47554	West of England
SN14DWO	63139	South Yorkshire	SN14EAG	47473	Manchester	SN14FGG	47555	West of England
SN14DWP	63140	South Yorkshire	SN14EAJ	47474	Manchester	SN14FGJ	47556	West of England
SN14DWU	63141	South Yorkshire	SN14EAM	47475	Manchester	SN14FGK	47557	West of England
SN14DWV	63142	South Yorkshire	SN14EAO	47476	Manchester	SN14FGM	47558	West of England
SN14DWW	63143	South Yorkshire	SN14EAP	47477	Manchester	SN14TPZ	33895	Hampshire & B
SN14DWX	63144	South Yorkshire	SN14EAW	47478	Manchester	SN14TRV	33896	Hampshire & B
SN14DWY	63145	South Yorkshire	SN14EAX	47479	Manchester	SN14TRX	33897	Hampshire & B
SN14DWZ	63181	Hampshire & B	SN14EAY	47480	Manchester	SN14TRZ	33834	Manchester
SN14DXA	63182	Hampshire & B	SN14EBA	47481	Manchester	SN14TSO	33835	Manchester
SN14DXB	63183	Hampshire & B	SN14EBC	63190	Hampshire & B	SN14TSU	33836	Manchester
SN14DXC	63184	Hampshire & B	SN14EBD	63191	Hampshire & B	SN14TSV	33837	Manchester
SN14DXD	63185	Hampshire & B	SN14EBF	63192	Hampshire & B	SN14TSX	33838	Manchester
SN14DXE	63186	Hampshire & B	SN14ECZ	63193	Aberdeen	SN14TSY	33839	Manchester
SN14DXF	63187	Hampshire & B	SN14EDC	63194	Aberdeen	SN14TSZ	33840	Manchester
SN14DXG	63188	Hampshire & B	SN14EDF	63195	Aberdeen	SN14TTE	33841	Manchester
SN14DXH	63189	Hampshire & B	SN14EDJ	63196	Aberdeen	SN14TTF	33842	Manchester
SN14DXJ	63156	Manchester	SN14EDK	63197	Aberdeen	SN14TTJ	33843	Manchester
SN14DXK	63146	Manchester	SN14EDL	63198	Aberdeen	SN14TTK	33844	Manchester
SN14DXL	63147	Manchester	SN14EDO	63199	Aberdeen	SN14TTO	33845	Manchester
SN14DXM	63148	Manchester	SN14EDP	63200	Aberdeen	SN14TTU	33846	Manchester
SN14DXO	63149	Manchester	SN14EDR	63212	Aberdeen	SN14TTV	33847	Manchester
SN14DXP	63150	Manchester	SN14EDU	63213	Aberdeen	SN14TTX	33848	Manchester
SN14DXR	63151	Manchester	SN14EDV	63214	Aberdeen	SN14TTY	33849	Manchester
SN14DXS	63152	Manchester	SN14FDP	63201	Aberdeen	SN14TTZ	33850	Manchester
SN14DXT	63153	Manchester	SN14FDU	63202	Aberdeen	SN14TUA	33851	Manchester
SN14DXU	63154	Manchester	SN14FDV	63203	Aberdeen	SN14TUH	33852	Manchester
SN14DXV	63155	Manchester	SN14FDX	63204	Aberdeen	SN14TUJ	33853	Manchester
SN14DXW	63219	Scotland East	SN14FDY	63205	Aberdeen	SN14TUO	33854	Manchester
SN14DXX	63220	Scotland East	SN14FDZ	63206	Aberdeen	SN14TUP	33855	Manchester
SN14DXY	63221	Scotland East	SN14FEF	63207	Aberdeen	SN14TUV	33856	Manchester
SN14DXZ	63222	Scotland East	SN14FEG	63208	Aberdeen	SN14TUW	33857	Manchester
SN14DYA	63223	Scotland East	SN14FEH	63209	Aberdeen	SN14TUY	33873	West Yorkshire
SN14DYB	63224	Glasgow	SN14FEJ	63210	Aberdeen	SN14TVA	33874	West Yorkshire
SN14DYC	63225	Glasgow	SN14FEK	63211	Aberdeen	SN14TVC	33875	West Yorkshire
SN14DYD	63226	Glasgow	SN14FEM	63215	Aberdeen	SN14TVD	33876	West Yorkshire
SN14DYF	63227	Glasgow	SN14FEO	63216	Aberdeen	SN14TVE	33877	West Yorkshire
SN14DYG	63228	Glasgow	SN14FEP	63217	Aberdeen	SN14TVF	33878	West Yorkshire
SN14DYH	63229	Glasgow	SN14FET	63218	Aberdeen	SN14TVJ	33879	West Yorkshire
SN14DYJ	63230	Glasgow	SN14FEU	47595	Hampshire & B	SN14TVK	33880	West Yorkshire
SN14DYM	63231	Glasgow	SN14FEV	47596	Hampshire & B	SN14TVL	33881	West Yorkshire
SN14DYO	63232	Glasgow	SN14FEX	47597	Hampshire & B	SN14TVM	33882	West Yorkshire
SN14DYP	63233	Glasgow	SN14FFA	47598	Hampshire & B	SN14TVO	33883	West Yorkshire
SN14DYS	63234	Glasgow	SN14FFC	47599	Hampshire & B	SN14TVP	33884	West Yorkshire
SN14DYT	63235	Glasgow	SN14FFD	47600	Hampshire & B	SN14TVT	33885	West Yorkshire
SN14DYU	63236	Glasgow	SN14FFE	47601	Hampshire & B	SN14TVU	33886	West Yorkshire
SN14DYV	63237	Glasgow	SN14FFG	47602	Hampshire & B	SN14TVV	33887	West Yorkshire
SN14DYW	63238	Glasgow	SN14FFH	47603	Hampshire & B	SN15ABK	47661	Cymru
SN14DYX	63239	Glasgow	SN14FFJ	47604	Hampshire & B	SN15ABO	47662	Cymru
SN14DYY	63240	Glasgow	SN14FFK	47605	Hampshire & B	SN15ABU	47663	Cymru
SN14DZA	47618	Glasgow	SN14FFL	47606	Hampshire & B	SN15ABV	47664	Cymru
SN14DZB	47619	Glasgow	SN14FFM	47607	Hampshire & B	SN15ACF	47665	Hampshire & B
SN14DZC	47620	Glasgow	SN14FFO	47608	Hampshire & B	SN15ACJ	47666	Hampshire & B
SN14DZD	47621	Glasgow	SN14FFP	47609	Hampshire & B	SN15ACO	47667	Hampshire & B
SN14DZD	47624	Glasgow	SN14FFR	47610	Hampshire & B	SN15ACU	47668	Hampshire & B
SN14DZE	47622	Glasgow	SN14FFS	47611	Hampshire & B	SN15ACV	47669	Hampshire & B
SN14DZE	47625	Glasgow	SN14FFT	47612	Hampshire & B	SN15ACX	47670	Hampshire & B
SN14DZF	47623	Glasgow	SN14FFU	47544	West of England	SN15ACY	47671	Hampshire & B
SN14DZF	47626	Glasgow	SN14FFV	47545	West of England	SN15ACZ	47672	Hampshire & B
SN14DZK	47627	Glasgow	SN14FFW	47546	West of England	SN15ADO	47629	Cymru
SN14DZL	47628	Glasgow	SN14FFX	47547	West of England	SN15ADU	47630	Cymru
SN14DZM	47466	Manchester	SN14FFY	47548	West of England	SN15ADV	47631	Cymru

Reg	No	Region	Reg	No	Region	Reg	No	Region
SN15ADX	47632	Cymru	SN54KDJ	65709	Scotland East	SN57JBE	37269	Scotland East
SN15ADZ	47633	Cymru	SN54KDK	65710	Scotland East	SN57JBO	37270	Scotland East
SN15AEA	47634	Cymru	SN54KDO	65711	Scotland East	SN57JBU	37271	Scotland East
SN15AEB	47635	Cymru	SN54KDU	65712	Scotland East	SN57JBV	37272	Scotland East
SN15AEC	47636	Cymru	SN54KDV	65713	Scotland East	SN57JBX	37273	Scotland East
SN15AED	47637	Cymru	SN54KDX	65714	Scotland East	SN57JBZ	69281	Scotland East
SN15AEE	47638	Cymru	SN54KDZ	65715	Scotland East	SN57JCJ	69282	Scotland East
SN15AEF	47639	Cymru	SN54KEJ	65716	Scotland East	SN57JCO	69283	Scotland East
SN15AEG	47640	Cymru	SN54KEK	65717	Scotland East	SN57JCU	69284	Scotland East
SN15AEJ	47641	Cymru	SN54KEU	65718	Scotland East	SN57JCV	69285	Scotland East
SN15AEK	47642	Cymru	SN54KFA	65719	Scotland East	SN57JCX	69286	Scotland East
SN15AEL	47643	Essex	SN54KFC	65720	Scotland East	SN57JCY	69287	Scotland East
SN15AEM	47650	Essex	SN54KFD	65721	Scotland East	SN57JCZ	69288	Scotland East
SN15AEO	47651	Essex	SN54KFE	65722	Scotland East	SN57JDF	69289	Scotland East
SN15AEP	47652	Essex	SN54KFF	65723	Scotland East	SN57JDJ	69290	Scotland East
SN15AET	47653	Essex	SN55CXE	43848	Essex	SN57JDK	69291	Scotland East
SN15AEU	47654	Essex	SN55CXF	43846	Essex	SN57MSU	69280	Scotland East
SN15AEV	47655	Essex	SN55CXH	43845	Essex	SN58CFK	33544	Midlands
SN15AEW	47656	Essex	SN55CXJ	43847	Essex	SN58CFL	33545	Midlands
SN15AEX	47657	Essex	SN55HDZ	32669	Scotland East	SN58CFM	33546	Midlands
SN15AEY	47658	Essex	SN55HEJ	32670	Scotland East	SN58CFO	33547	Midlands
SN15AFA	47644	Essex	SN55HEU	32671	Scotland East	SN58CFP	33548	Midlands
SN15AFE	47645	Essex	SN55HEV	32672	Scotland East	SN58CFU	33549	Midlands
SN15AFF	47646	Essex	SN55HFA	32673	Scotland East	SN58CFV	33550	Midlands
SN15AFJ	47647	Essex	SN55HFB	32674	Scotland East	SN58CFX	33551	Midlands
SN15AFK	47648	Essex	SN55HFC	32675	Scotland East	SN58CFY	33552	Midlands
SN15AFL	47649	Essex	SN55HFD	32676	Scotland East	SN58CFZ	33553	Midlands
SN51MSU	62356	Scotland East	SN55HFE	32677	Scotland East	SN58CGE	33554	West of England
SN51MSV	62355	Scotland East	SN55HFF	32678	Scotland East	SN58CGF	33555	Midlands
SN51MSX	62358	Scotland East	SN55HFG	32679	Scotland East	SN58CGG	33556	Midlands
SN51MSY	62357	Scotland East	SN55HFH	32680	Scotland East	SN58CGK	33557	Midlands
SN51UXX	65665	Essex	SN55HFJ	32681	Scotland East	SN58CGO	33558	Midlands
SN51UXY	65666	Essex	SN55HFK	32682	Scotland East	SN58CGU	33559	Midlands
SN51UXZ	65667	Essex	SN55HFL	32683	Scotland East	SN58CGV	33560	West of England
SN51UYA	65668	Essex	SN55JVA	65750	Scotland East	SN58CGX	33561	Midlands
SN51UYB	65669	Essex	SN55JVC	65751	Scotland East	SN58CGY	33562	Midlands
SN51UYC	65670	East	SN55JVD	65752	Scotland East	SN58CGZ	33563	Midlands
SN51UYD	65671	Essex	SN55JVE	65753	Scotland East	SN58CHC	33564	West of England
SN51UYE	65672	Essex	SN55JVG	65742	Scotland East	SN58CHD	33565	West of England
SN51UYG	65673	Essex	SN55JVH	65743	Scotland East	SN58CHF	33566	West of England
SN51UYH	65674	Essex	SN55JVJ	65744	Scotland East	SN58CHG	33567	Midlands
SN51UYJ	65675	Essex	SN55JVK	65745	Scotland East	SN58CHH	33568	Midlands
SN51UYK	65676	Essex	SN55JVL	65746	Scotland East	SN58CHJ	33569	Midlands
SN51UYL	65677	Essex	SN55JVM	65747	Scotland East	SN58CHK	33570	Midlands
SN53ESU	43837	Cymru	SN55JVO	65748	Scotland East	SN58CHL	33571	Midlands
SN53ESV	43836	Cymru	SN55JVP	65749	Scotland East	SN58CHO	33572	Midlands
SN53ESY	43838	Cymru	SN55KKE	36029	Scotland East	SN58ENR	33573	Midlands
SN53ETD	43839	Cymru	SN55KKF	36030	Scotland East	SN58ENT	33574	Midlands
SN53ETE	43840	Cymru	SN57HCP	37135	Scotland East	SN59AWV	33425	Essex
SN53ETF	43841	Cymru	SN57HCU	37136	Scotland East	SN60EAA	67701	Glasgow
SN53KHH	65693	Glasgow	SN57HCV	37137	Scotland East	SN60EAC	67702	Glasgow
SN53KHJ	65694	Scotland East	SN57HCX	37138	Scotland East	SN60EAE	67703	Glasgow
SN53KHK	65695	Scotland East	SN57HCY	37139	Scotland East	SN60EAF	67704	Glasgow
SN53KHL	65696	Glasgow	SN57HCZ	37140	Scotland East	SN60EAG	67705	Glasgow
SN53KHM	65697	Glasgow	SN57HDA	37141	Scotland East	SN60EAJ	67706	Glasgow
SN53KHO	65698	Glasgow	SN57HDC	37142	Scotland East	SN60EAM	67707	Glasgow
SN53KHP	65699	Scotland East	SN57HDD	37143	Scotland East	SN60EAO	67708	Glasgow
SN53KJX	42488	Essex	SN57HDE	37144	Scotland East	SN60EAP	67709	Glasgow
SN53KJY	42489	Essex	SN57HDF	37145	Scotland East	SN60EAW	67710	Glasgow
SN53KJZ	42876	Devon & Cornwall	SN57HDG	37266	Scotland East	SN60CAA	33423	East
SN53KKA	42871	Devon & Cornwall	SN57HDH	37133	Scotland East	SN61BDU	33911	Glasgow
SN53KKB	42872	Devon & Cornwall	SN57HDJ	37134	Scotland East	SN61BDV	33912	Glasgow
SN53KKC	42873	Devon & Cornwall	SN57HZX	69292	Scotland East	SN61BDX	33913	Glasgow
SN53KKD	42874	Devon & Cornwall	SN57HZY	69293	Scotland East	SN61BDY	33914	Glasgow
SN53KKE	42875	Devon & Cornwall	SN57HZZ	69294	Scotland East	SN61BDZ	33915	Glasgow
SN53KKY	67600	Midlands	SN57JAO	37267	Scotland East	SN61BEJ	33916	Glasgow
SN54KDF	65708	Scotland East	SN57JAU	37268	Scotland East	SN61BEO	33917	Glasgow

Reg	No	Location	Reg	No	Location	Reg	No	Location
SN61BEU	33918	Glasgow	SN62AWA	39133	West of England	SN64CHF	47493	West Yorkshire
SN61BEY	33919	Glasgow	SN62AWF	39134	West of England	SN64CHG	47494	West Yorkshire
SN61BFA	33920	Glasgow	SN62AWG	39135	West of England	SN64CHH	47495	West Yorkshire
SN61BFE	33921	Glasgow	SN62AWO	39137	West of England	SN64CHJ	47496	West Yorkshire
SN61BFF	33922	Glasgow	SN62AWR	39138	West of England	SN64CHK	47497	West Yorkshire
SN61BFJ	33923	Glasgow	SN62AWY	39139	West of England	SN64CHL	47498	West Yorkshire
SN61BFK	39101	Glasgow	SN62AXB	39140	West of England	SN64CHO	47499	West Yorkshire
SN61BFL	39102	Glasgow	SN62AXC	39141	West of England	SN64CHV	47500	West Yorkshire
SN61BFM	39103	Glasgow	SN62AXH	67773	Scotland East	SN64CHX	63161	Essex
SN61BFO	39104	Glasgow	SN62AXK	67774	Scotland East	SN64CHY	63162	Essex
SN61BFP	39105	Glasgow	SN62AXO	67775	Scotland East	SN64CHZ	63163	Essex
SN61BFU	39106	Glasgow	SN62AXU	67776	Scotland East	SN64CJE	63164	Essex
SN61BFV	39107	Glasgow	SN62AXW	67777	Scotland East	SN64CJF	63165	Essex
SN61BFX	39108	Glasgow	SN62AXY	67778	Scotland East	SN64CJJ	63166	Essex
SN61BFY	39109	Glasgow	SN62AXZ	67779	Scotland East	SN64CJO	63167	Essex
SN61BFZ	39110	Glasgow	SN62AYA	67780	Scotland East	SN64CJU	63168	Essex
SN62ABU	67711	Glasgow	SN62AYB	67781	Scotland East	SN64CJV	63169	Essex
SN62ABV	67712	Glasgow	SN62AYJ	67782	Scotland East	SN64CJX	63170	Essex
SN62ABX	67713	Glasgow	SN62AYV	44527	Hampshire & B	SN64CJY	47531	Scotland East
SN62ABZ	67714	Glasgow	SN62AYZ	44528	Hampshire & B	SN64CJZ	47532	Scotland East
SN62ACX	67715	Glasgow	SN62AZA	44529	Hampshire & B	SN64CKA	47533	Scotland East
SN62ACZ	67716	Glasgow	SN62AZB	44530	Hampshire & B	SN64CKC	47534	Scotland East
SN62ADU	67717	Glasgow	SN62AZW	44531	Hampshire & B	SN64CKD	47613	Scotland East
SN62ADV	67718	Glasgow	SN62DBO	44532	Hampshire & B	SN64CKE	63157	Scotland East
SN62AEA	67719	Glasgow	SN62DBV	44533	Hampshire & B	SN64CKF	63158	Scotland East
SN62AEF	67720	Glasgow	SN62DCX	44534	Hampshire & B	SN64CKG	63159	Scotland East
SN62AEK	67721	Glasgow	SN62DCY	44535	Hampshire & B	SN64CKJ	63160	Scotland East
SN62AET	67722	Glasgow	SN62DCZ	44536	Hampshire & B	SN64CKK	63241	Scotland East
SN62AEU	67723	Glasgow	SN63MYH	33825	West of England	SN64CKL	63242	Scotland East
SN62AEY	67724	Glasgow	SN63MYJ	33826	West of England	SN64CKO	63243	Scotland East
SN62AFE	67725	Glasgow	SN63MYK	33827	West of England	SN64CKP	63244	Scotland East
SN62AFJ	67726	Glasgow	SN63MYL	33828	West of England	SN64CKU	47614	Scotland East
SN62AFK	67727	Glasgow	SN63MYM	33829	West of England	SN64CKV	47615	Scotland East
SN62AFU	67728	Glasgow	SN63MYO	33830	West of England	SN64CKX	47616	Scotland East
SN62AFY	67729	Glasgow	SN63MYP	67870	Glasgow	SN64CKY	47617	Scotland East
SN62AFZ	67730	Glasgow	SN63MYR	67871	Glasgow	SN64CLF	47559	West of England
SN62AGV	67731	Glasgow	SN63MYS	67872	Glasgow	SN64CLJ	47560	West of England
SN62AGY	67732	Glasgow	SN63MYT	67873	Glasgow	SN64CLO	47561	West of England
SN62AHD	67733	Glasgow	SN63MYU	67874	Glasgow	SN64CLU	47562	West of England
SN62AHF	67734	Glasgow	SN63MYV	67875	Glasgow	SN64CLV	47563	West of England
SN62AHL	67735	Glasgow	SN63MYW	67876	Glasgow	SN64CLX	47564	West of England
SN62AHV	67736	Glasgow	SN63MYX	67877	Glasgow	SN64CLY	47565	West of England
SN62AHX	67737	Glasgow	SN63MYY	67878	Glasgow	SN64CLZ	47566	West of England
SN62AJU	67738	Glasgow	SN63MYZ	67879	Glasgow	SN64CME	47567	West of England
SN62AJV	67739	Glasgow	SN63MZD	67880	Glasgow	SN64CMF	47568	West of England
SN62AKG	67740	Glasgow	SN63MZE	67881	Glasgow	SN64CMK	47569	West of England
SN62AKJ	67741	Glasgow	SN63MZF	67882	Glasgow	SN64CMO	47570	West of England
SN62AKO	67742	Glasgow	SN63MZG	67883	Glasgow	SN64CMU	47571	West of England
SN62AKP	67743	Glasgow	SN64CFM	47513	Midlands	SN64CMV	47521	Essex
SN62AMV	67744	Glasgow	SN64CFO	47514	Midlands	SN64CMX	47522	Essex
SN62ANR	67745	Glasgow	SN64CFP	47515	Midlands	SN64CMY	47523	Essex
SN62ANU	67746	Glasgow	SN64CFU	47516	Midlands	SN64CMZ	47524	Essex
SN62AOA	67747	Glasgow	SN64CFV	47517	Midlands	SN64CNA	47525	Essex
SN62AOC	67748	Glasgow	SN64CFX	47518	Midlands	SN64CNC	47526	Essex
SN62AOF	67749	Glasgow	SN64CFY	47519	Midlands	SN64CNE	47527	Essex
SN62AOG	67750	Glasgow	SN64CFZ	47520	Midlands	SN64CNF	47528	Essex
SN62ASO	67755	Glasgow	SN64CGE	63171	Midlands	SN64CNJ	47529	Essex
SN62ASU	67756	Glasgow	SN64CGF	63172	Midlands	SN64CNK	47530	Essex
SN62ASX	67757	Glasgow	SN64CGG	63173	Midlands	SN64CNO	47482	South Yorkshire
SN62ASZ	67758	Glasgow	SN64CGK	63174	Midlands	SN64CNU	47483	South Yorkshire
SN62ATZ	67759	Glasgow	SN64CGO	63175	Midlands	SN64CNV	47484	South Yorkshire
SN62AUC	67760	Glasgow	SN64CGU	63176	Midlands	SN64CNX	47485	South Yorkshire
SN62AUH	67761	Glasgow	SN64CGV	63177	Midlands	SN64CNY	47486	South Yorkshire
SN62AUJ	67762	Glasgow	SN64CGX	63178	Midlands	SN64CNZ	47487	South Yorkshire
SN62AUK	67763	Glasgow	SN64CGY	63179	Midlands	SN64COA	47488	South Yorkshire
SN62AUU	67764	Glasgow	SN64CHC	47491	West Yorkshire	SN64COH	47489	South Yorkshire
SN62AUW	67765	Glasgow	SN64CHD	47492	West Yorkshire	SN64COJ	47490	South Yorkshire

SN64COU	63245	Scotland East	SV08FXW	37638	Aberdeen	T653SSF	65653	Essex
SN64CPE	63246	Scotland East	SV08FXX	37639	Aberdeen	T654SSF	65654	Essex
SN64CPF	63247	Scotland East	SV08FXY	37640	Aberdeen	T660VWU	30840	West Yorkshire
SN64CPK	63248	Scotland East	SV08FXZ	37641	Aberdeen	T661VWU	30841	West Yorkshire
SN64CPO	63249	Scotland East	SV08FYA	37642	Aberdeen	T663VWU	30843	West Yorkshire
SN64CPU	47501	East	SV08FYB	37643	Aberdeen	T664VWU	30844	West Yorkshire
SN64CPV	47502	East	SV08FYC	37644	Aberdeen	T665VWU	30845	West Yorkshire
SN64CPX	47503	East	SV54CFY	68518	Aberdeen	T701JLD	20201	Midlands
SN64CPY	47504	East	SV54CFZ	68519	Aberdeen	T701PND	40437	Manchester
SN64CPZ	47505	East	SV57EYH	69265	Aberdeen	T702JLD	20202	Midlands
SN64CRF	47506	East	SV57EYJ	69266	Aberdeen	T702PND	40438	Manchester
SN64CRJ	47507	East	SV57EYK	69267	Aberdeen	T703PND	40439	Manchester
SN64CRK	47508	East	T12TRU	43812	Devon & Cornwall	T704PND	40440	Manchester
SN64CRU	47509	East	T154OUB	60821	West Yorkshire	T705JLD	20205	Aberdeen
SN64CRV	47510	East	T156OUB	60823	West Yorkshire	T705PND	40441	Manchester
SN64CRX	47511	East	T157OUB	60824	West Yorkshire	T707JLD	20207	Aberdeen
SN64CRZ	47512	East	T158OUB	60825	West Yorkshire	T707PND	40443	Manchester
SN64CSF	35101	South Yorkshire	T162BBF	40009	Midlands	T708PND	40444	Manchester
SN64CSO	35102	Manchester	T163BBF	40010	Midlands	T727REU	42727	Midlands
ST09JPT	45118	East	T167BBF	40683	Manchester	T728REU	42728	Hampshire & B
ST58JPT	45117	East	T20TVL	53402	Devon & Cornwall	T730REU	42730	West of England
SV05DXA	10154	Aberdeen	T255GUG	60822	West Yorkshire	T731REU	42731	West of England
SV05DXC	10155	Aberdeen	T265JLD	41265	Cymru	T77TRU	53206	Hampshire & B
SV05DXD	10156	Aberdeen	T282JLD	41282	West Yorkshire	T801LLC	32801	Essex
SV05DXE	10157	Aberdeen	T283JLD	41283	West Yorkshire	T801RHW	48201	Devon & Cornwall
SV05DXF	10158	Aberdeen	T315VYG	40566	West Yorkshire	T802LLC	32802	Devon & Cornwall
SV05DXG	10159	Aberdeen	T32JCV	42232	Hampshire & B	T803LLC	32803	Devon & Cornwall
SV05DXH	10160	Aberdeen	T336ALR	41336	Hampshire & B	T804LLC	32804	Essex
SV05DXJ	10161	Aberdeen	T343ALR	41343	Cymru	T806LLC	32806	Essex
SV05DXK	10162	Aberdeen	T34JCV	42234	Hampshire & B	T808LLC	32808	Devon & Cornwall
SV05DXL	10163	Aberdeen	T356VWU	42656	Hampshire & B	T809LLC	32809	Essex
SV05DXM	10164	Aberdeen	T35JCV	42235	Devon & Cornwall	T810LLC	32810	Essex
SV05DXO	10165	Aberdeen	T365NUA	40154	Midlands	T811LLC	32811	Scotland East
SV05DXP	10166	Aberdeen	T366NUA	42841	Devon & Cornwall	T813LLC	32813	Scotland East
SV05DXR	10167	Aberdeen	T367NUA	42842	Devon & Cornwall	T814LLC	32814	Scotland East
SV05DXS	10168	Aberdeen	T368NUA	42843	Devon & Cornwall	T815MAK	60633	South Yorkshire
SV05DXT	10169	Aberdeen	T369NUA	42844	Devon & Cornwall	T816MAK	60634	South Yorkshire
SV05DXU	10170	Aberdeen	T370NUA	42845	Cymru	T817LLC	32817	Devon & Cornwall
SV05DXW	10171	Aberdeen	T372NUA	40155	Midlands	T817MAK	60635	South Yorkshire
SV05DXX	10172	Aberdeen	T373NUA	42673	Hampshire & B	T818LLC	32818	Essex
SV05DXY	10173	Aberdeen	T375NUA	40721	Hampshire & B	T818MAK	60636	South Yorkshire
SV06GRF	69110	Aberdeen	T421GUG	61022	Glasgow	T819MAK	60637	South Yorkshire
SV06GRK	69122	Aberdeen	T424GUG	61025	Glasgow	T820LLC	32820	Glasgow
SV06GRU	69123	Aberdeen	T426GUG	61027	Glasgow	T820MAK	60638	West Yorkshire
SV06GRX	69124	Aberdeen	T427GUG	61028	Glasgow	T821JBL	65621	Hampshire & B
SV07EHB	69125	Aberdeen	T428GUG	61029	West Yorkshire	T821LLC	32821	Scotland East
SV07EHC	69126	Aberdeen	T429GUG	61030	West Yorkshire	T821MAK	60639	South Yorkshire
SV07EHD	69127	Aberdeen	T430GUG	61031	West Yorkshire	T822JBL	65622	Hampshire & B
SV07EHE	69128	Aberdeen	T431GUG	61032	West Yorkshire	T822MAK	60640	South Yorkshire
SV07EHF	69129	Aberdeen	T469JCV	42469	Devon & Cornwall	T823LLC	32823	Scotland East
SV07EHG	69130	Aberdeen	T470JCV	42470	Devon & Cornwall	T823MAK	60641	South Yorkshire
SV07EHH	69131	Aberdeen	T471JCV	42471	Devon & Cornwall	T823SFS	60065	West Yorkshire
SV07EHJ	69132	Aberdeen	T472YTT	42472	Devon & Cornwall	T824MAK	60642	South Yorkshire
SV07EHK	69133	Aberdeen	T473YTT	42473	Devon & Cornwall	T824SFS	60066	West Yorkshire
SV07EHL	69134	Aberdeen	T563BSS	60217	West Yorkshire	T825MAK	60643	South Yorkshire
SV08FHA	69351	Aberdeen	T566BSS	60220	Scotland East	T825SFS	60067	West Yorkshire
SV08FHB	69352	Aberdeen	T567BSS	60221	Scotland East	T826MAK	60644	South Yorkshire
SV08FHC	69353	Aberdeen	T576JNG	65576	Essex	T826SFS	60068	Midlands
SV08FHD	69354	Aberdeen	T578JNG	65578	Midlands	T827SFS	60069	Midlands
SV08FHE	69355	Aberdeen	T579JNG	65579	East	T828MAK	60646	South Yorkshire
SV08FHF	69356	Aberdeen	T627SEJ	42327	Cymru	T829MAK	60647	South Yorkshire
SV08FHG	69357	Aberdeen	T628SEJ	42328	Cymru	T830LLC	32830	Scotland East
SV08FXP	37633	Aberdeen	T630SEJ	42330	Cymru	T830MAK	60648	South Yorkshire
SV08FXR	37634	Aberdeen	T631SEJ	42331	Cymru	T831LLC	32831	Scotland East
SV08FXS	37635	Aberdeen	T650SSF	65650	Essex	T831MAK	60649	South Yorkshire
SV08FXT	37636	Aberdeen	T651SSF	65651	Essex	T832MAK	60650	South Yorkshire
SV08FXU	37637	Aberdeen	T652SSF	65652	Essex	T833MAK	60651	Manchester

Reg	No	Area	Reg	No	Area	Reg	No	Area
T834LLC	32834	Scotland East	T884ODT	60702	South Yorkshire	V433HBY	41333	West of England
T835MAK	60653	South Yorkshire	T889KLF	34089	Manchester	V527ESH	62385	Scotland East
T836MAK	60654	South Yorkshire	T890KLF	34090	South Yorkshire	V528ESH	62386	Scotland East
T837LLC	32837	Scotland East	T891KLF	34091	Devon & Cornwall	V530ESH	62388	Scotland East
T837MAK	60655	South Yorkshire	T892KLF	34092	Devon & Cornwall	V531ESH	62389	Scotland East
T838LLC	32838	Scotland East	T893KLF	34093	Devon & Cornwall	V532ESH	62390	Scotland East
T838MAK	60656	South Yorkshire	T894KLF	34094	Manchester	V586DVF	65586	Essex
T839MAK	60657	South Yorkshire	T895KLF	34095	Manchester	V587DVF	65587	Essex
T840MAK	60658	South Yorkshire	T896KLF	34096	Devon & Cornwall	V588DVF	65588	East
T841LLC	32841	Scotland East	T897KLF	34097	Devon & Cornwall	V589DVF	65589	Essex
T841MAK	60659	South Yorkshire	T898KLF	34098	Devon & Cornwall	V590DVF	65590	East
T842LLC	32842	Scotland East	T899KLF	34099	Devon & Cornwall	V601GGB	10044	Aberdeen
T842MAK	60660	Manchester	T902KLF	34102	Manchester	V602GGB	10045	Aberdeen
T843LLC	32843	West of England	T904KLF	34104	Devon & Cornwall	V608GGB	10108	Aberdeen
T843MAK	60661	South Yorkshire	T905KLF	34105	Manchester	V610GGB	10110	Aberdeen
T844LLC	32844	West of England	T907KLF	34107	West Yorkshire	V701FFB	32701	Hampshire & B
T844MAK	60662	South Yorkshire	T918SSF	60171	Midlands	V71GEH	40304	Midlands
T845LLC	32845	Aberdeen	T919SSF	60172	West Yorkshire	V721UVY	60828	West Yorkshire
T845MAK	60663	Manchester	T990KLF	34100	Manchester	V732FAE	42732	West of England
T846LLC	32846	Devon & Cornwall	TJI4838	34195	Devon & Cornwall	V733FAE	42733	West of England
T846MAK	60664	South Yorkshire	TL54TVL	53403	Devon & Cornwall	V734FAE	42734	West of England
T847LLC	32847	Essex	TO54TRU	53401	West of England	V735FAE	42735	West of England
T847MAK	60665	Midlands	TT03TRU	42860	Devon & Cornwall	V736FAE	42736	West of England
T848MAK	60666	South Yorkshire	TT04TRU	20556	Devon & Cornwall	V737FAE	42737	West of England
T849LLC	32849	Essex	TT05TRU	20557	Devon & Cornwall	V738FAE	42738	West of England
T850LLC	32850	Essex	TT07TRU	20561	Devon & Cornwall	V759UVY	60826	West Yorkshire
T850MAK	60668	West Yorkshire	TT54TVL	53404	Devon & Cornwall	V760UVY	60827	West Yorkshire
T851MAK	60669	South Yorkshire	TT55TRU	20558	Devon & Cornwall	V762UVY	60829	West Yorkshire
T852LLC	32852	Midlands	TU04TRU	53204	West of England	V763UVY	60830	West Yorkshire
T852MAK	60670	South Yorkshire	UHW661	40582	Devon & Cornwall	V764UVY	60831	West Yorkshire
T853MAK	60671	South Yorkshire	UKT552	34198	Devon & Cornwall	V765UVY	60832	West Yorkshire
T854KLF	32854	Midlands	URS318X	31528	Aberdeen	V767UVY	60834	West Yorkshire
T854MAK	60672	South Yorkshire	V118FSF	61669	Glasgow	V768UVY	60835	West Yorkshire
T855MAK	60673	South Yorkshire	V122DND	60174	Midlands	V769UVY	60836	West Yorkshire
T856MAK	60674	South Yorkshire	V124DND	60176	Midlands	V770UVY	60837	West Yorkshire
T857MAK	60675	South Yorkshire	V124LGC	32027	West of England	V771UVY	60838	West Yorkshire
T858MAK	60676	South Yorkshire	V128DND	60180	Scotland East	V772UVY	60839	West Yorkshire
T859MAK	60677	South Yorkshire	V129DND	60181	Manchester	V773UVY	60840	West Yorkshire
T860MAK	60678	South Yorkshire	V133ESC	61034	West Yorkshire	V801KAF	53001	West of England
T861MAK	60679	South Yorkshire	V134ESC	61035	West Yorkshire	V808EFB	48208	Hampshire & B
T862MAK	60680	South Yorkshire	V135ESC	61036	West Yorkshire	V810EFB	48210	Devon & Cornwall
T863MAK	60681	South Yorkshire	V136DND	60188	Manchester	V826FSC	65626	Essex
T864KLF	32864	Essex	V136ESC	61037	West Yorkshire	V827FSC	65627	Essex
T864MAK	60682	South Yorkshire	V137DND	60189	Midlands	V830FSC	65630	Essex
T865KLF	32865	Aberdeen	V137ESC	61038	West Yorkshire	V830GBF	60072	Midlands
T865ODT	60683	South Yorkshire	V138ESC	61039	West Yorkshire	V831FSC	65631	Essex
T866KLF	32866	West of England	V139ESC	61040	West Yorkshire	V831GBF	60073	Midlands
T866ODT	60684	South Yorkshire	V140ESC	61041	West Yorkshire	V832DYD	42832	Devon & Cornwall
T867ODT	60685	South Yorkshire	V141DND	60193	Midlands	V832FSC	65632	East
T868ODT	60686	South Yorkshire	V141ESC	61042	West Yorkshire	V832GBF	60074	Midlands
T869ODT	60687	South Yorkshire	V142DND	60173	Midlands	V833DYD	42833	Devon & Cornwall
T870KLF	32870	Scotland East	V311GBY	41311	Glasgow	V835DYD	42835	Devon & Cornwall
T870ODT	60688	South Yorkshire	V314GBY	41314	Glasgow	V855HBY	32855	Essex
T871ODT	60689	South Yorkshire	V330DBU	60175	Midlands	V856HBY	32856	Essex
T872ODT	60690	South Yorkshire	V346DLH	41346	Hampshire & B	V859HBY	32859	Essex
T873ODT	60691	South Yorkshire	V347DLH	41347	Cymru	V863HBY	32863	Essex
T874ODT	60692	South Yorkshire	V348DLH	41348	Hampshire & B	V867HBY	32867	Manchester
T875ODT	60693	South Yorkshire	V356DVG	43356	Essex	V869HBY	32869	Manchester
T876ODT	60694	South Yorkshire	V357DVG	43357	Essex	V887HBY	32887	Essex
T877ODT	60695	South Yorkshire	V359DVG	43359	Essex	V889HLH	32889	Scotland East
T878ODT	60696	South Yorkshire	V35ESC	62392	Scotland East	V892HLH	32892	Scotland East
T879ODT	60697	South Yorkshire	V360DVG	43360	Essex	V893HLH	32893	Scotland East
T880ODT	60698	South Yorkshire	V362CNH	65662	Scotland East	V895HLH	32895	Scotland East
T881ODT	60699	South Yorkshire	V363CNH	65663	Scotland East	V896HLH	32896	Scotland East
T882ODT	60700	South Yorkshire	V364CNH	65664	Scotland East	V897HLH	32897	Scotland East
T883KLF	32883	Essex	V370KLG	41070	Midlands	V898HLH	32898	Scotland East
T883ODT	60701	South Yorkshire	V42DTE	40181	Manchester	V899HLH	32899	Manchester

VJT738	34193	Devon & Cornwall	W118CWR	10035	West of England	W348RJA	60270	Manchester
VOO273	34200	Devon & Cornwall	W119CWR	10036	West of England	W349RJA	60271	Manchester
VT09JPT	45116	East	W122CWR	10037	West of England	W351RJA	60273	Manchester
VT59JPT	33424	Essex	W122DWX	10039	West Yorkshire	W352RJA	60274	Manchester
VU02PKX	53040	Midlands	W124DWX	10041	West Yorkshire	W353RJA	60275	Manchester
VU02PKY	53041	Midlands	W126DWX	10043	West Yorkshire	W354RJA	60276	Manchester
VU03YJT	53042	Midlands	W127DWX	10038	West Yorkshire	W356RJA	60278	Manchester
VU03YJV	53043	Midlands	W128DWX	10040	West Yorkshire	W357RJA	60279	Manchester
VU03YJW	53044	Midlands	W129DWX	10042	West Yorkshire	W358RJA	60280	Manchester
VU03YJX	53045	Midlands	W132VLO	32950	West of England	W359RJA	60281	Manchester
VU03YJY	53046	Midlands	W179BVP	60283	Manchester	W361RJA	60262	Manchester
VU03YJZ	53047	Midlands	W213XBD	32053	Midlands	W362RJA	60272	Manchester
VU03YKB	53048	Midlands	W214XBD	32054	Midlands	W363RJA	60255	Manchester
VU03YKC	53049	Midlands	W215XBD	32055	Midlands	W364EOW	66164	Hampshire & B
VU03YKD	53050	Midlands	W216XBD	32056	Midlands	W364RJA	60282	Manchester
VU03YKE	53051	Midlands	W217XBD	32057	Midlands	W365EOW	66165	Essex
VX05JWW	42894	Midlands	W218XBD	32058	East	W365RJA	60267	Manchester
VX05LVS	67652	Midlands	W219XBD	32059	East	W366EOW	66166	West of England
VX05LVT	67653	Midlands	W221XBD	32061	East	W366RJA	60277	Manchester
VX05LVU	67654	Midlands	W223XBD	32063	East	W367EOW	66167	West of England
VX05LVV	67655	Midlands	W224XBD	32064	East	W368EOW	66168	Essex
VX05LVW	67656	Midlands	W2FAL	10047	Aberdeen	W369EOW	66169	Essex
VX05LVY	67657	Midlands	W301JND	60223	Manchester	W371EOW	66171	West of England
VX05LVZ	67658	Midlands	W302JND	60224	Manchester	W373EOW	66173	West of England
VX05LWC	67659	Midlands	W303JND	60225	Manchester	W374EOW	66174	West of England
VX05LWD	67660	Midlands	W304JND	60226	Manchester	W376EOW	66176	Hampshire & B
VX05LWE	67661	Midlands	W307DWX	50276	Devon & Cornwall	W377EOW	66177	Essex
VX05LWF	67662	Midlands	W307JND	60229	Manchester	W378EOW	66178	West of England
VX05LWG	67663	Midlands	W308DWX	50277	West of England	W378JNE	60247	Manchester
VX05LWH	67664	Midlands	W308JND	60230	Manchester	W379EOW	66179	Essex
VX53OEN	53059	Midlands	W309DWX	50278	West of England	W379JNE	60250	Manchester
VX53OEO	53060	Midlands	W311JND	60233	Manchester	W381EOW	66181	Hampshire & B
VX53OEP	53061	Midlands	W312DWX	50281	Midlands	W3FAL	10048	Aberdeen
VX53OER	53062	Midlands	W312JND	60234	Manchester	W422SRP	32062	East
VX53OET	53063	Midlands	W313JND	60235	Manchester	W425SRP	32065	East
VX53OEU	53064	Midlands	W314JND	60236	Manchester	W431CWX	34111	East
VX53OEV	53058	Midlands	W315DWX	50284	Devon & Cornwall	W432CWX	34112	East
VX53VJV	67601	Midlands	W315JND	60237	Manchester	W433CWX	34113	East
VX53VJZ	67602	Midlands	W317JND	60239	Manchester	W434CWX	34114	East
VX53VKA	67603	Midlands	W319JND	60241	Manchester	W435CWX	34108	East
VX53VKB	67604	Midlands	W322DWX	50291	Devon & Cornwall	W436CWX	34109	East
VX54MOV	67631	Midlands	W322JND	60244	Manchester	W437CWX	34110	East
VX54MPE	67632	Midlands	W326JND	60248	Manchester	W474SVT	40015	Midlands
VX54MPF	67633	Midlands	W327DWX	50296	Midlands	W475SVT	40016	Midlands
VX54MPO	67634	Midlands	W327JND	60249	Manchester	W478SVT	40019	Midlands
VX54MPU	67635	Midlands	W329DWX	50279	Devon & Cornwall	W4FAL	10049	East
VX54MPV	67636	Midlands	W329JND	60251	Manchester	W4TRU	56000	Devon & Cornwall
VX54MPY	67637	Midlands	W331DWX	50290	Devon & Cornwall	W577RFS	62170	Aberdeen
VX54MPZ	67638	Midlands	W331JND	60252	Manchester	W578RFS	62171	Aberdeen
VX54MRO	67639	Midlands	W331RJA	60253	Manchester	W579RFS	62172	Aberdeen
VX54MRU	67640	Midlands	W332RJA	60254	Manchester	W581RFS	62173	Aberdeen
VX54MRV	67641	Midlands	W334JND	60238	Manchester	W582RFS	62174	Aberdeen
VX54MRY	67642	Midlands	W334RJA	60256	Manchester	W583RFS	62175	Aberdeen
VX54MSO	67643	Midlands	W335RJA	60257	Manchester	W584RFS	62176	Aberdeen
VX54MTF	67647	Midlands	W336DWX	50285	Devon & Cornwall	W585RFS	62184	Scotland East
VX54MTJ	67648	Midlands	W336RJA	60258	Manchester	W586RFS	62185	Scotland East
VX54MTK	67649	Midlands	W337DWX	50292	Devon & Cornwall	W587RFS	62186	Scotland East
VX54MTO	67650	Midlands	W337JND	60242	Manchester	W588RFS	62187	Scotland East
VX54MTU	67651	Midlands	W337RJA	60259	Manchester	W589RFS	62188	Scotland East
VX54MTV	33401	Midlands	W338JND	60240	Manchester	W591RFS	62189	Scotland East
VX54MTY	33402	Midlands	W338RJA	60260	Manchester	W591SNG	65591	Glasgow
VX54MTZ	33403	Midlands	W339JND	60245	Manchester	W592RFS	62190	Scotland East
VX54MUA	33404	Midlands	W339RJA	60261	Manchester	W592SNG	65592	Glasgow
VX54MUB	33405	Midlands	W341JND	60243	Manchester	W593RFS	62205	Scotland East
VX54MUU	42892	Midlands	W342RJA	60264	Manchester	W593SNG	65593	Glasgow
VX54MUV	42893	Midlands	W346RJA	60268	Manchester	W594RFS	62206	Scotland East
VX57CYO	53405	Midlands	W347RJA	60269	Manchester	W594SNG	65594	Scotland East

Reg	No	Area	Reg	No	Area	Reg	No	Area
W595RFS	62207	Scotland East	W717RHT	32717	Devon & Cornwall	W803PAE	32003	West of England
W595SNG	65595	Scotland East	W718CWR	30863	West Yorkshire	W804DWX	60844	West Yorkshire
W596RFS	62208	Scotland East	W718ULL	41718	Cymru	W804EOW	32034	Hampshire & B
W596SNG	65596	Glasgow	W719CWR	30864	West Yorkshire	W804PAE	32004	West of England
W597RFS	62209	Scotland East	W719ULL	41719	Cymru	W805DWX	60845	West Yorkshire
W597SNG	65597	Scotland East	W721CWR	30866	West Yorkshire	W805EOW	32035	Hampshire & B
W598RFS	62210	Scotland East	W722CWR	30867	West Yorkshire	W805PAE	32005	West of England
W598SNG	65598	Scotland East	W723CWR	30868	West Yorkshire	W806DWX	60846	West Yorkshire
W599RFS	62211	Scotland East	W724CWR	30869	West Yorkshire	W806EOW	32036	Hampshire & B
W599SNG	65599	Scotland East	W726CWR	30870	West Yorkshire	W806PAE	32006	West of England
W5FAL	10050	Aberdeen	W726DWX	30871	Manchester	W807DWX	60847	West Yorkshire
W601PAF	48261	Devon & Cornwall	W727DWX	30872	Manchester	W807EOW	32037	Cymru
W601RFS	62219	Scotland East	W727ULL	41727	Cymru	W807PAE	32007	West of England
W601SNG	65601	Scotland East	W728DWX	30873	Manchester	W807PAF	53007	Devon & Cornwall
W602PAF	48262	Devon & Cornwall	W729DWX	30874	Manchester	W808DWX	60848	West Yorkshire
W602RFS	62220	Scotland East	W731DWX	30876	Manchester	W808EOW	32038	Hampshire & B
W603PAF	48263	Devon & Cornwall	W732DWX	30877	Manchester	W808PAE	32008	West of England
W603RFS	62221	Scotland East	W733DWX	30878	Manchester	W808PAF	53008	Essex
W604PAF	48264	Devon & Cornwall	W734DWX	30879	Manchester	W809DWX	60849	West Yorkshire
W604RFS	62222	Scotland East	W735DWX	30880	Manchester	W809EOW	32039	Hampshire & B
W605PAF	48265	Devon & Cornwall	W736DWX	30881	South Yorkshire	W809PAE	32009	West of England
W605RFS	62223	Scotland East	W737DWX	30882	South Yorkshire	W809PAF	53009	West of England
W606PAF	48266	Devon & Cornwall	W738DWX	30883	South Yorkshire	W809VMA	42358	Hampshire & B
W607PAF	48267	Devon & Cornwall	W739DWX	30884	South Yorkshire	W811DWX	60850	West Yorkshire
W607RFS	62225	Scotland East	W741DWX	30886	East	W811EOW	32041	Cymru
W608RFS	62226	Scotland East	W742DWX	30887	Essex	W811PAE	32011	West of England
W609PAF	48269	Devon & Cornwall	W743DWX	30888	East	W811PAF	53011	Devon & Cornwall
W609RFS	62227	Scotland East	W744DWX	30889	East	W811PFB	48211	Devon & Cornwall
W667CWT	30855	West Yorkshire	W745DWX	30890	West Yorkshire	W812DWX	60851	West Yorkshire
W668CWT	30865	West Yorkshire	W746DWX	30891	West Yorkshire	W812EOW	32042	Cymru
W681RNA	62204	Scotland East	W747DWX	30892	West Yorkshire	W812PAE	32012	West of England
W682RNA	62212	Scotland East	W748DWX	30893	West Yorkshire	W812PAF	53012	West of England
W683RNA	62213	Scotland East	W751DWX	30896	West Yorkshire	W812PFB	48212	West of England
W683ULL	41683	Glasgow	W752DWX	30897	West Yorkshire	W813DWX	60852	West Yorkshire
W684ULL	41684	Glasgow	W753DWX	30898	South Yorkshire	W813EOW	32043	Hampshire & B
W685ULL	41685	Glasgow	W754DWX	30899	South Yorkshire	W813PAE	32013	West of England
W6FAL	10051	Aberdeen	W756DWX	30901	East	W813PAF	53013	West of England
W701CWR	30846	South Yorkshire	W757DWX	30902	Essex	W813PFB	48213	West of England
W702CWR	30847	West Yorkshire	W758DWX	30903	Essex	W814DWX	60853	West Yorkshire
W702PHT	32702	Hampshire & B	W759DWX	30904	South Yorkshire	W814EOW	32044	Cymru
W703CWR	30848	West Yorkshire	W761DWX	30906	South Yorkshire	W814PAE	32014	West of England
W703PHT	32703	Hampshire & B	W762DWX	30907	South Yorkshire	W814PAF	53014	West of England
W704CWR	30849	West Yorkshire	W766HBT	60833	West Yorkshire	W814PFB	48214	West of England
W704PHT	32704	Hampshire & B	W768DWX	30913	West Yorkshire	W815DWX	60854	West Yorkshire
W705CWR	30850	West Yorkshire	W769DWX	30914	West Yorkshire	W815EOW	32045	Hampshire & B
W705PHT	32705	Hampshire & B	W771DWX	30875	Manchester	W815PAE	32015	West of England
W706CWR	30851	West Yorkshire	W771KBT	30916	West Yorkshire	W815PAF	53015	Devon & Cornwall
W706PHT	32706	Hampshire & B	W772DWX	30885	South Yorkshire	W816DWX	60855	West Yorkshire
W707CWR	30852	West Yorkshire	W772KBT	30917	West Yorkshire	W816EOW	32046	Hampshire & B
W707PHT	32707	Hampshire & B	W773DWX	30895	West Yorkshire	W816PAE	32016	West of England
W708CWR	30853	West Yorkshire	W773KBT	30918	West Yorkshire	W816PFB	48216	West of England
W708PHT	32708	Hampshire & B	W774DWX	30900	East	W817PAE	32017	West of England
W709CWR	30854	West Yorkshire	W774KBT	30919	West Yorkshire	W817PFB	48217	West of England
W709RHT	32709	Devon & Cornwall	W776DWX	30905	South Yorkshire	W818PAE	32018	West of England
W711CWR	30856	West Yorkshire	W776KBT	30921	West Yorkshire	W818PFB	48218	West of England
W711RHT	32711	Devon & Cornwall	W778DWX	30910	West Yorkshire	W819PAE	32019	West of England
W712CWR	30857	West Yorkshire	W787KBT	30920	West Yorkshire	W819PFB	48219	West of England
W712RHT	32712	Devon & Cornwall	W788KBT	30922	West Yorkshire	W821PAE	32021	West of England
W713CWR	30858	West Yorkshire	W7FAL	10052	Aberdeen	W821PFB	48221	Devon & Cornwall
W713RHT	32713	Devon & Cornwall	W801DWX	60841	West Yorkshire	W822PAE	32022	West of England
W714CWR	30859	West Yorkshire	W801EOW	32031	Hampshire & B	W822PFB	48222	West of England
W714RHT	32714	Devon & Cornwall	W801PAE	32001	West of England	W823PAE	32023	West of England
W715CWR	30860	West Yorkshire	W802DWX	60842	West Yorkshire	W823PFB	48223	West of England
W715RHT	32715	Devon & Cornwall	W802EOW	32032	Hampshire & B	W824PAE	32024	West of England
W716CWR	30861	South Yorkshire	W802PAE	32002	West of England	W824PFB	48224	West of England
W716RHT	32716	Devon & Cornwall	W803DWX	60843	West Yorkshire	W825PFB	48225	Devon & Cornwall
W717CWR	30862	South Yorkshire	W803EOW	32033	Hampshire & B	W826PFB	48226	Devon & Cornwall

Reg	No.	Location	Reg	No.	Location	Reg	No.	Location
W827PFB	48227	Devon & Cornwall	WA56FTZ	42969	West of England	WX05RSZ	53809	West of England
W828PFB	48228	Devon & Cornwall	WA56FUB	33411	West of England	WX05RTO	53810	West of England
W829PFB	48229	Devon & Cornwall	WA56FUD	33412	West of England	WX05RTU	53811	West of England
W831PFB	48231	Devon & Cornwall	WA56FUE	33413	West of England	WX05RTV	53812	West of England
W832PFB	48232	Devon & Cornwall	WA56OAO	42941	Manchester	WX05RTZ	53813	West of England
W833PFB	48233	Devon & Cornwall	WA56OAP	42942	Devon & Cornwall	WX05RUA	53814	West of England
W834PFB	48234	Devon & Cornwall	WA56OAS	42943	Devon & Cornwall	WX05RUC	53815	West of England
W840VLO	32940	West of England	WA56OAU	42944	Manchester	WX05RUJ	53816	West of England
W895VLN	32910	Scotland East	WA56OAV	42945	Manchester	WX05RUO	53817	West of England
W896VLN	32911	Manchester	WJ55CRX	32761	Devon & Cornwall	WX05RUR	53818	West of England
W897VLN	32920	Glasgow	WJ55CRZ	32762	Devon & Cornwall	WX05RUU	53819	West of England
W898VLN	32925	Glasgow	WJ55CSF	32763	Hampshire & B	WX05RUV	53820	West of England
W899VLN	32930	West of England	WJ55CSO	32764	Hampshire & B	WX05RUW	42895	West of England
W904VLN	32904	Scotland East	WJ55CSU	32765	Hampshire & B	WX05RUY	42896	West of England
W905VLN	32905	Essex	WJ55CSV	32766	Hampshire & B	WX05RVA	42897	West of England
W906VLN	32906	Manchester	WJ55CTE	32767	Hampshire & B	WX05RVC	42898	West of England
W907VLN	32907	Scotland East	WJ55CTF	32768	Hampshire & B	WX05RVE	42899	West of England
W908VLN	32908	Manchester	WK02TYD	48270	Hampshire & B	WX05RVF	42900	West of England
W909VLN	32909	Scotland East	WK02TYF	48271	Devon & Cornwall	WX05RVJ	42901	West of England
W912VLN	32912	Manchester	WK02TYH	48272	Hampshire & B	WX05RVK	42902	West of England
W913VLN	32913	Manchester	WK06AEE	43850	Cymru	WX05RVL	42903	West of England
W914VLN	32914	Scotland East	WK06AEF	43851	Cymru	WX05RVM	42904	West of England
W915VLN	32915	Manchester	WK06AFU	43852	Cymru	WX05RVN	42905	West of England
W916VLN	32916	Manchester	WK06AFV	43853	Cymru	WX05RVO	42906	West of England
W917VLN	32917	Scotland East	WK08ESV	64049	Devon & Cornwall	WX05RVP	42907	West of England
W918VLN	32918	Scotland East	WK10AZU	64050	Devon & Cornwall	WX05RVR	42908	West of England
W919VLN	32919	Scotland East	WK52SYE	32755	Devon & Cornwall	WX05RVT	42909	West of England
W921VLN	32921	Scotland East	WK52WTV	43811	Devon & Cornwall	WX05RVV	42910	West of England
W922VLN	32922	Scotland East	WK56ABZ	44500	Cymru	WX05RVW	42911	West of England
W923VLN	32923	Scotland East	WM04NZU	23208	Devon & Cornwall	WX05RVY	42912	Cymru
W924VLN	32924	Scotland East	WR03YZL	32279	West of England	WX05RVZ	42913	Cymru
W926VLN	32926	Manchester	WR03YZM	32280	West of England	WX05RWE	42914	West of England
W927VLN	32927	Glasgow	WR03YZN	32281	West of England	WX05RWF	42915	West of England
W928VLN	32928	Aberdeen	WR03YZP	32282	West of England	WX05SVD	42916	West of England
W931ULL	32931	West of England	WR03YZS	32283	West of England	WX05SVE	42938	West of England
W934ULL	32934	Scotland East	WR03YZT	32284	West of England	WX05UAF	42939	West of England
W935ULL	32935	West of England	WR03YZU	32285	West of England	WX05UAG	32636	West of England
W936ULL	32936	West of England	WR03YZV	32286	West of England	WX05UAH	32637	West of England
W937ULL	32937	West of England	WR03YZW	32287	West of England	WX05UAJ	32638	West of England
W939ULL	32939	West of England	WR03YZX	32288	West of England	WX05UAK	42552	West of England
W941ULL	32941	West of England	WR03ZBC	32291	West of England	WX05UAL	42553	West of England
W942ULL	32942	West of England	WR03ZBD	32292	West of England	WX05UAM	42554	West of England
W946ULL	32946	West of England	WSU489	20021	Aberdeen	WX05UAN	42555	West of England
W947ULL	32947	West of England	WU02KVE	30564	South Yorkshire	WX05UAO	42556	West of England
W948ULL	32948	Scotland East	WU02KVF	30565	South Yorkshire	WX06OMF	42557	West of England
W949ULL	32949	Scotland East	WU02KVH	30567	South Yorkshire	WX06OMG	42949	Hampshire & B
W951ULL	32951	Scotland East	WU02KVJ	30568	South Yorkshire	WX06OMH	42950	Hampshire & B
WA05UNE	20352	Aberdeen	WU02KVK	30569	South Yorkshire	WX06OMJ	42951	Hampshire & B
WA05UNF	20353	Aberdeen	WU02KVL	30570	South Yorkshire	WX06OMK	42952	Hampshire & B
WA05UNG	20351	Aberdeen	WU02KVM	30571	South Yorkshire	WX06OML	42953	Hampshire & B
WA08MVE	33420	Devon & Cornwall	WU02KVO	30572	South Yorkshire	WX06OMM	42954	Hampshire & B
WA08MVF	33421	Devon & Cornwall	WU02KVP	30573	South Yorkshire	WX06OMO	42955	West of England
WA08MVG	33422	Devon & Cornwall	WU02KVR	30574	South Yorkshire	WX06OMP	42956	West of England
WA54OLN	32759	Devon & Cornwall	WU02KVS	30575	South Yorkshire	WX06OMR	42957	West of England
WA54OLO	32756	Devon & Cornwall	WU02KVT	30576	South Yorkshire	WX06OMS	42958	West of England
WA54OLP	32757	Devon & Cornwall	WU02KVV	30577	South Yorkshire	WX06OMT	42959	West of England
WA54OLR	32760	Devon & Cornwall	WU02KVW	30578	South Yorkshire	WX06OMU	42960	West of England
WA54OLT	32758	Devon & Cornwall	WV02EUP	20514	East	WX06OMV	42961	West of England
WA56FTK	33414	West of England	WV02EUR	20515	East	WX06OMY	42962	West of England
WA56FTN	33415	West of England	WX05OZF	20307	Scotland East	WX06OMZ	42963	West of England
WA56FTO	33416	West of England	WX05RRV	53802	Cymru	WX06OMY	42964	West of England
WA56FTP	33417	West of England	WX05RRY	53803	Devon & Cornwall	WX06ONA	42965	West of England
WA56FTT	33418	West of England	WX05RRZ	53804	Cymru	WX06ONB	42966	West of England
WA56FTU	33419	West of England	WX05RSO	53805	Devon & Cornwall	WX06ONC	42967	West of England
WA56FTV	42946	Devon & Cornwall	WX05RSU	53806	West of England	WX06ONC	42968	West of England
WA56FTX	42947	West of England	WX05RSV	53807	West of England	WX08LNN	44902	West of England
WA56FTY	42948	West of England	WX05RSY	53808	West of England	WX08LNO	44903	West of England

Reg	Fleet	Region	Reg	Fleet	Region	Reg	Fleet	Region
WX08LNP	44904	West of England	WX55TZU	66957	East	WX57HLF	37345	West of England
WX09KBK	37757	West of England	WX55TZV	66958	Cymru	WX57HLG	37346	West of England
WX09KBN	37758	West of England	WX55TZW	66959	East	WX57HLH	37347	West of England
WX09KBO	37759	West of England	WX55TZY	66960	Cymru	WX57HLJ	37348	West of England
WX09KBP	37760	West of England	WX55TZZ	66961	Cymru	WX57HLK	37349	West of England
WX09KBU	37761	West of England	WX55UAA	66934	West of England	WX57HLM	37350	West of England
WX09KBV	37762	West of England	WX55UAB	66935	West of England	WX57HLN	37351	West of England
WX09KBY	37763	West of England	WX55UAC	66936	West of England	WX57HLO	37352	West of England
WX09KBZ	37764	West of England	WX55UAD	66937	West of England	WX57HLP	37353	West of England
WX09KCA	37765	West of England	WX55VHK	37001	West of England	WX57HLR	37354	West of England
WX09KCC	37766	West of England	WX55VHL	37002	West of England	WX57HLU	37355	West of England
WX09KCE	37767	West of England	WX55VHM	37003	West of England	WX57HLV	37356	West of England
WX09KCF	37768	West of England	WX55VHN	37004	West of England	WX57HLW	37357	West of England
WX09KCG	37769	West of England	WX55VHO	37005	West of England	WX57HLY	37358	West of England
WX09KCJ	37770	West of England	WX55VHP	37006	West of England	WX57HLZ	37359	West of England
WX09KCK	37771	West of England	WX55VHR	37007	West of England	WX58JWU	37587	West of England
WX09KCN	37772	West of England	WX55VHT	37008	West of England	WX58JWV	37588	West of England
WX53UKK	32289	West of England	WX55VHU	37009	West of England	WX58JWW	37589	West of England
WX53UKL	32290	West of England	WX55VHV	37010	West of England	WX58JWY	37590	West of England
WX54XCM	66727	West of England	WX55VHW	37011	West of England	WX58JWZ	37591	West of England
WX54XCN	66728	West of England	WX55VHY	37012	West of England	WX58JXA	37592	West of England
WX54XCO	66729	West of England	WX55VHZ	37013	West of England	WX58JXB	37593	West of England
WX54XCP	66730	West of England	WX55VJA	37014	West of England	WX58JXC	37594	West of England
WX54XCR	66731	West of England	WX55VJC	37015	West of England	WX58JXD	37595	West of England
WX54XCT	66732	West of England	WX55VJD	37016	West of England	WX58JXE	37596	West of England
WX54XCU	66733	West of England	WX55VJE	37017	West of England	WX58JXF	37597	West of England
WX54XCV	66734	West of England	WX55VJF	37018	West of England	WX58JXG	37598	West of England
WX54XCW	66735	Glasgow	WX55VJG	37019	West of England	WX58JXH	37599	West of England
WX54XCY	66736	Glasgow	WX55VJJ	37020	West of England	WX58JXJ	37600	West of England
WX54XCZ	66737	Glasgow	WX56HJZ	32684	West of England	WX58JXK	37601	West of England
WX54XDA	66716	Cymru	WX56HKA	32685	West of England	WX58JXL	37602	West of England
WX54XDB	66718	Cymru	WX56HKB	32686	West of England	WX58JXM	37603	West of England
WX54XDC	66719	Cymru	WX56HKC	32687	West of England	WX58JXN	37604	West of England
WX54XDD	66717	Cymru	WX56HKD	32688	West of England	WX58JXO	37605	West of England
WX54XDE	66721	West of England	WX56HKE	32689	West of England	WX58JXP	37606	West of England
WX54XDF	66720	West of England	WX56HKF	32690	West of England	WX58JXR	37607	West of England
WX54XDG	66724	West of England	WX56HKG	32691	West of England	WX58JXS	37608	West of England
WX54XDH	66723	West of England	WX57HJO	37315	West of England	WX58JXT	37609	West of England
WX54XDJ	66725	West of England	WX57HJU	37316	West of England	WX58JXU	37610	West of England
WX54XDK	66726	West of England	WX57HJV	37317	West of England	WX58JXV	37611	West of England
WX54XDL	66722	West of England	WX57HJY	37318	West of England	WX58JXW	37612	West of England
WX54ZHM	20300	Scotland East	WX57HJZ	37319	West of England	WX58JXY	37613	West of England
WX54ZHN	20301	Scotland East	WX57HKA	37320	West of England	WX58JXZ	37614	West of England
WX54ZHO	20302	Scotland East	WX57HKB	37321	West of England	WX58JYA	37615	West of England
WX55HVZ	10174	West of England	WX57HKC	37322	West of England	WX58JYB	37616	West of England
WX55HWA	10175	West of England	WX57HKD	37323	West of England	WX58JYC	37617	West of England
WX55HWB	10176	West of England	WX57HKE	37324	West of England	WX58JYD	37618	West of England
WX55HWC	10177	West of England	WX57HKF	37325	West of England	WX58JYE	37619	West of England
WX55TYZ	66938	West of England	WX57HKG	37326	West of England	WX58JYF	37620	West of England
WX55TZA	66939	West of England	WX57HKH	37327	West of England	WX58JYG	37621	West of England
WX55TZB	66940	West of England	WX57HKJ	37328	West of England	WX58JYH	37622	West of England
WX55TZC	66941	West of England	WX57HKK	37329	West of England	WX58JYJ	37623	West of England
WX55TZD	66942	West of England	WX57HKL	37330	West of England	WX58JYK	37624	West of England
WX55TZE	66943	West of England	WX57HKM	37331	West of England	WX58JYL	37625	West of England
WX55TZF	66944	Hampshire & B	WX57HKN	37332	West of England	WX58JYN	37626	West of England
WX55TZG	66945	Hampshire & B	WX57HKO	37333	West of England	WX58JYO	37627	West of England
WX55TZH	66946	Glasgow	WX57HKP	37334	West of England	WX58JYP	37628	West of England
WX55TZJ	66947	Glasgow	WX57HKT	37335	West of England	WX58JYR	37629	West of England
WX55TZK	66948	Glasgow	WX57HKU	37336	West of England	WX58JYS	37630	West of England
WX55TZL	66949	Glasgow	WX57HKV	37337	West of England	WX58JYT	37631	West of England
WX55TZM	66950	East	WX57HKW	37338	West of England	WX58JYU	37632	West of England
WX55TZN	66951	Glasgow	WX57HKY	37339	West of England	WX59BYM	69435	Midlands
WX55TZO	66952	Glasgow	WX57HKZ	37340	West of England	WX59BYN	69436	Midlands
WX55TZP	66953	Hampshire & B	WX57HLA	37341	West of England	WX59BYO	69437	West of England
WX55TZR	66954	Glasgow	WX57HLC	37342	West of England	WX59BYP	69438	West of England
WX55TZS	66955	Glasgow	WX57HLD	37343	West of England	WX59BYR	69439	West of England
WX55TZT	66956	West of England	WX57HLE	37344	West of England	WX59BYS	69440	West of England

Reg	No.	Location	Reg	No.	Location	Reg	No.	Location
WX59BYT	69441	West of England	X391HLR	41391	Cymru	X616NSS	62137	Aberdeen
WX59BYU	69442	West of England	X392HLR	41392	Cymru	X616OBN	40313	Manchester
WX59BYV	69443	West of England	X393HLR	41393	Cymru	X618NSS	62139	Essex
WX59BYW	69444	West of England	X394HLR	41394	West of England	X618OBN	40315	Manchester
WX59BYY	69445	West of England	X395HLR	41395	Cymru	X619NSS	62140	Aberdeen
WX59BYZ	69446	West of England	X398HLR	41398	Cymru	X619OBN	40316	Manchester
WX59BZA	69447	West of England	X399HLR	41399	Cymru	X621NSS	62149	Aberdeen
WX59BZB	69448	West of England	X401CSG	10017	Manchester	X622NSS	62150	Aberdeen
WX59BZC	69449	Midlands	X424UMS	61675	Glasgow	X623NSS	62151	Aberdeen
WX59BZD	69450	Midlands	X425UMS	61676	Glasgow	X624NSS	62152	Aberdeen
WX59BZE	69451	West of England	X426UMS	61677	Glasgow	X627OBN	40317	Manchester
WX59BZF	69452	West of England	X429UMS	61679	Glasgow	X683ADK	62182	Scotland East
WX59BZG	69453	West of England	X431UMS	61680	Glasgow	X684ADK	62183	Devon & Cornwall
WX59BZH	69454	West of England	X432UMS	61681	Glasgow	X688ADK	62194	West of England
WX59BZJ	69455	West of England	X433UMS	61682	Glasgow	X689ADK	62195	Essex
WX59BZK	69456	West of England	X434UMS	61683	Glasgow	X691ADK	62196	Aberdeen
WX59BZL	69457	West of England	X436UMS	61685	Glasgow	X692ADK	62197	Essex
WX59BZM	69458	West of England	X437UMS	61686	Glasgow	X693ADK	62198	Scotland East
WX59BZN	69459	Midlands	X439UMS	61688	Glasgow	X694ADK	62199	Scotland East
WX59BZO	69460	West of England	X441UMS	61689	Glasgow	X695ADK	62200	Scotland East
X103NSS	31560	Scotland East	X442UMS	61690	Glasgow	X696ADK	62201	Aberdeen
X104NSS	31561	Scotland East	X443UMS	61691	Glasgow	X697ADK	62202	Aberdeen
X132NSS	31558	Scotland East	X446UMS	61693	Glasgow	X698ADK	62203	Scotland East
X136FPO	10136	Aberdeen	X448UMS	61695	Glasgow	X699ADK	60405	Manchester
X136NSS	31562	Scotland East	X449UMS	61696	Glasgow	X69NSS	62131	Scotland East
X137NSS	31563	Scotland East	X451UMS	61697	Glasgow	X732HLF	41732	Essex
X138FPO	10138	Aberdeen	X452UMS	61698	Glasgow	X735HLF	41735	Essex
X141FPO	10141	Aberdeen	X453UMS	61699	Glasgow	X736HLF	41736	Essex
X144FPO	10144	Aberdeen	X454UMS	61700	Glasgow	X737HLF	41737	Essex
X193HFB	20463	Essex	X457UMS	61701	Glasgow	X749VUA	30894	West Yorkshire
X201HAE	43821	Devon & Cornwall	X458UMS	61702	Glasgow	X751JLO	41751	Scotland East
X202HAE	43822	Devon & Cornwall	X461UMS	61704	Glasgow	X752HLR	41752	Scotland East
X203HAE	43823	Devon & Cornwall	X474SCY	42474	Devon & Cornwall	X753HLR	41753	Scotland East
X239AMO	42339	Hampshire & B	X475SCY	42475	Devon & Cornwall	X754HLR	41754	Scotland East
X244AMO	42344	Hampshire & B	X476SCY	42476	Devon & Cornwall	X756HLR	41756	Scotland East
X247AMO	42347	Hampshire & B	X477NSS	62153	Aberdeen	X761HLR	41761	Essex
X253USH	60196	Midlands	X477SCY	42477	Devon & Cornwall	X762HLR	41762	Essex
X256USH	60199	Scotland East	X501BFJ	32751	Devon & Cornwall	X763VUA	30908	West Yorkshire
X257USH	60201	Midlands	X502BFJ	32752	Devon & Cornwall	X764VUA	30909	West Yorkshire
X261USH	60205	Midlands	X503BFJ	32753	Devon & Cornwall	X766VUA	30911	West Yorkshire
X269USH	60213	West Yorkshire	X503JLO	41730	Essex	X767VUA	30912	West Yorkshire
X272USH	60204	Scotland East	X504BFJ	32754	Devon & Cornwall	X771NSO	31559	Scotland East
X289FFA	40020	Midlands	X506HLR	41755	Scotland East	X776HLR	41776	Glasgow
X291FFA	40021	Midlands	X511HLR	41775	Glasgow	X778HLR	41778	Glasgow
X292FFA	40022	Midlands	X512HLR	41777	Glasgow	X779HLR	41779	Glasgow
X293FFA	40023	Midlands	X513HLR	41780	Manchester	X779VUA	30915	West Yorkshire
X294FFA	40024	Midlands	X514HLR	41786	Manchester	X781HLR	41781	Manchester
X295FFA	40025	Midlands	X578RJW	32052	West of England	X782HLR	41782	Manchester
X296FFA	40026	Midlands	X601NSS	62122	Aberdeen	X783HLR	41783	Manchester
X297FFA	40027	Midlands	X602NSS	62123	Aberdeen	X784HLR	41784	Manchester
X298FFA	40028	Midlands	X603NSS	62124	Aberdeen	X785HLR	41785	Manchester
X299FFA	40029	Midlands	X604NSS	62125	Scotland East	X787HLR	41787	Manchester
X303JGE	66233	Glasgow	X605NSS	62126	Scotland East	X788HLR	41788	Manchester
X351VWT	30931	West Yorkshire	X606NSS	62127	Scotland East	X78HLR	41390	Cymru
X352VWT	30932	West Yorkshire	X606RFS	62224	Scotland East	X791NWR	30923	West Yorkshire
X353VWT	30933	West Yorkshire	X607NSS	62128	Scotland East	X792NWR	30924	West Yorkshire
X354VWT	30934	West Yorkshire	X608NSS	62129	Glasgow	X793NWR	30925	West Yorkshire
X356VWT	30935	West Yorkshire	X609NSS	62130	Glasgow	X794NWR	30926	West Yorkshire
X357VWT	30936	West Yorkshire	X611HLT	32955	South Yorkshire	X795NWR	30927	West Yorkshire
X358VWT	30937	South Yorkshire	X611NSS	62132	Aberdeen	X796NWR	30928	West Yorkshire
X359VWT	30938	South Yorkshire	X612HLT	32960	Glasgow	X797NWR	30929	West Yorkshire
X381HLR	41381	Cymru	X612NSS	62133	Aberdeen	X798NWR	30930	West Yorkshire
X382HLR	41382	Cymru	X613HLT	32970	Aberdeen	X856UOK	30561	South Yorkshire
X383HLR	41383	Cymru	X613NSS	62134	Aberdeen	X857UOK	30562	South Yorkshire
X385HLR	41385	Cymru	X614HLT	32980	Glasgow	X858UOK	30563	South Yorkshire
X386HLR	41386	Cymru	X614NSS	62135	Scotland East	X944NSO	62141	Aberdeen
X387HLR	41387	Hampshire & B	X615NSS	62136	Scotland East	X954HLT	32954	West of England

Reg	No.	Region	Reg	No.	Region	Reg	No.	Region
X956HLT	32956	Glasgow	Y634RSA	62169	Aberdeen	YG02DHL	60904	West Yorkshire
X957HLT	32957	South Yorkshire	Y634RTD	60214	West Yorkshire	YG02DHM	60903	West Yorkshire
X958HLT	32958	Aberdeen	Y635RSA	62177	Aberdeen	YG02DHN	60906	West Yorkshire
X959HLT	32959	Manchester	Y636RSA	62178	Aberdeen	YG02DHO	60905	West Yorkshire
X961HLT	32961	West of England	Y637RSA	62179	Aberdeen	YG02DHP	40592	Devon & Cornwall
X962HLT	32962	Aberdeen	Y638RSA	62180	Aberdeen	YG02DHU	60928	York
X964HLT	32964	Glasgow	Y639RSA	62181	Aberdeen	YG02DHV	60907	West Yorkshire
X965HLT	32965	Glasgow	Y661UKU	60703	South Yorkshire	YG02DHX	40599	South Yorkshire
X967HLT	32967	Scotland East	Y701RSA	62165	Aberdeen	YG02DHY	40593	Devon & Cornwall
X968HLT	32968	Scotland East	Y774TNC	60406	South Yorkshire	YG02DKO	40614	Devon & Cornwall
X969HLT	32969	Glasgow	Y794XNW	30939	West Yorkshire	YG02DKU	60916	Devon & Cornwall
X971HLT	32971	Aberdeen	Y795XNW	30940	West Yorkshire	YG02DKV	60917	Devon & Cornwall
X972HLT	32972	Manchester	Y796XNW	30941	West Yorkshire	YG02DKX	40598	South Yorkshire
X973HLT	32973	Aberdeen	Y797XNW	30942	West Yorkshire	YG02DKY	40597	South Yorkshire
X974HLT	32974	Aberdeen	Y798XNW	30943	West Yorkshire	YG02DLD	60912	West of England
X975HLT	32975	Aberdeen	Y901KND	40318	Manchester	YG02DLE	40596	South Yorkshire
X977HLT	32977	Glasgow	Y902KND	40319	Manchester	YG02DLF	40595	South Yorkshire
X978HLT	32978	Glasgow	Y903KND	40320	Manchester	YG02DLJ	60918	Devon & Cornwall
X981HLT	32981	Glasgow	Y904KND	40321	Manchester	YG02DLK	40594	Devon & Cornwall
XFF283	40581	Devon & Cornwall	Y905KND	40322	Manchester	YG02DLN	60921	York
XSS344Y	31577	Aberdeen	Y932NLP	32990	Glasgow	YG02DLO	60911	Devon & Cornwall
Y148ROT	10148	Aberdeen	Y933NLP	32999	Glasgow	YG02DLU	60920	York
Y181BGB	66281	Glasgow	Y934NLP	33000	Glasgow	YG02DLV	48273	Hampshire & B
Y182BGB	66282	Glasgow	Y937CSF	62232	South Yorkshire	YG02DLX	60919	York
Y1EDN	42801	Devon & Cornwall	Y939CSF	62242	West of England	YG02DLY	60913	West of England
Y223NLF	32976	Aberdeen	Y941CSF	62231	Manchester	YG02DLZ	60915	Devon & Cornwall
Y224NLF	32979	Glasgow	Y942CSF	62233	Manchester	YJ04FYB	32432	West Yorkshire
Y251HHL	50232	Scotland East	Y943CSF	62234	South Yorkshire	YJ04FYC	32433	West Yorkshire
Y252HHL	50233	Scotland East	Y944CSF	62236	Manchester	YJ04FYD	32434	West Yorkshire
Y253HHL	50234	Scotland East	Y945CSF	62237	South Yorkshire	YJ04FYE	32435	West Yorkshire
Y254HHL	50235	West Yorkshire	Y946CSF	62235	South Yorkshire	YJ04FYF	32436	West Yorkshire
Y256HHL	50236	West Yorkshire	Y947CSF	62238	West of England	YJ04FYG	32437	West Yorkshire
Y2EDN	42802	Devon & Cornwall	Y948CSF	62239	South Yorkshire	YJ04FYH	32438	West Yorkshire
Y301RTD	61705	Glasgow	Y949CSF	62240	South Yorkshire	YJ04FYK	32439	West Yorkshire
Y302RTD	61706	Glasgow	Y949RTD	61710	Glasgow	YJ04FYL	32440	West Yorkshire
Y303RTD	61707	Glasgow	Y951CSF	62241	Manchester	YJ04FYM	32441	West Yorkshire
Y304RTD	61708	Glasgow	Y952CSF	62244	South Yorkshire	YJ04FYN	32442	West Yorkshire
Y307RTD	61709	Glasgow	Y953CSF	62243	South Yorkshire	YJ04FYP	32443	West Yorkshire
Y343XBN	60195	Scotland East	Y984NLP	32984	Glasgow	YJ04FYR	32444	West Yorkshire
Y344NLF	32983	Glasgow	Y985NLP	32985	Glasgow	YJ04FYS	32445	West Yorkshire
Y344XBN	60198	Scotland East	Y986NLP	32986	Glasgow	YJ04FYT	32446	West Yorkshire
Y346NLF	32982	Glasgow	Y987NLP	32987	Glasgow	YJ04FYU	32447	West Yorkshire
Y346XBN	60202	Midlands	Y988NLP	32988	Glasgow	YJ04FYV	32448	West Yorkshire
Y347XBN	60208	Midlands	Y989NLP	32989	Glasgow	YJ04FYW	32449	West Yorkshire
Y351AUY	42351	Midlands	Y991NLP	32991	Glasgow	YJ04FYX	32450	West Yorkshire
Y352AUY	42352	Midlands	Y992NLP	32992	Glasgow	YJ04FYY	32451	West Yorkshire
Y353AUY	42353	Midlands	Y993NLP	32993	Glasgow	YJ04FYZ	32452	West Yorkshire
Y354AUY	42354	Midlands	Y994NLP	32994	Glasgow	YJ04FZH	32460	West Yorkshire
Y356AUY	42356	Midlands	Y995NLP	32995	Scotland East	YJ04FZK	32461	West Yorkshire
Y445CUB	60876	York	Y996NLP	32996	Glasgow	YJ04FZL	32462	West Yorkshire
Y446CUB	60877	West Yorkshire	Y997NLP	32997	Glasgow	YJ04FZM	32463	West Yorkshire
Y447CUB	60878	West Yorkshire	Y998NLP	32998	Glasgow	YJ04FZN	32464	West Yorkshire
Y449CUB	60880	York	YA05SOJ	66792	West Yorkshire	YJ04FZP	32465	West Yorkshire
Y451CUB	60881	York	YA05SOU	66790	West Yorkshire	YJ04FZR	32466	West Yorkshire
Y546XNW	53034	West Yorkshire	YA54WBK	68528	West Yorkshire	YJ04FZS	32467	West Yorkshire
Y547XNW	53035	West Yorkshire	YA54WBL	68527	West Yorkshire	YJ04FZT	32468	West Yorkshire
Y597KNE	60197	Scotland East	YA54WBN	68530	West Yorkshire	YJ04FZU	32469	West Yorkshire
Y598KNE	60206	Essex	YA54WBO	68529	West Yorkshire	YJ04FZV	32470	West Yorkshire
Y626RSA	62154	Aberdeen	YG02DGY	60926	York	YJ04FZX	32471	West Yorkshire
Y627RSA	62155	Aberdeen	YG02DGZ	60909	York	YJ04FZY	32472	West Yorkshire
Y628RSA	62163	Aberdeen	YG02DHA	60908	West Yorkshire	YJ04FZZ	32473	West Yorkshire
Y629RSA	62164	Aberdeen	YG02DHC	60927	York	YJ05KNV	66754	York
Y631RSA	62166	Aberdeen	YG02DHD	60925	West Yorkshire	YJ05KNW	66755	York
Y632RSA	62167	Aberdeen	YG02DHE	60924	West Yorkshire	YJ05KNX	66756	York
Y632RTD	60203	Scotland East	YG02DHF	60923	West Yorkshire	YJ05KNY	66757	York
Y633RSA	62168	Aberdeen	YG02DHJ	60922	York	YJ05KNZ	66758	York
Y633RTD	60212	West Yorkshire	YG02DHK	60902	York	YJ05KOB	66750	West Yorkshire

YJ05KOD	66751	West Yorkshire	YJ06XLO	32696	West Yorkshire	YJ08CDU	69334	West Yorkshire
YJ05KOE	66752	West Yorkshire	YJ06XLP	32697	West Yorkshire	YJ08CDV	69335	West Yorkshire
YJ05KOH	66753	West Yorkshire	YJ06XLR	19012	West Yorkshire	YJ08CDX	69336	West Yorkshire
YJ05VUW	32538	West Yorkshire	YJ06XLS	19013	West Yorkshire	YJ08CDY	69337	West Yorkshire
YJ05VUX	32537	West Yorkshire	YJ06XLT	37043	West Yorkshire	YJ08CDZ	69338	West Yorkshire
YJ05VUY	32532	West Yorkshire	YJ06XLU	37044	West Yorkshire	YJ08CEA	69339	West Yorkshire
YJ05VVA	66759	York	YJ06XLV	37045	York	YJ08CEF	69340	West Yorkshire
YJ05VVB	66760	York	YJ06XLW	37046	West Yorkshire	YJ08CEK	69341	West Yorkshire
YJ05VVC	66761	York	YJ06XLX	37047	West Yorkshire	YJ08CEN	69342	West Yorkshire
YJ05VVD	66762	York	YJ06XLY	37048	West Yorkshire	YJ08CEO	69343	West Yorkshire
YJ05VVE	66763	York	YJ06XLZ	37049	West Yorkshire	YJ08CEU	69344	West Yorkshire
YJ05VVF	66764	West Yorkshire	YJ06XMA	37050	West Yorkshire	YJ08CEV	69345	West Yorkshire
YJ05VVG	66765	West Yorkshire	YJ06XMB	37051	West Yorkshire	YJ08CEX	69346	West Yorkshire
YJ05VVH	66766	West Yorkshire	YJ06XMC	37052	West Yorkshire	YJ08CEY	69347	West Yorkshire
YJ05VVK	66767	West Yorkshire	YJ06XMD	37053	West Yorkshire	YJ08CFA	69348	West Yorkshire
YJ05VVL	66768	West Yorkshire	YJ06XME	37054	West Yorkshire	YJ08CFD	69349	West Yorkshire
YJ05VVM	66769	West Yorkshire	YJ06XMF	37055	West Yorkshire	YJ08CFE	69350	West Yorkshire
YJ05VVN	66770	Glasgow	YJ06XMG	37056	West Yorkshire	YJ08GVE	37071	West Yorkshire
YJ05VVO	66771	Glasgow	YJ06XMH	37057	West Yorkshire	YJ08GVF	37072	West Yorkshire
YJ05VVP	66772	West Yorkshire	YJ06XMK	37058	West Yorkshire	YJ08GVG	37073	West Yorkshire
YJ05VVR	66773	West Yorkshire	YJ06XML	37059	West Yorkshire	YJ08GVK	37074	West Yorkshire
YJ05VVS	66774	West Yorkshire	YJ06XMM	37060	West Yorkshire	YJ08GVL	37075	West Yorkshire
YJ05VVT	66775	West Yorkshire	YJ06XMO	37061	West Yorkshire	YJ08GVM	37076	West Yorkshire
YJ05VVU	66776	West Yorkshire	YJ06XMP	37062	West Yorkshire	YJ08GVN	37077	West Yorkshire
YJ05VVW	66777	West Yorkshire	YJ06YSK	53503	West of England	YJ08GVO	37078	West Yorkshire
YJ05VVX	66778	West Yorkshire	YJ07EHO	53907	West Yorkshire	YJ08GVP	37079	West Yorkshire
YJ05VVY	66779	West Yorkshire	YJ07EHR	53909	West Yorkshire	YJ08GVR	37080	West Yorkshire
YJ05VVZ	66780	West Yorkshire	YJ07FLP	68709	West Yorkshire	YJ08GVT	37081	West Yorkshire
YJ05VWA	68545	West Yorkshire	YJ07LVL	19019	West Yorkshire	YJ08GVU	37082	West Yorkshire
YJ05VWE	32540	West Yorkshire	YJ07LVM	19020	West Yorkshire	YJ08GVV	37083	West Yorkshire
YJ05VWF	32541	West Yorkshire	YJ07LVN	19021	West Yorkshire	YJ08GVW	37084	West Yorkshire
YJ05VWG	32539	West Yorkshire	YJ07LVO	19022	West Yorkshire	YJ08GVX	37085	West Yorkshire
YJ05VWH	32542	West Yorkshire	YJ07LVR	19023	West Yorkshire	YJ08GVY	37086	West Yorkshire
YJ05XOP	53140	Hampshire & B	YJ07LVS	19024	West Yorkshire	YJ08GVZ	37087	West Yorkshire
YJ06WTV	68628	West Yorkshire	YJ07LVT	19025	West Yorkshire	YJ08GWA	37088	West Yorkshire
YJ06WTX	68626	West Yorkshire	YJ07LVU	19026	West Yorkshire	YJ08GWC	37089	West Yorkshire
YJ06WTZ	68630	West Yorkshire	YJ07LVV	19027	West Yorkshire	YJ08GWD	37090	West Yorkshire
YJ06WUA	68631	West Yorkshire	YJ07LVW	19028	West Yorkshire	YJ08GWE	37091	West Yorkshire
YJ06XEK	68640	West Yorkshire	YJ07LWC	66995	West Yorkshire	YJ08GWF	37092	West Yorkshire
YJ06XEL	68641	West Yorkshire	YJ07LWD	66996	West Yorkshire	YJ08GWG	37093	West Yorkshire
YJ06XFR	68608	West Yorkshire	YJ07LWE	66997	West Yorkshire	YJ08GWK	37094	West Yorkshire
YJ06XKK	37021	South Yorkshire	YJ07LWF	66998	West Yorkshire	YJ08GWL	37095	West Yorkshire
YJ06XKL	37022	South Yorkshire	YJ07WBK	68711	West Yorkshire	YJ08GWM	37096	West Yorkshire
YJ06XKM	37023	South Yorkshire	YJ07WBL	68700	West Yorkshire	YJ08GWN	37097	West Yorkshire
YJ06XKN	37024	South Yorkshire	YJ07WFM	69245	Hampshire & B	YJ08GWO	37098	West Yorkshire
YJ06XKO	37025	South Yorkshire	YJ07WFN	69246	Hampshire & B	YJ08GWP	37099	West Yorkshire
YJ06XKP	37026	South Yorkshire	YJ07WFO	69247	Hampshire & B	YJ08GWU	37100	West Yorkshire
YJ06XKS	37027	South Yorkshire	YJ07WFP	69248	Hampshire & B	YJ08GWV	37101	West Yorkshire
YJ06XKT	37028	South Yorkshire	YJ07WFR	69249	Cymru	YJ08GWW	37102	West Yorkshire
YJ06XKU	37029	South Yorkshire	YJ07WFS	69250	Cymru	YJ08GWX	69299	West Yorkshire
YJ06XKV	37030	South Yorkshire	YJ07WFT	69251	Cymru	YJ08GWY	69300	West Yorkshire
YJ06XKW	37031	South Yorkshire	YJ07WFU	69252	Cymru	YJ08XCN	68692	West Yorkshire
YJ06XKX	37032	South Yorkshire	YJ07WFV	69253	West of England	YJ08XCO	68690	West Yorkshire
YJ06XKY	37033	South Yorkshire	YJ07WFW	69270	West Yorkshire	YJ08XCP	68691	West Yorkshire
YJ06XKZ	37034	South Yorkshire	YJ07WFX	69271	West Yorkshire	YJ08XCR	68689	West Yorkshire
YJ06XLA	37035	South Yorkshire	YJ07WFY	69272	West Yorkshire	YJ08XCS	68693	West Yorkshire
YJ06XLB	37036	West Yorkshire	YJ07WFZ	69273	West Yorkshire	YJ08XXW	69379	York
YJ06XLC	37037	West Yorkshire	YJ07WGA	69274	West Yorkshire	YJ08XYB	69363	York
YJ06XLD	37038	West Yorkshire	YJ07XMB	68697	West Yorkshire	YJ08XYC	69364	York
YJ06XLE	37039	West Yorkshire	YJ07XND	68708	West Yorkshire	YJ08XYD	69365	York
YJ06XLF	37040	West Yorkshire	YJ07XWF	68710	West Yorkshire	YJ08XYE	69366	York
YJ06XLG	37041	West Yorkshire	YJ07XWG	68698	West Yorkshire	YJ08XYF	69367	York
YJ06XLH	37042	West Yorkshire	YJ08CDE	69329	West Yorkshire	YJ08XYG	69368	York
YJ06XLK	32692	West Yorkshire	YJ08CDF	69330	West Yorkshire	YJ08XYH	69369	York
YJ06XLL	32693	West Yorkshire	YJ08CDK	69331	West Yorkshire	YJ08XYK	69370	York
YJ06XLM	32694	West Yorkshire	YJ08CDN	69332	West Yorkshire	YJ08XYL	69371	York
YJ06XLN	32695	West Yorkshire	YJ08CDO	69333	West Yorkshire	YJ08XYM	69372	York

Reg	Fleet No	Location	Reg	Fleet No	Location	Reg	Fleet No	Location
YJ08XYN	69373	York	YJ09OAA	37687	West Yorkshire	YJ12MZD	49220	Manchester
YJ08XYO	69374	York	YJ09OAB	37688	West Yorkshire	YJ12MZF	49222	Manchester
YJ08XYP	69375	York	YJ09OAC	37689	West Yorkshire	YJ13GUE	29006	Aberdeen
YJ08XYR	69376	York	YJ09OAD	37690	West Yorkshire	YJ13GUF	29007	Aberdeen
YJ08XYS	69377	York	YJ09OAE	37691	West Yorkshire	YJ13HLR	49301	Cymru
YJ08XYT	69378	York	YJ09OAG	37692	West Yorkshire	YJ13HLU	49302	Cymru
YJ08ZGL	69358	York	YJ09OAH	37693	West Yorkshire	YJ13HLV	49303	Cymru
YJ08ZGM	69359	York	YJ09OAL	37694	West Yorkshire	YJ13HLW	49304	Cymru
YJ08ZGN	69360	York	YJ09OAM	37695	West Yorkshire	YJ13HLX	49305	Cymru
YJ08ZGO	69361	York	YJ09OAN	37696	West Yorkshire	YJ13HLY	49306	Cymru
YJ08ZGP	69362	York	YJ09OAO	37697	West Yorkshire	YJ13HLZ	49307	Cymru
YJ09FVE	37684	West Yorkshire	YJ09OAP	37698	West Yorkshire	YJ13HMA	49308	Cymru
YJ09FVF	37685	West Yorkshire	YJ09OAS	37699	West Yorkshire	YJ13HMC	49309	Cymru
YJ09FVG	37676	West Yorkshire	YJ09OAU	37700	West Yorkshire	YJ13HMD	49002	Cymru
YJ09FVH	37677	West Yorkshire	YJ09OAV	37701	West Yorkshire	YJ13HME	49003	Cymru
YJ09FVK	37678	West Yorkshire	YJ09OAW	37702	West Yorkshire	YJ13HMF	49004	Cymru
YJ09FVL	37679	West Yorkshire	YJ09OAX	37703	West Yorkshire	YJ13HMG	49005	Cymru
YJ09FVM	37680	West Yorkshire	YJ09OAY	37704	West Yorkshire	YJ13HMH	49006	Cymru
YJ09FVN	37681	West Yorkshire	YJ09OAZ	37705	West Yorkshire	YJ13HMK	49007	Cymru
YJ09FVO	37682	West Yorkshire	YJ09OBA	37706	West Yorkshire	YJ13HMU	49008	Cymru
YJ09FVP	37683	West Yorkshire	YJ09OBB	37707	West Yorkshire	YJ13HMV	49009	Cymru
YJ09FWA	69306	York	YJ09OBC	37708	West Yorkshire	YJ13HMX	49010	Cymru
YJ09FWB	69307	West Yorkshire	YJ09OBD	37709	West Yorkshire	YJ14BHA	49901	York
YJ09FWC	69308	West Yorkshire	YJ09OBE	37710	West Yorkshire	YJ14BHD	49902	York
YJ09FWL	69316	West Yorkshire	YJ09OBF	37711	West Yorkshire	YJ14BHE	49903	York
YJ09FWM	69317	West Yorkshire	YJ09OBG	37712	West Yorkshire	YJ14BHF	49904	York
YJ09FWN	69318	West Yorkshire	YJ09OBH	37713	West Yorkshire	YJ14BHK	49905	York
YJ09FWO	69319	West Yorkshire	YJ09OBK	37714	West Yorkshire	YJ14BHL	49906	York
YJ09FWP	69320	West Yorkshire	YJ09OBL	37715	West Yorkshire	YJ14BJX	49921	Manchester
YJ09FWR	69321	West Yorkshire	YJ09OBM	37716	West Yorkshire	YJ14BJY	49923	Manchester
YJ09FWS	69322	West Yorkshire	YJ09OBN	37717	West Yorkshire	YJ14BJZ	49922	Manchester
YJ09FWT	69323	West Yorkshire	YJ09OBO	37718	West Yorkshire	YJ14BKA	53601	Hampshire & B
YJ09FWU	69324	West Yorkshire	YJ09OBP	37719	West Yorkshire	YJ14BKD	53602	Hampshire & B
YJ09FWV	69325	Manchester	YJ09OBR	37720	West Yorkshire	YJ14BKE	53603	Hampshire & B
YJ09FWW	69326	Manchester	YJ09OBS	37721	West Yorkshire	YJ14BKF	53604	Hampshire & B
YJ09FWX	69327	Manchester	YJ09OBT	37722	West Yorkshire	YJ14BKG	53605	Hampshire & B
YJ09FWY	69328	Manchester	YJ09OBU	37723	West Yorkshire	YJ14BKK	53606	Hampshire & B
YJ09FWZ	69412	West Yorkshire	YJ09OBV	37724	West Yorkshire	YJ14BKL	53607	Hampshire & B
YJ09FXA	69413	West Yorkshire	YJ09OBW	37725	West Yorkshire	YJ14BKN	53608	Hampshire & B
YJ09FXB	69414	West Yorkshire	YJ09OBX	37726	West Yorkshire	YJ14BKO	53609	Hampshire & B
YJ09FXC	69415	West Yorkshire	YJ09OBY	37727	West Yorkshire	YJ14BPF	49232	Manchester
YJ09FXD	69416	West Yorkshire	YJ09OBZ	37728	West Yorkshire	YJ14BPK	49231	Manchester
YJ09FXE	69417	West Yorkshire	YJ09OCA	37729	West Yorkshire	YJ14BPO	49230	Manchester
YJ09FXF	69418	West Yorkshire	YJ09OCB	37730	West Yorkshire	YJ14BVA	53610	Hampshire & B
YJ09FXG	69419	West Yorkshire	YJ09OCC	37731	West Yorkshire	YJ14BVB	53611	Hampshire & B
YJ09FXH	69420	Manchester	YJ09OCD	37732	West Yorkshire	YJ14BVC	53612	Hampshire & B
YJ09NYA	69466	West Yorkshire	YJ09OCE	37733	West Yorkshire	YJ14BVD	53613	Hampshire & B
YJ09NYB	69467	West Yorkshire	YJ09OCF	37734	West Yorkshire	YJ14BVE	53614	Hampshire & B
YJ09NYC	69468	West Yorkshire	YJ09OCG	37735	West Yorkshire	YJ14BVF	53615	Hampshire & B
YJ09NYD	69469	West Yorkshire	YJ12GXV	49228	Manchester	YJ15AOW	53751	Glasgow
YJ09NYF	69470	West Yorkshire	YJ12GXZ	49227	Manchester	YJ15AOX	53752	Glasgow
YJ09NYG	69471	West Yorkshire	YJ12MYF	49202	Manchester	YJ15AOY	53753	Glasgow
YJ09NYH	69472	West Yorkshire	YJ12MYG	49203	Manchester	YJ15AOZ	53754	Glasgow
YJ09NYK	69473	West Yorkshire	YJ12MYH	49204	Manchester	YJ15AYK	49907	York
YJ09NYM	69474	West Yorkshire	YJ12MYK	49205	Manchester	YJ15AYL	49908	York
YJ09NYN	69475	West Yorkshire	YJ12MYL	49206	Manchester	YJ15AYM	49909	York
YJ09NYO	69476	West Yorkshire	YJ12MYN	49208	Manchester	YJ15AYN	49910	York
YJ09NYP	69477	West Yorkshire	YJ12MYO	49209	Manchester	YJ15AYO	49911	York
YJ09NYR	69478	West Yorkshire	YJ12MYP	49210	Manchester	YJ15AYP	49912	York
YJ09NYS	69479	West Yorkshire	YJ12MYR	49211	Manchester	YJ51PZT	60882	York
YJ09NYT	69480	West Yorkshire	YJ12MYS	49212	Manchester	YJ51PZU	60883	York
YJ09NYU	69481	West Yorkshire	YJ12MYT	49213	Manchester	YJ51PZV	60884	York
YJ09NYV	69482	West Yorkshire	YJ12MYU	49214	Manchester	YJ51PZW	60885	South Yorkshire
YJ09NYW	69483	West Yorkshire	YJ12MYV	49215	Manchester	YJ51PZX	60886	South Yorkshire
YJ09NYX	69484	West Yorkshire	YJ12MYW	49216	Manchester	YJ51PZY	60887	South Yorkshire
YJ09NYY	69485	West Yorkshire	YJ12MYX	49217	Manchester	YJ51PZZ	40570	Devon & Cornwall
YJ09NZY	37686	West Yorkshire	YJ12MYY	49218	Manchester	YJ51RAU	30964	Manchester

Reg	No	Location	Reg	No	Location	Reg	No	Location
YJ51RAX	30965	Manchester	YJ54XUD	32515	West Yorkshire	YJ57VTV	68685	West Yorkshire
YJ51RCO	30959	Manchester	YJ54XUE	32516	West Yorkshire	YJ57VVA	68686	West Yorkshire
YJ51RCU	30955	Manchester	YJ54XUF	32517	West Yorkshire	YJ57VYX	68684	West Yorkshire
YJ51RCV	30956	Manchester	YJ54XUG	32518	West Yorkshire	YJ57VYY	68687	West Yorkshire
YJ51RCX	30957	Manchester	YJ54XUH	32519	West Yorkshire	YJ57WKB	68707	West Yorkshire
YJ51RCZ	30958	Manchester	YJ54XUK	32520	West Yorkshire	YJ57WKC	68706	West Yorkshire
YJ51RDO	30954	Manchester	YJ54XUM	32521	West Yorkshire	YJ57YSK	69268	West Yorkshire
YJ51RDU	30960	Manchester	YJ54XUN	32522	West Yorkshire	YJ57YSL	69269	West Yorkshire
YJ51RDV	30961	Manchester	YJ54XUO	32523	West Yorkshire	YJ57YSM	69276	York
YJ51RDX	30962	Manchester	YJ54XUP	32524	West Yorkshire	YJ57YSN	69275	York
YJ51RDY	30963	Manchester	YJ54XUR	32525	West Yorkshire	YJ57YSO	69277	York
YJ51RDZ	60888	South Yorkshire	YJ54XUT	32526	West Yorkshire	YJ57YSP	69278	York
YJ51REU	60894	South Yorkshire	YJ54XUU	32527	West Yorkshire	YJ57YSR	69279	York
YJ51RFE	60895	Devon & Cornwall	YJ54XUV	32528	West Yorkshire	YJ58CEV	53065	Hampshire & B
YJ51RFF	60896	York	YJ54XUW	32529	West Yorkshire	YJ58GMO	37361	West Yorkshire
YJ51RFK	60910	Devon & Cornwall	YJ54XUX	32530	West Yorkshire	YJ58GMU	37363	West Yorkshire
YJ51RFL	60899	York	YJ54XUY	32531	West Yorkshire	YJ58GMV	37365	West Yorkshire
YJ51RFN	60900	York	YJ54XVA	32533	West Yorkshire	YJ58GNP	37360	West Yorkshire
YJ51RFO	60901	York	YJ54XVB	32534	West Yorkshire	YJ58GNU	37362	West Yorkshire
YJ51RFX	60898	York	YJ54XVC	32535	West Yorkshire	YJ58GNV	37364	West Yorkshire
YJ51RFY	60897	York	YJ54XVD	32536	West Yorkshire	YJ58GNX	37366	West Yorkshire
YJ51RFZ	40587	West Yorkshire	YJ54XVM	66738	West Yorkshire	YJ58RNN	37645	West Yorkshire
YJ51RGO	40588	Devon & Cornwall	YJ54XVN	66739	West Yorkshire	YJ58RNO	37646	West Yorkshire
YJ51RGV	40590	Devon & Cornwall	YJ54XVO	66740	West Yorkshire	YJ58RNU	37647	West Yorkshire
YJ51RGX	40591	Devon & Cornwall	YJ54XVP	66741	West Yorkshire	YJ58RNV	37648	West Yorkshire
YJ51RGY	60893	South Yorkshire	YJ54XVR	66742	West Yorkshire	YJ58RNX	37649	West Yorkshire
YJ51RGZ	60891	South Yorkshire	YJ54XVT	66743	West Yorkshire	YJ58RNY	37650	West Yorkshire
YJ51RHE	60889	South Yorkshire	YJ54XVU	66744	West Yorkshire	YJ58RNZ	37651	West Yorkshire
YJ51RHF	60892	South Yorkshire	YJ54XVW	66745	Devon & Cornwall	YJ58ROH	37652	West Yorkshire
YJ51RHK	60890	South Yorkshire	YJ54XVX	66746	West Yorkshire	YJ58ROU	37653	West Yorkshire
YJ51RHO	40577	West Yorkshire	YJ54XVY	66747	West Yorkshire	YJ58RPO	37654	West Yorkshire
YJ51RHU	40578	West Yorkshire	YJ54XVZ	66748	West Yorkshire	YJ58RPU	37655	West Yorkshire
YJ51RHV	40579	West Yorkshire	YJ54XWA	66749	West Yorkshire	YJ58RPV	37656	West Yorkshire
YJ51RJV	40585	Devon & Cornwall	YJ54YCO	68515	West Yorkshire	YJ58RPX	37657	West Yorkshire
YJ51RJX	40586	Devon & Cornwall	YJ54YCP	68516	West Yorkshire	YJ58RPY	37658	West Yorkshire
YJ51RKO	40571	York	YJ55CAO	68546	West Yorkshire	YJ58RPZ	37659	West Yorkshire
YJ51RKU	40572	York	YJ55CAU	68548	West Yorkshire	YJ58RRO	37660	West Yorkshire
YJ51RKV	40573	York	YJ55CAV	68547	West Yorkshire	YJ58RRU	37661	West Yorkshire
YJ51RPY	30944	West Yorkshire	YJ56AOT	53504	Devon & Cornwall	YJ58RRV	37662	West Yorkshire
YJ51RPZ	30945	West Yorkshire	YJ56AOU	53505	Devon & Cornwall	YJ58RRX	37663	West Yorkshire
YJ51RRO	30946	West Yorkshire	YJ56EAA	19014	West Yorkshire	YJ58RRY	37664	West Yorkshire
YJ51RRU	30947	West Yorkshire	YJ56EAC	19015	West Yorkshire	YJ58RRZ	37665	West Yorkshire
YJ51RRV	30948	West Yorkshire	YJ56EAE	19016	West Yorkshire	YJ58RSO	37666	West Yorkshire
YJ51RRX	30949	West Yorkshire	YJ56EAF	19017	West Yorkshire	YJ58RSU	37667	West Yorkshire
YJ51RRY	30950	West Yorkshire	YJ56EAG	19018	West Yorkshire	YJ58RSV	37668	West Yorkshire
YJ51RRZ	30951	West Yorkshire	YJ56LJE	68651	West Yorkshire	YJ58RSX	37669	West Yorkshire
YJ51RSO	30952	West Yorkshire	YJ56LJF	68652	West Yorkshire	YJ58RSY	37670	West Yorkshire
YJ51RSU	30953	West Yorkshire	YJ56LJK	68653	West Yorkshire	YJ58RSZ	37671	West Yorkshire
YJ51RSV	40574	York	YJ56LJL	68655	West Yorkshire	YJ58RTO	37672	West Yorkshire
YJ51RSX	40575	York	YJ56LJN	68654	West Yorkshire	YJ58RTU	37673	West Yorkshire
YJ51RSY	40576	West Yorkshire	YJ56LJY	68664	West Yorkshire	YJ58RTV	37674	West Yorkshire
YJ54BSV	53201	Glasgow	YJ56LKC	68667	West Yorkshire	YJ58RTX	37675	West Yorkshire
YJ54BVA	53301	West Yorkshire	YJ56LKD	68668	West Yorkshire	YJ58RVA	69315	West Yorkshire
YJ54BVB	53302	West Yorkshire	YJ56LKE	68663	West Yorkshire	YJ59KSO	37752	West Yorkshire
YJ54BVC	53303	West Yorkshire	YJ56LLG	68656	West Yorkshire	YJ59KSU	37753	West Yorkshire
YJ54XTO	32503	West Yorkshire	YJ56LLK	68657	West Yorkshire	YJ59KSV	37754	West Yorkshire
YJ54XTP	32504	West Yorkshire	YJ56LLN	68659	West Yorkshire	YJ59KSY	37755	West Yorkshire
YJ54XTR	32505	West Yorkshire	YJ56LLO	68660	West Yorkshire	YJ59KSZ	37756	West Yorkshire
YJ54XTT	32506	West Yorkshire	YJ56LMX	68669	West Yorkshire	YJ60KCA	59001	Manchester
YJ54XTU	32507	West Yorkshire	YJ56LNA	68662	West Yorkshire	YJ60KCC	59002	Manchester
YJ54XTV	32508	West Yorkshire	YJ56LRL	68672	West Yorkshire	YJ60KCE	59003	Manchester
YJ54XTW	32509	West Yorkshire	YJ56LRN	68671	West Yorkshire	YJ60KCF	59004	Manchester
YJ54XTX	32510	West Yorkshire	YJ56LRU	68670	West Yorkshire	YJ60KCG	59005	Manchester
YJ54XTZ	32511	West Yorkshire	YJ56WGA	68674	West Yorkshire	YJ60KCK	59006	Manchester
YJ54XUA	32512	West Yorkshire	YJ56ZMU	68675	West Yorkshire	YJ60KCN	59007	Manchester
YJ54XUB	32513	West Yorkshire	YJ56ZTM	68704	West Yorkshire	YJ60KCO	59008	Manchester
YJ54XUC	32514	West Yorkshire	YJ57NFF	68705	West Yorkshire	YJ60KCU	49101	Manchester

Reg	Fleet	Location	Reg	Fleet	Location	Reg	Fleet	Location
YJ60KCV	49102	Manchester	YK07AYG	37109	South Yorkshire	YM52UVL	61215	Scotland East
YJ60KDF	49106	Manchester	YK07AYH	37110	South Yorkshire	YM52UVN	61216	Scotland East
YJ60KDK	49107	Manchester	YK07AYJ	37111	South Yorkshire	YM52UVO	61217	Scotland East
YJ60KDN	49108	Manchester	YK07AYL	37112	South Yorkshire	YM52UVP	61218	Scotland East
YJ60KDO	49109	Manchester	YK07AYM	37113	South Yorkshire	YM52UVR	61219	Scotland East
YJ60KDU	49110	Manchester	YK07AYN	37114	South Yorkshire	YM52UVS	61220	Scotland East
YJ60KDV	49111	Manchester	YK07AYO	37115	South Yorkshire	YM52UVT	61221	Scotland East
YJ60KDX	49112	Manchester	YK07AYP	37116	South Yorkshire	YM52UVU	61222	Scotland East
YJ61JDO	59009	Manchester	YK07AYS	37117	South Yorkshire	YM52UVZ	61224	Scotland East
YJ61JDZ	59012	Manchester	YK07AYT	37118	South Yorkshire	YM52UWA	61225	Scotland East
YJ61JEO	59013	Manchester	YK07AYU	37119	South Yorkshire	YM52UWB	61226	Scotland East
YJ61JFU	49117	Manchester	YK07AYV	37120	South Yorkshire	YM52UWD	61227	Scotland East
YJ61JFV	49118	Manchester	YK07AYW	37121	South Yorkshire	YM52UWF	61228	Scotland East
YJ61JFX	49119	Manchester	YK07AYX	37122	South Yorkshire	YM52UWG	61229	Scotland East
YJ61JHK	49113	Manchester	YK07AYY	37123	West Yorkshire	YM52UWH	61230	Scotland East
YJ61JHL	49114	Manchester	YK07AYZ	37124	West Yorkshire	YM52UWJ	61231	Scotland East
YJ61JHO	49115	Manchester	YK07BJX	68694	West Yorkshire	YM52UWK	61232	Scotland East
YJ61JHU	49116	Manchester	YK07BJY	68695	West Yorkshire	YM52UWN	61233	Scotland East
YJ64	49907	York	YK07BJZ	68696	West Yorkshire	YN03ZVW	53151	Hampshire & B
YJ64	49908	York	YK07FTP	68682	West Yorkshire	YN03ZVX	50407	West Yorkshire
YJ64	49909	York	YK07FTT	68683	West Yorkshire	YN04AJU	23013	Devon & Cornwall
YJ64	49910	York	YK07FTU	68676	West Yorkshire	YN04AJV	23015	Hampshire & B
YJ64	49911	York	YK07FTX	68699	West Yorkshire	YN04GLV	36005	Hampshire & B
YJ64	49912	York	YK07FUA	68680	West Yorkshire	YN04GME	65705	Midlands
YJ64DYX	49233	Manchester	YK07FUD	68677	West Yorkshire	YN04GMF	65706	Midlands
YK04EZG	66713	West Yorkshire	YK53GXR	66707	West Yorkshire	YN04GNV	36001	Hampshire & B
YK04EZH	66715	West Yorkshire	YK53GXT	66708	West Yorkshire	YN04GNX	36002	Hampshire & B
YK04EZJ	66711	West Yorkshire	YK53GXU	66709	West Yorkshire	YN04GNY	36003	Hampshire & B
YK04EZL	66712	West Yorkshire	YK53GXV	66710	West Yorkshire	YN04GNZ	36004	Hampshire & B
YK04EZM	66714	West Yorkshire	YK54ENL	69001	York	YN04YHW	23202	Devon & Cornwall
YK04KWR	53801	Devon & Cornwall	YK54ENM	69002	York	YN04YHY	23201	Devon & Cornwall
YK05CDN	53826	Devon & Cornwall	YK54ENN	69003	York	YN04YHZ	23204	Devon & Cornwall
YK05CDO	53827	Devon & Cornwall	YK54ENO	69004	York	YN04YJC	65001	Midlands
YK05FJE	66784	West Yorkshire	YK54ENP	69000	West Yorkshire	YN04YJD	65002	Midlands
YK05FJF	66783	West Yorkshire	YK55AAJ	68603	West Yorkshire	YN04YJE	65003	Midlands
YK05FJJ	66781	West Yorkshire	YK55AAN	68610	West Yorkshire	YN04YJF	65004	Midlands
YK05FLB	66782	West Yorkshire	YK55AUE	68614	West Yorkshire	YN04YJG	65005	Midlands
YK05FLC	66786	West Yorkshire	YK55AUF	68615	West Yorkshire	YN05GXF	65759	Devon & Cornwall
YK05FOP	66791	West Yorkshire	YK55AUH	68616	West Yorkshire	YN05GXR	65760	Devon & Cornwall
YK05FOT	66789	West Yorkshire	YK55AUP	68606	West Yorkshire	YN05GYA	12001	Manchester
YK05FOU	66788	West Yorkshire	YK55AUU	68609	West Yorkshire	YN05GYB	12002	Manchester
YK05FOV	66787	West Yorkshire	YK55AVF	68621	West Yorkshire	YN05GYC	12005	Manchester
YK05FPA	66785	West Yorkshire	YK55AVG	68622	West Yorkshire	YN05GYD	12006	Manchester
YK06AOU	19001	West Yorkshire	YK55AVJ	68623	West Yorkshire	YN05GYE	12007	Manchester
YK06ATO	68642	West Yorkshire	YK55AVM	68625	West Yorkshire	YN05GYF	12008	Manchester
YK06ATU	19003	West Yorkshire	YK55ENM	53905	West Yorkshire	YN05GYG	12009	Manchester
YK06ATV	19002	West Yorkshire	YK55ENN	53906	West Yorkshire	YN05GYH	12003	Manchester
YK06ATX	19005	West Yorkshire	YK55ENR	53904	West Yorkshire	YN05GYJ	12004	Manchester
YK06ATY	19007	West Yorkshire	YK55JCN	68701	West Yorkshire	YN05GYK	12010	Manchester
YK06ATZ	19008	West Yorkshire	YK57CJF	37125	West Yorkshire	YN05GYO	12011	Manchester
YK06AUA	19010	West Yorkshire	YK57CJJ	37126	West Yorkshire	YN05GYP	12014	Manchester
YK06AUC	19011	West Yorkshire	YK57CJO	37127	West Yorkshire	YN05GYR	12015	Manchester
YK06AUL	19009	West Yorkshire	YK57CJU	37128	West Yorkshire	YN05GYS	12016	Manchester
YK06CZZ	68643	West Yorkshire	YK57CJV	37129	West Yorkshire	YN05GYT	12017	Manchester
YK06DAA	68646	West Yorkshire	YK57CJX	37130	West Yorkshire	YN05GYU	12013	Manchester
YK06DNN	68638	West Yorkshire	YK57CJY	37131	West Yorkshire	YN05GYV	12012	Manchester
YK06DTZ	68639	West Yorkshire	YK57CJZ	37132	West Yorkshire	YN05GYW	12018	Manchester
YK06DYJ	68635	West Yorkshire	YK57EZS	37063	West Yorkshire	YN05HCL	65027	Midlands
YK06EFR	68702	West Yorkshire	YK57EZT	37064	West Yorkshire	YN05HCO	65727	Midlands
YK06EFS	68703	West Yorkshire	YK57EZU	37065	West Yorkshire	YN05HCP	65728	Midlands
YK06EHE	68648	West Yorkshire	YK57EZV	37066	West Yorkshire	YN05HCU	65729	Midlands
YK07AYA	37103	South Yorkshire	YK57EZW	37067	West Yorkshire	YN05HCV	65730	Midlands
YK07AYB	37104	South Yorkshire	YK57EZX	37068	West Yorkshire	YN05HCX	65731	Midlands
YK07AYC	37105	South Yorkshire	YK57EZZ	37069	West Yorkshire	YN05HCY	65732	Midlands
YK07AYD	37106	South Yorkshire	YK57FAA	37070	West Yorkshire	YN05HCZ	65733	Midlands
YK07AYE	37107	South Yorkshire	YK57FCL	66999	West Yorkshire	YN05HGA	36006	Hampshire & B
YK07AYF	37108	South Yorkshire	YM52UVK	61214	Scotland East			

Registration	Fleet	Location
YN06CGU	23321	Cymru
YN06CGV	23322	Cymru
YN06CGX	23323	Cymru
YN06CGY	23324	Cymru
YN06CGZ	23325	Cymru
YN06NXP	65762	Devon & Cornwall
YN06NXW	65761	Devon & Cornwall
YN06TDO	65028	Essex
YN06TDU	65029	Essex
YN06TDV	65030	Essex
YN06TDX	65031	Essex
YN06TDZ	65032	Essex
YN06UPZ	37146	Midlands
YN06URA	37147	Glasgow
YN06URB	37148	Glasgow
YN06URC	37149	Glasgow
YN06URD	37150	Glasgow
YN06URE	37151	Glasgow
YN06URF	37152	Glasgow
YN06URG	37153	Glasgow
YN06URH	37154	Glasgow
YN06URJ	37155	Glasgow
YN06WME	65033	Midlands
YN06WMF	65034	Midlands
YN06WMG	65035	Midlands
YN06WMJ	65036	Midlands
YN06WMK	65037	Midlands
YN06WML	65038	Midlands
YN06WMM	65039	Midlands
YN06WMO	65040	Midlands
YN06WMP	65041	Midlands
YN06WMT	65042	Midlands
YN07MKD	37246	York
YN07MKE	37247	York
YN07MKF	37248	York
YN07MKG	37249	York
YN07MKJ	37250	York
YN07MKK	37251	York
YN07MKL	37252	York
YN07MKM	37253	York
YN07MKO	37254	York
YN07MKP	37255	York
YN07MKV	37256	York
YN07MKX	37257	South Yorkshire
YN07MKZ	37258	South Yorkshire
YN07MLE	37259	South Yorkshire
YN07MLJ	37261	South Yorkshire
YN07MLK	37262	South Yorkshire
YN07MLL	37263	South Yorkshire
YN07MLO	37264	South Yorkshire
YN07MLU	37265	South Yorkshire
YN08LCK	37230	South Yorkshire
YN08LCL	37231	South Yorkshire
YN08LCM	37234	South Yorkshire
YN08LCO	37235	South Yorkshire
YN08LCP	37237	South Yorkshire
YN08LCT	37238	Glasgow
YN08LCU	37239	Glasgow
YN08LCV	37240	Glasgow
YN08LCW	37241	Glasgow
YN08LCY	37242	Glasgow
YN08LCZ	37243	Glasgow
YN08LDA	37244	Glasgow
YN08LDC	37245	Glasgow
YN08LDD	37278	Glasgow
YN08NLL	37472	South Yorkshire
YN08NLM	37473	South Yorkshire
YN08NLO	37474	South Yorkshire
YN08NLP	37475	South Yorkshire
YN08NLR	37476	South Yorkshire
YN08NLT	37477	South Yorkshire
YN08NLU	37478	South Yorkshire
YN08NLV	37479	South Yorkshire
YN08NLX	37480	South Yorkshire
YN08NLY	37481	South Yorkshire
YN08NLZ	37482	South Yorkshire
YN08NMA	37483	South Yorkshire
YN08NME	37484	South Yorkshire
YN08NMF	37485	South Yorkshire
YN08NMJ	37486	South Yorkshire
YN08NMK	37487	South Yorkshire
YN08NMM	37488	South Yorkshire
YN08NMU	37489	South Yorkshire
YN08NMV	37490	South Yorkshire
YN08NMX	37491	South Yorkshire
YN08NMY	37492	South Yorkshire
YN08OWO	20801	Essex
YN08OWP	20802	Essex
YN08OWR	20803	Essex
YN08OWU	20804	Essex
YN08OWV	20805	Essex
YN08PLF	37493	South Yorkshire
YN08PLO	37495	South Yorkshire
YN08PLU	37496	South Yorkshire
YN08PLX	37498	South Yorkshire
YN08PLZ	37499	South Yorkshire
YN08PMO	37500	South Yorkshire
YN08PMU	37501	South Yorkshire
YN08PMV	37502	South Yorkshire
YN08PMX	37503	South Yorkshire
YN08PMY	37504	South Yorkshire
YN08PNE	37505	South Yorkshire
YN08PNF	37506	South Yorkshire
YN08PNJ	37507	South Yorkshire
YN08PNK	37508	South Yorkshire
YN09HFH	69461	South Yorkshire
YN09HFJ	69462	South Yorkshire
YN09HFK	69463	South Yorkshire
YN09HFL	69464	South Yorkshire
YN09HFM	69465	South Yorkshire
YN15AYK		York
YN53EFE	31787	Glasgow
YN53EFF	31788	Glasgow
YN53EFG	31789	Glasgow
YN53EFH	31790	Scotland East
YN53EFJ	31791	Scotland East
YN53EFK	31792	Scotland East
YN53EFL	31793	Glasgow
YN53EFM	31794	Glasgow
YN53EFO	31795	Glasgow
YN53EFP	31796	Glasgow
YN53EFR	31797	Glasgow
YN53EFT	31798	Glasgow
YN53EFU	31799	Glasgow
YN53EFV	31800	Glasgow
YN53EFW	31801	Glasgow
YN53EFX	31802	Glasgow
YN53EFZ	31803	Glasgow
YN53EGC	31804	Glasgow
YN53ELJ	50319	West Yorkshire
YN53ELO	50318	West of England
YN53EOA	31776	South Yorkshire
YN53EOB	31777	South Yorkshire
YN53EOC	31778	South Yorkshire
YN53EOD	31779	South Yorkshire
YN53EOE	31780	South Yorkshire
YN53EOF	31781	South Yorkshire
YN53EOG	31782	South Yorkshire
YN53EOH	31783	South Yorkshire
YN53EOJ	31784	South Yorkshire
YN53EOK	31785	South Yorkshire
YN53EOL	31786	South Yorkshire
YN53VBT	56001	Aberdeen
YN53VBU	56002	Devon & Cornwall
YN53VBV	56003	Scotland East
YN54APF	23021	Aberdeen
YN54APK	23020	Essex
YN54APX	23019	Essex
YN54NXV	23303	Devon & Cornwall
YN54NXZ	23307	Aberdeen
YN54NYU	23313	Devon & Cornwall
YN54NYV	23314	Aberdeen
YN54NZA	65006	Hampshire & B
YN54NZC	65007	Hampshire & B
YN54NZD	65008	Hampshire & B
YN54NZE	65009	Hampshire & B
YN54NZF	65010	Hampshire & B
YN54NZG	65011	Hampshire & B
YN54NZH	65012	Hampshire & B
YN54NZJ	65013	Hampshire & B
YN54NZK	65014	Hampshire & B
YN54NZM	65015	Hampshire & B
YN54NZO	65016	Hampshire & B
YN54NZP	65017	Hampshire & B
YN54NZR	65018	Hampshire & B
YN54NZT	65019	Hampshire & B
YN54NZU	65020	Hampshire & B
YN54NZV	65021	Hampshire & B
YN54NZW	65022	Hampshire & B
YN54NZX	65023	Hampshire & B
YN54NZY	65024	Hampshire & B
YN54NZZ	65025	Hampshire & B
YN54OCK	65026	Midlands
YN55PXF	23315	Cymru
YN55PXG	23316	Devon & Cornwall
YN55PXH	23317	Devon & Cornwall
YN55PXJ	23318	Cymru
YN55PXK	23319	Cymru
YN55PXL	23320	Cymru
YN56NHE	57001	Scotland East
YN56NHF	57002	Scotland East
YN57BVU	20321	Scotland East
YN57BVV	20322	Scotland East
YN57BVW	20323	Cymru
YN57BVX	20324	Cymru
YN57BVY	20325	Cymru
YN57BVZ	20326	Scotland East
YN57BWU	20327	Scotland East
YN57RJU	37228	South Yorkshire
YN57RJZ	37232	South Yorkshire
YN57RKA	37233	South Yorkshire
YN57RKJ	37236	South Yorkshire
YN58ERX	37494	South Yorkshire
YN58ERY	37497	South Yorkshire
YN58ESF	37509	South Yorkshire
YN58ESF	37510	South Yorkshire
YN58ESG	37511	South Yorkshire
YN58ESO	37512	South Yorkshire
YN58ESU	37513	South Yorkshire
YN58ESV	37514	South Yorkshire

YN58ESY	37515	South Yorkshire	YU52VYN	31137	South Yorkshire	YX13AFA	44556		Cymru
YN58ETA	37516	South Yorkshire	YU52VYO	31138	South Yorkshire	YX13AFE	44557		Cymru
YN58ETD	37517	South Yorkshire	YU52VYP	31139	South Yorkshire	YX13AHN	44538		Essex
YN58ETE	37518	South Yorkshire	YU52VYR	31140	South Yorkshire	YX13AHO	44539		Essex
YN58ETF	37519	South Yorkshire	YU52VYS	31141	South Yorkshire	YX13AHP	44540		Essex
YN58ETJ	37520	South Yorkshire	YU52VYT	31142	South Yorkshire	YX13AHU	44541		Essex
YN58ETK	37521	South Yorkshire	YU52VYV	31143	West Yorkshire	YX13AHV	44542		Essex
YN58ETL	37522	South Yorkshire	YU52VYW	31144	South Yorkshire	YX13AHZ	44543		Essex
YN58ETO	37523	South Yorkshire	YU52VYX	31145	South Yorkshire	YX13AKF	44544		Essex
YN58ETR	37524	South Yorkshire	YU52VYY	31146	West Yorkshire	YX13AKG	44545		Essex
YN58ETT	37525	South Yorkshire	YU52VYZ	31147	West Yorkshire	YX13AKJ	44546		Essex
YN58ETU	37526	South Yorkshire	YU52VZA	31148	South Yorkshire	YX13AKK	44547		Essex
YN58ETV	37527	South Yorkshire	YV03UBA	23008	Devon & Cornwall	YX13AKN	44548		Essex
YN58ETX	37528	South Yorkshire	YV03UBB	23009	Devon & Cornwall	YX13AKO	44549		Essex
YN58ETY	37529	South Yorkshire	YV03UBC	23010	Devon & Cornwall	YX13AKP	44550		Essex
YN62GXS	20809	Hampshire & B	YV03UBD	23011	Devon & Cornwall	YX13AKU	44558		Cymru
YN62GYR	20808	Hampshire & B	YV03UBE	23012	Devon & Cornwall	YX13AKV	44559		Cymru
YP02ABN	65678	Essex	YV03UOU	40976	South Yorkshire	YX13AKY	44551		Essex
YR02UVU	50239	West Yorkshire	YV03UOW	40975	South Yorkshire	YX13BNA	44573		Cymru
YR52VEH	65679	Essex	YV03UOX	40974	South Yorkshire	YX13BNB	44574		Cymru
YR52VEK	65680	Essex	YV03UOY	40973	South Yorkshire	YX13BND	44575		Cymru
YR52VEL	65681	Essex	YW04VAU	32431	West Yorkshire	YX13BNE	44576		Cymru
YR52VEP	65682	Essex	YX08HJF	44599	Essex	YX13BNF	44577		Cymru
YR52VEU	65683	Essex	YX09ACV	44516	East	YX13BNJ	44578		Cymru
YR52VEY	65684	Essex	YX09ACY	44517	East	YX13BNK	44579		Cymru
YR52VFO	65685	Essex	YX09ACZ	44518	East	YX13BNL	44580		Cymru
YS03ZKA	62406	Essex	YX09ADO	44519	East	YX13BNN	44581		Cymru
YS03ZKB	62407	Essex	YX09ADU	44921	West of England	YX14RUC	44602		Cymru
YS03ZKC	65686	Essex	YX09ADV	44922	Devon & Cornwall	YX14RUH	44603		Cymru
YS03ZKD	62409	Essex	YX09ADZ	44923	Devon & Cornwall	YX14RUJ	44604		Cymru
YS03ZKE	62408	Essex	YX09AFN	44905	West of England	YX14RUO	44605		Cymru
YS03ZKF	62410	Essex	YX09AFO	44906	West of England	YX14RUR	44606		Cymru
YS03ZKG	65687	Essex	YX09AFU	44907	West of England	YX14RUU	44607		Cymru
YS03ZKH	65688	Essex	YX09AFV	44908	West of England	YX14RUV	44608		Cymru
YS03ZKJ	65689	Essex	YX09AFY	44909	West of England	YX14RUW	44609		Cymru
YS03ZKK	65690	Essex	YX09AFZ	44910	West of England	YX14RUY	44610		Cymru
YS03ZKL	65691	Essex	YX09AGO	44911	West of England	YX14RVA	44611		Cymru
YS03ZKM	65692	Essex	YX09AGU	44912	West of England	YX14RVC	44612		Cymru
YS51JVA	61135	Hampshire & B	YX09AGV	44913	West of England	YX14RVE	44613		Cymru
YS51JVD	62228	Aberdeen	YX09AGZ	44914	West of England	YX14RVF	44614		Cymru
YS51JVE	68005	Hampshire & B	YX09AHA	44915	West of England	YX14RVJ	44615		Cymru
YS51JVH	68006	Hampshire & B	YX09AHC	44916	West of England	YX14RVK	44616		Cymru
YS51JVK	61136	Hampshire & B	YX09AHD	44917	West of England	YX14RVL	44617		Cymru
YT51EZW	50237	West Yorkshire	YX09AHE	44918	West of England	YX14RVM	44618		Cymru
YT51EZX	50238	West Yorkshire	YX09AHF	44919	West of England	YX14RVN	44619		Cymru
YU52VXH	61192	South Yorkshire	YX09AHG	44920	West of England	YX14RVO	44620		Cymru
YU52VXJ	61193	South Yorkshire	YX09AHK	44924	Devon & Cornwall	YX14RVP	44621		Cymru
YU52VXK	61194	South Yorkshire	YX10AXP	54302	Glasgow	YX14RVR	44622		Cymru
YU52VXL	61195	South Yorkshire	YX10AXT	54307	Glasgow	YX14RVT	44623		Cymru
YU52VXM	61196	South Yorkshire	YX10AYL	54304	Glasgow	YX14RVU	44624		Cymru
YU52VXN	61197	South Yorkshire	YX11HNW	44925	South Yorkshire	YX14RVV	44625		Cymru
YU52VXO	61198	South Yorkshire	YX11HNY	44926	South Yorkshire	YX14RVW	44626		Cymru
YU52VXP	61199	South Yorkshire	YX11HNZ	44927	South Yorkshire	YX14RVY	44627		Cymru
YU52VXR	61200	South Yorkshire	YX11HPO	20806	Hampshire & B	YX14RVZ	44628		Cymru
YU52VXS	61201	South Yorkshire	YX11HPP	20807	Hampshire & B	YX14RWE	44629		Cymru
YU52VXT	61202	South Yorkshire	YX12CHK	54401	Glasgow	YX14RWF	44630		Cymru
YU52VXV	61203	South Yorkshire	YX12CHL	54402	Glasgow	YX14RWJ	44631		Cymru
YU52VXW	61204	South Yorkshire	YX12CHO	54403	Glasgow	YX14RWK	44632		Cymru
YU52VXY	61206	South Yorkshire	YX12CJF	54404	Glasgow	YX58FRJ	45111	Devon & Cornwall
YU52VYE	31129	South Yorkshire	YX12CJJ	54405	Glasgow	YX58FRK	45112	Devon & Cornwall
YU52VYF	31130	South Yorkshire	YX12CJO	54406	Glasgow	YX58FRL	45113	Devon & Cornwall
YU52VYG	31131	South Yorkshire	YX12CJU	54407	Glasgow	YX58FRN	45114	Devon & Cornwall
YU52VYH	31132	South Yorkshire	YX13AEF	44537	Essex	YX58FRP	45115	Devon & Cornwall
YU52VYJ	31133	South Yorkshire	YX13AEV	44552	Cymru	YX58HVF	44076		Essex
YU52VYK	31134	South Yorkshire	YX13AEW	44553	Cymru	YX58HVG	44077		Essex
YU52VYL	31135	South Yorkshire	YX13AEY	44554	Cymru	YX58HVH	44078		Essex
YU52VYM	32278	West of England	YX13AEZ	44555	Cymru	YX58HVJ	44079		Essex

YX58HVK	44080	Essex	YX63LJO	33808	East	YX63LLD	44564	Hampshire & B
YX58HVL	44081	Essex	YX63LJU	33809	East	YX63LLE	44565	Hampshire & B
YX58HWF	44507	Hampshire & B	YX63LJV	33810	East	YX63LLF	44566	Hampshire & B
YX58HWG	44508	Hampshire & B	YX63LJY	33811	East	YX63LLG	44567	Hampshire & B
YX58HWH	44509	Hampshire & B	YX63LJZ	33812	East	YX63LLJ	44568	Cymru
YX58HWJ	44510	Hampshire & B	YX63LKA	33813	East	YX63ZUD	44582	Cymru
YX62DVM	44520	West of England	YX63LKC	33814	East	YX63ZVA	44583	Cymru
YX62DWG	44521	West of England	YX63LKD	33815	East	YX63ZVB	44584	Cymru
YX62DWM	44522	West of England	YX63LKE	33816	East	YX63ZVC	44585	Cymru
YX62DWO	44523	West of England	YX63LKF	33817	East	YX63ZVD	44586	Cymru
YX62DXC	44524	West of England	YX63LKG	33818	East	YX63ZVE	44587	Cymru
YX62DXF	44525	West of England	YX63LKJ	33819	East	YX63ZVF	44588	Cymru
YX62DXH	44526	West of England	YX63LKK	33820	East	YX63ZVG	44589	Cymru
YX63LHK	44591	Cymru	YX63LKL	33821	East	YX63ZVH	44590	Cymru
YX63LHL	44592	Cymru	YX63LKM	33822	East	YX64VPJ	44633	Cymru
YX63LHM	44593	Cymru	YX63LKN	33823	East	YX64VPK	44634	Cymru
YX63LHR	44569	Hampshire & B	YX63LKO	33824	East	YX64VPL	44635	Cymru
YX63LJF	33803	East	YX63LKU	44570	Cymru	YX64VPM	44636	Cymru
YX63LJJ	33804	East	YX63LKV	44560	Hampshire & B	YY63WBT	20810	Hampshire & B
YX63LJK	33805	East	YX63LKY	44561	Hampshire & B	YY63WBU	20811	Hampshire & B
YX63LJL	33806	East	YX63LKZ	44562	Hampshire & B			
YX63LJN	33807	East	YX63LLC	44563	Hampshire & B			

ISBN 9781904875246

© Published by British Bus Publishing Ltd, June 2015

British Bus Publishing Ltd, 16 St Margaret's Drive, Telford, TF1 3PH

Telephone: 01952 255669

web; www.britishbuspublishing.co.uk
e-mail: sales@britishbuspublishing.co.uk